Regenerative Design
for
Sustainable Development

THE WILEY SERIES IN SUSTAINABLE DESIGN

The Wiley Series in Sustainable Design has been created for professionals responsible for, and individuals interested in, the design and construction of the built environment. The series is dedicated to the advancement of knowledge in design and construction that serves to sustain the natural environment. Titles in the series cover innovative and emerging topics related to the design and development of the human community, within the context of preserving and enhancing the quality of the natural world. Consistent with their content, books in the series are produced with care taken in the selection of recycled and non-polluting materials.

GRAY WORLD, GREEN HEART
Technology, Nature and the Sustainable Landscape
Robert L. Thayer, University of California, Davis

REGENERATIVE DESIGN FOR SUSTAINABLE DEVELOPMENT
John T. Lyle, California State Polytechnic University, Pomona

Regenerative Design
for
Sustainable Development

■■■■■■■■■■■■■■■■■■■■■■■■

JOHN TILLMAN LYLE

JOHN WILEY & SONS, INC.

New York   Brisbane   Chichester   Toronto   Singapore

Library of Congress Cataloging in Publication Data:
Lyle, John Tillman.
    Regenerative design for sustainable development / John Tillman
  Lyle.
      p.   cm.
    Includes bibliographical references and index.
    ISBN 0-471-55582-7
    1. Environmental degradation.   2. Environmental policy.
  3. Sustainable development. I. Title.
  GE140.L95   1994
  333.73'15—dc20   93-21637

Arch.

Printed in the United States of America

10 9 8 7 6 5 4 3 2

For Harriett, Cybele, and Alex
with hope

Contents

Part III
Implementation and Its Implications

Preface

In shaping the places where we live, we shape the patterns of our own behavior. Over the past century or so, we have built into the landscape behavior patterns that derive from attitudes about the nature of the earth and the human relationship with it that go back at least to the Renaissance. Expanded and driven by fossil fuels and exploding population, they are now not only outmoded but dangerous. For our culture to survive, for the human environment to become sustainable, we will have to change some of those patterns, which means changing not only our behavior but our environment. It is not just a matter of fine tuning, not even a matter of overhaul. What is needed is redesign.

I use the word "design" here in a large and inclusive sense, not in the superficial fashion-conscious sense that has become a common parlance in the declining and decadent years of the industrial era. By design I mean conceiving and shaping complex systems. It has nothing to do with fashion statements and trendy labels of the sort that are often attached nowadays to clothing, appliances, and even some buildings conceived to project prestigious images. Environmental design is where the earth and its processes join with human culture and behavior to create form.

Design in this sense requires reestablishing some connections that began coming loose in the Renaissance and were entirely severed by industrialization. The first connection to be reestablished is that between people and nature; and next is that between art and science. At its best, environmental design is where people and nature meet, where art and science join. The principles and practices described in this book strive to accomplish the meeting and the joining, and thus draw heavily on both art and science. We can hardly shape anything useful or meaningful, particularly not anything so complex as a building or landscape without applying both rational and intuitive thought. We cannot afford not to use all the knowledge and skill we have at our disposal, and we certainly cannot ignore our feelings or our yearning for visible meaning.

Design is also the place where society and technology meet. During the industrial era, technology split apart from daily life. It became something physically separate, emotionally remote, hardly under human control, something inherently ugly. We will have to regain control of our means for supporting life. Indeed, we will have to embrace them and celebrate them, and design is one of the major means.

Design in this larger sense is clearly not the work of a single individual, though designers can certainly lead the way. Environmental design necessarily calls on the knowledge and skills of a great many people—architects, landscape architects, planners, scientists, artists, engineers, social scientists, as well as those affected. It is a team effort, truly interdisciplinary in applying collaborative process.

The development of this book followed the model of such a collaborative interdisciplinary design process. One would normally expect solar design and water conservation to be dealt with under separate covers in works devoted to those subjects alone. The conventions of the last few centuries predispose us to think of them as separate subjects, the provinces of separate specialists. In reality—that is, in nature—they are inextricably interrelated. Water requires energy to flow, and at the same time, water often also generates energy. The other life-support processes discussed—shelter, biotic production, and waste assimilation—are equally interrelated; by considering them together, we can take into account their commonalities as well as their interactions and overlaps, and we can benefit from their synergies. They all work together in nature, and with some thought we can shape the human landscape to follow nature's ways.

The book is organized in three parts. In the first, I have attempted to explain what regenerative design is and why it is important. Approaches, theories, principles, and strategies all come into play in these initial chapters.

The second section deals with applications, describing a broad sampling of practices and technologies that are regenerative (inherently self-renewing). The examples show how they have been applied through carefully conceived design in a variety of situations.

The third part explores the roles of regenerative design in the social, physical, economic, and political contexts. How do we implement regenerative design in the existing world, and how might these designs shape a different world in the future?

Through all three parts, the design for the Center for Regenerative Studies on the campus of the California State Polytechnic University (Cal Poly) provides a continuing case study, illustrating the design processes, concepts, practices, technologies, and forms discussed in each chapter. My colleagues and I have worked on this project over the past 7 years, and much of the content of this book took shape during that time.

The debts I have incurred in guiding the design of the Center and in writing this book are far more than I can ever repay. Four of my colleagues who worked with me in designing the Center worked closely and directly with me on certain chapters and reviewed most of the others. These are Dean Freudenberger, Professor at the Luther Theological Seminary in Minneapolis (Chapter 7); Arthur Jokela, Director of the Southern California Institute of Natural Resources (Chapter 6); William Stine, Professor of Mechanical Engineering at Cal Poly (Chapter 4); and Victor Wegrzyn, Professor of Plant and Soil Science at Cal Poly (Chapter 7). Literally hundreds of others, including all of the many students, colleagues, and administrators involved in one way or another with the Center, have contributed to the contents of this book in an endless variety of ways. While this was a highly integrative effort, responsibility for the shortcomings of the results is of course entirely mine.

Many conversations with my long-time friends and colleagues, Mark von Wodtke and Jeffrey Olson, influenced the development of the book. Both also reviewed the manuscript, as did Dean Freudenberger. Sharon Stine of Cal Poly, Robert Thayer of the University of California, Davis, and my wife, Harriett, reviewed certain chapters. Cathy DeMarzie worked patiently, endlessly, and most effectively in typing the manuscript. Dan Sayre of John Wiley & Sons was a most discerning editor.

Direct financial support also has come from a number of sources. The design work on the Center for Regenerative Studies was supported by grants from LandLab funds provided by the Los Angeles County Sanitation Districts under the Spadra agreement with Cal Poly, and from the Cal Poly Development Office. Construction of the first phase of the Center for Regenerative Studies is funded by a major grant from the Kellogg Foundation as well as by generous grants from the Ahmanson Foundation, the ARCO Foundation, the Hearst Foundation, the Simpson Paper Company, and the Bank of America.

A fellowship from the U. S. National Endowment for the Arts provided time and resources for collecting and organizing materials related to design and technology as well as funds for travel to visit many of the examples. A sabbatical leave granted by Cal Poly provided time to write.

JOHN TILLMAN LYLE

September 1993

Credits

DESIGN TEAM OF THE CENTER FOR REGENERATIVE STUDIES

John T. Lyle, Project Director (Architecture, Landscape Architecture)
Gregg D. Ander (Energy Analysis)
Barry A. Costa-Pierce (Aquaculture)
C. Dean Freudenberger (Agronomy)
Arthur W. Jokela (Geology, Hydrology)
Denise L. Lawrence (Anthropology)
Jeffrey K. Olson (Landscape Architecture)
Sharon Stine (Social Structure)
William Stine (Energy Conversion)
Barry L. Wasserman (Architecture)
Victor A. Wegrzyn (Agronomy)
James W. Weidman (Agricultural Economics)

Janith Johnson (Graduate Assistant, Architecture)
Simon Pastucha (Student Assistant, Landscape Architecture)

DESIGN TEAM FOR THE BATESON BUILDING

Office of the California State Architect
State Architect: Sym van der Ryn
Project Designers: Peter Calthorpe
Bruce Carson
Scott Mattews

DESIGN TEAM FOR SOUTHEAST LOS ANGELES

606 Studio Principals: John T. Lyle
Jeffrey K. Olson
Francis Dean
Arthur Jokela
Project Team: Charlotte Eubanks
Annette Gilg
Michael Heacox
Chia-Kuan Liao

DESIGN TEAM FOR THE ARROYO SECO

606 Studio Principals:	John T. Lyle
	Jeffrey K. Olson
	Francis Dean
	Arthur Jokela
Project Team:	Allyson G.
	Aultfather
	Kevin Trevor
	Talma
	Patricia Murphy
	Trap

DESIGN TEAM FOR ETIWANDA-DAY CANYON

606 Studio Principals:	John T. Lyle
	Jeffrey K. Olson
	Francis Dean
	Arthur Jokela
	Barry Wasserman
Project Team:	William Carlson
	Derrik Eichelberger
	Rosa Laveaga
	Alan Wong

DESIGN TEAM FOR THE SAN JACINTO WILDLIFE

606 Studio Principals:	John T. Lyle
	Jeffrey K. Olson
	Francis Dean
	Arthur Jokela
Project Team:	David W. Kelly
	Patricia V. Smith
	Tricia D. Thrasher

DESIGN TEAM FOR THE MANAGEMENT FRAMEWORK FOR THE TIJUANA RIVER VALLEY

606 Studio Principals:	John T. Lyle
	Jeffrey K. Olson
	Francis Dean
	Arthur Jokela
Project Team:	Sandra Cleisz
	Gregory Currie
	Ruth Ehrenkranz
	Jay Ziff
Assisted by:	John Hunt
	Carolyn Meredith

DESIGN TEAM FOR REGENERATION OF DEGRADED LANDSCAPES UTILIZING COMPOSTED ORGANIC WASTE

606 Studio Principals:	John T. Lyle
	Jeffrey K. Olson
	Francis Dean
	Arthur Jokela
	Royce Neuschatz
Consultants:	James Buras
	David Cote
	Luis Diaz

ROCKY MOUNTAIN INSTITUTE

Architects:	Steven Conger and the Aspen Design Group

ALBANY COUNTY AIRPORT

Architects:	The Fierning Group

I

Rethinking the
Mind in Nature

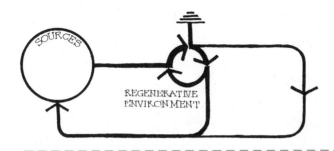

Chapter 1
Sustainability in the Neotechnic Era

When the phrase "sustainable development" came into widespread use in the last half of the 1980s, it signaled a new phase in our struggle with the twin catastrophes of resource depletion and environmental degradation. The shift may go very deep indeed. It could mean a change in course for the waning industrial age; it might even be a central part of one of those rare periods of metamorphosis in civilization itself.

The words seem innocuous enough in themselves; they hardly inspire revolutionary fervor. What's new here? Shouldn't all development be sustainable as a matter of course? Of course it should—but it isn't. That's why we can find lurking under the mundane associations of the word "sustainable" some profoundly important implications for the future.

A milestone in public acceptance of the term came when the World Commission on Environment and Development (WCED), which the United Nations General Assembly charged with formulating an "agenda for the future," based its proposals mostly on sustainable development. The WCED defined sustainable development as "development that meets the needs of the present without compromis-

ing the ability of the future to meet its own needs" (WCED, 1987, p. 42). We might say this means living on the interest yielded by our natural systems rather than on the capital. Considered in the light of the last hundred years, living on the interest is a revolutionary notion. But there is still more to it. Our ecological understanding developed over the last few decades makes it clear that we can only meet the needs of humans in an environment where the needs of other species—countless other species—are also met. This requires maintaining the integrity of nature's life-support processes. In this case, maintaining does not mean simply preserving. Development implies change—specifically modifying and adapting the landscape for human purposes. Among environmentally concerned people, the term "development" raises serious questions. Up to now, it has stood, more often than not, for destruction of nature for human gain. This need not be the case. Varied levels and types of development are possible.

Whether we like it or not, a considerable level of development—of change in the global landscape—will be necessary to meet the needs of the world's growing population and to redress present imbalances. The blending of continuity and change—

sustainability and development—will require approaches to reshaping the landscape quite different from those of the past two centuries. With its statement, the WCED has granted a kind of official acceptance to what many had been saying for some time: Conventional industrial development as practiced for nearly two centuries is inherently unsustainable; resource depletion and environmental degradation lie embedded in the design of our 20th-century landscape and especially in our cities. The assumption of unlimited resources that prevailed for so long has now been entirely discredited. Therefore, things cannot go on as they are.

Degenerative Patterns in Linear Flows

For all its fatal faults, there is much to admire in the grand pattern of industrial organization that we have imposed on the earth over the past two centuries. Judged by any standards, it is an impressive product of human ingenuity. Some of its parts are awesome indeed: Consider the powerful beauty of the Hoover Dam, or the Panama Canal, the long concrete ribbon of the Los Angeles Aqueduct (sloping slightly downhill through its entire 233-mile length), the twin ribbons of Interstate 70 twisting through the Rockies, or any three-level freeway interchange. Putting all the parts together, the accomplishment is no less than the replacing of billions of years of evolution with a simpler, more direct, and immensely powerful design of human devising. Where nature evolved an ever varying, endlessly complex network of unique places adapted to local conditions, human ingenuity has replaced it with a system of relatively simple forms and processes repeated with bold and consistent regularity over the face of the earth. Where nature evolved to a level of infinite diversity, humans have designed readily manageable uniformity. And most importantly, humans have replaced nature's endless cycling and recycling of materials, processes at the core of the earth's operating system, with an encompassing system of one-way flows, moving the materials that support life in vast quantities from source through consumption to sink.

It was an ambitious experiment indeed. As Lewis Mumford (1961) has pointed out, it began to take its present form in the 19th century with the railroads that connected coal mines with factories and cities. The connections expanded with technological improvement to include freeways, shipping and air lanes, pipelines, and powerlines. As the connections grew, the sources diminished, and the sinks increased, and toxicity accumulated.

Measured by the values of the marketplace and by 19th-century economic theory, the new design worked marvelously well. Success fed its expansion; by the beginning of the last quarter of the 20th century, the global landscape had been almost entirely reorganized to facilitate the artificial system of one-way flows. By 1988, source landscapes—including agricultural and grazing lands, oil fields, mines, production forests, watersheds, and a variety of other lands from which materials are taken to supply the consumption centers—covered about 61 percent of the world's land area (World Resources Institute [WRI], and International Institute for Environment and Development [IIED] 1988). These lands are no longer natural in the accepted sense; they are shaped by human intellect, human hands, and machines made by humans. Natural processes still operate in this human landscape, though in radically altered form. The remaining 39 percent that is still in a more or less naturally evolved state is mostly in Arctic or desert environments, though those have been affected by human actions as well.

Throughout the 20th century, consumption, the throughput of the one-way flows, became increasingly concentrated in large cities, demanding ever increasing volumes of material from the sources. Cities now cover less than 2 percent of the 61 percent, but they include over 42 percent of the world's population. These small, intense clusters of activity are the decision centers as well as the energy-consumption centers. They are determining what happens in the rest of the landscape, namely, a pattern of degeneration. With materials taken from the earth at rates far higher than they can be replaced, the sources must eventually diminish. Herein lies the modern crisis of resource depletion and degradation. The global statistics on deforestation, desertification, salinization, soil erosion, habitat loss and other landscape pathologies tell that story very clearly.

After being used by consumers, the materials coaxed from the earth in such prodigious amounts flow back to land, air, and water on the sink side of the sequence in even greater quantity. Sinks include the entire atmosphere, most streams, rivers, lakes, bays, estuaries and other wetlands, most groundwater, and the multitudinous but relatively small land areas where wastes are deposited. Strangely, the amount of waste outputs can be considerably greater than the amount of materials put in from the

source side. This disparity occurs because so many materials combine with air or water in the process of being used. For example, every pound of fuel carbon burned in combustion results in 3.3 lb of carbon dioxide emitted into the atmosphere. The amounts of carbon now being released are too great to be readily absorbed by nature's recycling mechanisms, which are primarily green plants. As a result, the carbon builds up in concentration to become pollutants. While sources are being depleted, the sinks are loaded far beyond their capacities. Consider, for example, urban smog; buildup of the greenhouse layer; depletion of the ozone layer; dying bays, lakes, and rivers; overflowing landfills; and toxic dumps. Even where residuals are smaller in amount, they can be highly biologically active in small concentrations.

What such situations are telling us is that the one-way throughput system, like most human inventions but unlike nature's recycling material flows, has a linear time dimension built in with a descending curve: Eventually a one-way system destroys the landscapes on which it depends. The clock is always running and the flows always approaching the time when they can flow no more. In its very essence, this is a degenerative system, devouring its own sources of sustenance. Eugene Odum (1993) puts it this way: ". . . . current cities are parasites that, unlike successful parasites in nature, have not evolved mutual aid relationships with their life-support host landscape that prevent the parasite from killing off its host and thereby itself."

Source landscapes will eventually run out of materials, and sinks will eventually become overloaded beyond the ability to function. For practical purposes, many are already plugged, thus no longer functioning as sinks. In the process of one-way flow, both sources and sinks are degraded to dysfunctional levels.

Past dysfunctions resulted in pressure on human populations to migrate. In recent decades, migrations have moved people into more and more marginal landscapes, accelerating degenerative processes such as desertification. At the same time, shortages of available land have forced more people to move to cities. This has hastened urban degeneration everywhere but especially in nonindustrial countries.

The one-way throughput system is a global system. Virtually every society on earth depends on it to some degree. Every landscape on the planet is affected by it to some degree. James Lovelock (1988) in his Gaia hypothesis, envisioned the earth as a single living organism. We might envision the worldwide one-way throughput industrial system in a very similar sense as a single all-encompassing global machine. Like Lovelock's concept of the earth as a single self regulating organism, which he called Gaia for the Roman goddess of earth, this is more literal reality than metaphor. Over two centuries, industrial technology imposed the throughput machine upon Gaia.

Even before sources or sinks fail entirely, cities may succumb to social or functional failure brought on by overconcentration of population combined with consumption gone amok. There are ample statistics to support predictions of any of these outcomes. We might wonder, for example, which will happen first: We run out of petroleum, the buildup of greenhouse gases reorganizes the earth's climate system, or cities grind to a halt from gridlocked streets or choking on smog. Other sources and sinks are engaged in similar races.

Perhaps industrial technology will simply become too expensive to build and operate. There are numerous cases of this having occurred already as the costs of industrial technology rise beyond human control. In 1988 a transportation study by the

Southern California Association of Governments estimated that at least $42 billion would have to be spent on freeway construction over the next 20 years just to keep traffic moving at its present (rather slow) pace (Roderick, 1988). If land-use patterns do not change during that time to limit sprawl and bring dwellings closer to jobs, the report said costs could run over $110 billion. Construction costs tend to go up beyond prediction. When the city of Los Angeles started construction in the late 1970s on a giant incinerator to burn its sewage sludge, the cost was estimated at $100 million. In 1988, when construction was substantially completed, the cost had risen to over $400 million. However, the incinerator still was not operational, and there were considerable doubts that it ever would be. In 1992 the work was still going on, and costs were still mounting. Even more costly was the debacle of the Washington Public Power Supply System, which had to halt construction on five half-completed nuclear generating plants because costs had gotten out of control. The loss amounted to about $6 billion, to be paid eventually by Washington electricity users.

Such situations are even more tragic in third-world countries than can ill afford them. The immense Itaipu Dam, for example, cost $19 billion and contributed in a major way to Brazil's hopeless national debt, not to mention its incalculable environmental impact. Its contribution to that nation's electrical supply is marginal.

The Progress of Environmental Change

By the 1960s these ecological dysfunctions were beginning to gain attention, and environmental activities began to make themselves heard. When the WCED (1987) published its report on environment and development, the environmental movement had been actively demanding change on a number of fronts for over 20 years, and it had what looks at first glance like a record of success. Concerned citizens had stopped a great many potentially damaging projects, including numerous dams, most notably two proposed for the Colorado River where it flows through the Grand Canyon, several nuclear power plants, and a number of freeways. Federal legislation had undertaken to protect endangered species. The area of protected wild lands in the United States had increased from 234,000 square kilometers in 1970 to nearly 800,000 in 1990 (Orga-

nization for Economic Cooperation and Development [OECD], 1991). The Clean Air and Clean Water acts established reasonably high standards for air and water quality. The percentage of the population served by sewage treatment plants with capacity for secondary treatment had more than doubled.

Nevertheless, despite enormous efforts by activist groups and governmental agencies and despite an impressive volume of environmental legislation, overall environmental quality has not dramatically improved since 1970. While there have been some considerable improvements, in other ways the situation has gotten worse. Our basic life support systems continue to decline. The statistics are well publicized and widely known. A brief review may help to bring them back into perspective. Since 1970 in the United States:

- Overall quality of surface waters has declined slightly (U.S. EPA, 1987).
- Groundwater quality has declined significantly, especially in agricultural regions, and most especially in the midwestern grain-belt states (Frederick, 1991).
- Overdrafts of groundwater have increased dramatically, especially in western and midwestern states (Rogers, 1985).
- Failure or inadequacy of sewage treatment plants and urban and agricultural runoff have increasingly polluted coastal waters. More than 2000 beaches in the United States were closed in 1991 for this reason (Stammer, 1992).
- Water quality in bays and estuaries has declined considerably for the same reason (WRI, 1992).
- Overall air quality has improved somewhat—20 to 30 percent for most pollutants and over 80 percent for lead (OECD, 1991). Nevertheless, 62 cities in the United States still failed to meet federal standards for ozone and carbon monoxide in 1987 (U.S. EPA, 1987).
- Emissions of greenhouse gases (mostly carbon dioxide and methane) have increased significantly (over 30 percent in the case of carbon dioxide) (WRI and IIED, 1988).
- Of the two main contributors to acid rain, emissions of sulphur oxides have decreased considerably (over 30 percent) and nitrogen oxide emissions have decreased slightly (WRI and IIED, 1988).
- The rate of soil erosion has increased (see, for example, Clark et al., 1985).

Globally, the situation is considerably worse with respect to both air and water quality. Depletion and degradation did not start to level off after 1970 but instead accelerated.

- Human use has reduced about 11 percent of the world's best agricultural soils to a badly degraded state over the past half century, mostly during the last 20 years (Oldeman et al., 1990).
- Abusive and exploitative land-use practices turn over 6 million hectares of productive semiarid land to desert each year (IUCN et al., 1991).
- Also each year, more than 180,000 square kilometers of tropical forest are cleared for unsustainable development (IUCN et al., 1991).

The trends are not encouraging; nowhere do they show the levels of improvement needed to achieve sustainability.

At the global level the increasing destruction is not so surprising. The means for controlling it hardly exist. Nobody ever thought rainforest destruction or desertification were under control. We have long known that achieving a sustained yield in the world's fisheries or forests would be a long, hard job. Yet in the United States, only 20 years ago it seemed we had turned a corner; solutions were in sight. The legislation of the 1970s was the triumph of the environmental movement. Why did it not accomplish more?

First, we should make it clear that, despite the numbers, the legislation was not entirely a failure. Given the population growth of the United States since the first Earth Day, we can reasonably claim that pollution levels per capita have decreased. Given that industrial and agricultural production were growing even faster than the population, it was a considerable accomplishment to prevent even greater deterioration. However, if we take sustainability of basic life-support processes as the most essential goal—as the minimum acceptable level of environmental quality and the basic criterion for success or failure of our environmental policies and practices—then we can certainly not pronounce the legislation a success.

As the realization dawned in the 1980s that the general trajectory of resource depletion and environmental degradation was continuing its downward course despite concerted efforts to solve the problems, some people began to ask why and some tried to answer. There were those who said our commitment was not strong enough, and there is undeniably some truth in that. The national political climate in the United States during the 1980s ran counter to environmental improvement. But that did not explain everything. Some said we had not been willing to spend enough money. Perhaps this was true, but the amounts spent were enormous by any reasonable standard: for example, over $100 billion was spent in the private and public sectors on water pollution control alone (Smith et al., 1987). On the contrary, it could be argued that we were relying too much on money to solve our problems.

Others blamed lax enforcement of environmental regulations. The agencies concerned replied that they were doing the best they could; staffs were too small for adequate enforcement, and besides, there just weren't many options. Given the magnitude and complexity of pollution problems, the uncertainty of causes, the multiplicity of sources, and the difficulties of monitoring, failures of enforcement are not surprising. The complexity of the prescriptive means commonly used for regulation probably pose an impossible task. Moreover, big industry begets big government for controlling it, and the governmental bureaucracy is itself difficult to control. On the other hand, there have certainly been signs of reluctance to fully shoulder regulatory responsibility, and this was especially evident during the 1980s. Until 1990, for example, the Environmental Protection Agency (EPA) allowed firms responsible for dumping toxic wastes to assess the health risks of their own dumping as well as determine the best means for cleaning them up. Moreover, the EPA did not—still does not—enforce penalties, such as loss of highway funds, for noncompliance with air-quality standards.

Barry Commoner (1990), representing a widely held view, argues persuasively that a basic problem lies in our means of production; to solve pollution problems, we have to change our ways of making things. Commoner's argument addresses the basic problem of linear flows; his logic is certainly right as far as it goes but is only part of the story. Even more deeply imbedded in our culture, in fact among the primary ingredients of culture, are our ways of shaping the human environment. The palliative approaches taken so far in environmental regulation have not been adequate to deal with the fundamental structure of one-way flows that we have built not only into our means of production but into the very design of our cities and our landscape—our fundamental sources of sustenance.

Inadequacy of Palliatives

The palliative approach is embedded in most of our environmental legislation beginning with the National Environmental Policy Act (NEPA) of 1969. At NEPA's heart is the requirement that an environmental impact statement be prepared for any project that might significantly affect the environment. In some ways this requirement was a revolutionary notion when NEPA was enacted. For the first time the simple and ancient moral imperative that we take responsibility for the results of our actions was extended beyond human relationships to include the physical environment. It was a major step into a new dimension of institutionalized morality and a clear manifestation of a new world view evolving in our time.

But amidst the good intentions, there is a reactive tone in the language of NEPA. In the very words "environmental impact" we hear the assumption, long a tenet of Western culture, that humans and nature swell in realms apart and thus human works must run counter to nature. "Impact" suggests an iron fist hammering on nature from outside. When it comes to dealing with the fist, there is a tone of ambivalence in the provisions of NEPA. Included are requirements for alternative plans and mitigation measures. These open the door to the necessity of more ecologically benign designs. Taken seriously, they could be combined to inspire new ways of shaping the environment. This must certainly be what the drafters of NEPA had in mind when they called in its introduction for "harmony between man and environment."

In practice, however, it rarely works that way. Conceptually different alternatives are rarely offered in impact reports, and mitigation measures are usually presented as means for softening the blows of the fist. They take a variety of different forms, common among which are pollution control devices. Here again there is an assumption that our means for changing the environment—our industrial processes and our land development practices—will remain essentially as they are, though with adjustments to render them environmentally acceptable.

At first hearing, that approach sounds reasonable enough. Why change any more than necessary a system that in so many ways serves our needs very well? But it depends for its reasonableness on another assumption: that we can predict accurately the impacts of our actions. To some degree, we can in most cases make such predictions, as least in a general way and up to a point. But nature is much too complex to be entirely predictable. Cause and effect are often not sequential but intertwined and dynamic in ways that defy analysis. Multiple causes can bring on single effects and vice versa, which can make prediction doubtful. Chaos theory has shown how very small perturbations can multiply in time to throw an entire system out of equilibrium. Tracing pollutants back to their sources sometimes proves virtually impossible. Studies by the Southern California Air Quality Management District have shown cancer risks in certain areas over 1000 times greater than levels considered acceptable by the state of California. Yet they have found no way of tracing these to particular pollutants.

Moreover, effects can take a long time to happen, and they can be almost invisible. Those who stored nuclear wastes around Hanford, Washington could not have predicted the horrors that the radiating materials eventually would bring, and the freeway builders of the 1950s and 1960s could not have known they were contributing to global warming. Impact reports in those situations would not have changed anything; such is the case with many of our most difficult environmental issues.

Nevertheless, predictions are at least good enough to be worth the effort; that approach derives from an intellectual tradition that is well developed and has proven useful. The failing of NEPA—and of other legislation that followed it—is that it does not reach beyond that prevailing tradition in pursuing its revolutionary purpose. It fails to ask us to make an effort to design a human environment that actually does result in "harmony between man and his environment." Albert Gore (1992) put it this way: "The problem is not our effect *on* the environment so much as it is our relationship *with* the environment" (p. 34). Rather than mitigating impacts, we might create ecologically harmonious development that by its very nature requires no mitigation, recognizing that humans are integrally part of the environment. NEPA instead demands only that we analyze our mistakes and apply patches.

The most commonly applied patches—the pollution control devices—made some immediate improvements, during the 1970s and 80s, especially when they were applied on large industrial plants with highly concentrated emissions. In the early years of pollution control (1970s), it was widely believed (or hoped) that most pollution came from such concentrated "point sources." In most cities, regulatory agencies demanded that industries hasten to install the proper equipment to reduce emissions. With billions of dollars per year involved in this effort, improvements in the technology came quickly.

Importance of Nonpoint Sources

Many, though by no means all, industries complied with the requirements and installed the "best available technology" for the purpose, which was what the legislation usually demanded. While improvement in some places was considerable, it gradually became obvious that these tactics were not turning the pollution tide. Increasing reductions of point-source emissions from such concentrated sources as manufacturing plants were making more obvious the even greater volume of nonpoint-source emissions from sources spread out over the urban and agricultural landscapes. In the case of air quality, especially in the cities with the greatest problems like Los Angeles, the automobile was the greatest culprit. In the industrialized nations, automobiles are responsible for about three-quarters of the carbon monoxide, half of the nitrogen oxides, and two-fifths of the hydrocarbons emitted. Reducing these by means of pollution control devices is vastly more difficult than reducing point-source emissions. Even if we assume that the devices are effective when they are working, which is only partially correct, checking catalytic converters and other smog devices on millions of cars takes many times the number of hours that it takes to monitor emission control devices on a small number of large industrial plants. The regulatory bureaucracy becomes an overwhelming organizational problem. Nevertheless, virtually all efforts so far to reduce air pollution have relied on end-of-the-pipe solutions.

In water pollution, the results have been similar: Industry again emerged as the lesser culprit, though still a major one. It has become increasingly clear that the greatest contributors to water pollution are nonpoint sources. Nevertheless, before 1982, 99 percent of federal funding for water pollution control went to dealing with point-source problems (Copeland and Zinn, 1986). Nationally, the greatest water polluter is agriculture, a widely dispersed nonpoint source. Agricultural pesticides and fertilizers are the chemicals most at fault in polluting lakes, streams, and groundwater.

What this means is that pollution is a problem that spreads out and permeates the landscape. In the case of automobiles, pollution is embedded in transportation systems, our daily habits, and our land-use patterns. In the case of agriculture it is spread over the approximately 11 percent of the earth's surface covered by cultivated farmland, integrally part of industrial farming practices that have been standard in much of the world since the 1950s. In both of these cases, as in so many others, *pollution and degradation derive fundamentally from our ways of using and abusing the land.*

Point and nonpoint sources aside, other short-comings in pollution control devices soon became obvious as well. The scrubbers added to industrial stacks to reduce emissions and the baghouses that collected particulates proved very expensive and not entirely reliable. On a smaller scale but in immensely greater numbers, the catalytic converters added to automobile exhausts have similar problems. While they reduce hydrocarbons, they also increase emissions of sulfates, sulfuric acid, and carbon dioxide. They increase gasoline consumption as well.

Moreover, even when working smoothly, pollution control devices often do no more than move pollutants from one place to another. The stacks on industrial plants grow taller to carry emissions out of local areas, but this gets them into regional patterns of air movement to be carried on the winds to distant lakes and forests, where they can fall as acid rain. Pollutants kept out of the stacks by the scrubbers and baghouses are collected on the ground and thus prevented from fouling the air, but then they have to be put somewhere. Often this means landfills, where they can build over years and decades into large concentrations, thus adding to the myriad problems of landfills.

It often happens that in controlling pollution, we simply convert one set of pollutants into a different, less visible set. An example is the commonly used air and water pollution control devices that transform organic materials into water vapor and carbon dioxide, which are usually considered harmless. But the carbon dioxide can make its way upward into the greenhouse layer, while the water vapor can affect local microclimates.

All in all, it has become discouragingly clear that the palliatives are not succeeding. They can be useful in the short term; perhaps they can help to prevent the environment from deteriorating to hopeless levels while we work on longer-range solutions. But they have brought us no closer to a sustainable biosphere. Probably they never will because the problems they are trying to set right go far deeper than such solutions. *The problems are manifestations of structural failure in the global infrastructure constructed over the past two centuries.*

Designing Regenerative Systems

Coming back to where we began, we can envision sustainable development as an antidote to this pattern of unsustainability. Since development in this context means modifying and adapting the landscape to support human populations, sustainable development does not result in landscapes that are "natural" in the generally accepted sense. Natural landscapes by definition have evolved without substantial human influence.

That large areas of the global landscape must be protected from development and thus preserved in their natural state is beyond doubt for a number of reasons that have been convincingly argued many times. Undisturbed nature provides our best source for understanding how natural processes work. It is the most fundamental part of our library of information for living on the earth. But it is important to recognize that most of the earth's surface is already in human use. Inevitable levels of population growth mean that even more of it will be modified over the next few decades and that the areas already modified will change further. That is, there will be a great deal of development. The character and quality of that development will determine the health of the biosphere. Karl-Henrik Robert (1991) puts it like this: "We must learn to deal with environmental problem at the systemic level; if we heal the trunk and the branches, the benefits for the leaves will follow naturally" (p. 7). *Sustainability depends primarily on environmental design.*

In supporting its population, the developed landscape has to provide ongoing supplies of energy and materials for habitat, daily living, and economic activity. The first law of thermodynamics makes it clear that the one-way throughput system in unsustainable energy and materials cannot be created or destroyed, only transformed from one state to another. This means that, in order to be sustainable, the supply systems for energy and materials must be continually self-renewing, or regenerative, in their operation. That is, sustainability requires ongoing regeneration.

The term "regenerative" was first promoted in relation to use of the land by Robert Rodale in an effort to symbolize the enlargement and expansion of his work in organic farming and gardening. He used the word with reference to the continuing organic renewal of the complex life of the soil that occurs in the absence of agricultural chemicals. The same principle of ongoing self-renewal can apply equally to all of the systems that support life. In this book we are concerned with the means for providing the necessities of daily life: energy, shelter, water, food, and waste processing. Since these are embedded in the landscape, dealing with them is largely a matter of designing and managing the landscape. *Regenerative design means replacing the present linear system of throughput flows with cyclical flows at sources, consumption centers, and sinks.*

The same principles, however, can apply to the economy as a whole. In a scientific sense, regeneration involves a set of demonstrable natural processes that we can make operational for human purposes. At this point a clearer definition may be useful. *A regenerative system provides for continuous replacement, through its own functional processes, of the energy and materials used in its operation.* Energy is replaced primarily by incoming solar radiation, while materials are replaced by recycling and reuse. Such a system generally has the following characteristics:

- operational integration with natural processes, and by extension with social processes;
- minimum use of fossil fuels and manmade chemicals except for backup applications;
- minimum use of nonrenewable resources except where future reuse or recycling is possible and likely;
- use of renewable resources within their capacities for renewal;
- composition and volume of wastes within the capacity of the environment to reassimilate them without damage.

The connotations of the term "regenerative system", however, go well beyond definition. John Dewey (1916) observed that "the most notable distinction between living and inanimate things is that the former maintain themselves by renewal" (p. 1). *Regeneration has to do with rebirth of life itself, thus with hope for the future.* In this sense we can apply it to the earth as a whole. That life on earth is diminished and threatened by degenerative practices and technologies is no longer a matter of dispute. Reversing the degenerative trend will be a long and difficult job that may well occupy the world's attention for the next century or more. The price of failure would be unthinkably high, probably not outright extinction of the human species but certainly unimaginable levels of human misery, and probably the end of civilization. A great many approaches and programs will be tried in the effort to change. Among these, regenerative systems deserve a prominent place, especially as a long-range solution. Pursuing this direction means that within a relatively short period of time, the world will have to move from a simple, highly mechanized technological base to one of great complexity, rooted in natural processes. Thus, regenerative systems can play a central role in global renewal. It has often been said (see, for example, Gore, 1992) that solving the environment/resource dilemma is not a matter of technology alone. The human relationship with nature is the core issue. In response to this argument, it is important to remember that technology is a clear manifestation of that relationship.

A Different Kind of Technology

Daniel Bell (1973) has defined technology broadly as "the use of scientific knowledge to specify ways of doing things in a reproducible manner" (p. 29). In these terms, technology did not originate with the industrial era. While regenerative systems represent a technological realm quite different in concept and basic operation from that of industrial systems, they are not new. In one sense they are as old as the human species. Since fossil fuels were not available until just two centuries ago, humans had to rely until then mostly on locally available resources. History provides a storehouse of experience on what works to the long-term benefit of humanity and what does not. There are numerous examples dating from the Bronze Age of civilizations that devoured their resource base, especially their forests and their soils, in ways as degenerative as any of our own time, though before the use of fossil fuels, they did so at a much more gradual pace. The early hydraulic civilizations of Mesopotamia and the exploitative practices of the Roman Empire are two examples. However, there are also historical examples of sustainable societies, some of which developed ingenious means of drawing on natural processes to provide food, water, and energy. Northern European and some meso-American cultures are examples. A number of other examples will be given in later chapters of this book.

Furthermore, traditional regenerative practices did not entirely disappear when fossil fuels came into use. Although industrial development spread over most of the world, traditional practices survived in a great many places. Highly sophisticated regenerative agriculture is still widely practiced in China, for example. In Indonesia there are examples of complex polycultures (diverse combinations of plants commonly used in traditional agricultural systems) side by side with rice monocultures managed in the industrial mode.

Even in the industrialized countries, regenerative practices have never entirely disappeared. Organic farms, while not common, have continued to exist and prosper. Enthusiasts like Rudolph Steiner, Louis Bromfield, and J. I. Rodale continued to expand and refine regenerative food growing techniques in the 20th century. In the more mechanical areas the technology of wind generators, solar collectors, bicycles, and other devices continued to develop, although very slowly and with little institutional support. With the growth of the environmental movement, both the number of people inventing and developing regenerative methods and the number using them increased rapidly. During the 1970s and 1980s, small organizations like the New Alchemy Institute (in Massachusetts), the Land Institute (in Kansas), and the Permaculture Institute (in Tasmania) advanced the theory and practice of sustainable systems in myriad promising ways. E. F. Schumacher (1973) coined the term "appropriate technology" to describe the many devices developed for use in nonindustrial countries. Appropriate technology is practical and within the skills and economic means of potential users. Under this banner, engineers and tinkerers have developed a broad range of devices, most of them for third-world applications.

At this point, then, the foundation on which to base regenerative systems is large and quite solid though it is hardly a complete or coherent body of knowledge. A great many examples of regenerative technologies are in place and working effectively. They have proven practical and economical. Chemical free farms, natural sewage treatment plants, passive solar buildings, and wind generators are hardly rarities anymore, although neither are they yet mainstream technology. Joining ancient traditions and practices with modern science and technology offers enormous potential for the future. Following the oil shortages of the 1970s, there was a widespread tendency to assume that the depletion of petroleum means returning to preindustrial levels of technology and standards of living. There is no reason why this should be so. Scientific knowledge and technological skills are even more applicable to regenerative systems than to industrial ones. Regenerative systems can encompass every level of technology from the very simple to the highly complex. Electronic communications and information processing will certainly play central roles. Computer modeling of complex systems and electronic tools for dynamic management are becoming more sophisticated and practical. The need to operate on sources of energy less concentrated than petroleum offers exciting challenges to creative design and engineering.

Thus technological development will certainly continue and perhaps for a time accelerate as new ways replace old ones, though probably with a different conceptual base and new ground rules. Given that regenerative systems must recognize natural limits, much of the research will probably have to do with accomplishing more with less. Mindless consumption of the sort that has characterized the last half of the 20th century is not likely to occur in a regenerative economy; concepts like planned obsolescence will probably have no place. It is plausible, however, that regenerative systems can provide enough energy and material goods for a comfort-able and dignified life for everyone if population growth can be controlled.

Is the Neotechnic Age Finally Beginning?

Whatever the technological underpinnings may be for the age that follows the fossil-fuel era, life is likely to be different in both material and nonmaterial aspects. There are good reasons to think that, for humanity as a whole, both can be better in the post-petroleum world, especially the nonmaterial life.

Almost since its beginnings, a great many thoughtful people have been deeply uneasy with industrial technology. Much of the literature and art dealing with science and technology, beginning with Mary Shelley's *Frankenstein* and continuing through the film era from Lang's *Metropolis* up to *Terminator II,* has featured the persistent notion that in industrial technology we have created a monster beyond our control, a monster that might very well end up destroying us. In the 20th century it has become a general assumption that technology is indeed out of control, and that it is in large measure responsible for the social deterioration, personal alienation, transitoriness, and general malaise that plague our society.

Throughout the 19th century, concern focused mostly on social ills: long hours required of workers laboring under barely livable conditions; child labor; crowded, unhealthy housing; and exploitative wages. There was some worry about environmental conditions as well, especially the noxious clouds of smoke that enveloped so many industrial towns. Around mid-century the urban-parks-and-walks movement became active in England, promoting the view that environmental improvements and connection with nature could do much to relieve the unhealthy conditions under which urban workers lived. In its concern with physical and mental health and revitalization, this approach was an essentially regenerative one. It grew and expanded, leading eventually to the park systems now accepted as essential to urban well-being. Around the beginning of the 20th century, Camillo Sitte (1901) first called parks the "lungs of the city," this was an impressive insight when we consider all we have since learned about the roles of plants in maintaining the composition of the atmosphere. At about the same time, Ebenezer Howard made his proposal for building "garden cities" to house the growing urban multitudes. These were neat and orderly, low-density new towns set within greenbelts of natural and agricultural lands, forests, orchards, and woodlots. Sewage and other organic wastes were to be treated and returned to the soils of the greenbelts. In its use of natural processes, this is clearly regenerative thinking.

A few years later Patrick Geddes (1915) published his study of the urban growth patterns stimulated by the evergrowing and multiplying factories, and the consequent mass movement of people from country to city. These were patterns never seen before in human experience: cities that spread in vast stretches over the landscape, covering hills and valleys, floodplains, farms, and whatever was in their path until they bumped into the spreading edges of neighboring cities. Here is his description of Greater London at the time: "This octopus of London, polypus rather, is something curious exceedingly, a vast irregular growth without previous parallel in the world of life—perhaps likest to the spreadings of a great coral reef" (ibid., p. 26). Geddes was a biologist by profession, and this shows in his description as well as his perceptions. His was the first fundamentally organic understanding of cities, and he had little liking for the chaotic growth that he saw resulting from industrialization: "Such swift multiplication of the quantity of life, with correspondingly swift exhaustion of the material resources on which this life depends has been too much . . . like that of the mould upon the jam-pot" (ibid., p. 52).

Geddes's antidote was planning at the regional scale, based on a solid analytical understanding of the natural features and processes of the landscape and its resources. His notions of planning influenced regional planning movements in other parts of Europe and in the United States.

Geddes did not expect the industrial era as he described it to last. Rather, he envisioned a division like the distinction that historians make between the Old and the New Stone ages or between the Paleolithic and the Neolithic.

The period between the emergence of machinery in the late 18th century and his own time he called the Paleotechnic era which was as crude in its way as the Paleolithic, though with more impressive hardware. Geddes believed he could see this period beginning to give way to a new era, which he called the Neotechnic age:

> . . . Just as our paleotechnic money-wealth and real property is associated with the waste and dissipation of the stupendous resources of energy and materials and power of using them, which the growing knowledge of Nature is ever unlocking for us, so their better neotechnic use brings with it potentialities of wealth and leisure beyond past Utopian dreams. This time the Neotechnic order, if it means anything at all, with its better use of resources and population towards the bettering of man and his environment together, means these as a business proposition—the creation, city by city, region by region, of its Eutopia, each a place of effective health and well-being even of glorious and in its way unprecedented beauty, renewing and rivalling the best achievements of the past and all this beginning here, there, and everywhere—even where our paleotechnic disorder seems to have done its very worst (ibid., p. 72).

Published in the early 20th century, his study expresses an unmistakably regenerative vision of the future. From the vantage point of the late 20th century, it also seems hopelessly naive. Hardly anyone has dared to be so optimistic since. The great Neotechnic era that Geddes thought he saw emerging has not happened; the Paleotechnic continued to flourish.

Geddes was not, however, the last to announce the demise of the industrial age. A number of writers have done that, always with high hopes. No one has mourned its passing. David Riesman (1958), who seems to have been the first to use the term "postindustrial," wrote of a society turning its major focus of attention from work to leisure. A few years later Daniel Bell (1973) also saw a postindustrial society emerging and defined it in terms of five dimensions. The first was the change from a goods-producing to a service economy. The other four had to do with knowledge and its uses. Bell predicted a shift from the industrial era's emphasis on practical knowledge to a new central role for theoretical knowledge as a basis for innovation and policy. Along with the primacy of theory, he suggested that society might achieve another fundamentally important dimension of change: the ability to plan and control its own technological development. As the control of technology became stronger, the professional and technical class would gain an increasingly preeminent position in society. This class would include the engineers and economists who dominated the industrial era but no longer would they be in control. The knowledge base and the decision-making apparatus would be much broader, and to deal with the increasing complexity Bell saw a new "intellectual technology" of decision making emerging.

Though numerous observers have followed Riesman and Bell in proclaiming the arrival of the postindustrial era and the term itself has entered the general vocabulary, in some ways they are all premature. From the employment point of view, Bell is unquestionably correct; the majority of jobs are now in the service sector and that percentage increases with each census. However, this results largely from automation and the movement of factories to different countries. Our goods-producing apparatus and our basic life-support systems still function mostly in the fossil-fuel-powered, degenerative industrial mode. The one-way flows of industrial society are still very much with us.

As for the control of technology and the ability to control technological development, the issue is still in doubt. We might see regenerative technologies as being in the forefront of the struggle to establish a socially and ecologically benign technological base, drawing on a broad fund of theoretical knowledge and susceptible to social control. Industrial technology, along with its tendency to proliferate beyond control, shows no signs of giving way easily. While the interests of a large majority are probably best served by a regenerative technological base, a powerful minority profits enormously from uncontrolled industrial technology. The question of who will make the important decisions on these matters remains open. Bell believed that the desire for participation in the decision-making processes that affect everyone's life would be a serious source of social conflict. Events have borne him out; public participation in decisions, especially decisions concerning the physical environment, has increased enormously over the past 20 years. Public-opinion polls consistently indicate serious concern over environmental quality—including, for example, a consistent preference for environmentally benign energy sources. The interests of future generations are also of grave concern. However, governmental institutions, which are beset by inflexibility, confusion, complexity, and conflict, have often been unable to make any decision at all. Short-term thinking, related to the length of terms in office, tends to pre-

vail, although environmental and resource issues inevitably involve very long term policy.

We should recognize, however, that the desires of the public are not usually based on complete knowledge of a situation. Ours is a time when a great deal of information is widely available. Indeed, many observers believe the postindustrial era is characterized primarily by the power of information rather than by either the importance of leisure or the change to a service economy. However, much—perhaps almost all—of the information that inundates our lives is either irrelevant to anything that truly matters or is misleading. Concerning the great questions of our time, most people—including most of the professional and technical class—remain poorly informed. The tendency to deny a difficult and ominous reality as long as possible is extremely tempting.

So it seems that we remain in the midst of Bell's last four dimensions of change, which involve information. While the outcomes are still in doubt, there are reasons for optimism, among them the growing acceptance of all that is summed up in the term "sustainable development."

Regenerative systems are coming into wider use, as I will show in the chapters that follow. Many of the technologies involved are tried and proven in practice; some of them are used everyday by mainstream organizations. These technologies are ready for widespread application. Putting them to use, integrating them into the natural and social environment, will require highly sophisticated levels of design. Perhaps it is not entirely too optimistic to join Geddes in his hopes and imagine, three-quarters of a century later, that the Neotechnic era is beginning at last. We might see Bell's dimensions of change as the social mechanics of its operation.

For the remainder of this book I will follow Patrick Geddes in referring to the first, fossil-fuel-powered industrial period of the past two centuries as the Paleotechnic, and the new period that may be emerging, founded partly on regenerative systems, as the Neotechnic.

CASE STUDY

■■■

The Center for Regenerative Studies
as a Neotechnic Community

What will a Neotechnic future look like? How will regenerative systems function? What will it be like to live in a regenerative community? The Center for Regenerative Studies to explore the possibilities and the implications of these questions. It has evolved from an idea that first took shape in 1976 through completion of the first phase of construction in 1993. In this book, the Center will serve —as a case study to illustrate application of the concepts and techniques in each chapter.

Because both the possibilities and the implications are intertwined with society, inseparable from people, the Center is a living community as well as a university-based setting for education, demonstration, and research in regenerative technologies. On a 16-acre site on the campus of the California State Polytechnic University (Cal Poly) in Pomona, it incorporates facilities for a broad range of practices and technologies dealing with energy, shelter, water, food, waste, and other essential functions. It is a community in which students work with regenerative technologies as integral parts of their daily lives, thus providing the means for studying these practices in ongoing daily routines. This is important because in some cases these practices require shifts in social organization of their users. For effective and benign application the relationships between regenerative practices and human attitudes and behavior are probably as important as the functioning of the technologies themselves (Lyle et al., 1987).

PURPOSES

The Center's community, which includes 20 residents in the first phase and will eventually increase to 90, grows food, generates energy, regulates its own thermal environment, and recycles wastes. In the process the students and faculty members learn about, demonstrate for others, and experiment with the practices and technologies involved.

Education in regenerative studies is the primary purpose of the Center. In the polytechnical tradition, graduate and undergraduate students learn by doing in laboratory courses conducted on the site. Students grow food using various regenerative agricultural and aquacultural techniques. They also build and operate devices for generating energy, disposing of wastes, and carrying out other basic tasks.

Because the Neotechnic understanding of the world is quite different from the Paleotechnic, it requires a different approach to education. The integration of learning with daily life and its merging with technology, the interdisciplinary structure and the ongoing interaction among teachers and students are all important aspects of this emerging culture.

Demonstration of these processes for the university community and the interested public is the Center's second major purpose. As the facilities develop and become operational, they will be open for visitors and tours, and demonstrations will be provided for educational groups. The Center will also offer guidance and consultation services to those interested in applications of practices within its areas of expertise. Such public education is an important part of the Center's mission. Public knowledge of regenerative technologies is presently very limited and is crucial to widespread acceptance and application.

Research is the Center's third purpose. While no less important than the first two, research programs will develop more slowly because they depend on having well developed, fully functioning facilities, and a fund of experience and knowledge about their operation. Ultimately, the Center's development will depend on research because both educational and demonstration programs can only grow from research. As the Center reaches this level of activity, it will offer varied opportunities for original contributions in a number of disciplines and combinations of disciplines, including several areas of agriculture, aquaculture, architecture, landscape architecture, engineering, and social science.

FACILITIES

It is extremely important that the physical facilities, the social organization, and the academic program of the Center be shaped to fit its purpose. Technologies can be successful only to the extent that they can adapt to human psyche and physique and to the extent that people are willing and able to adapt to their operational requirements. This is especially true of regenerative practices because they generally require more active human participation and more cooperative efforts than industrial technologies. This is why the Center is designed as a community that will explore the interactions between people and technological practices as well as the practices themselves.

Such exploration requires that the community be large enough to accomplish the necessary supporting tasks but small enough to form a

cohesive social unit. The Center is developing in phases. The initial increment, now in operation, includes 20 students, two visiting scholars, and a resident advisor.

Facilities include residential units to house students and resident advisors as well as dining and common facilities, educational and research space. There will also be storage, shop areas, and other ancillary facilities. Vehicular access is limited to those vehicles needed for service, work purposes, deliveries, and emergencies.

The physical order and visible form of the Center's buildings and landscape are important to its success. While industrial technologies often ignore the interactive relationships between physical form and environment, regenerative technologies depend on the correspondence of form and environment for their continually renewing qualities. By shaping the architecture of site and buildings for such correspondence, we can establish optimal conditions for the operation of regenerative technologies from the very beginning.

But the importance of form goes far beyond its functional role. By adapting to the diverse conditions of the environment, landscape and architecture can give visible expression to fundamental relationships between humans and nature implicit in regenerative practices.

Since the design of the Center is based upon the principles and practices explored in this book, it represents an inclusive example of their application. In each of the following chapters, a particular aspect of the Center will be described in some detail to illustrate and expand on the subject matter of that chapter.

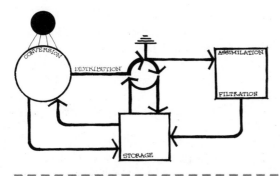

■■■

Chapter 2
Science, Design,
and Regeneration

Development, sustainable or otherwise, involves change in the landscape guided by human will— usually for agriculture, or urbanization, or recreation. Nature also develops the landscape, albeit more slowly; evolution and succession are developmental processes. When we reshape a landscape, we radically alter a system of forms and relationships that are the current manifestation of some 4.6 billion years of evolution. The results are unimaginably complex, interrupting countless interactions, destroying millions of creatures, most of which are unseen and hardly known. No one has ever succeeded in cataloging every organism present in even a few square yards of earth; thus we destroy what we don't even know.

The problem lies partly in our 20th-century habit of thinking of development as a matter of economics, or what Daly and Cobb (1989) call the "focus on mathematics in place of empirical attention to physical reality" (p. 39). The Paleotechnic emphasis on productivity and its quantitative measures has tended to place economic concerns at the center of human motivations. In this way of thinking, rationality and economic gain are synonymous. But the reality of the world is far greater than eco-

nomic abstractions. Though the purpose of development is usually economic and it always produces economic results, the essential physical reality of development is change in the ecology of the landscape.

Dilemma of Development

In our culture we are like children playing in a sandbox, undertaking development projects casually and routinely, usually with only the minimal thought for the consequences as required by law. However, the moral and philosophical implications are enormous. The practical implications are considerable as well, especially if we take the long-term perspective; in diminishing the natural environment, we threaten to destroy ourselves. The dilemma is this: Development is necessary to provide habitat and sustenance for our society, but development inevitably alters natural systems, usually for the worse.

On the one hand, we can adopt the view, often expressed in the environmental literature since the 1960s, that humans have no right to wreak such devastation on a natural community purely for human interest. The damage is in a sense irreparable: That particular natural community can never exist again. Moreover, the processes occurring in that landscape have been permanently disrupted; they will never function in exactly the same way again, and this is probably to the long-term disadvantage of humans as well as other species.

On the other hand, by adopting the view that humans are part of nature, we can reasonably say that developing the landscape for human purposes is not qualitatively different from alterations made by other species. Why should we regard a dam built by humans as ecologically destructive while we admire the dam building of beavers? Certainly, the environment is changed, but nature is enormously resilient; as soon as the development work is done, nature responds by starting to evolve new sets of relationships leading eventually to a new ecosystem.

There are obvious difficulties with both of these arguments. The former, or preservationist, view is challenged by the enormous number of people living on the earth. As of 1990 the number was about 5.5 billion. By the most conservatively hopeful U.N. estimate, it will level off at around 8 billion sometime in the 21st century. At that point, the earth's life-support capacities will be seriously tested. If the total reaches 14 billion, as some projections suggest, crises of resources and environment will probably be inevitable, regardless of how enlightened our approaches to development may become. In any case, since these people must live somewhere and their food must be grown somewhere, development will inevitably continue. Redevelopment and evolutionary change on lands already developed will continue as well. By the most hopeful estimates, it may be possible to preserve as much as 10 percent of the global landscape, or roughly one-quarter of the undisturbed 39 percent, in a state more or less unaltered by humans. Assuming that about 25 percent will remain essentially unusable, this means that the other 65 percent will be developed to some degree.

As for the conventional development argument, while it is certainly tenable to view humans as part of nature and their actions therefore as natural occurrences, there are critical differences between the development activities of humans and those of other species. Technology is the all-important difference; no other species has the power to reshape the landscape to a degree that is even comparable. Given the degenerative development patterns of the past two centuries, the prognosis is not favorable. Certainly, the 10 percent of the earth's land surface that may be preserved in a natural state is not enough to insure healthy ecological functioning at a global level if 65 percent is rendered ecologically dysfunctional by development.

Evolving Concepts of Nature

This is a complex dilemma made especially difficult by the fact that our understanding of nature and our concepts of the relationship between humans and nature are changing rapidly. As natural processes evolve, so does our understanding of them evolve. Long periods of more or less steady and gradual evolution in the human struggle to grasp nature's patterns are thrown into doubt and confusion by shorter periods of rapid intellectual change. Thomas Kuhn (1970) has shown that these periods of change develop slowly, but once new fundamental concepts take root, they give impetus to rapid shifts in our internalized models, or paradigms, of nature's fundamental workings. A number of observers (such as Capra, 1982, and Toffler, 1970) have argued convincingly that we are in the midst of such a shift right now.

All design of the human environment is based on some fundamental model of the essential character of nature deeply imbedded in the culture—the nature of nature. Much of our difficulty in dealing with resource and environmental issues is brought on by the fact that the human landscape, including the cities in which we live, was shaped according to a concept of nature that grew out of the Renaissance notion that humans are the measure of all things. Renaissance buildings and gardens placed humans firmly in the central position in their ordering of the environment, and thus gave form to a new conception of the human relationship with nature. The axial layout and strict geometry of the Renaissance garden expressed this new relationship between humans and nature with particular clarity.

The thinkers who followed expanded the symbolic statement into a basis for reshaping the world. Francis Bacon, René Descartes, and Isaac Newton are usually credited as originating the ideas that coalesced during the 17th and 18th centuries into a highly mechanistic world view. This view is best symbolized by the conception of the earth as a giant machine. The parts of the machine could be analyzed one at a time through rigorous and objective application of what came to be called the scientific method. Descartes (1647) advised that we should "reduce involved and obscure propositions step by step to those that are simpler, and then, starting with the intuitive apprehension of all those that are absolutely simple, attempt to ascend to the knowledge of all others by precisely similar steps." The knowledge thus gained could be applied through technology to gain power over nature and thus to control her processes. The attitude was given highly sophisticated form in the gardens of the French Baroque period, most notably those designed in the 17th century by André Lenotre at Vaux le Vicomte and Versailles. These imposed absolute geometric form on the landscape, expressing human-imposed

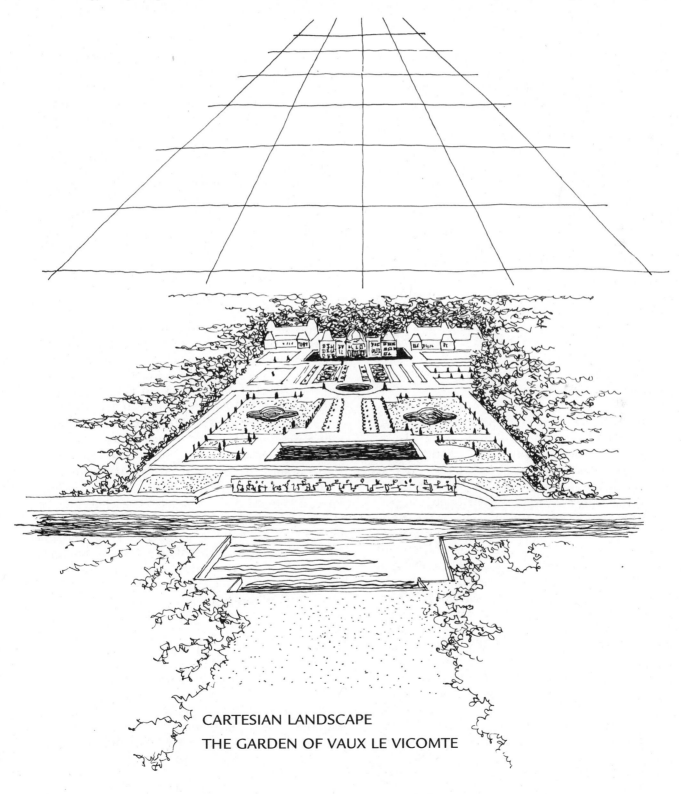

CARTESIAN LANDSCAPE
THE GARDEN OF VAUX LE VICOMTE

order down to the smallest detail, an order that allowed no deviation or evolution. As time went on, scientists studied ever smaller parts on the reductionist assumption that it was possible to understand nature only by understanding her most minute parts.

These ideas were waiting for wider application when the energy potential in fossil fuels was discovered and machines were invented to use that power. Industrialization then began its ambitious task of reshaping the global landscape, a task that was undertaken without plan or program and with only the most pragmatic of visions. This led inevitably to the one-way throughput world.

Throughout the 20th century, contrary concepts have emerged to challenge these assumptions, and these have led to quite different perspectives on nature's underlying order. The emerging understanding of nature views humanity within a more complex, less deterministic, more interdependent, multidimensional world with little resemblance to a machine. Among the important and revolutionary conceptions of nature's processes that have emerged in the 20th century are these:

- Einstein's theory of relativity
- Heisenberg's uncertainty principle
- the global perspective
- chaos theory
- the scale relationships of fractal geometry
- general systems theory

Exactly how these and other fundamental concepts might fit together to form a new model of nature is yet unclear. However, all are integrally related to one emerging, fundamental concept that has overwhelming importance for environmental design: the ecosystem concept. The ecological perspective had its origins just over a century ago in the observations of a few scientists working in Europe and the United States. Their early observations of consistent relationships among the species living in ponds led eventually to the understanding that the species present in any environment form consistent—though complex and not entirely predictable—sets of interactions. Thus they form an ecosystem, which is defined as the living species and nonliving materials and their interrelationships within a given landscape. The landscape can be of any size from a square foot of ground to the whole earth.

The ecosystem concept as first articulated by Tansley (1935) is profoundly important for several reasons. Especially significant among these is the revelation that nature's fundamental order does not lie entirely at the molecular level, as reductionist thinking implies, but at every level. An ecosystem has consistent order. It is also important because it gives scientific credence to the intuitions of such thinkers as Lao Tzu, Plato, Chief Seattle, and John Muir, all of whom have seen wholeness in nature. Everything is indeed "hitched to everything else" (in Muir's phrase), within a vast organic unity (as Plato believed), and humans are included. In clarifying the complex systems of relationships involved in natural processes, the ecosystem concept makes obvious the fundamental flaws in paleotechnology while at the same time establishing a theoretical foundation for neotechnology and regenerative life-support systems.

Our ecological understanding has rendered industrial paleotechnology incongruent with the prevailing model of the inner workings of the world. Who knows what currents of cognitive dissonance may be running through the collective psyche of a society functioning in continuous contradiction to its own knowledge of the world? Such conflicts between what we know and what we perceive can be unsettling indeed.

For the Neotechnic era the governing concept of relationship between humanity and nature is likely to be the ecosystem. It will certainly replace the Newtonian view of earth as a machine. If Bell is right in believing the technology of the future will be more firmly based in theory than that of the past, the ecosystem concept is likely to form an important part of the theoretical foundation. Since all ecosystems include human influence and most include human presence, we might well think of human ecosystems as the ordering systems of life on earth. In nature, ecosystems are continuously changing through the processes of evolution and succession, generally in a trajectory of increasing complexity and efficiency. Where humans dominate the ecosystem, the natural processes of change are, more often than not, severely altered. Nevertheless, ecosystematic order remains operational at some level.

Modes of Ecological Order

Ecosystematic order, while enormously complex in its infinite detail, is relatively simple in concept. In essence, ecosystems are defined by three modes of order, each of which has basic implications for regenerative design. We can think of the ecosystem as being like a house, as reflected in the word "ecology" itself: *ecos* means "house" in Greek, and *logy* refers to "study."

Ecosystematic order, then, is analogous to the order found in buildings. First, there is the structural order of posts, beams, walls, and roof. Second, there is the functional order of material and energy flows represented by the pipes, valves, wires, switches, circuit breakers, ducts, dampers, and other apparatus. Third, there is the locational order of the floor plan.

The ecosystem and its modes of order provide a conceptual model of the world that serves well as a basis for regenerative design. Any landscape, even the whole earth, is a large house.

Structural Order

Structural order describes the composition of living and nonliving elements: rocks, soil, and plant and animal species. In considering the structure of an ecosystem, we include all life and its interactions with nonlife. In natural ecosystems, structure is usually consistent in that each species inhabits a particular niche and maintains ongoing interactions with other species. We can understand ecosystem structure as a process in that it changes with time, either gradually through succession or rapidly through sudden perturbation. Natural structures are continually reorganizing themselves according to certain principles. For example, complex and diverse networks of interaction are generally associated with stability. Among ecologists, this relationship is a matter of ongoing controversy. While diversity and stability seem generally related, there are numerous exceptions. It has been shown that diversity does not necessarily produce stability (May, 1973, 1975). Cause and effect are unclear, though evidence of a relationship between diversity and stability is strong.

Eugene Odum (1975) hypothesized that infusions of energy can enable a simple system to maintain stability; this is what happens in an estuarine wetland, which is a relatively simple natural community, for example. Tidal action supplies the energy subsidy.

Industrial life-support systems are generally simple in terms of elements and interactions. While this is true of mechanical as well as biological systems, we can see it most clearly in industrial agriculture with its vast monocultures. It is not unusual to find a single crop covering most of a region, as with corn in some parts of the midwestern United States. Such monocultures are artificially sustained by heavy infusions of energy in the forms of fertilizers, pesticides, and gasoline for operating tractors. This seems to support Odum's hypothesis.

With their need to reduce energy input, regenerative systems tend to be much more diverse in structure, offering numerous means for accomplishing any particular task and using the interactions among elements or species within a system to benefit the system as a whole. Thus is resilience built into the structure. Polycultures provide one example. With their complex structures, these require little energy input to maintain stability. They need no chemicals and little if any gasoline.

The same principle holds true for other basic support systems. For conveying water, for example, industrial technology substitutes arrow-straight concrete channels for meandering streams with their diverse riparian communities.

Functional Order

The second mode of ecosystematic order derives from function: the flow of energy and materials that distribute the necessities of life to all of the species within the ecosystematic structure. These flows constitute the dynamics of the ecosystem and often explain the flux and change that it undergoes. As with structure, they operate within certain rules that define the behavior of ecosystems. Every landscape receives a new energy infusion from the sun every day. The incoming energy then undergoes a series of transformations, beginning with reflection, absorption, or photosynthesis. Energy absorbed or reflected at the earth's surface warms the atmosphere and contributes to the heat balance. Radiation striking surface waters warms them, eventually to the point of evaporation, thus powering the water cycle. Energy fixed into living matter by photosynthesis makes its way through the food web, supplying all living creatures with energy. Following the second law of thermodynamics, more energy is dissipated as heat with each transformation than is passed on as other forms of energy.

Water, nutrients, and other materials, by contrast, having no source of new supplies, are not lost or dissipated but instead are continually recycled. The cycling systems also work through the food web, closely paralleling the flow of energy and supplying all living creatures with the materials needed for bodily functions.

While both industrial and regenerative systems function within these basic processes, they do so in quite different ways. Industrial systems tend to short-circuit or bypass the natural flows by drawing on energy and materials accumulated in past eons and stored in the earth. Fossil fuels, for example, make it possible to make minimal use of solar energy and to maintain heat balance within a building virtually independent of the larger regional and global heat balance. Groundwater, much of which has been stored since the Ice Ages, makes similar bypassing of the water cycle possible in providing water supplies. In terms of the discussion in Chapter 1, since these sources are not replenished, they fall under the heading of degenerative practices. Regenerative technologies, by contrast, function within the flow systems evolved by nature, using nature's means of replenishment on a sustainable basis and maintaining their functional integrity, or working wholeness.

Locational Patterns

Even before life existed, the surface of the earth varied enormously in climate and geological composition. After life appeared, it was guided by these varied patterns into varied structural and functional compositions. At the extremes, a desert is very different in structure from a rainforest, and there are infinitely varied landscapes in between. The type and number of species that any ecosystem can support are determined largely by the environment in the particular place where it exists, which is in turn determined by the specific local conditions of topography, soil, and climate. An ecosystem is unique to its location.

Until the industrial era, human cultures and the landscapes, buildings, and cities they produced were also uniquely integral parts of their places on earth. Mass communications and transportation have done much to change that. Those along with infusions of fossil fuels have tended to create universal forms in buildings, cities, and landscapes. A highrise office building in São Paulo looks very much like one in New York, London, or San Francisco because fossil-fuel-driven heating and cooling systems, along with their elevators and water and sewage systems, override local climatic conditions. With these and other localized factors eliminated, forms tend to follow models promulgated in the international media.

Similar tendencies tend to prevail in other basic life-support processes. A cornfield plowed by tractors and fertilized and protected from pests by manufactured chemicals is much the same anywhere. Furthermore, universal distribution of hybrid seed varieties developed for the conditions of industrial agriculture has tended to eliminate locally adapted varieties evolved over long periods of time.

Thus corn plants, skyscrapers, and a great many other artifacts of industrial culture respond to contemporary currents of industrial civilization in similar ways and depend on the same nonrenewable resources. *Genius loci*, or spirit of place, becomes a matter of memory and museum exhibits. While the advantages and disadvantages of these universal patterns can be and have been debated at length (for example, see Hough, 1990), they clearly work against structural diversity; equally clearly, they tend to short-circuit energy and material flows. In any case, these patterns are heavily dependent on fossil-fuel infusions; unless new, massive, and cheap sources of energy appear soon, they will fade as fossil-fuel stores diminish.

Regenerative ways for accomplishing these tasks, being dependent on local processes and resources, vary widely with locale. Ways of generating renewable energy depend on levels of solar radiation, prevailing winds, the availability of running water, and in some cases on tides or geothermal activity. Suitable crops depend on soil quality and topography as well as climatic conditions. Such conditions vary according to global patterns, and they vary regionally and locally as well. While there are some consistent conditions within a region—this is what defines a region in the first place—there are also smaller local variations. Even within a single site, conditions can vary considerably, especially with respect to topography and microclimates. This rich, complex system of patterns and patterns within patterns offers a foundation for equally rich patterns of development. Here lie the means for reestablishing connections between people and place as well as between people and natural processes.

Utility and Limitations of Analysis

While scientific analysis is unquestionably essential in dealing with environmental issues, it is important to recognize its limitations. Correct use of the scientific method can produce results approaching certainty only when dealing with just one variable at a time. This is a major reason why so much scientific research deals with small questions, especially the essentially linear aspects of nature's processes at the cellular and molecular level. At this level, precise quantification and prediction are possible, though never with absolute certainty. By applying highly structured observation, science can also be effective in describing nature's larger processes in qualitative terms. These larger processes—like the effect of greenhouse gases on the global heat balance or the interactions among high nutrient loads in offshore waters—involve numerous variables and are therefore extremely difficult to quantify precisely. Causes and effects are not clear and linear but rather are intermixed in complex webs of interactions. A single cause may produce dozens of effects and vice versa. Statistical methods are useful in making reasonably accurate estimates and predictions, but these are never entirely reliable; moreover, statistics are easily manipulated, often unintentionally.

Despite its limitations, the past successes of reductionist analysis and its honored place in Western culture have led the public as well as government agencies to have abiding, often exaggerated, faith in its reliability. Environmental regulations are most easily enforced where precise limits can be established. The question is often asked: How much of this pollutant or that activity can the environment absorb before it becomes unacceptably damaging or life-threatening? This is like asking how many times one can beat a person over the head before he will die, or how much money one can steal from a bank before it will go bankrupt. This is difficult to answer with any accuracy and usually not the most useful question anyway.

Such questions often have led to highly sophisticated mathematical calculations and precisely quantified estimates and predictions based on limited and imprecise data. The reason has much to do with legal processes and formulating rules and regulations. For legal purposes any number, however questionable, is better than none, and if the mathematics behind it is complex enough and based on defensible methodology, it is commonly accepted regardless of the quality of data on which it is based.

Landscape as Process

This prevailing emphasis on analysis of certain partially quantifiable variables selected from the many variables that combine to describe the environment has diverted attention from the highly integrated functioning of the environment as a whole. From the perspective of the courtroom and the laboratory, there has been a tendency to forget that the health, esthetic quality, and sustainability of the environment are determined largely by the way we use the land.

In this context the term "land" presents difficulties. In general usage it usually refers to ownership or political control with connotations of commodity and inertness. What we really are referring to here is a piece of the earth including the rock underlying it, the water, the soil with its countless microorganisms, the plants rooted in it, the animals living on it, the air moving over it, and all the dynamic processes occurring within it. Land is a living ecosystem, but in human terms it is more than a system. We can walk through it, touch it, and form emotional attachments to it. In a sense we can become an integral part of it. Since such an encompassing view of a small piece of earth has developed in Western culture only recently, we have inherited no appropriate word for it. Landscape comes closest, although most definitions of landscape emphasize external appearances. To most people a landscape is a scene. This is probably a carryover from the days when we could perceive the seductive beauty of the surface but could not know the complex processes underlying it. We should update the word "landscape" to include all the life and nonliving materials within and on the land, both natural and human, invisible processes and visible forms, buildings, roads, and whatever else humans or others may have put there. Only if we do so will we have a term for this complex, dynamic living assemblage that is the essence of what we call environment and is an integral and essential part of our lives.

Thus landscape is the physical context of an ecosystem and its visible manifestation. It is a community. In its complex range of activities, this community carries on processes to support itself and others. The ecosystem concept provides a context for analyses of the component processes at whatever level of detail may be useful.

In effect, development means designing a new ecosystem, whether by intention or default. The order of this new ecosystem—its structure, function, and spatial distribution of activities—determines its effects in terms of both resource use and environmental quality. The behavior patterns of the community dwelling within it then further shape its relationship with the larger environment. To paraphrase Winston Churchill, we shape the landscape and then it shapes us.

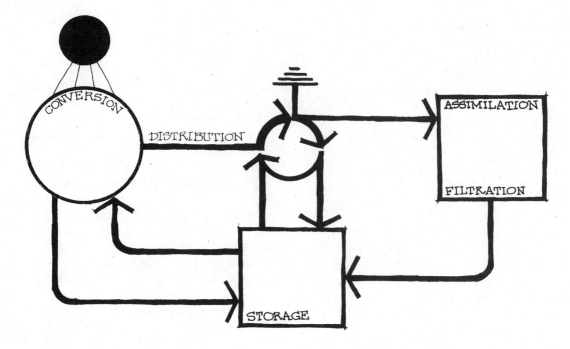

In nature, development means increasing complexity. During the Paleotechnic period, development of the landscape by humans has generally meant simplification—loss of complexity, diminishing of process. It could be otherwise. Although development inevitably alters the operation of natural processes, it is possible to integrate human development into their working order and thus to retain their essential operational integrity and their capacity for regeneration. The regenerative capacities of the landscape lie largely in six basic phases of ecosystem functioning: conversion, distribution, filtration, assimilation, storage, and, where human development occurs, human thought. These six basic processes of regeneration are the keys to the sustenance of life itself and thus to sustainability.

Conversion

In photosynthesis, solar rays become life. If nature's living processes can be said to have a beginning, this is it: the source of the food we eat and the oxygen we breathe. Interacting with other components of the atmosphere, the oxygen given off and the carbon dioxide absorbed during photosynthesis maintain the delicate blend of gases that makes life possible. In processes of conversion, one thing becomes something else.

After arriving at the earth's surface, the radiant energy of the sun goes through a series of conversions—to plant biomass, to animal biomass, to heat

in various forms—before being eventually dissipated back into space. Through this complex series of conversions, it supports all life.

Distribution

In order for energy and materials to reach the innumerable members of an ecological community spread over the landscape, means of distribution are needed. Nature provides a number of such means. The distribution patterns of winds cover the earth. Water itself is first distributed in the atmosphere by the wind and, after it falls back to earth, by gravity within a single watershed. It carries a great many other materials along on its journey. Moving animals, including migratory birds that may fly halfway around the world, also move energy and materials about. The human invention of trains, trucks, ships, and airplanes has added enormously to nature's power of distribution, carrying both natural and manufactured objects everywhere in the world. These distribution patterns bring on continual mixing, mingling, and cross-fertilization, but they also bring on some severe problems related to locational adaptation.

Filtration

As air and water flow over and through the landscape, plants and soil act as filters, removing materials that have been dissolved or otherwise taken up and carried along. The leaves, in effect, cleanse the air as it moves through them. Grasses and ground covers perform the same service for water flowing over the surface of the landscape. Soil and decomposing rock filter out most particles from water making its way from the surface to underground storage. These filtration functions restore the relative purity of the air and water in preparation for the next phases of their ongoing ecological roles. This is nature's waste treatment system.

Assimilation

Everything produced in the landscape returns to the landscape. The materials filtered out of air and water comprise a small portion of the materials returned to the earth for reassimilation. Most of these materials are either dead biomass or what we label as wastes. However, what humans call wastes are essential food for vast populations of decomposing organisms that include numerous species of insects, worms, bacteria, and fungi. These are the infinitely diverse, multitudinous, mostly unseen, often ignored, absolutely essential workhorses of regeneration; their activity comprises most of the earth's biological processes. Eugene Odum (1971) recognizes three stages of decomposition: (1) particulate detritus formed by a physical or biological action, (2) humus production and release of soluble organics, and (3) mineralization of humus, which is much slower. Thus decomposition, or reassimilation, enriches the soil with detritus and humus and provides nutrients for new plant growth. It is the basic process of revitalizing the earth.

Storage

In making their way through the ongoing cycles, materials are held inactive at some points awaiting eventual reuse. For example, water is stored for varying lengths of time in the soil, in the voids of underground rock strata called aquifers, and in lakes and ponds. For periods measured in geological time, some materials are stored as with minerals locked into rock structures or deposited on the ocean floor. Energy has been stored in coal, gas, and petroleum for thousands of years. Other storage periods may last only for hours or days. The detritus on the floor of a tropical rainforest, for example, is quickly broken down in the moist environment and taken up by trees. Thus in a tropical rainforest, nutrients are stored mostly in biomass.

Thought

These processes, indeed virtually all of nature's processes are guided primarily by human activity over more than 60 percent of the global landscape. The exceptions are protected areas and those stretches of Arctic and desert landscape inhospitable enough to be left alone, although humans strongly affect even those landscapes. Under present circumstances this far-reaching control is exerted mostly unintentionally, that is, as a peripheral result of pursuing other goals; nevertheless, sustainability requires that it be guided by thought. Thus nature's processes are joined by the human process of conscious thought, which in fact becomes the guiding force. We may well mourn the loss of free, untrammeled nature existing and evolving apart from human control, but in fact such nature exists only in the relatively small landscapes of protected reserves and even there only within limits. However we may feel about it—whether we wish it to be so or not—the human intellect has become a dominant force in the global landscape. Bill McKibbon (1989) wrote: "We have deprived nature of its independence, and that is fatal to its meaning. Nature's independence is its meaning" (p. 73). Given the far-reaching impact of human activities on atmosphere and water, there are probably no truly independent landscapes left in the world. Having inadvertently taken from nature its meaning, we are left with the grave responsibility of infusing new meaning in human terms. There is no turning back. Humanity has no choice but to provide the mind within nature.

Plato called it the *anima mundi,* and Teihard de Chardin called it the noosphere. Human intellect encompasses the earth. In the context of development, it becomes hard reality; human thought becomes part of the natural process. Here indeed we provide the mind *of* nature. This is a far more complex and subtle role than that envisioned by Bacon, who believed the human purpose was control of nature. In Neotechnic thought, mind and nature join in partnership. The human mind is nature's consciousness, not its master.

The scope and complexity of most development situations requires thought in the forms of cognition, planning, design, engineering, and ongoing management. By cognition, I mean internalized understanding of natural processes. Analysis has an important part to play, but only in the context of profound knowledge of the whole. Planning and design for regenerative development are founded on such understanding. They use information and concepts provided by science, but they are not in themselves scientific.

In emphasizing the importance of thought as applied in these varied ways, I mean analytical and creative intellectual activity. Through the Paleotechnic era, what has passed for thought has too often been the application of formulas, standard practices, and unexamined preconceptions. All professions have been guilty of this, and one result has been increasing challenges to their expertise by laypeople who think. This has given the professions a much-needed impetus to broaden their scope.

In going beyond the limitations—the narrow purpose and scope—of industrial technology and its linear engineering, regenerative systems draw on human creativity for invention and adaptation to ever-varying circumstances. They require creative planning and design to bring together diverse factors, human and natural, and weave them into a coherent whole that is essentially a new ecosystem. Within the whole they also require the operational function that only sound science and engineering can provide. In dealing with the complexities of ecosystems, planning, design, and engineering require more encompassing, more challenging processes of thought than does the linear, deterministic approach of the industrial period. Thought processes mesh with ecological processes; together, they transcend and ultimately determine form.

When the work of planning, design, and engineering is done, management takes over. Because regenerative systems continue to evolve after taking their initial form, management is necessarily a creative activity as well. Continuous monitoring, feedback, and conscious change replace the automatic control mechanisms of nature. Thus management of regenerative systems differs dramatically from the maintenance of industrial systems, the purpose of which is essentially to prevent change.

In this dynamic model of human thought interacting with natural processes, information plays an essential role as the fuel for thought. Computers have made the fuel more powerful and more widely available. Data networks encompass the earth, becoming integral parts of the global mantle of intellect that Teilhard called the noosphere. Networks like ECONET have begun to accomplish this. However, powerful though it may be, information is only the fuel, not the process itself. What is most significant here is that in regenerative development, human thought fuses with nature. Imagination, abstraction, and ecological function join to form a

unified process. In a practical way this is useful, perhaps essential, for achieving sustainability. More importantly, this unifying process can connect the human mind with the inner rhythms of the earth.

Merging of Disciplines

The way of understanding and ordering natural processes described here does not correspond with the conventional breakdown of knowledge into academic disciplines as they have developed since the Enlightenment. Academic disciplines are narrowly defined areas of knowledge and expertise with jealously guarded boundaries having little to do with the realities of natural processes. For this reason the thought required in understanding, planning, designing, and managing human ecosystems is necessarily multidisciplinary. It requires teams of people knowledgeable in a range of different disciplines. Even more importantly, it requires the ability to define the connections among disciplines and to organize the disparate fragments of information from different disciplines into coherent wholes. Moreover, it requires a level of interaction among experts that can deal with both the creative possibilities of regenerative systems and their inherent and inevitable limitations. It is inherently interdisciplinary.

Regenerative Systems and Landscape

Human life-support systems make use of basic processes in various ways. Industrial systems tend to apply strategies of concentration and subsidization; that is, energy and material flows are concentrated in small areas, and their operation is speeded up by infusions of additional energy and materials. For example, in usual engineering practices, runoff water in urban areas is concentrated as quickly as possible in channels and pipes. Thus contained, the water bypasses other landscape processes as it is conducted to a large body of water—a lake, river, or ocean—which can serve as storage. In the natural situation, by contrast, much of the rainwater soaks into the ground where it falls. Part of it is assimilated by plants as part of their growth, and another portion filters through the soil strata into the aquifer for temporary storage. The water remaining on the surface is distributed slowly over the land, filtering through grasses and groundcovers, moving into streams and swales, and then into larger streams and rivers. Along the way, part of it is assimilated by plants and animals to help feed their own growth. Eventually it reaches a larger storage, as did the urban runoff, but by a very different route.

Other industrially based systems are similarly founded on concentration and subsidies. Concentration requires power, which is provided by fossil fuels. The processes of regeneration are bypassed. The concentrated monocultures of industrial agriculture are subsidized by petroleum and petroleum-derived chemicals that make it possible to emphasize production to the exclusion of other processes. Sewage treatment is concentrated in a few highly mechanized facilities. Electricity is generated mostly in very large centralized plants, most of which are fossil-fuel-driven, with little attention to the productive capacities of the larger landscape.

In contrast, regenerative systems tend to follow a strategy of dispersal, or spreading out over the landscape, combined with some degree of augmentation. The effort is to make full use of basic landscape processes—even more complete use than nature herself makes. In dealing with runoff water, for example, regenerative technologies tend to slow the flow rather than speeding it. Among the commonly used devices are shallow depressions of retention basins, which hold the water for some periods of time while it filters into the ground, and swales, which allow the water to flow very slowly.

In summary, the industrial age replaced the natural processes of the landscape with the global machine discussed earlier, while regenerative design seeks now to replace the machine with landscape.

Whatever the means used, sustainability requires that the basic processes not be exploited beyond their capacity for renewal. Whether by industrial or regenerative means, the landscape processes can be used only up to a point. If a higher volume of conversion is demanded than the sustainably productive capacities of the environment can provide, then the resource will become depleted. An example is the erosion and depletion of soils resulting from overgrazing. When greater volumes of materials are introduced into the soil or water than they can filter or assimilate, the result is pollution. An example is eutrophication of groundwater throughout the midwestern grain belt due to overloading of fertilizers. Storages are highly susceptible both to depletion brought on by overuse and to pollution caused by overloading.

Largely because of their concentration and their intensive use of materials and energy subsidies, industrial technologies have extreme difficulty maintaining this balance between use and capacity of basic processes. Concentrations of materials tend to cause pollution simply by virtue of the volumes involved. While the assimilative capacity of land or water may be severely stressed at the point of concentration—the location of a waste treatment plant or a river, for example—it may go unused elsewhere.

By virtue of their distribution, regenerative systems have distinct advantages in matching use to capacity. They have the flexibility to distribute use according to the inherent characteristics of the landscape and to control the flows in such ways as to maintain them within given limits. Infiltration basins can be located in permeable soils above water-bearing aquifers, for example. Combinations of crops can be matched to landforms and qualities of soil. Solar collectors can be placed where incident radiation is high. Thus regenerative systems have the potential ability to make full use of the landscape's capacities for conversion, distribution, filtration, assimilation, and storage.

The word "use" is important in this context. Reliance on regenerative technologies does not mean limiting ourselves to what undisturbed or unaided nature provides. The sheer numbers of people in the world and the requirements for sustaining human culture long ago outgrew what nature could provide without human thought and stimulus. Supporting the human population and culture requires augmenting nature's processes through engineering and technology guided by planning, design, and management. Given the diversity of situations and the complexity of nature's processes, the activities involved in implementing regenerative systems are more complex than those involved in industrial systems. It is a simpler matter to design and manage a single, large coal-fired generating plant than an uncertain number of solar generators, wind-energy converters, and biomass plantations spread over a large area. A farmer will have less difficulty planting and harvesting a thousand acres of wheat than the same acreage covered with mixes of 20 different crops along with cows, pigs, and chickens. This is probably a major reason why Paleotechnic life-support systems still prevail long past the times when their degenerative tendencies became generally apparent.

Problem of Limits

Another serious difficulty with regenerative systems is that of defining limits. While sustainability requires using natural processes within their capacities, it is difficult to know what those capacities are. Natural resource managers developed the concept "carrying capacity" in order to have a reasonably accurate means for determining the number of grazing or browsing animals that a given area of land could support. Applying that concept to other systems has met with limited success, mostly due to the many variables involved. Especially where human activity or habitation is concerned, complex and almost unpredictable behavioral patterns (including esthetic preferences, material appetites, investment decisions, desire for profits, and others) enter the picture, making limits definable only in very general terms. The carrying capacity of the earth depends on consumption habits, which in turn depend on myriad social and cultural factors.

For the present the best means of defining limits has been through monitoring and response. It is necessary first to identify indicators of stress, and then, when stress brought on by overuse manifests itself, to reduce the volume of use. While this technique is useful in particular management situations, it provides only limited information for future planning. There is a great need for better understanding of the capacities of basic natural processes.

Along with its advocacy of sustainable development, the World Commission on Environment and Development (WCED, 1987) suggested that the global economy might grow to be five to 10 times more productive over the next few decades. Even if we assume that human life-support systems and means of production become entirely regenerative, such a level of growth is almost certainly unsustainable. The capacities of the global landscape for conversion, filtration, assimilation, and storage are already severely stressed in places of intensive population concentration; in cities like São Paulo or Mexico City they are in a state of collapse. With careful planning and design and some redistribution, these capacities can probably support the world's present population and perhaps a few billion more. Understanding these capacities better is an urgent need that will require a great deal of research. Without such information, it is unlikely that the global environmental management agencies can carry out their enormous task. The present state of the earth provides great opportunities for growth in the quality of the environment and everything it produces but only very limited opportunities for growth in quantity.

A few rough and very preliminary studies have been done to determine the total ultimately sustainable world population. Reed Bryson (1986) has made a rough calculation based on the earth's arable land area. Applying his estimate that each arable hectare can feed an average of 5.5 people, Bryson concludes that the ultimate global population is somewhat less than double the present number of 5.5 billion. Since the present doubling time is 35 years, Bryson's calculations suggest the population will reach the biosphere's capacity well before the year 2024. Bryson's carrying-capacity estimate is somewhat higher than the most conservative projections made by international agencies, but 4 billion lower than the most liberal projections. His estimate is extremely rough, better than a guess but hardly adequate as a basis for policy. It might be increased somewhat by improved agricultural methods and by intensive cropping of urban open space. However, it is even more likely to be reduced due to land degradation from salinization and erosion, both of which are causing marginal lands to be taken out of production. Furthermore, food production capacity is only one of many possible limiting factors. Regenerative systems have the potential to achieve sustainability, perhaps to stretch the limits of growth somewhat, but they definitely do not remove the limits. Hoping for technological fixes is most unwise.

A Regenerative Design Process

The team that developed the schematic design for the Center for Regenerative Studies included a core group of 12 people: two architects, two landscape architects, two agronomists (one of whom emphasizes third-world agriculture), an anthropologist, an aquaculturist, an energy analyst, a geologist-hydrologist, an agricultural economist, and two graduate assistants. Team members are listed on page xiii. A great many other people participated in important ways. These included a number of specialists in areas such as natural sewage treatment and civil engineering, several consultants from various parts of the world with experience in similar institutions, and a number of students who represented future residents.

The unifying concept for the Center is the human ecosystem. This is a developed landscape serving human purposes, but it is also an ecological system with life-support processes functioning as natural systems do. The design follows basic principles of ecological order related to structure, function, and locational pattern, all of which will develop and evolve over time, beginning with an initial basic increment. Through a series of discussions, the design team considered these modes of order in their applications to the 16-acre site of the Center. The concepts that emerged from these early explorations served as the foundations for design.

STRUCTURE

The principle of interactive diversity applies here in the intensive development of the site with a wide range of biological and cultural activity. Food-growing areas especially present a strong contrast with the single-crop monocultures characteristic of industrial agriculture. The complex topography of the site allows five distinctly different cropping systems, and within each of these are polycultural combinations of species growing at different levels from soil to tree level. A range of animal species will also be included.

FUNCTION

Within the complex structure of diverse species, the elements are connected by the network of energy and material flows. In its essential general operation, this network is identical with the functional pattern of a natural system. The species involved, however, are quite different, and most of it is regulated by human management. As the Center evolves, this network will develop in complexity and cohesion. The working concept and preliminary hypothesis are shown in the diagram showing flows of energy, water, and nutrients among the major elements of the Center's structure. In very gross form, these flows are as follows:

	Process
■ Food is produced in the agricultural areas,	Conversion
■ taken to the kitchen,	Distribution
■ consumed by residents,	Conversion/ assimilation
■ passed on as waste to treatment ponds, where it is taken up by microorganisms and aquatic plants.	Assimilation
■ The enriched water is stored in the ponds,	Storage
■ conveyed to the irrigation system	Distribution
■ used to irrigate the crops,	Assimilation
■ and the runoff is conveyed to the overflow reservoir.	Storage
■ The aquatic plants are harvested from the treatment ponds.	Distribution
■ Some of these plants are used for biogas digestion,	Conversion
■ and the gas is conveyed to the kitchen for cooking.	Distribution
■ Some aquatic plants are used to feed animals,	Conversion
■ and the meat and milk is used to feed residents.	Conversion
■ Animal manure is used to fertilize crops and enrich aquacultural ponds.	Assimilation
■ Fish from aquacultural ponds are used to feed residents,	Conversion
■ and the water from the ponds is used to irrigate crops.	Assimilation

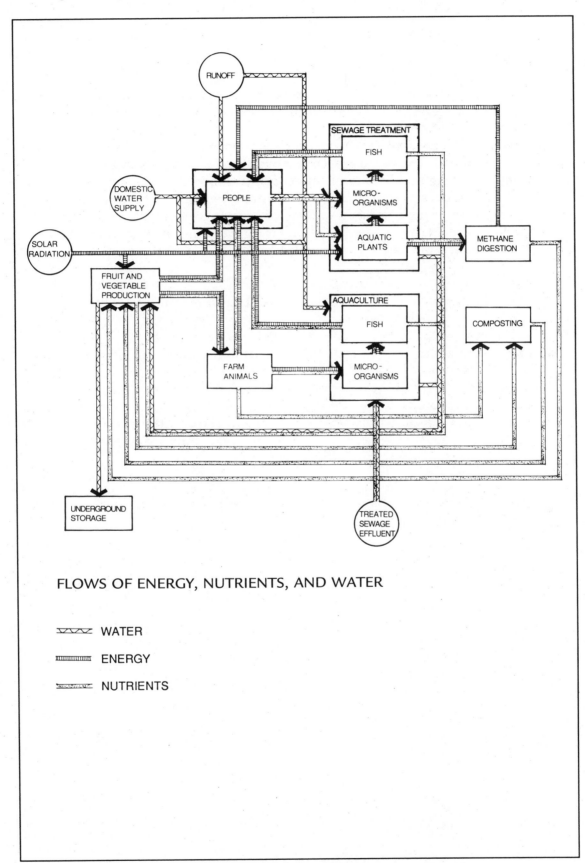

FLOWS OF ENERGY, NUTRIENTS, AND WATER

WATER

ENERGY

NUTRIENTS

LOCATIONAL PATTERN

The varied situations on the site represent on a small scale most of the topographic conditions found in most of the food-producing areas of the world. Thus we can view the site as a microcosm of the global agricultural landscape. With careful selections of specific locations within the site, it is possible to replicate a wide range of food-growing situations. In fitting buildings and other facilities into this topographically diverse microcosm, we can also demonstrate beneficial archetypal relationships that might exist in similar situations in various parts of the world (Lyle et al., 1987). The following is a general summary of land uses as determined primarily by topography.

Area	Slope	Use
Valley bottom	0–10%	Aquaculture and water-related crops
Knolltops	0–10%	Energy generation
Flatter knollsides	0–10%	Grain-growing, contour-plowed agriculture
Knollsides	10–40%	Terraced agriculture
South-facing knollsides	10–40%	Village
Steep slopes	40+%	Agroforestry (with permanent roots to stabilize soils)

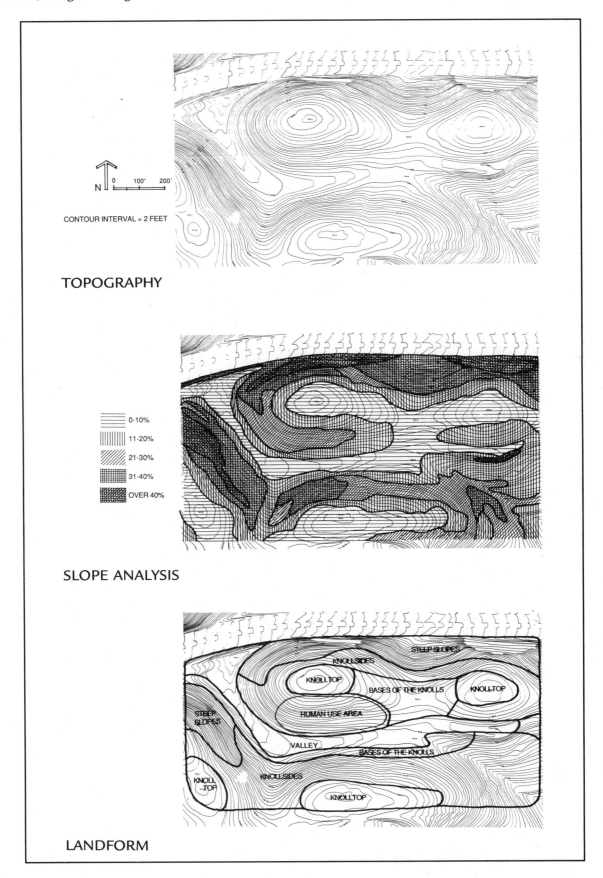

TOPOGRAPHY

SLOPE ANALYSIS

LANDFORM

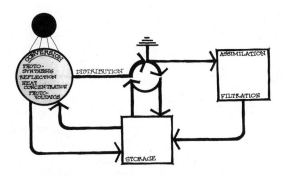

Chapter 3
Strategies for
Regenerative Design

Industrial systems are the products of recent Western technology in its purest form, shaped by engineering criteria that seek high levels of productivity and operational efficiency to the virtual exclusion of other concerns. Therein lies their utility and occasional grandiose beauty—and their incipient failure.

Regenerative systems by contrast are enmeshed in natural and social processes in ways that make their purposes far more complex. While technology remains the means for augmenting nature, it ideally becomes a factor within the larger social and ecological context rather than the engine driving that complex.

Furthermore, with the need to interrelate technology with society and nature, a broad and disparate body of knowledge enters the process. To further complicate matters, regenerative systems function as integral parts of the communities they serve. This means they necessarily involve those communities in their design and operation.

Thanks to the experience developed over the last century and especially since the beginning of World War II, there exists a considerable methodology for dealing with complex issues, bringing varied

expertise to bear. Ecosystem theory offers a framework for assembling the contributions of different scientific disciplines. Environmental impact analysis has also contributed ways of conceiving landscapes as interacting wholes. Systems science is especially useful in coordinating disciplines and in dealing with complex relationships among the parts of a system and of systems within systems. Information systems provide the means for dealing with large quantities of data. With the need for more public involvement, the planning and landscape architecture professions have developed effective means for working with the interested public. The participatory workshop format has proven especially workable.

With more interactions involved, more options available and far more flexible technologies to deal with, regenerative design provides virtually unlimited opportunities for invention and for devising varied ways of combining elements. In such situations, analysis and deterministic methods usually provide knowledge of parts and mechanisms, but they rarely yield adequate answers. Creativity enters the process in the key role of assembling diverse parts, often in unexpected ways. Regenerative design involves both art and science not separately but merging together.

Where we often find difficulty is in connecting means with ends. Industrial processes are very clear in this regard. The well-established ends of labor efficiency and productivity provide clear goals, and the means for shaping the system are geared to meet those goals. The processes of thought and human interaction applied in pursuing these goals are linear and logical, taking the shortest distance between two points.

The more complex multiple goals of regenerative systems, involving natural and social processes that are not entirely understood, present greater challenges for design. Paths to the goals can be winding and indirect. For guidance there are few rules, but there is an ancient fund of experience. Some researchers and practical experimenters have rediscovered much of the experience of preindustrial societies in recent years, while others have added a great deal from a contemporary perspective. However, as a way of thinking and a mode of technological development in the contemporary context, regenerative design is still very young; we are still feeling our way into the future. Regenerative design requires patterns of thought quite different from the patterns that have become customary. Einstein's advice that "the significant problems we face cannot be solved at the same level of thinking we were at when we created them" certainly applies here. The following list of design strategies, given in no particular order, is a tentative effort to summarize the experience to date. It is anything but definitive; more items could be added or some left out. What this list helps to do is define the character of regenerative systems as distinguished from industrial systems.

1. LETTING NATURE DO THE WORK

Virtually all of the human life-support functions dealing with energy, shelter, water, food, and waste are performed in undisturbed nature by the highly evolved natural processes of conversion, distribution, filtration, assimilation, and storage. Replacing these with engineered processes relying heavily on hardware and fossil fuels is a costly habit, both in terms of money and environmental disruption. Often the necessary services could be performed just as well by simply augmenting the already operational

natural process. Examples include the use of predator species to control agricultural pests (in preference to chemical pesticides), the use of landforms to guide and absorb the flow of runoff water (in preference to pipes and concrete channels), and the use of trees to control urban microclimates (in preference to mechanical heating and air conditioning).

In Cherry Creek Park near Denver, park managers introduced a small herd of cashmere goats to prevent invasive exotic weeds, such as spurge and thistle, from taking over the landscape from the native bunchgrasses. The goats prefer forbs (which include the weeds), over grasses and so eat the weeds first. Left in the same area, however, the goats will eat the grasses when the weeds are gone. This means that the goats must be moved on to another landscape at exactly the right time. A carefully devised rotational pattern covers the park's shortgrass prairie landscape. The goats are cheaper and more environmentally benign than the alternatives, which include chemical pesticides and hand weeding, and they produce a harvest of cashmere wool as well.

In each of these cases, the natural means is more resource-conserving, less environmentally damaging, and less expensive than the chemical means. However, each does require more careful consideration of the specific situation than the industrial alternative. Such is commonly the case when working with natural processes; dealing directly with nature on its own terms requires a great deal of thought.

Given the ingrained Paleotechnic habit of relying on hardware, we have now in our landscape a vast collection of steel-and-concrete devices that were constructed unnecessarily. As these wear out or otherwise present problems, at least some of them can be replaced by natural processes. An example is the proposal to remove a 50-year-old concrete flood-control channel in the Arroyo Seco in southern California and replace it with a meandering stream and a low earthen dam that will hold back the occasional floodwaters. The channel was unnecessary in the first place, and the stream and dam combination will provide higher assimilative capacity, thus better flood control and a far richer ecosystem. For more details, see pages 162 to 166.

Using nature's processes usually means using them on the site where they occur. Distribution routes are thus much shorter than those of most industrial processes, which usually require transport of both energy and materials. Mostly for this reason an essential early step in regenerative design is an inventory of on-site resources and processes.

2. CONSIDERING NATURE AS BOTH MODEL AND CONTEXT

When we develop the landscape for human purposes, whether by minor alteration or reconstruction, the larger landscape and ecosystem of which it is part form the operational and visual context. Maintaining or reestablishing continuity and connections is important. On a practical level the flow of water as it enters and leaves a given site is critical to the larger hydrologic system in terms of quality and quantity. In the Arroyo Seco example mentioned in item 1, the stream and earthen dam form part of a larger system; they receive the flows from a mountain watershed and an upstream reservoir, and they pass flows on to a downstream urban area. The Arroyo Seco is also a link in the regional pattern of wildlife habitat, serving as a riparian extension of the Angeles National Forest to the north and as a corridor linking the National Forest with other open areas.

Within the influences of the larger context, any natural landscape is the product of a long period of coevolution. If enough time passes since the last major upheaval, complex networks of energy and material flow will develop. Such an evolved system defines the particular character and capacities of the place: what will work here and what will not. Thus the evolved landscape provides a model for future development.

For purposes of regenerative design, biological processes of the landscape generally provide more useful models than physical processes. The primary scientific basis for Paleotechnic systems lay in physics; the basis for Neotechnic systems lies in biology.

In the Arroyo Seco the native plant communities had long since been destroyed by lack of water, which meant that the best models for ecosystemic structure were nearby streams in similar situations that were still relatively undisturbed. By analyzing the community structures in these examples and integrating those structures with the redefined stream location, it was possible to develop a model on which to base the design for the new stream.

Wes Jackson has applied the same principle in his research at the Land Institute in Kansas. In his search for a sustainable agricultural system appropriate for the environment of the Great Plains, Jackson has analyzed the typical native vegetation structures of the region. Using transects he has determined the proportion of grasses, legumes, sunflowers, and other types in a number of landscapes. He then undertook to design a mix of agricultural plants that would follow the same proportions. The research is ongoing, and the results are not yet clear.

David Hopcraft applies the natural model principle to ranching in Kenya. Hopcraft's ranch is essentially a native landscape on which he harvests native species of antelope. More details on this system, which has proven highly productive and financially successful, will be given on page 207.

Applications of natural models can be far less literal; they are often highly abstract, bearing little visible resemblance to the source. One example is the rock-and-reed sewage treatment system described on page 244. While this system applies the assimilative processes of a natural wetland, its form and species are entirely different from those of natural wetlands.

3. AGGREGATING, NOT ISOLATING

As recommended by Descartes, an essential step in science is dismantling any complex process to reveal the characteristics of each component part. Once the most basic elements are isolated, each of the various factors involved in their operation can usually be controlled; when all factors but one are controlled, then it is possible to study the functions of that one. In this way, one factor at a time, science builds its understanding. Paleotechnic practice applies this approach in design. It is easier to shape the parts than the whole; the technology for each part is often relatively simple, while that of the whole may be more complex, less predictable, and less controllable. Once the parts are separately designed, it is difficult if not impossible to combine them into an integrated whole. The result is a disaggregated world. Disaggregated cities have dwelling areas well separated from commercial areas, suburbs that are deserted in the daytime and downtowns deserted at night, affluent neighborhoods set apart from poor neighborhoods, nature apart from people. Disaggregated farming has one crop growing in isolation in one landscape another crop in another, and livestock separated from both in giant feedlots. Disaggregated universities have departments, each dealing with a single discipline and each isolated within its own boundaries. Since the parts of a system tend to feed each other, disaggregation requires energy to feed the parts separately. With the rich linkages of interactions missing, the integrity of the whole is diminished.

Regenerative design reaggregates. A regenerative city brings its varied activities together to share space, reinforce each other, and eliminate long trips from one area to the other. Regenerative buildings open their windows to make natural light, air, and solar radiation part of their interior environments. On a regenerative farm, polycultural plantings form communities in which each species helps to provide for the needs of the others. These needs might include nutrients, shade, protection from pests, and/or physical support.

In reaggregating the parts, regenerative design has to be as concerned with the interactions among parts, the connections, as with the parts themselves. The next five chapters will discuss in some detail the nature of these interactions and their roles in shaping an integrated environment.

4. SEEKING OPTIMUM LEVELS FOR MULTIPLE FUNCTIONS, NOT THE MAXIMUM OR MINIMUM LEVEL FOR ANY ONE

Some of the major difficulties with industrial systems are brought on by their tendency to maximize one goal, such as flood control, power, or food production, at the expense of all others. This leaves other landscape processes out of the picture. Furthermore, it usually means that environmental and social concerns are given low priority or ignored entirely, which can bring serious trouble later. Gregory Bateson (1979) observed that "for all objects and experiences, there is a quantity that has optimum value. Above the quantity, the variable becomes toxic. To fall below that value is to be deprived" (p. 59).

One problem lies in defining the optimum value, which is always elusive. It may be more useful to think in terms of a range of values lying between serious deprivation and serious toxicity. Defining that range is generally easier than defining a single number. A second problem stems from the fact that there is always a number of variables involved in any system and there are persuasive arguments for optimizing each of them. Regenerative systems always have more than one goal; often they have numerous goals, some of them in conflict with others. In such complex situations, quantification is difficult and almost always imprecise. Fuzziness and ambiguity are characteristic. Thus it is generally best not to seek precision but to accept approximations. The purpose of system design often becomes a matter of maintaining a set of variable values, which may be

in some degree of conflict, within approximately optimum ranges.

Had David Hopcraft, for example, followed usual Paleotechnic practice on his ranch, he would have established the antelope population at the level required for maximum productivity. Instead, he established the animal numbers at a level that allow for optimizing the vegetation community. He harvests only the surplus number of animals—that is, the number that might bring the antelope population up to a level that could begin to deplete the vegetation (Hopcraft, 1975).

5. MATCHING TECHNOLOGY TO NEED

The economics of industrial technology, involving low-cost fossil fuels and assumptions of unlimited material supplies and unlimited waste sinks, allowed overdesign of support systems, often to an absurd degree. Amory Lovins's characterized using nuclear power to heat water to generate electricity as being like using a chain saw to cut butter. His analogy might apply to any number of industrial support systems. As multiple goals enter design processes and as all the costs of operation become more apparent, the price of overdesign becomes too high. This state has been reached in a number of technological areas, notably in nuclear power. This situation encourages a rethinking of technological means.

Consider, for example, the problem of keeping the interior of a building within the human comfort range. During the peak Paleotechnic decades following World War II, this task was considered a job for mechanical heating and cooling devices powered by fossil fuels. During the 1970s, as incentives for saving energy were introduced, architects began using other devices for interior climate control, including insulation, operable ventilators, sunshades, and heat exchangers. Such means quickly lowered energy costs for heating and cooling by up to 50 percent and sometimes reduced initial costs as well. As energy costs continue to rise, we will see more use of such sophisticated devices as those used in the examples to be presented in Chapter 5. These include glass located for solar gain, various thermal storage materials, cooling tubes, and heat chimneys.

E. F. Schumacher's (1973) notion of appropriate technology applies particularly in the use of simpler devices suited to the needs of people who lack the resources or skills for industrial technologies. This principle is especially important in dealing with the development problems of the non-industrial countries, where attempts to introduce industrial practices have often led to disaster.

However, there are also situations in which high-quality energy or high technology is appropriate. In the irrigated agriculture of the southwestern states, sprinkler irrigation is commonly used because it is simple and cheap, even though it is wasteful and environmentally destructive. However, the volume of water use could be much reduced by using a number of more complex, highly developed technologies. These include drip and underground systems, and tensiometers, which provide feedback concerning soil moisture to guide in scheduling water applications. Such devices are often not used because they are relatively expensive and the price of water is kept low by heavy subsidies by the federal government.

From these examples it is clear that there is a close relationship between the cost and appropriateness of technology, a relationship that often works against an appropriate match between ends and means. This is often the result of manipulations of the price structure to benefit certain groups. Such manipulation often works in opposition to long-term sustainability. We will return to the often puzzling relationship between economics and sustainability in Chapter 11.

6. USING INFORMATION TO REPLACE POWER

Here, as with matching technology to need, we are concerned with the fit between means and ends. Industrial systems, with their access to virtually unlimited low-cost energy, tend to use the power available to them to be sure of their ability to meet any situation. The less that is known about possible situations, the more power is needed to gain this assurance. An automobile with a 400-horsepower engine will be able to move at any speed required of it and to climb virtually any hill; never mind that most of the time the car will be moving along city streets using less than 10 percent of that power and that it will burn an inordinate amount of fuel in moving at any speed. The situation is akin to that of the chainsaw and the butter.

If the potential situation can be more precisely described, the safety margin can be reduced and the system designed to suit the situation. This requires information. Given adequate information, we can achieve precise fits between system and function.

During the 1970s the Japanese used this strategy to increase their efficiency in energy use to the point where they were using half as much energy per unit of production as the United States.

In the formative stages of shaping an environment or system, we apply information through planning, design, and engineering. In the operational stage the means of application is management, which involves sensing and feedback.

The cybernetic principle of feedback as a means of controlling the operations of a system is widely applied in both industrial and regenerative systems. The difference is partly a matter of degree and partly a matter of scale.

Lewis Mumford (1966) has suggested a major reason for the overwhelming and frequently destructive role of industrial technology in modern society: the positive feedback concerning technological operations is usually stronger than the negative feedback, which may be nonexistent. That is, there are effective means in government and the marketplace for the beneficial aspects of technology to become known and encouraged, but few means for the negative aspects, especially those that are long-term and socially related, to become known and discouraged. Such technological devices as automobiles, automated production lines, and possibly computers, all of which bring considerable benefits to society, are allowed, in the absence of negative feedback, to proliferate to levels at which they bring more harm than good. Although an increasingly critical and vociferous public has begun to sound more danger signals, the power of technology continues to develop beyond thoughtful control.

At this larger level, regenerative systems incorporate feedback information primarily through active participation on the part of the public. Thus, from inception and during the course of a project, channels are open for expressions of both positive and negative effects.

At the smaller operational scales, feedback is a means of regulating energy and material flows to avoid excessive consumption. An example is the tensiometers that monitor soil moisture and thus regulate application of irrigation water. While such automatic devices are useful in a great many situations, direct human observation commonly plays a key part in regenerative systems. Integrated pest management (IPM), for example, relies heavily on the farmer watching for signs of pest infestation in the crops. Simple devices like insect traps can augment direct observation. When pest populations reach harmful levels, the farmer can take action. Consider this in contrast to the common practice in industrial agriculture of massive overapplication of pesticides to be sure of using enough. Thus, regenerative-system practice substitutes careful observation, acquired knowledge, and direct participation through feedback in place of the standardization of practices, which requires large safety factors. This is a major reason why the rapidly developing Neotechnic society with its strong emphasis on information is likely to be a low-energy society by contrast with the industrially based Paleotechnic society.

The high degree of human involvement relative to more mechanical procedures is another key difference between regenerative and industrial systems. Passive solar heating and cooling, for example, require people to open and close windows, shutters, and dampers and to operate sunshades. Along with human involvement goes a preference for direct observation over assumptions, deductions, general formulas, and high safety factors.

7. PROVIDING MULTIPLE PATHWAYS

In most cases, regenerative technologies are relatively small in scale and suited to specific applications under particular conditions. This contrasts with the large-scale, standardized, and more encompassing operations of industrial technologies. There are a number of continuously renewable means for generating electrical power, for example, all of which depend on particular sets of conditions such as sun, wind, ocean currents, or running water. As the large electrical supply grids adapt to using these sources in supplying power, they necessarily must diversify in their ability to shift among different combinations of sources depending on what is available. Photovoltaic cells might supply power on sunny days, and the source might shift to wind power when the wind is blowing. A building with its own photovoltaic array, such as the Rocky Mountain Institute (described in Chapter 5), can supply its own electricity most of the time, perhaps even feeding power back to the utility company when the sun is shining. After sunset, the building might depend on power bought from the utility company. In this way the distribution system develops multiple pathways with the ability to shift from one to the other according to the situation. This contrasts with typical Paleotechnic systems, which feature one-way flows from producer to consumer and rely on a small number of very large fossil-fuel- (or nuclear-)

powered generating plants. In Chapter 4 we will discuss further the energy grid and its diversification with new and varied energy sources.

Another example of multiple pathways is the regenerative farm with its varied combinations of crops and animals that change from year to year and season to season. In this case the multiplicity of pathways provides means for taking advantage of the different resources that can exist within the landscape of a single farm. They also assure the farmer that if one pathway is cut off by disease, weather, or some other unpredictable condition, others will remain open and thus provide some yields. At the same time, pathway multiplicity allows a flexible response to changing market conditions.

In both of these examples, multiple pathways involve greater complexity and the need for more decisions than the industrial alternatives. Such is often the case with regenerative systems.

8. SEEKING COMMON SOLUTIONS TO DISPARATE PROBLEMS

Industrial life-support systems tend to be clearly separated into distinct categories, such as supplying electrical power or disposing of solid waste. Even different parts of the same material flow pattern are usually managed separately, as happens in the case of water supply and stormwater drainage. Especially when reinforced by the lines or responsibility drawn for public agencies, such distinctions can become rigid, forcing each system to function entirely within its own arbitrarily defined boundaries.

Natural systems recognize no such distinctions. Being conceptually based on an understanding of natural ecosystems, regenerative systems are considered as encompassing whole patterns of flow. As outlined in strategy 2, for example, a problem of water supply is considered in the context of the whole pattern of flow, from the time the water strikes the earth as precipitation, to the time when it evaporates to reenter atmospheric storage. Considered in this way, both stormwater runoff and treated wastewater become potential contributors to the water supply.

At the same time, the ecological perspective illuminates interactions among systems. In the San Jacinto Wildlife Area example in Chapter 8, for example, two problems—returning treated wastewater to underground storage, and providing rich and diverse wildlife habitat in a dry and degraded landscape—are solved simultaneously by using the water to create a range of different landscape conditions. After playing its part in habitat enrichment, the water soaks into the ground and is filtered by the soil before it reaches groundwater storage. In other examples, similarly treated wastewater contributes to food production as irrigation water.

In other cases the relationships among systems are not so clear or obvious. Sometimes certain properties of one process are useful for a quite different process. In the composting greenhouse developed by the New Alchemy Institute, the heat given off in the composing process is directed into a greenhouse, where it helps to stimulate organic growth.

9. MANAGING STORAGE AS A KEY TO SUSTAINABILITY

While industrial systems tend to undervalue all processes occurring in the landscape, the one generally most undervalued is storage. Paleotechnic systems use stored materials such as petroleum and groundwater with little concern for sustaining yields for any length of time or for replenishment. That is, they treat storages not as the temporary fluctuating phenomena they are but as inexhaustible sources. Waste materials, on the other hand, are stored with little concern for their destructive effects or for the eventual means of returning them to useful circulation. The most unsettling example is the spent radioactive fuels being stored around nuclear power plants. While there may some day be ways of dealing with such problems, it seems that imbalances of storage like these lie at the core of industrial systems. Certainly, they are an inevitable result of one-way flow patterns.

Storage lies also at the core of regenerative systems. Maintaining adequate storage and balancing the rate of replenishment with the rate of use are important keys to sustainability. Since rates of productivity, assimilation and use all vary, storage is the essential, ever-varying maintainer of equilibrium. All natural processes have their storages: groundwater basins for water; the atmosphere for oxygen, nitrogen, and other gases; trees for biomass; and fatty tissue for animal energy. Regenerative systems either draw on these natural storages or incorporate other means of storage for their own use. Passive-solar heating systems use dense materials such as stone, brick, or water to store heat; the balance be-

tween solar radiation gain and thermal storage capacity is critical for effective operation. For regenerative agriculture, soil is the essential storage medium for water, nutrients, and minerals. In industrial agriculture, erosion gradually carries away the soil and with it the storage capacity of the landscape.

While providing adequate storage volume is always essential for a regenerative system, it is almost equally important to provide for appropriate rates of replenishment and release. In most cases the ideal is rapid replenishment and slow release. In replenishing groundwater storage, for example, the ideal is to collect runoff or treated wastewater in basins over highly permeable soils that can absorb it quickly and filter it down to storage. If the soil cannot absorb the water quickly enough, more surface storage is needed. As with groundwater, most storages can absorb materials only during brief and sporadic periods when they are available, while use or release takes place over a longer period. In a solar-heated building, heat can be stored only when the sun is shining, while the release of heat is needed over longer sunless periods, which can last several days. Thus, storage capacity, as well as replenishment and release rates, is matched to local conditions. Consider, for example, the extraordinary amount of thermal mass needed in the Lovins house (Rocky Mountain Institute described in Chapter 5) because of its location in the cold heights of the Rocky Mountains.

10. SHAPING FORM TO GUIDE FLOW

This principle could also be stated "flow follows form follows flow." Energy and material flows occur within the physical medium of the environment, and the medium largely determines the pace and direction of flow. By shaping the medium (the environment), we can guide the flow. As an example of the implications of this principle, consider the process of igniting charcoal for a barbecue fire. For some decades, most people have accomplished this simple task by saturating the charcoal with kerosene before applying a flame. The Southern California Air Quality Management District has found that the vapors released in this way contribute significantly to air pollution. An alternative that requires no fossil fuel and thus does not pollute is to first put several briquets of charcoal in a steel tube about 10 to 18 inches high and 8 inches in diameter.

Some people have used coffee cans with the ends cut out. At the bottom the charcoal rests on an open grate, allowing air to flow freely through the tube. When a flame is applied at the bottom, the warm air rises around the briquets, and more air follows up through the grate from the bottom. The flame and the oxygen thus supplied cause the charcoal to ignite almost immediately. Thus the form of the tube induces a flow that accomplishes the task of igniting the charcoal in a much more elegant way, as well as a more resource-conserving and nonpolluting way, then the use of kerosene. These devices are now being marketed as "charcoal starters," one small example of the vast entrepreneurial possibilities in regenerative technologies.

Similar principles are used in inducing flows of warm and cool air through buildings for heating and cooling. The form of the building and the location of openings within the form guide the movement of air. In controlling the flow of storm water, the form of the landscape can hold the water as in a bowl while it percolates in to underground storage. On agricultural lands, plowed furrows follow the contours of a hillside to minimize erosion. Thus, form guides the flows as it does in nature, rather than employing fossil fuels, steel, and concrete as in industrial systems.

11. SHAPING FORM TO MANIFEST PROCESS

Technology of any kind presents itself in ways that demand attention. The massive scale and harsh forms of industrial technology project a kind of grandeur that can inspire and repel, often at the same time. To most people, however, they are repellent. So industrial technology has lived in exile, located where it is seen no more than necessary, outside the course of the lives that it serves. Society's collective ambivalence on the subject is clearly expressed in its planning for industry. We want what industrial technology provides, but we do not want its reality to penetrate our consciousness. Most of all, we do not want to see it. Robert Thayer (1993) has called the two poles of this deep-seated ambivalence technophilia and technophobia: fascination with and attachment for the products of technology, on the one hand, and revulsion for its visible presence on the other.

If we cannot hide technology, then we clothe

and mask it in gaudy costumes that disguise its function. Near the Long Beach Harbor in southern California there are several small islands, clearly seen from shore. From a distance, they look like South Sea island resorts designed for the jet trade. Rectangular towers rise against the sky and palm trees sway lazily among them in the ocean breezes. Within the sleek facades are oil wells pumping oil from beneath the harbor bottom, with the steel framework of the derricks well hidden.

While it may be argued that such practices produce a more aesthetically satisfying landscape, they also tend to reinforce the alienation of technology, removing from view one means of understanding the processes that support our lives. In terms of information, paleotechnology tells us lies and the lies become part of our misunderstanding of the world. Not seeing the real face of industrial technology is among the factors that make it possible to ignore its presence until its effects become overwhelming.

Regenerative technologies are much harder to hide because they are by nature more integral to their context. Their operation usually requires specific attributes of form and location, and those attributes are often highly visible. Neighbors often protest the dramatically visible clusters of wind generators that adorn several mountain ridges in California. In Holland, however, where windmills have been integral parts of the landscape for centuries, people regard them as features of the cultural heritage.

Also tending to make regenerative technologies more visible is the fact that they generally function in ways that are more closely integrated with daily life than industrial technologies; they are not so easily set apart. The solar heating system for a building is necessarily an essential part of the building. If the building is heated by gas or electricity, by contrast, the apparatus for providing those fuels is far away, probably well out of sight, and the machinery for burning them is hidden in a mechanical room in the bowels of the building. Regenerative waste management works best on the local scale. Managing storm water in regenerative ways usually means retaining it near where the rain falls, which requires reshaping the landscape in ways that can be readily seen.

Altogether, much of the energy- and materials-processing work of the landscape—conversion, distribution, assimilation, filtration, and storage—occurs in and around the places where people live and is thus highly visible. Where form facilitates flow, as in strategy 10, it is part of the landscape where we see it. The forms of regenerative technology impart useful information and increase our understanding of the world. Being seen, the processing can become part of daily life. Being generally smaller in scale and less alien in form, it is more easily integrated with the surroundings.

This integration, however, is not achieved without difficulty. Regenerative forms often are highly distinctive in character, sometimes quite different from what is familiar or perceived as natural, and therefore difficult for many people to accept and relate to. Thus "technophobia" can apply to regenerative as well as industrial technologies. The contrast between this emotional response and technophilia, is striking. Thayer's research has also uncovered some displeasure with landscapes designed in regenerative ways, largely due to unfamiliarity of form.

Nevertheless, a healthy society with the ability to make informed decisions concerning its technological base will require the ability to live in harmony with that base. For such ability to develop, it is important that technology become an integral aspect of the common culture. The potentials for regenerative systems to heal the schism between culture and technology lie in sensitive planning and design. With understanding of the processes involved, it is possible to shape buildings and landscapes in such ways as to give visible form to those processes. The forms of buildings and landscapes have always been a major means of making connections between people and environment. Cultural habits and preconceptions change slowly, but if we can manifest the inherent elegance of ecological processes in visible forms, those forms will become symbols for the times. Even the wind generators that many find objectionable can be seen as an evocative kind of kinetic sculpture—unfamiliar perhaps and certainly not natural, but meaningful, even beautiful, in terms of process and context.

12. PRIORITIZING FOR SUSTAINABILITY

Although regenerative technologies have come increasingly into use in recent years, modern industrial technology still predominates and will certainly continue to do so for decades to come. An entirely regenerative world is a distant dream that might someday come about; in the meantime there will be a long period of transition. Through this period society will be supported by a mix—sometimes a strange, discordant mix—of industrial and regenerative systems, existing side by side, often interconnected. For every development project, there are choices to be made between the two approaches. Inertia, professional biases, innate conservatism, perceptions of risk, and sometimes economics favor industrial options. In purely practical terms, the set of resource and environmental concerns that we have grouped under the heading of sustainability, sometimes along with economics, favors regenerative systems. Such are the values and decision-making processes of the industrial society in which we still live that sustainability is rarely considered. If the transition is to be made—if the world is to make the change from the degenerative to the regenerative and thus sustainable mode—then priorities must change. If we take the point of view of society as a whole, then sustainability must have a high priority, perhaps an overriding priority. At the very least, sustainability will have to enter into every development decision, beginning with regional patterns, proceeding to the decisions of what and where to develop, and continuing on to such details as the species of trees to be planted and drainage methods to be used. The next five chapters will explore some of the practices and technological means that have become part of the repertoire for shaping the human environment. At the very least they are strong alternatives to industrial technologies and deserving of a place in decision-making processes. At best they will combine to constitute the technological underpinnings for a regenerative world.

CASE STUDY

Applying Regenerative Strategies

The design of the Center for Regenerative Studies applies these strategies in numerous ways in both concept and detail. The following summary lists as examples a number of conceptual applications of the strategies in very general outline form. The next five chapters will explain technological applications in detail.

1. Letting nature do the work
   - Passive solar heating and cooling systems use plants for microclimate control, thermal storage properties, and inducement of air movement within buildings.
   - Landforms guide the flow of water.
   - Predator species and companion planting are major means of pest control.
2. Nature as model and context
   - The location in a semiarid Mediterranean climate makes it essential to emphasize water efficiency, especially water reuse and recycling.
   - Distribution of food-growing areas on north- and south-facing hillsides follows the natural pattern of distribution in this region.
3. Aggregating, not isolating functions
   - The basic concept is an aggregation of functions that are usually isolated; these include energy generation, shelter, water management, food production, and waste recycling.
4. Optimum levels for multiple functions
   - Energy, shelter, water, food production, and waste all function interactively, each in equilibrium with the others and serving the others.
5. Matching technology and need
   - Several levels of technology operate within the Center, from the high technology of Dish–Sterling concentrating collectors to solar food-drying racks.
   - A 5-acre agricultural area, called the hand-technology (hand-tech) area, focuses on agricultural techniques appropriate for small farmers in nonindustrial countries.

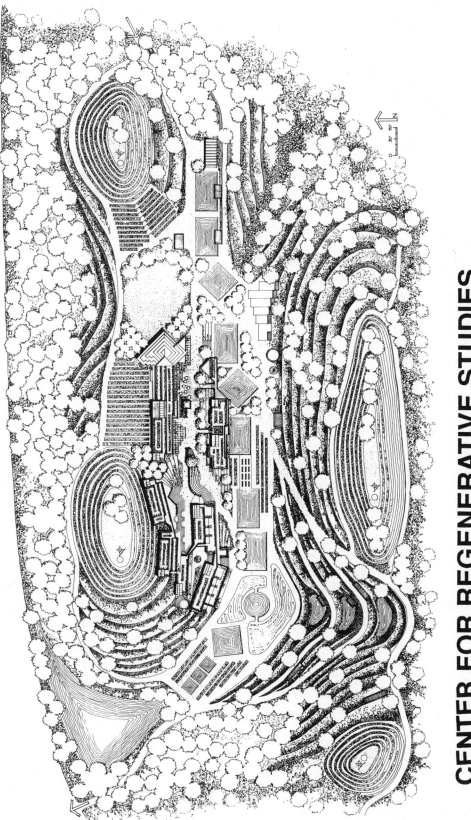

CENTER FOR REGENERATIVE STUDIES

THE VALLEY
Bottomlands
2.4 acres

BASES OF THE KNOLLS:
Planting Beds
.4 acres

KNOLLSIDES.
Terraced Slopes
3.5 acres

KNOLL TOPS
Upland Grain
2.4 acres

HUMAN USE AREA
The Village
2.2 acres

STEEP SLOPES
Agroforestry
5.1 acres

6. Using information to replace power
   —Residents are trained to systematically observe the operation of each system as part of everyday life.
   —Electronically operated sensing devices monitor some critical environmental variables such as soil moisture.
   —Water quality in the aquacultural ponds and sewage system are continuously monitored by laboratory tests.
7. Multiple pathways
   —More than one means is provided for most service systems.
   —For food production several different communities of plants supply each basic nutritional need.
   —Public utilities serve as backup for most service needs, including electricity, gas and sewage.
8. Common solutions to disparate problems
   —Greenhouses and solaria provide heat for buildings as well as growing plants and fish.
   —Roofs of buildings serve for growing food, collecting water, heating water, generating energy, circulation, and activity areas as well as for protection from the weather.
   —Trees and vines grown on trellises help to control microclimates near buildings as well as providing food.
9. Storage as a key to sustainability
   —Runoff water is stored for later use.
   —A variety of techniques—including drying, smoking and canning—aid in food storage.
   —Thermal-mass materials provide heat storage in buildings.
10. Form to facilitate flow
    —Building forms intercept maximum levels of solar radiation, with means for blocking it out when necessary.
    —Terraces and contour plowing in agricultural areas provide for maximum water retention.
11. Form to manifest process
    —Hilltop wind and solar generators are major features in the landscape.
    —Technological devices are in visible locations wherever possible.
12. Prioritize for sustainability
    —All systems provide means for on-site recycling, though this is not fully achieved until later stages.

II

Means: Regenerative Technology and Its Applications

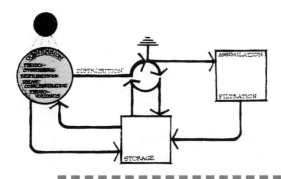

Chapter 4
Energy: The Heart of the Matter

William Stine, Coauthor

Primarily through altering and speeding up natural energy flows, industrial civilization has expanded over the last century to become a major force in the global ecosystem. While it has brought to humans a great many material benefits, this dominant position has not been a benign influence on the ecology of the biosphere. In the long term it may be disastrous for most forms of life including humanity.

Energy Flow in the Industrial Society

Inevitably, probably fortunately, industrial society is a temporary phenomenon. It is powered almost entirely by fossil fuels (Cook, 1971) in the throughput mode. As mentioned earlier, whether or not fossil-fuel stores will run out before the air pollution they cause makes cities uninhabitable is a question for debate. Global warming induced by the buildup of greenhouse gases will probably begin to alter the global climate before either of these occurs, if indeed it has not begun already. Most of the temperate-zone forests may succumb to acid precipitation within a few years.

Whatever the limiting factor may turn out to be, time is short. Most authorities agree that, if present consumption rates continue, U.S. petroleum re-serves will run out some time in the first half of the 21st century, and global reserves will last longer but certainly not beyond the century's end. Due to new discoveries in the 1980s, reserves of natural gas will last much longer; estimates of the depletion date at 1980s extraction rates average around 2200 (Smil, 1991). In fact, actually running out is unlikely. Long before the reserves are entirely depleted, the prices of fossil fuels will probably rise to levels at which few can afford to buy them.

Coal reserves will last much longer, and transporting coal presents fewer difficulties. Coal is likely to be available into the 23rd century and perhaps well beyond. However, coal cannot replace petroleum to any significant extent for several reasons. It is a less efficient energy source, requiring considerably more energy to be invested in the mining process. It is also more environmentally destructive both in the mining and the burning.

On the sink side of Paleotechnic energy flow, the problems are even more imposing, involving impending change in the planet's basic ecological processes. The warming effect brought on by the buildup of greenhouse gases is global in scope compared with the local effects of smog and the regional effects of acid precipitation. The scale of global warming makes it the most ominous result of fossil-fuel dependence. As long as we burn carbon-based fuels,

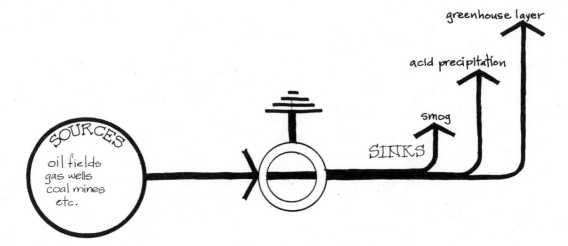

large quantities of carbon dioxide will rise into the atmosphere, add to the greenhouse effect, and thus contribute to global warming. Some authorities argue convincingly that global warming has already begun (Hansen et al., 1988; Kerr, 1989; Schneider, 1989). Regional climate shifts and sea level rises are likely to reach significant proportions by the mid-21st century.

Even if we set aside our concern for sources and sinks and ignore issues like the greenhouse effect, burning fossil fuels remains a highly questionable practice. Often ignored in our appetite for energy is the fact that oil and coal have even greater utility as materials. The uses of petroleum in the economy resemble in some ways the uses of food in the human body. Some petroleum, like carbohydrates, we burn for energy; some, like fats, we store for future use, and some of it, like protein, we add to the material substance of the human environment. The value of carbon-based fossil materials for the latter two purposes probably far outweighs its value as a fuel. Other fuels are available, but no other molecules are as adaptable to combining with various others for making synthetic materials as are the molecules of oil and gas.

The hydrocarbon molecules of oil and natural gas are uniquely versatile in their ability to serve as building blocks for making the array of materials known collectively as petrochemicals. Some petrochemicals are used directly—as detergents, drugs, or cosmetics, for example—while most form the raw materials for an enormous variety of plastics. While many of these are used in wasteful and frivolous ways, such as unnecessary packaging, most serve useful purposes, including paints, fabrics, insulation materials, adhesives, and structural materials. Though there are difficult problems of toxicity in their manufacture and some petrochemicals are dif-

ficult to recycle, their potential beneficial role is great. Light-weight, low-energy vehicles, including automobiles, aircraft, and human-powered devices, rely heavily on the use of plastics. Future historians will probably regard the inhabitants of the 20th century as foolish indeed for having thoughtlessly burned such valuable and irreplaceable materials.

Regenerative Energy Flow

As the industrial era falters, we can see emerging a few fragments of a new regenerative pattern of energy flow. While the details are far from clear, it seems certain that the new pattern will have to be based on continuously self-renewing sources. It will thus be a shift toward use of energy income rather than energy capital. In terms of form and the ways of life it engenders, this pattern of flow will be as different from those of preindustrial society as it will be from those of the current industrial culture. Regenerative energy technology is inherently different from fossil-fuel-driven technology, but it does not necessarily mean a lesser quality of life.

For all the problems that profligate use of energy has brought upon us, 20th-century science and technology have developed a highly refined understanding of energy and its behavior. We have to put this knowledge to good use. The challenge is to design systems of energy flow that meet society's needs and at the same time meet the criteria of sustainability, including low pollution. We can also hope to design an energy system that fosters social justice and general human well-being in ways that Paleotechnic energy flow does not. This seems well within the scope of our knowledge, though it is hardly a simple undertaking.

The all-important sustainable energy source, renewed daily and inexhaustible in human time spans, is the sun. Solar energy can be channeled by a number of means to provide usable energy in diverse forms that can replace all of the nonrenewable energy forms now in use for an indefinite period of time. The solar energy striking the earth in just 11 days equals all of the energy stored in fossil-fuel reserves (Smil, 1991).

Other sustainable sources, such as tidal and geothermal energy, are small by comparison. While useful in specific situations, they are geographically limited to certain locations and relatively narrow ranges of applications.

Geothermal energy is drawn from the intense heat of the earth's interior where it comes close enough to the surface to be tapped. Although this happens in relatively few places in the world, where it does occur, geothermal energy can make a sizable contribution. They include many locations around the Pacific Rim, in Iceland, along the Great Rift in East Africa, and around the edge of the Mediterranean Sea. Heat from such sources is most effectively used directly for space and water heating and process heating for industry. Generating electricity by using geothermal heat to make steam and turn turbines is less efficient but still economical.

Nuclear energy, which can be generated through fission or fusion, has always been problematic. Nuclear fission once seemed most likely to replace fossil fuels but has proven too expensive and too dangerous. Most important, it is not sustainable

due to limited stores of uranium and the unresolved problem of storing waste. Duplicating the sun's own energy-generating process through nuclear fusion remains a distant hope of unknown potential, and may not produce net energy.

Brief Review of the Science of Solar Energy

Solar energy originates with the ongoing process of nuclear fusion in the sun's core, which causes a continuing conversion of mass to energy. As a result the sun will burn itself out within a few billion years. Meanwhile, each fusion of two hydrogen nuclei to form one helium nucleus results in mass being converted to energy. The gamma radiation streaming out from this process in the sun's core is reduced first to X rays and then to photons composed primarily of visible light but also some ultraviolet and infrared rays. From the outer layer of the great glowing ball of the sun, these particles radiate out in every direction, and less than one-billionth of them eventually strike the earth. The ozone layer in the upper atmosphere filters out most of the ultraviolet rays, while water and carbon dioxide molecules in the lower atmosphere tend to filter some of the infrared rays. Thus about 45 percent of the photons of solar radiation striking the earth's surface are within the visible spectrum—that is, they are light rays. Several things can happen to the rays of sunlight when they reach the earth, including photosynthesis, heat absorption, reflection, and evaporation:

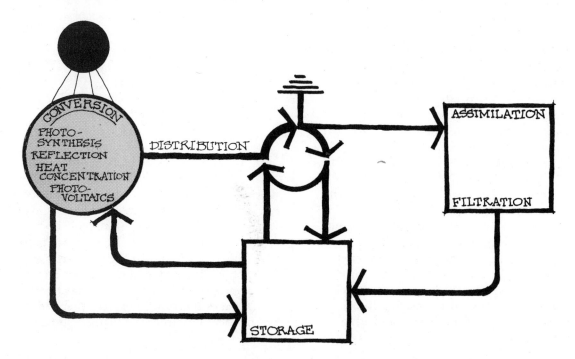

Photosynthesis. If the photons strike the green surface of a plant, that surface reflects the green wavelengths. Reaction with carbon dioxide and water converts the blue and red wavelengths in the process of photosynthesis into the stored energy of organic molecules, that is, molecules containing hydrogen and carbon. Of the photons that strike the earth every day, the process of photosynthesis uses a tiny portion, perhaps one-tenth of 1 percent.

Absorption and Reflection. The rest of the photons striking the earth are either absorbed, thus heating the absorbing material, or reflected. A dark surface, such as brick or calm water, absorbs over 90 percent of the photons striking it. The radiation that is absorbed and eventually reradiated, provides most of the earth's surface heat. If the photons strike a light-colored surface, such as the white wall of a building or a snow bank, over 80 percent of them are reflected. Thus the relative reflectivity of surfaces (called the albedo) on the earth's face has an enormous effect on the heat balance of the planet. This is as true for a small landscape or a city as it is for the earth as a whole. Differences in absorption and reflectivity over large landscapes—in effect, differences in color—determine the temperature of overlying air masses and thus direct global air movement.

Evaporation. Where the photons strike a water surface, they cause water to evaporate, or change to a gaseous form. The vapor rises and eventually falls back to earth as precipitation.

Conversion and Dissipation

According to the first law of thermodynamics, energy can change from one form to another but can never be created or destroyed. The second law of thermodynamics, also called the law of energy degradation, says that during this change, some of it is degraded to low-temperature heat, which is no longer useful. The balance between the photons incoming from the sun and those reflected and radiated back to space from the lower temperature of the earth maintains the heat equilibrium; that is, it keeps the temperature of the land and the atmosphere within a more or less consistent range. Even in the process of photosynthesis, far more energy is reflected as heat than is locked into biomass. Marshes are the most efficient biomass converters; about 1.5 percent of the solar radiation striking an average marsh is fixed in plant matter, and a highly

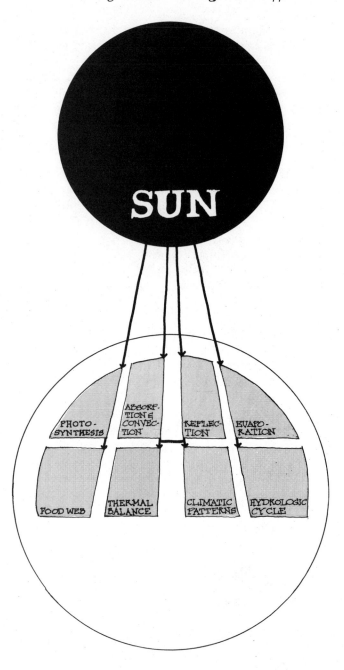

efficient marsh can fix twice that much. The most efficient temperate forest converts about the same amount as an average marsh and grasslands fix between 0.13 and 1.2 percent (Smil, 1991).

Thus, we can think of the natural pattern of energy flow as the rapid or gradual conversion of solar energy into low-temperature heat and its eventual reradiation back into the atmosphere. For a small but all-important portion of that energy, however, the route is neither direct nor fast. Between the time it reaches the earth and the time it leaves the atmosphere, the energy flow that emanates from the sun drives four basic processes that, along with geological forces, shape the environment for life on earth. First, the sun energizes life through photosynthesis by initiating the food web. Thus is life is created. This primary biomass is the essential funnel through which the earth's fundamental energy distribution system pours out to support all life. A second portion imparts heat to the earth's surface and the atmosphere, thus maintaining the global heat balance within a range that permits life. Third, some areas absorb more heat than others, depending on surface cover and declination; the earth's surface releases this heat into the atmosphere by convection. The warm air rises. Its temperature varies, and regional differences in temperature and atmospheric pressure thus drive the pattern of wind and climate. Fourth, where solar energy happens to strike the surfaces of lakes and seas, it evaporates water and thus energizes the hydrologic cycle.

With continuous renewal by the sun and continuous dispersal into space, this is the ultimate regenerative system. A regenerative energy system to do the work required for human activities must necessarily tap into this flow, working in concert with these vital processes, using the energy that is abundantly available along the pathways between energy's arrival and its departure. Thus, these four basic solar driven processes—photosynthesis, heat balance, air movement, and the hydrologic cycle—form the foundation on which our efforts to provide energy to the human environment can be based.

Energy Concentration

Along its pathways of flow, a number of processes convert energy into various forms. The energy in plant biomass produced by photosynthesis, for example, is converted into animal biomass if an animal eats the plant matter. Occasionally, when organic matter is buried under oxygen-deficient conditions, which prevent complete oxidation and decay, it will slowly undergo another transformation: Over a period of thousands or millions of years, this organic matter becomes fossil fuels—coal, petroleum, and natural gas. If the fossil fuel is burned to generate electricity, the result is electrical energy.

Industrial societies have come to depend heavily on electricity and fossil fuels for almost all their energy uses because of their convenience and flexibility. However, this reliance is extremely costly in energy terms, if not in present economic terms, because of the energy expended in the series of conver-

sions required to make fossil fuels and electricity. The second law of thermodynamics tells us that most of the energy in a given form is dissipated as unusable heat when it undergoes conversion to another form. About 96 to 99 percent of the solar energy striking an average landscape is lost as unusable heat while the rest is fixed in biomass. When an animal eats the plant matter, roughly 10 times as much energy is dissipated as heat as is fixed in animal biomass.

Entropy is the measure of the degree to which energy is dissipated in a transformation. Industrial society until very recently ignored entropy because energy in the form of fossil fuels was so widely available that it seemed to matter little if entropy was high in relation to the work performed. That is, energy inefficiency did not seem a critical concern. Nevertheless, the effects of entropy have long been evident. Entropy represents increasing disorder, expressed in physical, ecological, and social terms. The industrial system and the society, cities, and landscape it produced are, by the very nature of how they use energy, high in entropy.

Largely due to increased entropy, cities are several degrees warmer than the surrounding countryside, a phenomenon called the heat island effect. Almost certainly, the intensity and randomness of energy concentration and entropy also have profound social effects on cities and the people who live in them. Ivan Illich (1970) wrote that "high quanta of energy degrade social relations just as inevitably as they destroy the physical milieu" (p. 50). We might well view the social disintegration, unemployment, homelessness, drugs, and crime prevalent in cities as to some degree entropic effects. Certainly, concentrations of energy have much to do with the increasing size and monolithic character of both public and private institutions and their inability to deal with the lives and needs of large segments of the human population. Important though they are, the connections between energy and social dysfunction are obscure; causes and effects are entangled with myriad other conditions. However, our lack of understanding does not alter the fact that social disintegration could well bring disruption to the industrial pattern of energy flow even before depletion or pollution does.

A Low-Entropy Society

Breaking society's dependence on fossil fuels, in using effectively the energy available along the pathway of dissipative flow, will require that we make full use of energy from the sun in its various forms.

Since this energy is less concentrated, uses will have to be more efficient and lower in entropy. We might say that regenerative energy systems simultaneously reduce entropic disorder and build ecosystematic order. In general, where there are no subsidies of stored energy, the more efficient a system or organism is in converting and using energy, the greater will be its chances of survival—its sustainability.

Counteracting the ever-increasing disorder of entropy is the order-building process of photosynthesis, the first step in the ecosystematic order of nature. Green plants embody structural and functional order. Their growth represents expanding order. Thus, while entropy occurs with each conversion of energy within an ecosystem, entropic disorder is balanced through photosynthesis to some degree by increasing organic order, which contributes to the matrix of life. While increasing photosynthesis increases organic order, reducing fossil-fuel use decreases entropic disorder. We can further reduce entropy and increase sustainability by increasing energy efficiency.

Regenerative design can promote a shift over time from a high-entropy to a low-entropy society. There are many advantages in a low-energy technology, social as well as economic and technological. Illich insists that "participatory democracy postulates low energy technology" (ibid., p. 51). The lesson that excess energy is both physically and socially destructive has been a difficult one for Paleotechnic society to accept. Addicts are reluctant to face the fact that their preferred drugs are dangerous and unhealthy.

It may help when we recognize that a low-entropy society does not mean a deprived or uncomfortable society. There is no reason to think there is not enough energy available on the pathways to support a high standard of living for a population kept within reasonable limits. On the other hand, there are reasons to think a low-entropy society will be considerably more stable and comfortable simply because so many of the sources of instability and discomfort can be traced to the disorder resulting from high entropy.

While minimizing entropy requires calling into play all of the key strategies of regenerative systems discussed in Chapter 3, three of them are especially important. Especially relevant is the sixth strategy of using information to replace power. By applying accurate knowledge of energy needs and processes we can minimize the use of energy. Industrial society is enormously wasteful of energy. The industrial nations with about one-quarter of the world's population account for over 80 percent of global energy use, while the poorest (nonindustrial) quarter use about 2.5 percent (Smil, 1991). There is general agreement among energy experts, even those who advocate continued reliance on industrially based energy systems, that U.S. society could function essentially as it does now on far less energy, certainly less than one-half, by applying a few simple conservation measures. At our present stage of energy development, each joule of energy saved costs far less than each joule of energy generated by any means.

Also of particular relevance here is the ninth strategy—managing storage for sustainability. This is especially hard to apply to energy systems because energy use is notoriously sporadic, rising and falling through the day and from season to season. At the same time, partly because it does not have material substance, energy is inherently elusive in character and thus difficult to store. Despite its volatility, gasoline is among the most storable of energy sources, which partially accounts for its usefulness. On the other hand, electrical energy is difficult to store. The most common means of storing electricity is the storage battery, which is bulky and expensive; moreover, most batteries use dangerous and toxic acids. Solar energy is also difficult to store before being converted into a different form. Biomass is nature's major storage medium, but for human purposes its energy content is relatively low. Inert materials can store heat quickly, but they also tend to dissipate it quickly. However, this same property is the basis for passive solar heating, which uses a storage medium such as rock or water to store heat when the sun is shining and to release it as the surrounding air cools.

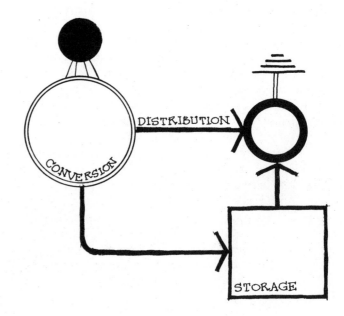

The difficulty of storing energy directly makes indirect means of storage useful. For example, energy generated by wind turbines can pump water uphill to holding tanks when the wind is blowing. Water stored in the tanks can then be distributed by gravity at any time. Water flowing from the tanks downhill can then drive hydropower turbines to generate electricity when there is no wind. It has also been suggested that hydrogen fuel could be easily and safely stored as a component of water and separated out by electrolysis powered by the sun or wind when available. It is also possible to store hydrogen in metal hydrides for quick release. Inventors often propose other devices for storage, such as large springs tightened by energy when available and released to supply energy when it is not. Possible storage media are virtually unlimited.

Devices like these will assume increasing importance as regenerative energy systems come into wider use simply because so many regenerative devices depend on sporadic phenomena such as sun or wind. In fact, storage devices will probably be as important as the conversion devices themselves and will present an equally fertile field for invention.

Another strategy of key importance is the fifth—matching technology to need or energy source to use, that is, using energy of the type required for the task at hand. Solar energy, for example, is free and plentiful but relatively dispersed. Heating a room can be accomplished by solar energy rather than by natural gas or electricity with far less entropy and fuel cost.

Energy Quality

The concept of energy quality is especially useful in applying the strategy of matching source to use. The quality of an energy source relates to its ability to do work; the greater the ability to do useful work, the higher the quality. Most authorities equate energy quality with concentration; that is, the more concentrated the energy is in a particular source, the higher the quality. By this measure, electricity is at the top of the quality scale. In general terms the more conversions an energy form has undergone to achieve its present state, the higher its quality. Thus animal biomass is higher in quality than plant biomass, charcoal is higher than wood, and petroleum higher than any of these. However, solar energy can be converted directly to the highest-quality electrical energy by photovoltaics, thus bypassing the series of conversions required to generate electricity by combustion.

The strategy of matching technology and need (means and ends) is related to the concept of energy quality. Amory and Hunter Lovins (1982) have estimated that only about 8 percent of our uses of energy require high-quality electrical energy. If the other 92 percent were served by lower-quality sources, our existing power plants could fill our electrical demands twice over.

Converting Solar Energy

Each of the natural conversions that solar radiation undergoes on reaching the earth plays an essential role in supporting earthly life, and each has the potential to provide far more energy for human purposes. The chains of transformation associated with each of the four can be summarized as shown in the table below.

Source	Conversion Process	Global System	Energy Form	Utility
Solar Radiation	Photosynthesis	Food web	Biomass	Food Fiber Fuel Waste treatment
	Absorption and convection	Thermal balance Climatic patterns	Heat Mechanical energy	Space heating Electrical power Water heating Process heating
	Reflection Evaporation	Reradiation Water cycle	Visible light Mechanical energy	Daylight Electrical power

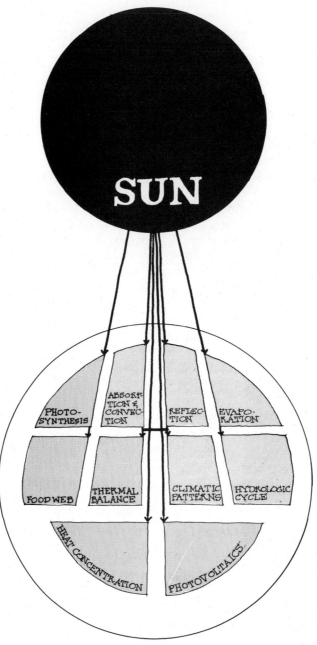

Thus, while powering the earth's basic processes, solar energy can also be transformed into all of the energy forms required by civilization: food, heat, liquid and gaseous fuels, light, and electricity. In addition to these natural means of transformation, human ingenuity has contributed other technologies of transformation. Most prominent among these are photovoltaics and heat concentration. So to the above list we can add the following:

Source	Conversion Process	Energy Form	Utility
Solar radiation	Photovoltaic reaction	Electricity	Electrical power
	Heat concentration	Process heat	Industrial power
		Biological activity	Waste treatment
		Mechanical energy	Electrical power
			Movement

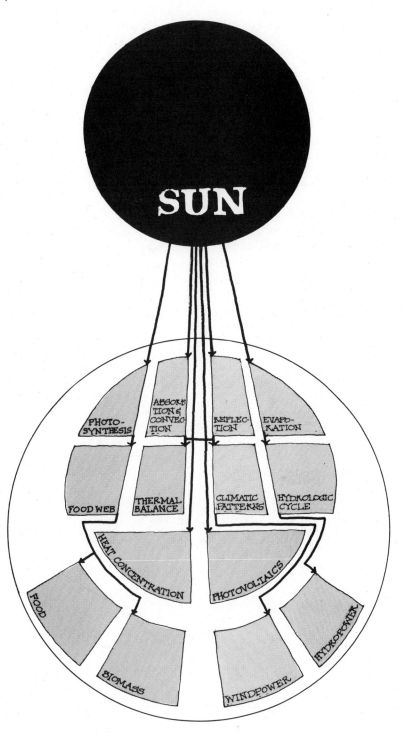

Regenerative Conversion Technology

In all of these energy-flow patterns, the point where solar energy is initially changed to another form determines what can happen from that point on. That is, conversion devices are the pivot points of energy flow, determining the energy's usefulness. Ef-

ficient and economic conversion technology is the most essential components of regenerative energy systems. Following are general descriptions of a number of regenerative conversion devices presently in operation or development and testing. We might consider these a beginning. As societies make the transition to sustainable technological bases, technological development will produce a far greater range of devices, some of which may eventually render most of these described here obsolete. Nevertheless, the following are quite practical and useful now. They can form the elemental parts for building a regenerative energy system. Economic feasibility is a complex question to which we will return in some detail in Chapter 11.

Heat Absorption from Solar Radiation

In using solar energy directly, we apply at smaller scale the same process by which solar radiation maintains the global heat balance: assimilation and distribution of energy by materials with varied heat-holding capacities. The most common uses for heat in the temperature range that can be provided by direct solar means are space heating and water heating. Solar space heating is accomplished by two fundamentally different approaches: passive and active.

Passive Space Heating orients the building form to trap incoming solar radiation through carefully placed transparent surfaces and uses it to heat interior space. At the same time, it uses materials with high heat-absorption capacities to store heat for release later when direct radiation is no longer available. Natural processes are thus applied to control and distribute energy. Forms and devices for carrying out these simple functions are endlessly varied, offering a fertile field for architectural invention and innovation. We will explore some of the possibilities further in the Chapter 5.

Active Space Heating uses a heat-transport medium—typically air, water, or an antifreeze solution—which circulates through collector panels exposed to solar radiation. The heated medium then transfers its heat for space heating to a storage medium, which is usually a storage tank or rock bed. This provides heat to interior air when direct radiation no longer is available. Active systems require fans, pumps, and other mechanical operations for moving the transport medium and air.

Water Heating is usually accomplished by active means. As with active space heating, water circulates continuously through panels in direct sunlight. The heated water is then stored in a tank and distributed for use as needed. Solar water-heating systems are commonly used to provide domestic hot water and low-temperature industrial process heat.

Food Drying is among the more common of other tasks accomplished using direct solar radiation. This can be done by simply laying food out to dry or by using glass-covered boxes to store heat. In large-scale examples, solar collectors and heat-storage materials supply hot air to drying chambers.

Photosynthesis and Biomass Conversion

Through photosynthesis, nature does work to store solar energy in the molecules of plant matter; biomass conversion takes advantage of this work already accomplished. The gaseous, liquid, or solid fuel produced can be as flexible in its uses as natural gas or petroleum. It can be burned to power internal

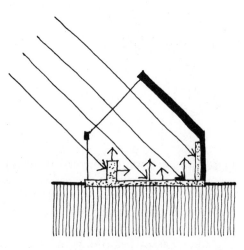

PASSIVE SOLAR HEATING

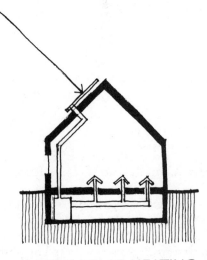

ACTIVE SOLAR HEATING

combustion engines or industrial processes or to generate electricity. As with primary conversion, the potential means for using energy derived from biomass are many and varied. Among the most useful or promising are the following.

Direct Combustion

Direct combustion accounts for most of the use of biomass fuels worldwide, wood having been for eons the predominant—often the only—fuel source for most societies. It is still the major energy source in most nonindustrial countries, which has led to disastrous levels of deforestation. However, if harvested on a sustained-yield basis, and if burned in efficient wood stoves with complete combustion, wood could continue to provide a large part of the world's energy needs, especially for cooking and space heating. Masonry heaters and other devices with very high heat-storage capacity can use wood very efficiently. Enclosing combustion in wood stoves with catalytic devices or masonry heaters reduces particulate pollution produced by wood burning by as much as 90 percent and increases combustion efficiency, making wood an entirely acceptable heat source. However, its great bulk per unit of energy and its relatively low combustion temperatures reflect its low position within the quality hierarchy and limit its range of uses. Making charcoal from the wood raises the quality of wood. It takes about 4 tons of wood to make 1 ton of charcoal, which contains the energy of 2 tons of wood. Thus 50 percent of the wood's energy is lost in the conversion process.

Anaerobic Digestion

Anaerobic digestion uses acid-forming bacteria to convert organic materials into fatty acids, alcohols, and aldehydes. Methane-forming bacteria then convert the acid to a biogas, which is a mixture of methane (65 percent) and carbon dioxide (35 percent) with traces of nitrogen, hydrogen, and hydrogen sulfide. This mix makes it an excellent fuel. The technology is simple and direct, the principal requirement being an oxygen-free environment of almost any size. All biomass can be digested, leaving a rich fertilizer as residue; all nutrients in the original material are retained through the digestion process. Wood is more difficult to digest, but scientists are working on optimizing this process. Most waste materials, including animal manure, are readily digested; in fact, digesters are commonly used in sewage treatment processes. Anaerobic digesters are widely used in India and China. There are believed to be more than 7 million digesters now in operation in China. One plant that lends itself well to biogas digestion is the water hyacinth, which is also among the most useful plants in the aquacultural sewage treatment processes described in Chapter 8. This suggests a strong potential for linking the two processes. Hyacinths grown in the process of drawing nutrients out of wastewater can then be harvested and digested to make biogas.

Fermentation

Fermentation of biomass materials produces alcohols that are like petroleum in their potential use as liquid fuels. In practice, ethanol and methanol are often mixed with gasoline to fuel internal combustion engines. Service stations in some places commonly sell mixtures of 90 percent gasoline and 10 percent ethanol. Pure methanol fuels all cars in the Indianapolis 500 race. Alcohol fuels can be made from biomass crops specifically for that purpose or from organic wastes produced in agriculture, food processing, and other industries.

In Brazil, ethanol is made from sugarcane and to some extent from cassava. In 1990, ethanol powered 23 percent of the cars in Brazil (Schiller, 1990). However, fluctuations in the sugarcane market have seriously affected its availability.

In the United States the crop usually proposed for ethanol production is corn, which with its high sugar content ferments readily. A bushel of corn yields about 2.5 gallons of ethanol (Grinnell, 1988). With current agricultural and distillation techniques, the net energy (energy produced minus energy consumed in its production) of this process is small: 1 joule expended in the high-quality forms of petroleum and electricity is required to produce 3.3 joules in the lower-quality form of corn kernels.

Producing ethanol from corn has other serious disadvantages as well. Corn production as commonly practiced also uses large volumes of fertilizers and pesticides. Ethanol production from corn also competes with food production.

For these reasons, the U.S. Department of Energy's Solar Energy Research Institute favors using plant fibers—lignocellulose—for making ethanol. The process is slower and more expensive because lignocellulose has to be broken down into sugars before it can be fermented. On the other hand, lignocellulose is widely and cheaply available as a waste material from agriculture. Some experts believe that enough ethanol could be made from presently available lignocellulose waste available in the United States to replace all of the petroleum presently consumed, with enough left over for returning nutrients to the soil.

Genetic engineering may reduce the cost of producing ethanol from cellulose substantially. A bacterium developed at the University of Florida by implanting two genes from one bacterium into another is able to produce ethanol from virtually any organic material including agricultural residues, plant trimmings, corncobs, and newspapers.

In Sweden, where long-term national policy calls for phasing out fossil-fuel use in favor of sustainable, domestic sources with low environmental impacts, energy plantations are expected to have a major role. There the most promising system involves willows grown in 2- or 3-year rotations. Some foresters see coppicing as a most useful practice. Coppicing is an ancient technique that involves harvesting most of the woody growth of trees at frequent intervals while leaving the trunks in place to produce new wood. In the tropics, a number of very fast growing species show promise for using the high natural productivity of rainforest ecosystems to produce biomass for energy while maintaining the integrity of the forest.

In Minnesota, scientists have analyzed the energy potential of cattails grown in wetland areas. Calculations suggest that if all of Minnesota's 10 million acres of land suitable for growing cattails were devoted to the purpose, they could provide for all of Minnesota's energy needs indefinitely. However, since most cattail areas are ecologically important wetlands, any large-scale use of cattails will probably depend on constructing new wetlands, which would compete with agriculture for land.

Oil-Producing Plants

Algae growth, which can take place in shallow saltwater ponds, is capable of producing enormous volumes of biomass. After drying, about 50 percent of the algae biomass consists of oil that can be used as a fuel.

Another intriguing possibility involves growing oil-producing plants on marginal semiarid lands. Professor Melvin Calvin has identified several plants of the genus *Euphorbia* with high hydrocarbon contents that grow rapidly in such areas. His research suggests that euphorbias could produce 10 to 50 barrels of oil per year in a desert landscape. Calvin estimates that an area of desert the size of Arizona planted with *Euphorbia* could replace the U.S. petroleum supply (Miller, 1975).

Several problems are likely to seriously limit biomass conversion as a substitute for fossil fuels.

First, since conversion efficiencies are generally less than 1 percent, estimates of their potential usually include assumptions of very large land areas devoted to energy crops. The Minnesota wetlands present one example. Using land areas of these magnitudes, energy crops would have to compete with both established agriculture and natural reserves. It has been estimated that powering the world's cars, trucks, and buses with ethanol would require about 25 percent of the world's arable land and that powering U.S. cars with methanol derived from corn would use five times the present area of U.S. cropland (Smil, 1991). If agricultural land area continues to decline in the developed countries, energy plantations might replace some of them, but given likely levels of population growth, this is doubtful. Moreover, if energy plantations follow industrial agricultural practices, they will cause more soil erosion and depletion, more water consumption for irrigation, and increased fertilizer and pesticide use. Following regenerative practices in growing energy crops would avoid these problems but would probably lower production density.

The second major problem is that, as already mentioned in the case of corn, the production processes for liquid biofuels require so much energy that the net energy of the resulting fuel is low. Experts disagree as to exactly how low it is; some say there is no net energy at all in most biofuels. This is probably an exaggeration. Nevertheless, if ethanol or methanol needs to be transported very far, the small net energy margin is very likely expended in transportation.

A third problem is air pollution. While they pollute less than fossil fuels, biofuels still do pollute. Sulfur dioxide emissions are much lower than those of coal or petroleum due to the low sulfur content. Large particles are considerably less. Carbon dioxide production is a net zero because carbon dioxide absorbed in growing the fuel equals that emitted in burning it. However, methanol-powered vehicles emit several times as much formaldehyde as gasoline-powered vehicles (Schiller, 1990), and methanol is twice as toxic as gasoline. Other pollutants vary with the specific fuel but are roughly similar to those of petroleum (Grinnell, 1988).

These problems combine to suggest that fuels produced by biomass conversion, especially the liquid fuels, may be useful as interim energy sources while the world is in the process of converting to a regenerative resource base. In the longer term, however, they probably will be limited to those applications that cannot be served by other energy sources, where direct substitutes for petroleum are needed, or where they can be used close to where they are grown and distilled.

Converting Wind Energy

Wind turbines represent the latest manifestation of an ancient technology. In operation, they are quite similar to the windmills that have been used since the 12th century for turning mills and pumping water. The rotary mechanical energy induced when the wind turns the blades is converted by a generator into electrical power. The process is simple and low in cost.

In general, wind turbines require minimum wind speeds of about 7 miles per hour to function. Higher power-output ratios are achieved as wind speed increases because power output is proportional to wind speed cubed. However, most machines can no longer operate safely when wind speeds exceed about 50 miles per hour. Wind turbines of the current generation are computer-controlled to produce steady amounts of power regardless of wind speed. Variable-pitch fiberglass blades can produce electricity at wind speeds of 9 to 60 miles per hour.

Wind turbines vary in size from machines about 100 to 200 feet tall with power ratings in the 100- to 1000-kilowatt range, to the giant machines that can reach heights of 400 feet (including blades, which usually span about 100 feet on current models) and produce over 1 megawatt of electricity. Power output increases with height because wind speeds in-

crease with distance above the ground. Larger machines are more economical both in cost and in their use of land, but the very large wind turbines have been plagued by problems of structural failure. Probably, there is a practical limitation on size.

Most regions of the United States have some locations with winds adequate for wind-energy conversion. According to U.S. Windpower, the major U.S. wind turbine manufacturer, five states each have enough wind to generate enough electricity to supply the entire country. These are Kansas, Montana, North Dakota, South Dakota, and Texas (Wald, 1992).

Water Power

Hydroelectric power—use of falling water to turn turbines that generate electricity—is the one ostensibly renewable energy source widely exploited by present industrial technology. During the period between the two world wars, the many immense hydroelectric dams built in the Tennessee Valley and the western states came to represent progress through technological might. After World War II this attitude spread overseas, especially to third-world countries. As people observed the results of the dams built during the first half of the 20th century, however, it became clear that they brought drastic and far-reaching ecological change. Not only are large land areas covered by water; the entire water regime downstream of a large dam is altered, which in turn affects the surrounding landscape. Many of the early environmental battles centered on dam projects, including the Hetch Hetchy dam in Yosemite National Park, the proposed Green River dam in Dinosaur National Monument, the Glen Canyon Dam, and the dams proposed for the Grand Canyon. Even after dam building virtually ceased in the United States, international agencies continued to build large dams in third-world countries with few objections. But in some cases these have also brought on severe environmental and financial problems. Examples are the Aswan Dam on the Nile and several dams in Brazil that inundated vast areas of rainforest and indigenous communities.

It is important to recognize also that the lakes behind large dams fill with silt over time, thus eventually becoming dry land and losing their power-generating potential. Though the lifetime of a well-located, carefully designed dam can often be measured in hundreds of years, it is never indefinitely sustainable. Since ideal dam sites are rare, dams are often built in less than optimal locations.

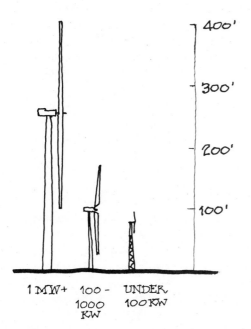

A survey carried out by the World Bank examined 200 dams built over 45 years. The average loss in capacity due to siltation was 2 percent of the original capacity per year (Myers, 1987). This suggests an average life of about 50 years with steadily diminishing capacity. Given such brief periods of effective life along with their widespread environmental impacts (see the example in Chapter 6 of the water resources plan for Sardinia), large dams do not generally qualify as regenerative technologies.

Small Hydropower Impoundments

Small hydroelectric plants, however, are different from large ones in both respects. Earthen or rock dams less than about 3 meters high generally bring only minor and temporary environmental change if carefully located. While they do cause siltation and tend to be even shorter lived than large dams, streams can quickly reestablish their courses through silted-up areas after a small dam is breached.

The technology of power generation by small impoundments is ancient, essentially the same as that used to turn wheels for grinding grain since before the time of Christ. The dam impounds water, which in turn is diverted from the impoundment into a small human-made channel or raceway in which the flow is rapid. A water wheel or turbine turned by the moving water spins a generator to generate electricity.

Though the downstream changes wrought by such devices are small, they can be serious in especially sensitive areas or where stream flows vary or where a stream is impounded at several points too close together. Fish populations can be affected by fluctuations in flow, by turbulence, and by siltation.

Given such problems, along with their necessarily small generating capacity, the potential contribution of small hydroelectric plants is small, generally limited to supplying power for single houses or small communities in isolated locations.

Photovoltaic Conversion

Photovoltaic cells use a semiconductor material, such as silicon, to create a voltage differential, which makes it possible to convert sunlight to electricity in one step. When a photon strikes the surface of the semiconductor, which is usually negatively charged and has loosely bound electrons, the electrons become excited, and often one of them jumps out of orbit. This leaves a positively charged "hole" that can migrate, as can the loose electron. If the hole reaches a position on the opposite side of the semiconductor material from the position of the loose electron, a current of electrons flows through a connection with an external load which can capture the current.

A typical photovoltaic cell is about 4 inches square, and each one can generate about 1 watt of electricity with maximum sunlight. Banks of cells can be assembled to generate the number of watts needed. Ideally, the banks of cells are south-facing to capture the maximum sunlight. They can be mounted on movable panels programmed to track the sun so that the cells are always perpendicular to the sun's rays for maximum interception of solar radiation. A further refinement provides each cell with a lens that focuses the light rays striking the larger area of the lens directly onto the silicon semiconductor. The efficiency of photovoltaic cells generally runs about 10 to 15 percent; that is, 10 to 15 percent of the solar energy striking them becomes usable electrical energy. A photovoltaic generator can achieve a high level of technological sophistication, but the cost is commensurately high.

Photovoltaic converters have the important advantage of being easily integrated into a building structure or other parts of the human environment. An array of cells can be very small or very large.

Heat Concentration and Solar Thermal Conversion

Solar thermal converters use reflective surfaces to force photons from a large area to a point or surface. Here the concentrated heat raises the temperature of a fluid to very high levels. The heated fluid then turns water into steam that operates a turbine to generate electricity.

Installations in California, France, Japan, Russia, Spain, and New Mexico have used tracking reflectors called heliostats—that is, reflectors that move to keep their reflecting surfaces aimed so that sunlight is reflected to a central tower. The reflected rays heat the heat-transfer medium located at the top of this tower to temperatures of over 1000°F (Fahrenheit).

Simpler and less costly are systems half cylindrical trough-shaped reflectors that present their concave surfaces to the sun and bounce the photons to a pipe running down the center of the semicylinder. This pipe carries a heat-transfer oil that is heated to several times the boiling temperature of water and then used to convert water to steam to drive turbine generators.

A number of variations on this basic concept have been tried in various parts of the world, generally with success. So far, solar thermal systems have proven the lowest-cost means of primary solar conversion. Their efficiency can be as high as 23 percent on a sunny day.

Dish–Stirling Converters

The Dish–Stirling system manufactured by Cummins Power Generation, is typical solar-thermal conversion technology. It uses a solar concentrator which moves on two axes to track the sun through the day. The concentrator consists of an array of concave, mirror-surfaced disks mounted in a space frame. The mirrors are made of thin sheets of reflective plastic stretched over both sides of a ring with a slight vacuum forming a concave (and thus concentrating) shape. These surfaces reflect solar radiation, concentrating it on a free-piston Stirling engine, which drives a linear alternator to convert thermal energy into electrical energy. The result is an efficient, relatively inexpensive solar energy-conversion device. The world's record for conversion efficiency was recorded by a Dish–Stirling converter at 29 percent.

Solar Ponds

Several natural solar ponds exist in widely separated parts of the world. The water in a solar pond is naturally stratified in several layers of varied salinity from clear on top to very salty and correspondingly heavy on the bottom. The upper levels allow solar radiation to pass through and also serve as insulation, while the lower levels collect the heat sometimes to the point of boiling. This heat can be transferred through a heat-transfer device to a liquid with a low boiling point such as ammonia or freon, and then used to drive a turbine and generate electricity in the same way as steam.

Solar ponds can be constructed for this purpose, or sections of larger bodies of water isolated by

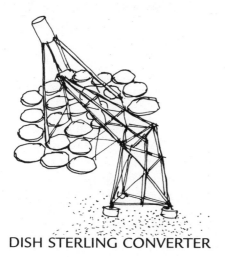

DISH STERLING CONVERTER

dikes can be used. Scientists have proposed converting portions of the Dead Sea and the Salton Sea (in California) to solar ponds. As with other solar conversion technologies, desert locations are best. Small experimental ponds have been built at the University of Texas at El Paso and other places. Efficiencies are generally around 1 percent. Although the technology is simple and inexpensive and apparently has little impact on the environment, it has been little exploited up to now.

Hydrogen Fuel

By coincidence or grand design, the substance most likely to replace petroleum as a multipurpose, widely distributed, highly adaptable fuel is the same gas that plays the key role in emitting radiant energy from the sun: hydrogen. Highly volatile, light in weight, and odorless, hydrogen gas can power internal combustion and other types of engines. It does not exist as a free element in the earth's environment, but can be obtained by separating it from the oxygen in water. This is accomplished by electrolysis or high levels of heat, which means that another energy source must be used. Thus the potential of hydrogen as a fuel is closely coupled with solar energy to provide electric current or heat.

Once freed, hydrogen gas can be stored or transported, though not easily. Pipelines can carry it hundreds of kilometers with little loss and without the environmental threats posed by oil spills. It can be stored in pressurized tanks, liquified and stored at ambient temperatures, or absorbed into metallic compounds. Some researchers have suggested that hydrogen might be injected into the voids of depleted oil fields for long-term storage. However, the gas is very low in density, thus bulky to store. Its volatility requires extreme care in handling, as the explosion of the Hindenberg dirigible demonstrated.

At present, it appears that the most energy-efficient means for using hydrogen to power automobiles and other machines is to "burn" it in a fuel cell that converts chemical energy into low-voltage, direct-current electricity which can then drive an electric motor. Overall efficiency, even with the two conversions, is very high—about twice that of an internal combustion engine.

Hydrogen's principal virtue is its lack of pollution. A hydrogen engine emits only water vapor, nitrogen, and a small amount of nitrogen oxides. In a complete system the vapor can be condensed and again decomposed by heat or electrolysis to repeat the process.

EXAPMLE

■■

Conservation and Renewable Energy in the Southern California Edison System

Public utility companies, by and large, have not been quick to accept regenerative energy technologies. Most have continued to base their plans on nuclear, gas, and coal-fired power.

Conservation approaches have found more acceptance. A number of utilities have adopted conservation programs, applying the principle, pioneered by Amory Lovins that the cost of energy-saving measures should be accounted for as the equivalent of the generating capacity not built. Lovins applied in a sophisticated way Benjamin Franklin's notion that a penny saved is a penny earned (Lovins, 1977). In this case, a penny saved is considerably more. The Pacific Gas and Electric Company has estimated that the cost of building 1 kilowatt-hour of generating capacity is about seven times the cost of saving 1 kilowatt through its conservation program.

The Southern California Edison Company (SCE), which provides electricity to most of southern California, excluding the cities of Los Angeles and Pasadena, has adopted a more forward-looking approach than most utility companies in preparing for the transition to renewable sources. SCE has maintained active conservation programs and has also invested considerably in experiments with renewable sources. Renewable energy sources account for 20.7 percent of SCE's generating capacity, which is about twice the figure for all utilities nationwide. Large-scale hydroelectric facilities account for over half of this, however. As pointed out earlier, hydroelectric power is not truly renewable in the long term. Other technologies used by SCE include solar thermal conversion, photovoltaics, wind-energy conversion, refuse-to-energy conversions, methane recovery, biomass conversion, and geothermal energy. The company pursues a policy of preparing itself for a major shift away from fossil-fuel-generating plants in the future.

Solar Thermal Conversion

Two different types of solar thermal-conversion systems have contributed to SCE's knowledge base and generating capacity, one a highly sophisticated central receiver system and the other a relatively simple trough reflector system. Both are located in the Mojave Desert, where insolation levels are among the world's highest.

Solar One and Two

Solar One, which operated for several years in the Mojave Desert near Barstow, California, used an array of computer-controlled tracking mirrors called heliostats spread out in a roughly circular form in the desert landscape. The heliostats reflected solar rays to a solar absorber in the peak of a 300-foot-tall central power tower. There the concentrated heat boiled water to 1000°F to make high-temperature steam, which then turned generating turbines, producing 10 megawatts of electrical energy. While this is not a great deal of power, it proved the technology feasible, though costly.

At present, Solar One is out of operation while engineers are making preparations to convert the facility to Solar Two, which will use molten salt as the working fluid in the solar absorber rather than steam. A hot and a cold storage tank will be added. This change is expected to result in a more flexible and cost-effective plant that will continue to produce the power from the stored heat until about 3 hours after sunset. It requires rebuilding the heat receiver unit in the tower as well as the piping system. More heliostats will also be added to improve energy distribution.

The U.S. Department of Energy, which has built smaller plants to test the technology, is paying half its cost. Several other utilities are forming a consortium with SCE to pay the other half. If all goes well, engineers expect to build plants of the Solar Two type with generating capacities of 100 to 200 megawatts by the end of the 1990s.

SEGS II (Solar Energy Generating System)

Generating far more energy on an everyday working basis than Solar One or Two are eight solar generating plants built in the Mojave Desert by the Luz International Corporation. These plants feature the Solar Electric Generation System (SEGS), which uses long rows of parabolic trough reflectors that track the sun along one axis (rather than two as with Solar One's heliostats).

The total generating capacity of the eight plants is about 280 megawatts, nearly 1.5 percent of SCE's total generating capacity. In the Mojave the sun shines almost every day of the year, and the Luz plants work on solar energy as long as the sun is shining. The sunlight hours correspond to SCE's peak-load hours except in the late evening. When the sun goes down, and on cloudy days, the plants shift to natural-gas-fired operation for their last few hours of the day.

The Luz solar thermal plants are examples of the kind of energy innovation and development made possible by the Public Utilities Regulatory Policies Act (PURPA), passed by the federal government in 1978. This act requires public utilities to buy power generated by alternative means from independent energy producers at the cost of electricity produced by a new oil-fired plant. However, the oil glut of the early 1990s resulted in unrealistically low fuel prices. The cost of solar thermal power is roughly the same as that generated by nuclear plants but at least half again that of oil- or coal-fired plants. Unable to pay its costs at

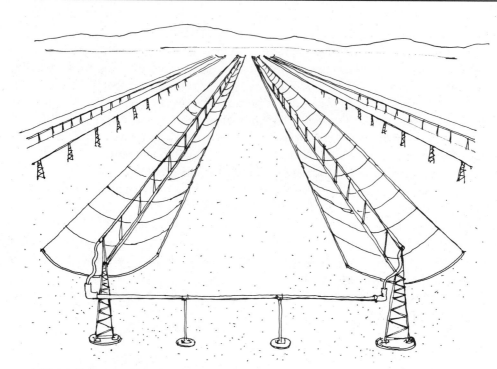

LUZ SOLAR THERMAL SYSTEM

these prices Luz International declared bankruptcy in late 1991, but the SEGS plant is still in operation, managed now by the Daggett Leasing Corporation.

In addition, SCE has invested in Dish–Sterling technology, having purchased rights to make and sell Dish–Sterling thermal solar generators. However, none of these is yet operating on line.

Photovoltaics

SCE has also worked jointly with other companies and agencies in several areas of photovoltaic-cell development. One of these is the "solar spheral" technology being developed in conjunction with Texas Instruments. The solar spheral system features small spherical cells mounted in metal mesh for installation on building roofs.

The solar spheres are tiny; about 17,000 of them can be mounted on a 4-inch-square surface. Each of these tiny cells functions independently, so the failure of one or a few has little effect on the performance of the whole. They can be made from low-grade silicon, which costs about $\frac{1}{35}$ as much as the high-grade silicon required for conventional cells.

A 17-foot-square array (a little smaller than a typical two-car garage) of spheral cells mounted on a south-facing roof can provide about 6000 kilowatt-hours of electricity per year, roughly the amount of power used in an average southern California residence.

A second device being tested is a solar-powered recharging carport for electric cars. The initial pilot unit is a 3000-square-foot (approximately 15-car) carport installed in the parking area of the southern California Air Quality Management District (AQMD), which is SCE's partner in the venture. This facility uses an array of flat photovoltaic panels facing south with a capability of generating about 24 kilowatts for charging the batteries of cars parked underneath. When not charging the vans, the solar-cell arrays feed power into the SCE grid through a DC/AC inverter. SCE will monitor the system's performance. Once the system is tested and proven reliable, SCE and AQMD plan to begin installing them in public parking areas such as shopping centers.

Wind-Energy Conversion

There are three large wind farms in California, located at the Altamont Pass near San Francisco and the Tehachapi and San Gorgonio passes in southern California. All three wind farms were privately developed with money from investors taking advantage of the tax credits offered for sustainable energy development in the late 1970s and early 1980s. The latter two contribute a peak of about 900 megawatts to SCE's capacity. Studies indicate that there exist within SCE's service area suitable sites for an additional 4000 megawatts. Wind turbines are presently the lowest-cost regenerative energy-conversion technology, and they probably will be so long into the future.

Since the average machine produces about 200 kilowatts, it takes a great many machines to generate a significant level of power, so a wind farm makes a very large mark on the landscape. The Altamont farm is about 8 miles long, and the other two are only a little smaller. This has brought on a great many impassioned complaints about their visual impact on the landscape. There is no question that the long rows of wind-energy converters dominate the rolling hills on which they sit. But we can also see them as a form of kinetic sculpture, one that provokes a strong response. The strategy of making the process visible is at work here, of necessity. In a dramatic way, they make us aware of the dominant role of energy in our society and the consumption patterns that require such vast arrays of machinery to support it. In this light, they compare favorably to the noxious emissions, immense machinery, and gas flares of an oil refinery.

Despite their visual dominance, the physical and ecological impacts of wind farms are relatively minor when the sites are carefully planned and the installations well designed. Although wind farms occupy large areas of land, it can be shared with other uses. At Altamont Pass, for example, cows graze in the shadows of the wind machines.

However, especially at the two southern installations, the machines were not carefully sited to fit wind patterns and the landscape. As a result, many of the machines stand on unsuitable slopes, and poorly graded access roads are causing soils to erode away. At San Gorgonio especially, a large number of the machines rarely operate even in high winds. A careful land-suitability analysis

carried out before the development showed that less than 20 percent of the land on which wind machines were eventually installed was actually functionally suitable for them (Lyle, 1985).

Refuse-to-Energy Conversion

SCE has designed a system for separating out recyclable materials, including metals, glass, plastic, rocks, and dirt, from household and commercial refuse, and then shredding the rest to make a refuse-derived fuel (RDF). The fuel will move to a fluidized bed gasifier, which will convert most of it at 1500°F to a gas, which will then cool to about 200°F in a heat exchanger. The heat given off by the cooling gas will be converted to stream for generating electricity, while the gas itself can be used as a fuel in other applications. Researchers expect it to produce lower emissions than natural gas. Water used in the process is cleaned after each use and recycled. The ash residue—about 7 percent of the fuel volume—can be used for various purposes.

If this system, called Advanced Integrated Recycling (AIR), works as predicted when it goes into operation (probably in 1995), it will have three major advantages over most refuse-to-energy plants. The first is that it uses only materials considered not recyclable as compared to conventional mass-burn-type facilities. However, the design calls for removing only 50 tons of the initial 200 tons of refuse for recycling, which leaves 150 tons of fuel. Some programs have succeeded in recycling over 50 percent of urban refuse, and rates of over 80 percent are theoretically possible. There is little doubt that some portion of the refuse stream, probably between 10 and 35 percent, is unrecyclable, and for this portion, refuse-to-energy is a promising option. A question remains as to whether this is enough to allow for economical operation of a refuse-to-energy facility.

The second advantage is the modular nature of the gasifier technology. Plants of almost any size can be built to serve small or large communities.

The third important advantage of the AIR system is that the gasifier technology is expected to produce no air emissions. If this expectation is borne out, then it will have solved the problem that has prevented most of the refuse-to-energy plants proposed in the past from being built. If the first AIR plant demonstrates when it goes into operation that it can operate on a small fraction of the waste stream without polluting the air, then it will probably be an important regenerative technology for the future.

Methane Recovery

Several landfills in southern California are equipped with methane gas recovery systems, which collect the gases produced by the decomposition of refuse. The gases are drawn into a network of perforated pipes buried in the landfill by means of a vacuum. Gases are piped to a generator that burns them to make steam, which turns turbines to generate electricity. SCE then buys the electricity under the terms of PURPA and feeds it into the grid.

Biomass Conversion

In its Highgrove Generating Station, SCE developed a wood gasifier that converts up to 1500 pounds of wood per day into a gas used as a fuel for the power plant boiler. The gasifier is a downdraft fixed-bed device that operates at about 90 percent thermal efficiency. However, about 5 percent of the wood weight remains as a nontoxic char for which no use has been found.

SCE estimates that about 5000 tons of wood waste, which could be converted to energy by this process, go into landfills within its service area everyday. This includes 65 tons trimmed from trees within the company's own distribution rights-of-way. However, after operating the gasifier for 3 years to develop and refine the technology, SCE took it out of operation because the cost of producing gas was higher than that of buying natural gas at current prices. Since gas prices will certainly rise within a few years, the gasifier will almost certainly operate again.

Hydroelectric Energy

About 12 percent of SCE's generating capacity comes from hydroelectric sources. Most of that comes from a series of six dams in the Big Creek drainage on the western slope of the Sierra Nevada. The lakes created by the dams are heavily used for recreation, and the land around them is managed for its wildlife and forest value.

SCE also purchases about 188 megawatt-hours per day from small-scale hydroelectric suppliers. This is about 2 percent of the power the company buys under the terms of PURPA, enough to supply about 30,000 houses.

Geothermal Energy

Over half of the power purchased by SCE under PURPA is geothermal. This is because the company's service area happens to include a number of areas where the unusual conditions for geothermal energy production exist. Altogether, SCE buys power from 22 geothermal generating plants. These are located on sites where the molten rock of the earth's core is relatively close to the surface (within 3000 to 6000 feet) and is saturated with water. This very hot water is brought to the surface, and as the pressure on it is reduced, part of it flashes into steam, which then runs turbines to generate electricity. Excess water is injected back into the ground.

The geothermal process is low in cost, but the process does produce some sulfur, hydrogen sulfide, radon, dissolved minerals, and noise. It requires only a small surface area and causes no disruption in the surrounding community. However, some geothermal plants have found that energy production declines over time, and it is not clear how long they can be productive. SCE engineers believe this problem might be overcome by limiting the amount of water extracted each day, and that geothermal plants can be productive on a sustainable basis. They are conducting research for this purpose.

From this brief survey, it is clear that SCE is preparing for the time when fossil fuels run short by experimenting with a broad range of renewable technologies. The commitment is long-range; for the present SCE has no plans to expand any of these systems into a major contributor. These renewable energy program seems far-sighted when compared to those of other public utilities. Seen in the light of our looming energy issues, however, they seem only a very tentative first step.

Regenerative Conversion as a New Realm of Technology

Though some conversion technologies are based on ancient practices, a great many have emerged since the first glimmering of awareness of an energy crisis in the 1960s. As the SCE examples show, sustainable energy has proven a fertile field for human inventiveness and will certainly continue to do so even if research funds continue to be scarce. Exploration of the possibilities has only begun.

Taken as a group, regenerative conversion devices form a new realm of technology quite different in character from the energy technology of the industrial era. The difference in character suggests differences in application with far-reaching social implications.

Multiple Means

With so many different technologies that apply in so many different situations, it seems unlikely that a single energy source will ever again be as predominant as coal was at the beginning of the industrial period and as petroleum has been in later decades. The seventh strategy for regenerative design listed in Chapter Three—using multiple pathways—applies especially to supplying energy.

Energy pathways are many and varied. The SCE system gives some notion of the variety of means available for generating electricity and how the means depend on the local landscape. SCE has taken advantage of the desert, the windy ridges, and the geothermal sites within its service area. Climate and land availability also enter the picture. Even within the realm of a single technology, the means can vary greatly. Photovoltaic devices, for example, can be used in large, complex tracking generators, as tiny rectangles on the face of a pocket calculator, or as period-sized units mounted in a mesh to form part of the roof of a building.

The forms of liquid and gaseous fuels also vary, and their sources are even more diverse. Fuels can be made from a number of different plant species, kelp and other seaweed, industrial or agricultural wastes, and sewage or animal manure. Thus the feasibility of a source is likely to depend on the context. What is readily available or easily produced nearby is likely to be a feasible energy source.

Most regenerative energy technologies are closely related to processes serving other purposes. Biomass conversion is inseparable from agriculture, forestry, and waste treatment. Photovoltaic devices are often integrated with architectural form; passive solar heating is mostly a matter of architectural form. Wind farms are often also grazing lands. Biogas production and sewage treatment can be integrated. Cogeneration uses the surplus heat from industrial processes. The eighth strategy—finding common solutions to seemingly disparate problems—applies widely in regenerative energy planning.

Using multiple means and integrating diverse processes mean greater complexity, not in the technology, which is relatively simple, but in the system. Regenerative energy systems are likely to be complex in their operational diversity and in their many interrelationships. The linking of technologies leads to complexity. Powering an automobile with hydrogen gas using the most efficient means, for example, requires four energy conversions: solar radiation to heat or electric current, decomposition of water, hydrogen gas to electrical power and electrical to mechanical power.

The range of options and the systemic complexity mean a great many decisions have to be made in the design and operation of a regenerative energy system. In most cases the decisions are not highly technical but tend to be more economic and social in character, closely linked with the general well-being of the society they serve. Thus human participation in technological systems becomes essential.

The costs of the various energy technologies will have a great deal to do with their success in practice. While some regenerative technologies are already competitive with conventional technologies powered by fossil fuels, others are not. However, cost comparisons depend on what is included in the estimates, which makes them difficult to derive and often misleading. We will return to this subject in Chapter 11.

Scale Implications

In contrast to industrially based energy technologies, which tend to grow ever larger, regenerative energy technologies tend to be smaller and more localized in their operation. This is especially true of those regenerative technologies that apply low-density energy. In applying solar radiation directly for heat, the use must be where the sunlight strikes; there is no extra energy for moving it about. This means that solar space and water heating are local matters: The heat is collected and used within the site.

The scale of biomass use is somewhat broader but still limited. Firewood is usually moved no more than a few miles from where it is cut. Since the low net energy of alcohol fuels allows little to spare for transportation, producing them from biomass probably will also be more localized than petroleum production. Their production is also dependent on the biomass that the local landscape can provide. While there may be some minor benefits in using large plantations rather than small ones to produce biomass for alcohol fuels, the waste-material sources for the more promising alcohol-fuel technologies are dispersed. The alcohol-making process itself can be very small in scale.

The scale implications of electrical energy are more disparate. Electrical energy generated by fossil fuels is highly concentrated and centralized, thus large in scale. In contrast, most regenerative technologies are modular in nature, photovoltaic cells being an obvious example. The basic unit is small, ranging from the tiny cells used in pocket calculators to those about 4 to 5 inches square that are assembled in arrays for power generation. This small basic unit does all of the work; it contains the entire process of generating electricity within itself. For tracking collectors it is practical to assemble a number of units into a movable panel, which then becomes the module. Yet the number is still small, typically less than three or four thousand units.

The modular character of wind turbines and solar Dish–Stirling converters are equally apparent. Wind turbines vary in size, the larger ones being more effective in use of resources, but there are certain limitations. Within the size range, each machine functions as an independent unit. While numbers of units are connected in series to generate any given amount of power, one unit operating alone can be just as cost-effective if it is located near the point of energy use.

What this means is that most regenerative energy technologies have few or no economies of scale, and in fact often operate more efficiently and economically at smaller scales. They also have little or no distribution cost and thus can respond to other factors in determinations of size and location. This inherent flexibility has far reaching implications for planning. Not only are choices among energy sources available, but so are choices among means of tapping those sources. A single residence might have its electrical energy supplied by a wind generator, by a bank of solar cells on its roof, or by a combination of both. Or it might share in a small community system with 10, 20, or 100 other houses.

The same community might share a biogas digester or a woodlot from which to take firewood.

Given this inherent difference, electrical energy from regenerative sources will be less centralized, more community-based. Communities may then be more dispersed, more closely related to the local landscape. There are economic advantages as well. Transmission and distribution costs will be much reduced. Amory Lovins has estimated that the cost of transmission and distribution of equipment, operation, and maintenance account for nearly 70 percent of the average electric bill with only 19 percent going to the actual cost of power generation (Lovins, 1977).

Given the range of options, in designing communities planners can choose the most suitable combination of sources as well as the most appropriate scale for their application. They can take advantage of local resources, such as sunny locations, windy ridges, or highly productive soils. Thus regenerative energy systems can be endlessly varied and closely related to local landscape and social order.

Energy Systems

In just a century, electricity has become the most versatile and one of the two most widely used forms of energy. Since processes for converting solar energy to electrical power are the most efficient of regenerative energy-conversion processes—more efficient by far than photosynthesis or biomass conversion—the importance of electricity is likely to be ever greater in a regenerative future.

Though diverse, usually small in scale, dispersed, and localized, regenerative energy technologies will still interact to form larger systems. In general, the systems they form are less monolithic, more flexible than those of current industrial energy production, and therefore more varied and complex. Few people expect that regenerative technologies will quickly assume predominance. Rather, they will necessarily be evolving extension of industrially based systems for some years to come. Large systems and the large organizations that manage them are not likely to suddenly disappear. Probably they will give way gradually. Three existing, highly developed systems likely to evolve rapidly over the next few decades as regenerative energy becomes more prevalent are the electrical distribution system, the transportation system, and the information system. The evolution of these three energy-based systems, along with the more dispersed use of energy for heating and cooling, is likely to profoundly influence the shape of the human landscape over the next few decades.

Transmission Grids

The vast electrical transmission grids that the perform the distribution function for electric power have spread during the 20th century to cover whole continents. They have proven effective in providing power where needed, when needed, usually in the quantities needed. Their major disadvantages are high cost, environmental damage in varied forms, social problems related to centralized operation, and the still-unknown health dangers of electromagnetic radiation.

Grids are networks of transmission lines spreading over large areas of landscape. In the United States, two grids cover the entire country—one west of the Rocky Mountains and one east. They evolved during the industrial period to transmit electricity from large generating plants, which are mostly outside cities, to users of electricity, who are mostly inside cities. The giant coal-fired Four Corners generators in New Mexico and the turbines at Hoover Dam in Nevada were both built to supply power to the city of Los Angeles hundreds of miles away, for example; through the grid, they can supply other cities as well, albeit at high environmental cost.

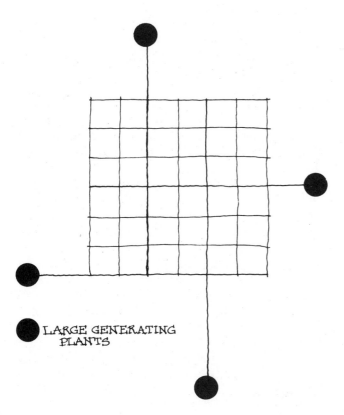

LARGE GENERATING PLANTS

The potentials of energy grids, however, go far beyond such centralized organization. In effect, as shown in the SCE example, energy can be put into the grid at any point and used at any other point. Thus a grid can accommodate energy inputs of varied sizes from different sources in widely dispersed locations. Such widespread flexibility is a fairly recent phenomenon. Until mid-century it was possible to transmit energy only about 300 to 400 miles from its generating source. In the 1960s, by using ultrahigh voltage and improved conductivity, this distance increased to over 1500 miles. More recently, the transmission range has stretched out to 4000 miles for direct current and 3000 miles for alternating current. Super conductivity offers even greater potential. Buckminster Fuller (1981) saw in these advances the potential for a global energy grid that would interconnect all of the world's major sources of electrical energy. Fuller's World Game foresaw important advantages in a global grid. For example, the trading of energy among different time zones could level peak demands and thus reduce the amount of generating capacity needed. Generators using an almost unlimited range of energy sources could contribute to the global electrical energy supply. The World Game projections foresaw gains in electrical energy availability almost everywhere with a net reduction in large generating plants. Third-world nations in particular would benefit. Based on its analyses, in fact, the World Game made the global grid the top-priority project in moving toward its goal of making "the world work for 100 percent of humanity in the shortest possible time through spontaneous cooperation without ecological damage or the disadvantage of anyone" (Fuller, 1981, p. 198).

Today, officials in the United States and Russia are considering plans for extending the first link in what might eventually become a global grid across the Bering Strait to link the grids of the two countries. The political difficulties, once formidable, now seem easily surmountable in light of evolving East-West relations.

Whatever eventually comes of such plans, the advantages even of the more modest regional grids are considerable. Their breadth and coverage make it possible for them to accommodate energy from sources that can operate only at certain times—for example from solar generators or photovoltaics during the daytime and from wind generators when and where the wind is blowing. They can also compensate for unequal geographic distribution of energy resources. Deserts are likely to loom very important in future global energy systems because they are so well suited for solar conversion. A grid can function with inputs from many diverse sources of varied sizes better than it can with a few large central generating stations.

This potential was rendered more significant in 1978 when the federal government passed PURPA, which required utility companies to purchase, at the "avoided cost" (which means the cost of electricity generated from the most expensive fossil fuel), electrical power generated by anyone who wants to feed it into the grid. Though the price was set much too low, the implications of this are large and far reaching. In effect, PURPA makes it possible for the power grid to become a basis for regenerative development. Entrepreneurs can go into the energy business even on a very small scale, applying a whole range of new renewable energy sources. As fuel prices rise and different generating technologies become more economically feasible, we might find large generating plants fading into history; in its place the grid can become a highly flexible and pervasive system that collects and delivers electrical energy from diverse and scattered sources of different sizes to locations that could eventually encompass the whole earth. An energy grid might develop into a network of linkages among widespread local energy units, a vehicle for cooperation rather than a monolithic delivery system. Thus might the one-way flow pattern of Paleotechnic technology evolve into a network of interaction.

For all the flexibility that they offer, electrical grids also have serious disadvantages. One is the energy lost in transmission, and another, already mentioned, is the high cost of transmission and distribution facilities. Where local sources are not available or where they are significantly more costly than more distant ones, these may be small prices to pay. But where local sources are available in sun, wind, or geothermal forms, it is better to make use of them.

The local-global balance envisioned in this scenario of electrical energy will be one of the underlying themes of the Neotechnic era. We will see it in politics, trade, and technology transfer as well as in the more obvious areas of transportation and information exchange. The local community will assume increasing importance as it relies more heavily on the resources of the local landscape. At the same time, connections between the community of the world will expand. It is likely to be a tense and productive relationship characterized by cooperation and competition.

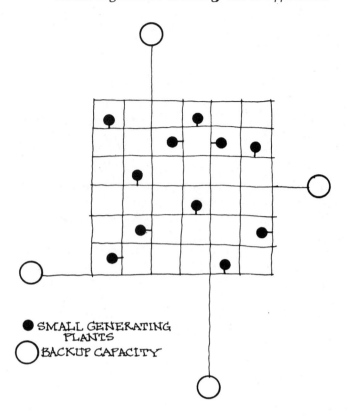

● SMALL GENERATING PLANTS
◯ BACKUP CAPACITY

Transportation Systems

Petroleum presently supplies about 97 percent of the energy for transportation in the United States (Schiller, 1990), an obviously unsustainable situation. Although hydrogen is promising, it is most unlikely that any renewable fuel will replace gasoline in its adaptability and low cost. Rather, we will draw on a variety of energy sources for transportation, and the modes of movement will be as varied as the energy sources. Scale is the most important factor in determining the appropriate mode. Following the fifth strategy, the technology should match the need.

The smallest scale of transportation is that which one can cover on foot, the scale of a small community or neighborhood. The next smallest is the area of a few square miles, which one can cover by bicycle. At these scales, biomass is the appropriate energy source, supplied in the form of food, which powers the human body, but only where the infrastructure makes it possible.

At the next level of scale, which might be that of a large town or small city, industrial technology has provided few options beyond the automobile, which is too powerful and energy-intensive to be entirely appropriate at this scale. Hydrogen, electrical power, and biofuels can replace some portion of the petroleum that fuels cars. But higher costs will probably limit their use. A combination of mass transit and small, highly efficient vehicles will be needed for urban use. The small electric carts commonly used on golf courses give some indication of the kind of transport mode that can be suitable at this scale. Charged by photovoltaic cells, such carts could be an appropriate mode for individual intercity movement.

At the scale of larger cities and regions, mass-transit systems using trains and buses are far more suitable than individual modes such as bicycles, for which the distances are too great, or automobiles, which occupy too much space, use too much energy, and produce too much pollution. Intercity mass transit uses less than $\frac{1}{10}$ as much fuel energy per passenger mile as automobiles, and intracity transit uses less than one-sixth as much (Lowe, 1990). Air pollution produced by transit systems is also less than that of automobiles, but the reduction is much less than the reduction in energy consumption.

For travel between cities and regions, automobiles, mass transit, and airplanes all have their appropriate roles. The enormous potentials of high-speed electric trains like the Japanese Shinkansen have hardly been explored outside Japan. The same trains that have been traveling between Fukuoka and Tokyo in 3 hours for more than 20 years could travel between Boston and Washington or between Los Angeles and San Francisco in the same time, or between Los Angeles and New York in 24 hours using electrical energy generated by wind or sun. For travel to rural areas and remote towns, for getting to know the landscape, the automobile will probably remain the best mode. Electric cars cause less pollution than gasoline-powered cars, even when we consider the source of electricity. They probably have an important role to play. When time is critical, the airplane will remain the best way for intercity and intercontinental travel.

As modes of transportation diversify, the strategy of multiple pathways is likely to be literally expressed in urban form. Making the transition will be a formidable, long-term, and expensive task because the cities of the late 20th century are so clearly designed around automobile movement. In Paleotechnic urban design the streets come first and all else follows. The automobile, more than any other cause, has given rise to the entropic city and remains embedded in modern urban culture. Wide, well-paved streets, large parking areas, bold signs meant for reading at 40 miles per hour or more, and an absence of pedestrian spaces are all hallmarks of entropic cities. Pedestrian paths and plazas, bicycle routes, transit vehicles of varied types, and perhaps other modes not yet imagined, all knitted together in intricate patterns, will characterize regenerative cities.

Information Systems

Designing regenerative systems for energy, shelter, water, food production, and waste requires a great deal of information concerning technical and scientific processes, people and their habits, past performance and future prediction, and the characteristics of physical context such as climate, soils, and topography. In contrast with industrial systems, which require information primarily concerning technical operation and which tend to be energy- and materials-intensive, regenerative systems are information-rich. In their ongoing management this is even more true; their functioning requires constant feedback. As suggested by the sixth strategy, whereas industrial systems rely on power that is readily available for the time being in the form of fossil fuels, regenerative systems rely on information.

Since they function in close concert with the local environment, regenerative systems require information concerning that environment. Because they also usually function in close conjunction with people, they also require information on human needs and idiosyncrasies. Since environments and people change, the information requires frequent updating. And since regenerative operation is necessarily dependent on feedback and response, it requires ongoing information about its own functioning.

In this context it is important to recognize that our funds of information include that which is remembered and that which is recorded in books and databases. Trial-and-error processes have been going on for eons in the natural world and within human societies. Wes Jackson (1987) has argued that far from experiencing an information explosion in the past few decades, we have actually undergone an impoverishment of information. His argument rests on the loss of species along with their genetic information and on the loss of traditional cultures and practices along with the information they have collected over generations. Jackson makes a compelling case and his point is especially relevant to regenerative systems, which draws heavily on the evolved wisdom of numerous cultures and which are enmeshed in complex interactions with many species.

Regenerative systems are integrally interrelated with the world of evolved culture and the world of electronic information processing as well as with the natural world.

Energy and information are inextricably intertwined. It requires energy to generate information, to transmit it, and to store it. With the use of electronic media, which operate on very high quality energy but in small quantity, the energy investment per unit of information decreases. This means the amount of information that we can afford to generate and use has increased as electronics has developed and is still increasing. Thus, designing and managing complex systems of all types becomes more feasible, which is important to this discussion because regenerative systems are usually complex. At the same time, the low cost of information leads to its proliferation, often to information overload, and to further energy cost for separating the meaningful from the meaningless. Electronic media particularly tend to promulgate enormous quantities of meaningless and even inaccurate information, which can inhibit the use of regenerative practices.

Nature's processes of self-organization operate primarily by trial and error. It may take millions of mutations that don't work to produce a single one that becomes the starting point for a new species. Howard Odum (1988) contends that the solar energy used in the trial-and-error process is a measure of the quantity of information expended. By this measure, nature's information is very costly indeed, though we rarely treat it that way. He also points out that it requires considerably more energy to generate new information than to copy existing information.

One of the great strengths of human thought is the ability to bypass the trial-and-error process by applying imagination and forethought. This is based on information drawn from diverse sources and situations in contrast with nature's information feedback process, which is limited to the situation at hand. That is the fundamental nature and value of planning and design. By storing and exchanging information from an immense range of sources and using it judiciously, we have the potential to use energy more economically in the process of organizing the ecology of human environment than has ever been possible before. For any design of a new environment we can develop models of its physical form and performance in relation to people and nature. There are several simple examples of such models in this book. For other examples of the use of such models in design processes, see my earlier book, *Design for Human Ecosystems* (1985b) and subsequent articles on roles of the mind (1985a) and applications of models (1991) in design processes. Mark von Wodtke (1993) has explored the potentials of shaping alternative designs in virtual reality before shaping them in actual reality. The primitive beginnings of technical means for accomplishing this are available, but the information cost is high, and it increases with increasing precision. However, the entropy level of both the design process and the real physical environment that ultimately results will be correspondingly much lower. Ultimately, the cost will also be much lower.

While global exchange of information concerning technical matters is an ancient practice, communication became fast, cheap, widespread, and habitual only during the 20th century. This has allowed industrial technologies to spread very quickly. The exchange of information on industrial technologies is relatively easy, however, because designs can be copied whole. A high-rise glass-box office building that works in New York can also work in Rio de Janeiro because fossil-fuel-powered mechanical systems can compensate for differences in climate. The same is true for a manufacturing plant or an industrial sewage treatment facility. Regenerative technologies by contrast are closely related to local context, both social and physical. A building that depends on solar radiation for heating and cooling will have a different form in New York than in Rio. Technologies that vary so much with context require more detailed information from both natural and cultural sources and more judgment applied in selecting information. While much of the information required for regenerative design is universal in potential applications most is specific to certain regions or locales. This is another example of the information richness of regenerative systems. It is another example also of the relationship between local environment, which largely determines the operational character of regenerative systems, and the global context from which they draw information.

Large-scale networks for exchange of ecological information began to appear in the 1970s and some, such as ECONET, have become quite large and sophisticated. The information available for design and operation of the human environment is both sparse and abundant: sparse when measured against what we don't know and want to know, but abundant for a beginning.

Energy Future

With the broad range of regenerative conversion technologies already available and under development, with the various systems for distributing and applying energy becoming more flexible and practical, and with information technology developing rapidly in sophistication and capacity, the sustainable-energy basis for society and culture seems promising. With so many areas of energy development open for exploration, they will certainly attract inventive minds and entrepreneurs. The big questions involve the abilities of the very large economic interests now benefiting from Paleotechnic energy patterns to change and the abilities of government to shape rational far-sighted energy policies. If business and government are able to evolve in the public interest, regenerative energy is likely to be abundant and inexpensive within a few decades and far more benign in its relationship with society than the energy patterns of the past century. We will return to these questions of economics and policy in Chapter 11.

CASE STUDY
■■

The Energy System of the Center for Regenerative Studies

The energy-flow pattern of the Center for Regenerative Studies is in many ways analogous to that of a larger society. It is by no means complete since the Center leaves out the whole realm of industrial production, which accounts for about 30 percent of total energy use in the United States. Nor does it include the commercial realm to any significant degree. In focusing on the basic element of life support, the Center directs attention to the essential core of the energy-flow system—the heart of the heart of the matter.

This does not mean the system is basic or primitive in the technological sense. Rather, it makes use of a broad range of technologies from simple and basic to highly sophisticated.

The goals for the Center's energy system are essentially the same as those for any community in the postpetroleum era:

■ supply adequate quantities of energy;
■ minimize use of nonrenewable resources, especially fossil fuels;
■ minimize waste, including none that is hazardous or toxic;
■ provide sustainability into the indefinite future;
■ maximize community participation and control.

While it would be technologically feasible to achieve these goals in the initial development, this would not fulfill the Center's purpose, which calls for experimentation. Thus it is preferable to begin with the basic elements of a regenerative system and experiment with a number of different technologies for providing energy as well as with the means for using less. This allows for wide-ranging exploration and comparison. New components will be added on a selective basis as funding is available and as research proves their workability. For this reason, the Center will rely in the beginning on public utilities for a major part of its gas and electrical service, gradually weaning away from these as regenerative technologies are added. In general outline it is a strategy that a much larger community, perhaps a whole society, might follow in making the shift from an industrial to a regenerative energy base.

The energy-planning process for the Center involved eight basic steps in a sequence that can be applied to any energy-planning problem. It is most important to begin with energy uses (or demand).

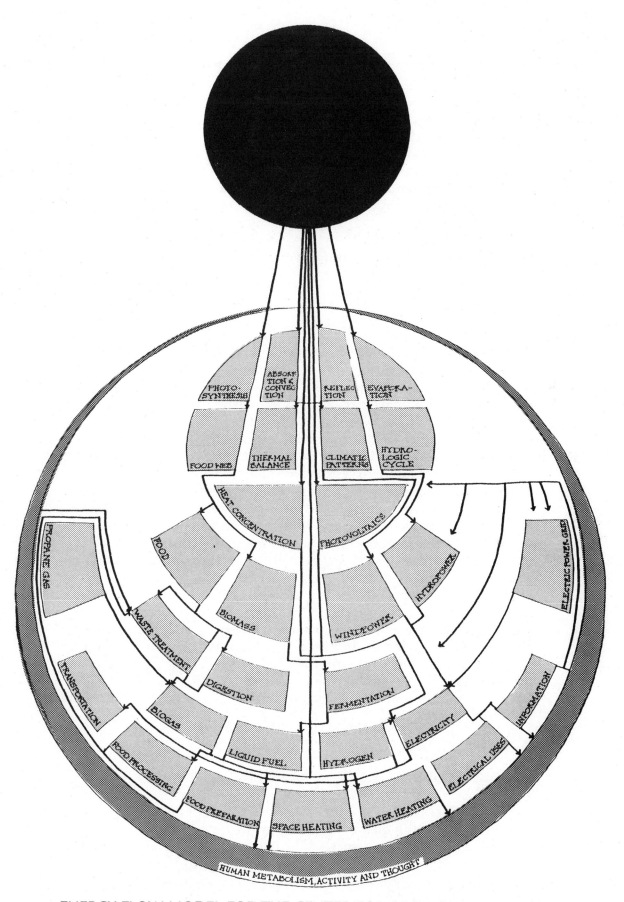

ENERGY FLOW MODEL FOR THE CENTER FOR REGENERATIVE STUDIES

1. Determine *energy uses* (demand).
2. Determine potential *means for conversion.*
3. Develop a *energy-flow model,* showing sources, conversions, and uses and the flows among them.
4. Estimate quantities for *energy uses.*
5. Estimate quantities for *energy sources and conversions.*
6. Develop an *energy budget,* matching quantities for uses, sources, and conversions.
7. *Evaluate* sustainability.
8. Define the *role* of community in energy processes.

ENERGY-FLOW MODEL

To conceptualize processes of energy flow through the Center, a qualitative energy-flow model (page 81) serves as a working hypothesis. The system described by the model can eventually meet the energy goals. By representing the flow pattern as an integral whole, the model engenders an awareness of the relationships among the parts.

In the model there are four sources: the sun, the electrical utility company (Southern California Edison), the gas company, and gasoline suppliers. Over time the roles of these sources will evolve, with the sun increasing its contribution and the other two reducing theirs. Eventually, SCE will become a buyer as well as a seller of electrical power; ultimately, it might become only a buyer from the Center.

Following the sources in the line of flow are the means of conversion. Of the six means discussed earlier in the chapter, only water power will not be applied in the Center.

From the conversion devices, energy spreads out in a number of directions to do diverse kinds of work. The model reflects a careful matching of energy quality to the task to be performed. The ordering of energy-conversion devices and uses corresponds roughly to demand and supply. However, there are important distinctions to be made. The Center community will examine the potential uses and make an effort to serve those important to the quality of life. It will not necessarily respond to all demands.

ENERGY USES

Beyond qualitative description, the next step in energy planning is estimating the potential quantities of energy involved in each use. Thus, the process begins with the demand side. For each use the researchers established a baseline by estimating the amount of energy that would be used if practices now prevalent in the society were followed. In most cases the data on which these estimates were based were rough and highly aggregated. In some cases, special studies were undertaken to obtain somewhat better data (Stine and Lyle, 1992).

The researchers next estimated the amount by which energy consumed for each use could be reduced without serious inconvenience. These estimates then became working assumptions for preliminary budgeting purposes. Future efforts to reduce energy use by either behavioral or technical means can be measured against these.

As reflected in the energy-flow model, the general categories of energy use within the Center are the following.

Human habitat
- Food conversion (metabolic processes)
- Electricity (including lighting and appliances)
- Water heating
- Space heating

Food production
Food processing and preparation
Transportation (people and goods)

Human Habitat

Included in this category is the energy used by residents of the Center within the Center environment in the course of their daily lives, other than that consumed in food production, food processing and preparation, and transportation.

Food Conversion

Through metabolism the human body converts food into living protoplasm and energy. The food energy required is easily estimated on the basis of average daily intake of food calories: 90 people $\times$ 2400 calories per day $\times$ 365 days = 79×10^6 = calories per year = 79,000 kilocalories per year = 3.1×10^8 Btu = 3.3×10^{11} joules = 3.3×10^8 kilojoules per year.

Electricity Used by Individuals

Consumption of electrical energy by residents in their daily routines is a major factor in the energy budget and one that may vary greatly with behavior patterns. It will probably be the subject of much experimentation and observation. However, there is very little information available on the subject. For these reasons a limited survey was conducted to obtain baseline data. Nine students living in university dormitories recorded in detail their energy and water use and travel for a week. From these responses the researchers drew a quantitative picture of how a dorm-dwelling student uses electrical energy. The responses are summarized in Table 1 and shown also in bar-graph form.

Table 1.   *Typical Dorm Resident's Electrical Use Survey*

Item	Number Using	Power (watts)	Use Time (hr/day)	Energy (kJ/day)	Energy (% total)
Room/Appliances					
Room lights	9	50	6.9	1245	11%
Clock radio	9	8	24.0	690	6%
Desk lamp	9	100	2.1	585	5%
Answering machine	4	7	24.0	275	2%
Battery recharger	1	16	7.1	45	<1%
Desk fan	1	6	9.1	20	<1%
Electric eraser	1	50	0.1	1	<1%
Entertainment					
Radio/stereo	7	28	3.5	270	2%
Television	3	37	1.3	55	<1%
CD player	2	12	2.9	30	<1%
Personal					
Hair dryer	6	1168	0.2	625	5%
Electric shaver	3	100	0.2	30	<1%
Curling iron	2	175	<0.1	2	<1%
In-Room Food					
Refrigerator	5	126	12.0	3050	26%
Popcorn popper	1	1000	0.4	14	<1%
Clothes Maintenance					
Clothes dryer	5	4856	0.43	4195	36%
Clothes washer	5	372	0.5	390	3%
Clothes iron	1	1100	0.1	40	<1%
Cleaning					
Vacuum cleaner	2	660	0.2	100	1%
TOTAL				11,665 (=3.24 kWh/day)	

Source: Stine and Lyle (1992)

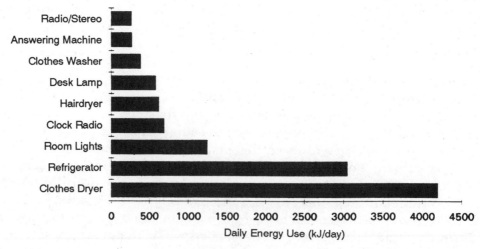

Daily energy use of a typical Cal Poly dorm student. Source: *Stine and Lyle (1992).*

By taking these data and suggesting energy conservation measures that can be practiced at the Center, a picture of energy use by a "typical" Center resident emerges. For example, the largest energy use, that of clothes drying, could be significantly reduced by encouraging the use of clothesline drying rather than electric dryers. Also, the students will probably not need individual refrigerators, especially if they have to forgo other energy uses to be able to use a personal refrigerator.

On the other hand, students will need room and desk lighting. Although less of a necessity, hair drying and clothes washing are associated with personal care. Hair drying is certainly less essential. Such uses will be matters for community decisions. Students will also see that some nonessential items such as CD and tape players, popcorn poppers, and electric erasers (used for drafting projects) use such small amounts of energy that their inclusion in the Center resident's lifestyle is acceptable.

Following this thinking, it will be possible to reduce energy use by Center residents to a level considerably below that of the present dormitory residents. Table 2 shows predicted energy use for a typical resident at the Center, 1.12 megajoules per year. Instrumentation to be installed by SCE will monitor actual electricity consumption for every space and use in the Center.

Table 2. *Typical Center Resident's Expected Electrical Energy Use*

| | Power | Use Time | Energy | |
Item	(watts)	(hr/day)	(kJ/day)	(% of use)
Room/Appliances				
Room light	50	6.9	1245	37%
Desk lamp	100	2.1	585	17%
Battery recharger	16	7.1	45	1%
Desk fan	6	9.1	20	1%
Electric eraser	50	0.1	1	<1%
Entertainment				
Radio/stereo	28	3.5	270	8%
CD player	12	2.9	30	1%
Personal				
Hair dryer	1168	0.2	625	18%
Electric shaver	100	0.2	30	1%
In-Room Food				
Popcorn popper	1000	0.4	15	<1%
Clothes Maintenance				
Clothes washer	372	0.5	390	12%
Clothes iron	1100	0.1	40	1%
Cleaning				
Vacuum cleaner.	660	0.2	100	3%
TOTAL			3395	
			(=0.943 kWh/day)	

Source: Stine and Lyle (1992).

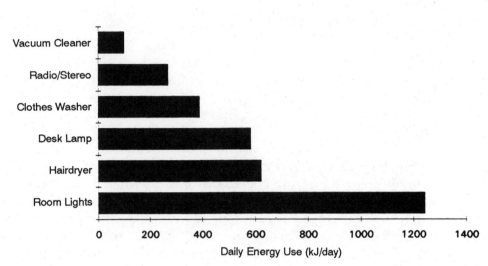

Projected daily energy use by a resident of the Center for Regenerative Studies. Source: Stine and Lyle (1992).

Electricity in Common Areas

In addition to individuals' use of electricity discussed previously, a considerable amount of electrical energy will be consumed within the Center's common areas and academic facilities within the village complex. This includes the lighting of indoor space as well as shared computers, televisions, office and laboratory equipment and other apparatus, and outdoor lighting around the building walkways. Table 3 quantifies these uses.

Water Heating

The second major energy use by students found in the survey was the energy required to heat water for showers. To determine the energy used for this purpose, the researchers assumed that low-flow (2 gpm) showers would be installed at the Center and the water temperature would be 60°C (140°F). A smaller use of hot water was for shaving; however, many survey participants indicated that they use an electric razor.

Assuming that the shower time can be reduced by half, the energy consumption for water heating for personal use can be estimated at 15,600 kilojoules per day, or 4.9×10^5 megajoules per year.

Space Heating

The Center's buildings are passively solar heated and cooled. This implies that they function as both solar collectors and heat-storage units in the winter, and use natural cooling in the summer without mechanical systems for heat transfer. The means for accomplishing this will be further discussed in Chapter 5.

The energy expended in heating buildings is equal to the heat lost through the building envelope, which must be replaced by outside

Table 3.   Electricity Use in Common Areas

	Illumination Level (lumens/ft²)	Number of Units	Unit Power (Watts)	Weekly Usage (hr/wk)	Average Energy Use (kWh/day)
Common Rooms					
Illumination	80	126	40	56	40.3
Local lighting	Spot	21	22	56	3.7
Television sets	Zero	7	40	15	0.6
Teaching and Research Areas					
Illumination	100	157	40	30	26.9
Equipment	—	—	600	30	2.6
Faculty and Administrative Offices					
Illumination	100	77	40	30	13.2
Equipment	—	—	400	40	2.3
Service Areas					
Illumination	100	54	40	28	8.6
Equipment	—	—	500	12	0.9
Outdoor Lighting					
Illumination	1	20	35	84	8.4
Illumination	1	47	35	35	8.2
TOTAL average daily energy use					115.7

Source: Stine and Lyle (1992).

sources. The heat lost by well-insulated, partially earth-sheltered buildings of this type in the southern California climate is approximately 250 megajoules per square meter per year. The total building area is about 3000 square meters, resulting in a total heating demand of 750,000 megajoules per year.

Food Production

For purposes of estimating the amount of energy used in food production at the Center, researchers have divided the agricultural operations into the major growing categories and evaluated each for its energy inputs (Kern, 1991).

It is assumed that field crops such as small grains, legumes, corn, and forage crops will be grown on 0.97 hectares (2.4 acres). Energy consumption for this sector will include ground preparation, planting cultivation, and harvest. There will also be approximately 0.16 hectares (0.4 acres) of raised-bed vegetable gardens. Energy consumption for the vegetable gardens is estimated to be about one-third that of field vegetable crops.

A small number of animals, including dairy cows, beef cattle, goats, sheep, swine, and poultry, will be kept at the Center. These require energy for food processing, water heating (sterilization for milk handling), and waste handling.

Annual irrigation water needs for the Center have been estimated at 3,700,000 liters (30 acre-feet) for all agricultural purposes. Raising this water (60 feet) from the aquacultural ponds or the reservoir to tanks on top of the four knolls, and from there pumping it to appropriate locations with adequate distribution pressure, requires energy.

By far the greatest energy input to the agriculture section of the Center will be in transportation. It is assumed that a single half-ton gasoline-powered truck will be required, operated 4 hours per day. This high consumption of a nonsustainable resource is an ideal target for developing new farm transportation techniques using regenerative fuels such as digester gas, ethanol, or electricity.

Energy consumption in food production is summarized in Table 4.

Food Processing and Preparation

Processing and preparing food are energy-intensive activities. In the United States, nearly 5 percent of total fossil-fuel use is for food processing and preparation including distribution, while only a little over 3 percent is for food production. This energy now comes directly from nonrenewable sources. Of the energy used in processing and preparation, about half comes from natural gas, about 15 percent from fuel oil, and 13 percent from electricity.

The figures in Table 5 provide an indication of the consumption at the Center using conventional practices and technologies. However, as discussed below, significant reductions are expected with the implementation of energy-conservative practices and technologies.

Table 4.   *Agricultural Energy and Water at the Center for Regenerative Studies*

Energy Usage	
Field crops	3,270 MJ/year
Raised-bed vegetable gardens	3,020 MJ/year
Animal production	1,790 MJ/year
Irrigation	1,000 MJ/year
Farm transportation	191,000 MJ/year
TOTAL	200,080 MJ/year
Daily Average:	548 MJ/year
	(=152 kWh/day)
Water Usage	
Irrigation:	3,700,000 L/year
Daily Average:	10,000 L/day

Source: Stine and Lyle (1992).

Table 5. *Typical Energy Use for Food Processing and Preparation*

Food processing	9,500 MJ/person/year
Food preparation	5,800 MJ/person/year
TOTAL	15,300 MJ/person/year
	(=4,250 kWh/person/year)

Type of Energy Used:	*Percentage*
Electricity	40%
Gas	30%
Heated water	30%

For the purposes of this study, it is necessary to identify the types of energy sources that will supply this. A rough approximation is presented in Table 5.

Using a variety of means it will probably be possible to reduce energy consumption for food processing and preparation well below the national average. In the absence of better means, we can reasonably assume that, with careful application of energy-efficient devices now available, the Center's energy use for food processing can be 25 percent of the national average, and for preparation 50 percent of the average for restaurants. This gives the annual consumption rates shown in Table 6.

Transportation

A major potential use of energy will be the transport of students from the Center to the center of the Cal Poly campus for activities and classes. Assuming every student were to drive individually to campus an average of three times daily, as might be done in usual circumstances, this would require 18,000 megajoules per day (6,620,000 megajoules per year). It is obvious that it will be necessary to avoid this level of energy expenditure in order to achieve energy sustainability.

Table 6. *Food Processing and Preparation Energy at the Center for Regenerative Studies*

Total Energy Usage	
Food processing	585 MJ/day
Food preparation	715 MJ/day
TOTAL	1,300 MJ/day
	(=361 kWh/day)
Types of Energy Sources	
Electricity	520 MJ/day (=144 kWh/day)
Gas	390 MJ/day
Heated water	390 MJ/day

Source: Stine and Lyle (1992).

The most important mode of student transport to be encouraged is walking. It is about a 15-minute walk from the Center to the core of campus. For most this will require time planning, with the gain of aerobic exercise transferred from the workout room to the walking path. To discourage automobile use the Center will not provide parking lots, and those students having cars will use campus parking lots about 2000 feet away.

Regenerative Vehicle Development

Since transportation energy use forms a significant portion of the Center's energy demand, a portion of the energy curriculum will be focused on developing specialized vehicles operating on sustainable sources of energy. These will become part of the "Regenerative Vehicle Pool" of resource-efficient vehicles. Students will select them based on their appropriateness (the least energy for the task).

Probably the most regenerative transport vehicle in existence is the bicycle since it requires only human energy input for rapid, low-effort transport over relatively long distances. The Center will provide a number of these for student and faculty use for trips beyond walking range.

The Center's research program plans to develop small motor-aided bicycles for situations requiring less human input or more speed. These will be modified to run on biofuels such as ethanol, methanol, or digester gas made at the Center. In parallel development, researchers plan to develop an electric-motor-aided bicycle (using solar power to charge its battery) and compare its performance with the internal combustion engines mentioned above.

The Center's research plans also include a small fleet of solar-powered golf-cart-type vehicles. These will be both for personal transport (four seats) and hauling (flatbed with two seats). In experiments the university's Mechanical Engineering Department found that an unoptimized commercial golf cart with solar cells installed on its roof to charge its batteries could operate approximately 1 hour for every 6 hours it was in the sunlight. This is approximately the duty cycle of many delivery and service vehicles. Researchers estimate that with little effort, this operation-to-charge ratio could be improved to 2 or 3 hours of charging for every hour of operation.

A small pickup truck and possibly a van operating on digester gas from Center digesters will be incorporated into the regenerative motor pool. These will form the power/convenience portion of the transport vehicle mix. Although these vehicles are expected to be capable of operating on streets, their purpose will be travel around the Center for maintenance and agricultural transport needs, and to campus for occasional special transport of individuals. This is important since the operating radius of digester-powered vehicles should be limited in order to reduce the size of fuel tank.

ENERGY RESOURCES

To serve the electrical energy needs, the Center's energy plan calls for converting solar radiation to useful work through five means: direct use of solar heat, concentration of solar heat, photovoltaics, and biomass and wind conversion. In addition to these, plans call for sources used in the beginning to initiate operations to be used later for backup. These include electricity from the local utility (Southern California Edison) grid, propane as stored in containers on the site, and petroleum purchased locally.

Solar Resource

The solar radiation input varies over each day and from day to day and is generally not predictable from one day to the next. However, monthly averages of typical years are useful for design purposes. The closest available data are for Long Beach (about 30 miles away as the crow flies). Pomona has similar or slightly better insolation conditions.

Averages of the daily irradiation for each month for a typical year are given in the bargraph below. Shown here are the two important measures of solar energy, beam normal irradiation and total horizontal irradiation. Beam normal irradiation represents the energy coming directly from the sun, onto a surface constantly kept pointed toward the sun, over a specific period of time. Total horizontal irradiation represents the energy coming both directly from the sun and from the rest of the sky, onto a horizontal surface over a specified period of time.

Over a typical year this input averages over 18 megajoules per square meter per day. For the 6.5 hectare (16-acre) land area of the Center, this totals 11×10^6 megajoules per day.

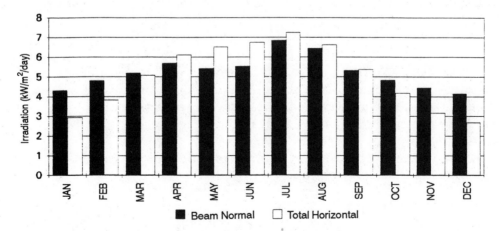

Daily average beam normal and total horizontal solar radiation estimates for the Center for Regenerative Studies. Source: *Stine and Lyle (1992).*

Direct Heat
Heat produced by solar radiation will be used directly for space and water heating and for crop and clothes drying. Calculations indicate that available radiation will be more than adequate for all these purposes.

WATER HEATING. / Flat-plate collectors mounted on the building roofs will heat water for personal use and food preparation. Rooftop locations will be as close as possible to the point of use.

The present energy use for water heating for personal use as determined by the survey and reduced by potential conservation is 678 megajoules per day. The energy required for hot water for clothes washing and food processing and preparation is approximately the same. Thus the total predicted energy use for water heating is 1355 megajoules per day. To supply this will require approximately 155 square meters of collector surface. Assuming solar radiation at 18 megajoules per square meter per year, total energy use for water heating will be 2790 megajoules per year.

Providing for the difference between times of solar radiation and times of hot-water use will require insulated water-storage tankage. The volume required is approximately 4.23 square meters (1125 gallons).

SPACE HEATING. / Using direct solar radiation to passively heat the buildings requires the use of a number of devices within the architectural forms to collect, store, and distribute heat. Passively cooling the building requires devices for cooling air and distributing it through the buildings. Means for accomplishing these tasks are many and complex. They involve not only the buildings themselves but the surrounding landscape. This subject will be discussed in detail in Chapter 5.

Since the solar radiation potentially striking the exterior glass surfaces each day during the colder seasons is more than 20 times the estimated heat loss, the solar heating potential is more than adequate.

Electricity

CONCENTRATED HEAT. / Two Dish-Stirling engine-driven electric generators heated by reflective parabolic dishes will be located on the site before buildings are occupied. These have a generating capacity of about 6 kilowatts each on a clear day at noon.

PHOTOVOLTAIC CONVERSION. / Two photovoltaic tracking collectors are now in place on the site:

- A 3-kilowatt unit manufactured by Martin Marietta that uses an array of photovoltaic cells with Fresnel lenses to focus solar rays. The photovoltaic array is mounted on two rectangular arms about 20 feet long, which rotate on a pedestal through the day so as to remain continuously perpendicular to the sun's rays. Their movement is guided by a shadow sensor, with backup by a program that computes the correct solar azimuth and declination for every minute of every day.

■ A smaller flat-plate unit with a peak generating capacity of about 50 watts.

In addition to the tracking collectors, arrays of spheral photovoltaic cells mounted in metal mesh will be installed on south-facing building roofs.

WIND CONVERSION. / Since the site is in an area with generally low wind speeds, a long-term program is collecting data to determine the feasibility of wind generators. Preliminary data (see graph) indicate an average wind speed adequate for water pumping and probably some power generation. Water can be pumped from the ponds in the valley to the knolltop tanks when the wind is blowing. There it can be stored for release to the irrigation system as needed.

Biofuels
Ethanol and methanol will be produced using small stills and agricultural wastes; actual productivity will probably be small.

METHANE DIGESTERS. / Agricultural and food wastes as well as animal manure will be digested to produce methane gas mixed with carbon dioxide. Preliminary calculations indicate the amount produced will be adequate to meet cooking needs.

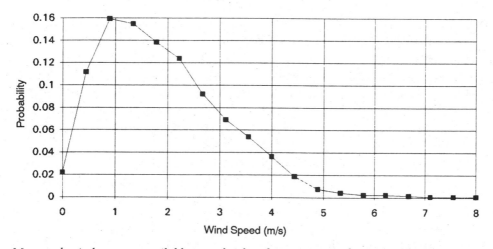

Measured wind energy available at a height of 3 meters, at the Center for Regenerative Studies. Source: *Stine and Lyle (1992).*

Table 7.   *Energy Usage by Type and User (MJ/day)*

	Electrical	Gas	Hot Water	Gasoline	Percent
Student residential	305	0	1355	0	25%
Shelter	416	0	0	0	6%
Agriculture	0	0	0	548	8%
Food processing	1510	1132	1132	0	57%
Transport	80	0	0	155	4%
TOTAL	2311	1132	2487	703	
%	35%	17%	37%	11%	100%

Grand total energy use: 6633 MJ/day

Source: Stine and Lyle (1992).

The Energy Budget

Table 7 shows estimates of energy consumption at the Center on the basis of estimated feasible reductions. Predicted need is higher than the expected capacity. The difference between the two represents the margins for research and development required to meet the operational good of functioning with on-site energy.

SOLAR PARK

All of the analyses up to this point suggest that energy conversion and distribution will be smaller in scale, more locally controlled, and more functionally integrated in regenerative communities than they ever were in industrial communities. If this is so, the different relationship should be expressed in physically and symbolically different ways as well. Following the 11th strategy we can shape the forms of energy conversion to give visible expression to the processes involved. Replacing the power lines and substations that are the visible manifestations of energy in the Paleotechnic landscape, we might envision seeing the actual technologies of energy expressed in a way that manifests their central role.

The design of the Solar Park provides such an expression for the Center. The location is the top of a knoll where access to sun and wind is greatest, and where vistas stretch out over the Center and the surrounding landscape. It is also a prominently visible place.

The integral community role of energy technology demands that it be seen, experienced, and understood. In the Solar Park people can see two tracking photovoltaic converters and the wind generator up close, touch them, and mingle with them. Plans call for adding two Dish-Sterling converters in late 1993. Displays will explain their operation. There is also a complete weather station with its instruments prominently displayed. Data from these instruments is recorded by a central

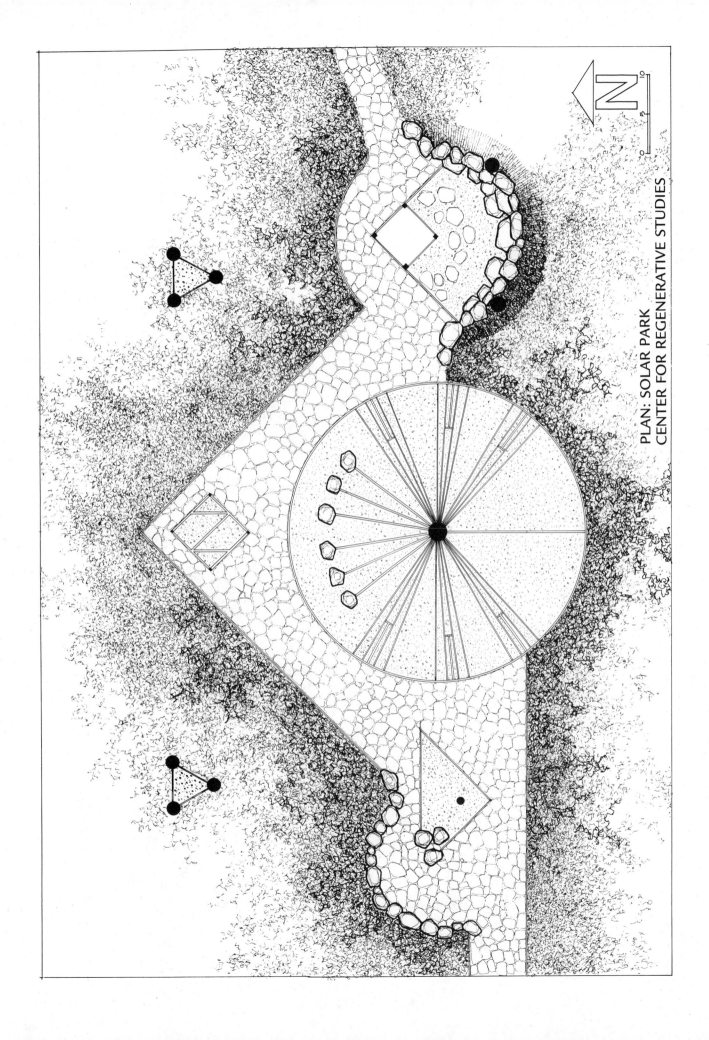

PLAN: SOLAR PARK
CENTER FOR REGENERATIVE STUDIES

computer in order to have a comprehensive profile of the microclimate of the site. This is essential for operating the Center's energy system (and other systems) at optimal efficiency.

The landscape features the rough primal forms of rocks and gravel contrasting with the highly finished technology of the machines, con-

necting them with the earth. Paved surfaces are made of recycled concrete. Lines and points on the ground surface mark the directions of the sun at the key points in the earth's annual cycle: summer and winter solstices, spring and fall equinoxes.

The Solar Park is intended to be a place where earth, sun, people, and technology meet in a simple and undemanding way.

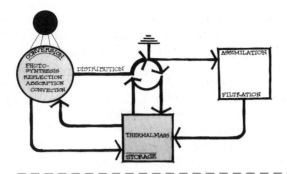

Chapter 5
Habitat, Culture, and Energy Flow

While the history and traditions of architecture are rich in beauty and meaning—usually interesting, sometimes inspiring—since the 15th century the art of architecture has followed a course ever diverging from the realm of nature. Paleotechnic society has come to view buildings as cultural artifacts, with their forms referring only to symbols of human devising, not to the forces of sun, wind, and earth. The result is alienation of architecture and cities from nature, like a tree severed at the trunk from its roots. The severed tree slowly decomposes.

During the industrial era, technology and fossil fuels provided the means for making the separation from nature not only apparent but real. Shelter is largely a matter of controlling energy flow, and machines made it possible to accomplish this mechanically. The interior environment became entirely divorced from the larger complex world outdoors, maintained at constant temperature by heating and cooling apparatuses driven by fossil fuels. Thus, shelter was separated from its environs and, in larger terms, from the processes of the global ecosystem and its heat balance. In the 20th-century city, people began to think of landscape as the frame around a picture—the picture being the building—rather than the source of life.

With mass production and transportation, also powered by fossil fuels, and mechanical heating and air-conditioning systems, it became possible to use the same materials everywhere. A steel structure could be fabricated in Pennsylvania and shipped to Nairobi for assembly. An apartment tower in San Francisco became much the same as one in Paris or Sydney.

Cut off from the guidance—or the tyranny, depending on one's point of view—of nature's processes, architecture entered the industrial era with the emergence of modernism, which sought to impart coherent form to industrial processes. When modernism fell before the onslaught of discontent with its austere and heartless forms, architecture entered a phase of form making that brought the noble and ancient art into close alignment with fashion design. Since mid-century, shapes and symbols appearing in one place have been picked up and reproduced in dozens of other places, and then left in the shadows of succeeding fashions like last year's hats. The cost of turning architecture and landscape into matters of industrial production and fashion has been high in terms of energy and materials consumption and ecological dysfunction, and in human terms as well.

Even buildings that stand aloof from nature and use fossil fuels for heating and cooling can be far more energy-efficient than they were in the energy-binge years of the 1950s and 1960s. The energy awareness that emerged in the early 1970s led to a number of improvements in construction, including better and thicker insulation, tighter sealing of joints and cracks, and the use of less heat-conductive materials such as reflective glass and double glazing. The average new office building of 1980 used less than half as much energy per square foot for heating and cooling as the average new building of 1970 (Rosenfeld and Hafemeister, 1988). It is clear that this is a significant saving when we consider the roles of buildings in the larger pattern of energy flow. Buildings are the largest or second-largest consumers of energy in all industrial countries. In the United States, buildings account for about 75 percent of electricity consumption; most of this is for heating and cooling.

Really dramatic improvements in energy-efficient building will require that we go beyond building materials and construction to the next level: the realm of design. A long history of shaping the human habitat, including a number of more recent highly sophisticated experiments, has demonstrated that through passive solar heating and cooling it is possible to design the landscape and buildings within it as comfortable places for humans with little or no resort to fossil fuels. Passive solar heating and cooling function with few or no mechanical devices; they are mostly matters of designing the form of landscape and building in relation to each other and to sun, earth, and air movement. Going to this level, we find the form of the human habitat being shaped less by the dictates of fashion and stylistic dogma and more by the processes of nature. Buildings become again part of the earth.

Shelter and Ecological Processes

Achieving regenerative human habitat will require fundamental change in the way we think about design. Practicalities aside, there are important implications in this for the basic environmental relationships that establish equilibrium in our lives. Since most of us live most of our lives in and around buildings, many of our interactions with the environment are determined by the design of buildings and cities. If these interactions present us with false impressions of the world—impressions that exclude

natural processes and include only an artificial environment—then our relationship with the world is stunted. Our gut-level understanding of its richness and complexity and our own roles in the rich, complex fabric are limited. In a fundamental sense, they are unreal. It has been argued that the environmental crisis is happening largely because humanity has lost contact with the natural world. By living in an artificial environment for so long we may have lost our ability to perceive that something is wrong when natural processes become dysfunctional.

In order to try and reestablish a primal equilibrium in which nature is the fundamental reality, we will discuss shelter in this chapter by starting with the basic relationships between the human and the natural environment and working our way back to architecture. The first goal for regenerative habitat is to design shelters in which everyone can lead a comfortable, productive, secure, and meaningful life without depleting resources or damaging natural systems.

There are any number of ways to do this, but all of them converge on the need to make human shelter rejoin nature's processes and play harmonious roles within them. We can design our environments to continue the ecological functions of the land they displace. They can carry on the flows of energy and materials, and they can incorporate complex communities of organisms. Doing this requires that they become partners in the ecological community, joining in the web of interactions that is landscape. We might state the second goal like this: to join buildings with the earth again.

A third goal, following the 11th strategy for regenerative design described in Chapter Three (shaping form to manifest process) is to give visible and meaningful form to that relationship. With this goal, architecture becomes something quite different from the industrial expressions of the modern period or the fashion and formalism that have prevailed since.

It is widely accepted, though hard to prove, that there is a close relationship between the health and cohesiveness of the human community in terms of its social relationships, and its relationship with nature. The highly entropic character of industrially based society has tended to push people apart and to loosen community structure. The smaller scale and participatory character of many regenerative practices tends to pull them together. Thus we might reasonably hope for a reintegration of communities as regenerative systems replace industrial ones. While building and urban forms cannot create community, and a great many complex factors are involved in the social character of communities, physical form can undoubtedly encourage or impede social cohesion. The tenth strategy applies here; in social as well as physical situations, form can guide flow. Thus, a fourth goal for regenerative habitat is to shape building and urban form so that they foster community interaction. This is a subject we will discuss at greater length in Chapter 9.

Practices and Technologies for Regenerative Shelter

Human habitat includes both indoor and outdoor environments. From the perspective of an individual human being seeking comfort, security, and meaning in life, we might think of the environment about him or her as a "shell within a shell within a shell within a shell": The outermost shell is the whole earth with its global systems of heat balance, air movement, water distribution, and living communities. Within that is the shell of the local landscape, modifying and augmenting global patterns to shape local conditions. Within the local landscapes a building shell controls interior environments, and within the buildings are people whose clothing forms the innermost shell. In keeping with the strategy of letting nature do the work, we can begin with the shell of the local landscape, where photosynthesis and organic growth, heat absorption and reflection, and related natural processes,

functioning within global systems, do the work of environmental control.

Sheltering Roles of Plants

In the farm belt of the American Midwest, as in most farming country, one sees vast flat fields of crops stretching to the horizon with here and there a small grove of trees, usually deciduous trees like elms or cottonwoods, breaking the endless horizontal skyline. Near each grove there is a barn and scattered around it an array of other farm buildings. Peering into the dark places within the shade of the trees, one can usually see the dim shape of a house. The trees are like a large shell enveloping the farmhouse; in fact, that is how they work. Trees and building form the living environment for the farm family; the trees within their shading branches create a cool zone in summer within which the family can carry on its daily activities. Children can play; the washing can dry; people can sit and talk. And within this cool zone it is not difficult to keep the interior of the house cool as well. When it rains, the leaves intercept the rain, filter some of it through and store some on their surfaces. Two hours after a hard rain, water is still dripping from the trees, soaking slowly into the ground. Given this much time, the plants and soil can absorb most of the water and thus keep it on the site. The slow release also minimizes soil erosion. Moreover, the trees help to fend off the winds that whistle across the plains and catch much of the dust borne on the wind.

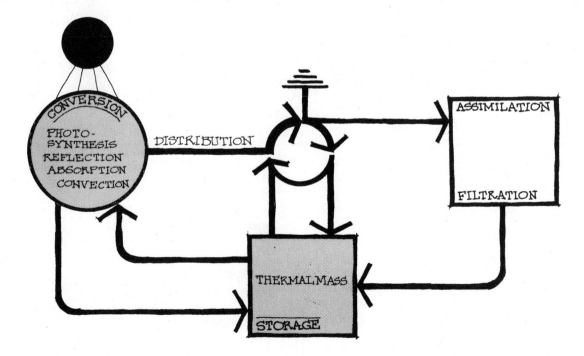

In the winter they lose their leaves allowing most of the sun's rays to pass through and helping to keep the building warm.

Thus building and landscape form a unit, working together to create a living environment in a region known for climatic extremes. The same principle works in other places, in suburbs and perhaps most importantly in cities, where trees can help to reduce pollution and cool the air. Nature is doing the work.

On this smaller scale of local landscape and human environment, plants can perform the same services they perform for the global ecosystem. They are natural processors of air, taking in carbon monoxide, emitting oxygen, absorbing pollutants, creating microclimates.

Plants for Microclimate Control

Because most building and paving surfaces tend to retain and release more heat than vegetated areas, and because heating and air-conditioning equipment releases a great deal of heat into the environment, urban areas are generally several degrees warmer than vegetated areas. One of the earliest and best studies of the subject showed downtown St. Louis to be 13°F warmer in the winter and 9°F warmer in June than the large, tree-canopied Forest Park 5 miles away. Numerous other studies have shown similar patterns; see for example Duckwork

and Sandberg (1954); Bernatzky (1969); and Bryson and Ross (1972).

Tree cover can moderate this heat island effect, as it has come to be called, helping to control microclimate in three different ways. The first is simply by absorbing and reflecting solar radiation. A tree in full leaf intercepts between 60 and 90 percent of the radiation that strikes it, depending on its canopy density. This creates cool shade beneath. A deciduous tree in the wintertime reflects between 25 and 50 percent. Thus, clusters of trees spaced closely together can reduce ambient summer temperature in large areas. Placed directly adjacent to buildings on the south, east, and west sides, they can reduce incoming solar radiation in the summer and, if deciduous, allow most of it to pass through in the winter.

The second way trees moderate the heat island effect is by creating a still zone or zone of calm air under the canopy. Around the edges of a tree canopy is a band of air turbulence where the cooler air within and the warmer outside air meet and mix. This turbulent zone seems to form a kind of containing frame for the still, cool air within the canopy.

The third cooling mechanism provided by trees is the release of cooling water vapor from their leaf surfaces through evaporation and transpiration.

Altogether the cooling effects of trees are considerable. According to data developed by Pinkard

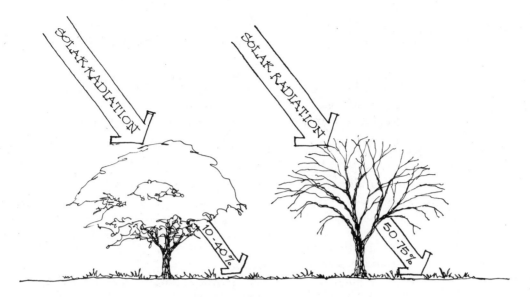

(1970), one large tree can provide the same cooling effect as 10 room-size air conditioners working 20 hours per day. A study of a mobile home in Florida showed that well-placed plantings could reduce cooling costs by over 50 percent (Hutchinson et al., 1983).

The hotter and longer the summers are in a region, the greater are the energy savings afforded by well-placed trees. A California study showed that one 25-foot-tall tree on the west side of a house in the coastal town of El Toro, which has warm but rarely extremely hot summers, would reduce cooling energy use by 146 kilowatt-hours each year. In the inland desert town of China Lake, the savings would be twice that much. In both areas the same tree planted on the west side of a building saved twice as much energy as the same tree planted on the south or east side. In all cases, between one-half and two-thirds of energy savings occurred during peak use hours (McPherson and Sacamano, 1992). Calculations of electrical energy saved by tree planting suggest that this is one of the most cost-effective means of reducing the heat island effect and thus electrical energy consumption. According to initial studies by Gregory McPherson and Biedenbender (1991), the Urban Releaf program to plant 500,000 desert-adapted trees in the city of Tucson over an 8-year period will eventually save over 144 million kilowatt-hours per year in electricity for operating air conditioners.

These examples illustrate how landscape can modify microclimate at both small and large scales. At the smaller scale, effectiveness depends on specific location of plants with respect to buildings and other use areas. At larger scales it depends on the location of planting masses in relation to regional climatic patterns, especially wind.

The Tucson program is a massive effort to reduce urban temperatures for both indoor and outdoor comfort. Some cities have gone further in attempting to guide the whole pattern of urban air movement. The German city of Stuttgart, for example, had a serious problem with stagnant air, which tended to sit over the city. With industrial plants emitting various materials into the air, pollution tended to build up along with heat, creating extremely uncomfortable and unhealthful conditions. The city undertook a large-scale tree-planting program that included the entire urban area. Tree masses were located in such a way as to guide prevailing breezes through the city and periodically flush out the air. The effort so far seems to be achieving its purpose.

Plants for Pollution Control

Though the capacity of plants to absorb carbon dioxide is often cited as a reason for planting urban trees, the actual quantity absorbed by each tree is small. Boer's (1972) studies estimate that it takes about 75 trees to absorb the carbon dioxide breathed out by one human being. McPherson (1990) estimates that about 97 percent of the total carbon conserved annually by a tree is in reduced power-plant emissions resulting from reduction in electrical energy use rather than in carbon dioxide absorbed.

The effectiveness of plants in controlling air pollution has long been known. In the 17th century

John Evelyn proposed large plantings of shrubs to cleanse London's polluted air. But the cleansing effects are difficult to quantify. As air moves through the branches of trees, it leaves dust and other particles trapped on stems and leaves. One study carried out in Germany showed that a two-and-one-half-acre stand of beech trees had removed about 4 tons of dust every year (Meldan, 1959). The dust particles were eventually washed from the leaves and stems by the rain, which carried them to the ground to be absorbed back into the soil. Other studies have shown much higher amounts of particulates suspended in the air in treeless city centers than in areas with heavy tree cover.

In general, plants are also able to absorb some gaseous air pollutants through the stomata (breathing pores) in their leaves; the more stomata the leaves have, the more polluting gases are absorbed. A study of the effectiveness of the green "sanitary clearance zones" sometimes provided around industrial areas in Russia showed that a band of trees 500 meters wide reduced sulphur dioxide (SO_2) by 22 percent and nitrogen oxides (NO_x) by 27 percent. A computer model developed by Murphy et al. (1977) confirmed that a forest belt around an industrial plant with high SO_2 emissions can absorb most of those emissions. Studies by Jenson and Kozlowski (1975) showed that several deciduous forest species including bigtooth aspen can absorb large amounts of SO_2.

Ozone, which is also among the most common of air pollutants, is also readily taken in by a number of tree species. Townsend (1974), for example, demonstrated both the high ozone sorption capacity and the high pollution tolerance of the sugar maple.

Choice of Species

These studies and others confirm that the environmental value of plantings depends heavily on the species used and on the form and density of the design. Plants can easily require more energy and other resources to keep them going than they return in benefits. In fact, most present-day urban plantings are poorly designed and ill-adapted to their settings.

It has long been known that plants emit some hydrocarbons, thus contributing to some degree to air pollution. A study carried out at the University of California at Riverside showed that the actual level of hydrocarbon emissions varied greatly according to species. At the lower end of the scale, with negligible emissions of hydrocarbons in the form of isoprene, were crape myrtle (*Lagerstroemia indica*), camphor (*Cinnamomum camphora*), Aleppo pine (*Pinus halepensis*) and stone pine (*Pinus pinea*). At the upper end, with emissions as much as 1600 times higher than these, were sweetgum (*Liquidambar* spp.) and carrotwood (*Cupaniopsis anacardiopsis*).

Ill-adapted plantings in arid western cities are especially ecologically expensive: They require inputs in the form of irrigation water, pesticides, fertilizers, and fossil fuels for maintenance that considerably exceed the benefits they provide in the forms of microclimate and drainage control, air filtering, and habitat value. Both of the hydrocarbon emitters mentioned in the UC-Riverside study are exotic species ill-adapted to southern California with its unusually high water requirements. In Los Angeles, for example, each acre of a typical park consumes over 1 million gallons of water and 200 pounds of nitrogen each year, along with numerous other materials. Since the plant materials involved are mostly exotic types that provide few ecological benefits, the investment is clearly far greater than the return. Poor design can turn the landscape into an environmental liability.

This is why the Tucson Releaf program specifies desert-adapted trees. Plants adapted to the conditions of the local environment can live on the water and nutrients available there. If they are species native to the region and coevolved with other species there, they will also support the region's wildlife communities.

Adaptations to local conditions necessarily include conditions created by humans. Especially in cities these can be extremely stressful. Air pollution is especially damaging to plants, and some cannot adapt. Particulates settling on leaves can clog their breathing pores and eventually choke a whole tree. Some deciduous trees with tough leaves, such as mountain-ash (*Sorbus* spp.), beech (*Fagus*), elm (*Ulmus*), ginkgo (*Ginkgo*) and plane (*Platanus*), are remarkably resistant. Since most cities have their greatest need for both cooling and pollution reduction during the summer months, the deciduous pattern fits well. However, some cities, such Milan, experience their most serious pollution during the winter; for such places, the effectiveness of trees for this purpose is limited. Most conifers, which retain their needles for at least two years, are highly susceptible to air-pollution damage.

Effectiveness in ambient cooling and in filtering air pollution depends on the density of the canopy. Thus large trees with closely packed leaves are most effective. Trees should be closely spaced over large areas to create continuous canopy cover, maximizing the still air zone and minimizing the zone of turbulence around the edges. Canopy coverage of 20 to 50 percent of an urban area is needed to overcome even partially the heat island effect. At least two studies have agreed that urban temperatures are reduced by about 1°F for every 10 percent increase in tree canopy (McPherson and Sacamans, 1992).

For a planting of any size, species diversity is important. The danger of relying entirely on one species has been demonstrated by infestations like the Dutch elm disease. If a number of species are mixed, as in most natural forests, then most of them will survive any disease or pest that may attack. Different species also play different ecological roles; it is important that the plantings form a community that includes all the interactions of a natural community.

Building as Mediator between Sun and Earth

Within the green outer shell of the landscape, buildings enclose space in which the temperature range is such that we can carry out our daily lives without being threatened or distracted by heat or cold. This comfort range is roughly between 66° and 80°F though some would narrow that to 68° to 76°F. Since heat is energy, maintaining the comfort range is matter of controlling the flow of energy.

At this level, shelter is a mediator between sun and earth; designing shelter is a matter of shaping energy flow. The processes involved are smaller versions of those that drive the global heat balance and climate patterns: reflection, absorption, and release of heat by various materials, and air movement by differences in pressure and temperature. The 10th strategy for regenerative design, shaping form to guide flow, applies especially to architectural form. Thus it is useful to think of a building and its immediate environs as a microcosm of the earth operating on the same fundamental basis.

Building Form and Energy Flow

If we follow this strategy and this analogy, controlling the heat balance of a building is a matter of guiding the reflection, absorption, and release of heat and the movement of air. To explore this further, consider three basic building forms that use these three principles to guide the flow of energy

in three quite different ways. We might see these as three archetypes for shelter as energy flow. Each developed in response to the need to create living space within specific climatic conditions. Each works in ways quite different from the others; together they illustrate a wide range of means for controlling energy flow through the shaping of shelter. The first building form is the raised structure, or building on stilts. The second form is the earth-sheltered structure, which is dug into the earth becoming part of it and sharing in its thermal balance. The third form is the sunspace, which is a portion of a building specifically shaped to collect and store solar radiation.

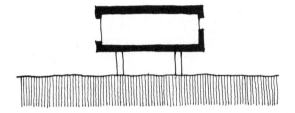

The strategy of the building on stilts, or "pilotis" to use the Corbusian term, is to allow movement of air all the way around the structure. Raising the structure creates a shaded cool zone underneath, which helps to keep the floor of the building cool and serves also as an outdoor living space. Air moving around the structure helps to prevent pockets of warm air from forming, and the movement of air generally keeps the structure somewhat cooler than its surroundings. Raised structures often have broad overhangs to increase the shaded zone, and they commonly feature cross-ventilation through the building as well. Raised structures are much more effective in creating a cooler interior in a warm climate than in creating a warm interior in a cool climate. They are most commonly found in the tropics.

Earth-sheltered structures use the earth as a kind of thermal governor. Since the temperature a few feet below ground level in fairly constant at about 12° to 15° Centigrade (about 54° to 59°F), they are able to release heat to the ground through

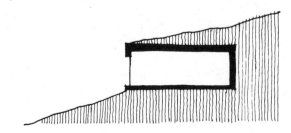

conduction when their interiors are warmer and draw heat from it when they are cooler. The earth also serves as insulation from temperature extremes.

Earth-sheltered structures are most effective in areas with climatic extremes, either very hot or very cold or both. The desert Indians of the American Southwest commonly built earth-sheltered villages. In this they may have been influenced by the many burrowing animals of the desert, which dig deep holes in which they stay cool while the surface temperatures range above 100°F.

The sunspace works like a greenhouse, and in fact often is a greenhouse. It has a sizable area of south-facing glass through which short-wavelength solar radiation flows when the building needs warming. Typically a sunspace has shading devices such as deciduous trees or vines to block out the heat when not wanted. Once admitted, the short-wavelength solar radiation is either absorbed by the surfaces it strikes or reflected as long-wavelength radiation, which cannot so easily penetrate through transparent surfaces and is therefore trapped inside the structure.

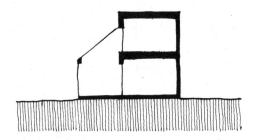

Though each of these archetypes represents a distinctly different means of controlling energy flow, they can be combined in one structure, and often are in practice. A structure on stilts can incorporate a sunspace, for example, or at least use the sunspace principle in providing south-facing glass for its interior spaces. These three basic concepts of energy/earth form can be used in various ways and almost unlimited combinations. The key lies in the fifth strategy of matching technology to need.

Interior Energy Flow

In controlling the flow of energy within a building, it is important that the materials and the details of their assembly augment the form. Five elements of a building are particularly important for their roles in the thermal regime:

- insulation to contain or exclude heat as needed;

- transparent surfaces to admit solar radiation as needed;
- thermal mass to store heat and release it as needed;
- shading materials to block solar radiation from transparent surface when desired;
- openings to control air movement.

Insulation

Human comfort often demands spaces with temperatures either warmer or cooler than the outside air. In nature, however, following the entropy law (the second law of thermodynamics), the warmer air is always trying to release its heat to the cooler air until both are at the same temperature. Insulating materials slow this energy flow, either to conserve heat within a space or to prevent heat from entering. If we include devices for sealing cracks around openings, insulation is probably the most cost-effective energy-conserving device.

An important consideration with insulation is its placement with respect to the two areas to be thermally separated. It is essential to determine where the separation should best occur and to place the insulation there. For example, on exterior concrete walls, the insulation is often placed on the inside face of the wall, whereas it would function more effectively on the outside, where it would reduce the amount of heat entering the building before it entered the concrete. Insulating curtains and panels are likewise best placed outside rather than inside buildings.

Transparent Surfaces

The size, placement, and material properties of transparent surfaces are critically important to any energy-flow system that uses solar radiation. Transparent materials readily allow the short wavelengths of solar radiation (which includes almost all of it) to

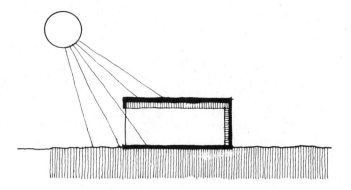

pass through. However, after striking interior surfaces, the reflected rays are long in wavelength, and these do not pass through so readily. This way of trapping heat is called the greenhouse effect. Here again the building functions as a microcosm of the whole earth, which has a layer of gases in the upper atmosphere, holding heat in like the glass of a greenhouse.

Nevertheless, transparent materials are poor insulators and thus readily lose heat by exchange with outside air. For this reason, with transparent surfaces there is a problem of net effectiveness; transparent surfaces may lose more heat than they gain. Maintaining the balance between incoming and outgoing heat to keep interiors within the comfort zone requires careful sizing and placement of transparent areas. Usually it is best for transparent surfaces to face the direction of maximum solar radiation: south in the northern hemisphere, north in the southern hemisphere. The heat gain needed to maintain the comfort zone within a building can be calculated and the area of translucent surface matched to that number (See Mazria, 1979; Watson and Labs, 1983).

Thermal Mass

Once admitted through the transparent surfaces, solar radiation can maintain warmth within a building as long as the sun is shining in. To store the heat and reradiate it when solar radiation is no longer coming in requires a storage medium called "thermal mass." As in most other processes of energy and material flow, storage capacity is essential for operation and is often the limiting factor for effectiveness of the system. Ideally, thermal mass absorbs a great deal of heat rapidly and releases it slowly. Materials vary greatly in their capacity for storing heat. Brick, stone, and water make excellent thermal mass. Wood, wallboard, and most metals do not. The most effective thermal mass tends to be dense, heavy, bulky, and relatively expensive. However, its

effectiveness has been demonstrated through a long history. Buildings with heavy stone, brick, or clay walls are notably constant in their indoor temperature. Witness, for example, the cool interior of a stone cathedral or an adobe pueblo on a hot summer day.

Such naturally heavy materials are not the only options, however. The technology of thermal storage materials has shown notable signs of improvement since energy consumption first became a matter of concern in the 1960s. Among the more interesting developments is the use of phase-change materials such as Glauber's salt. These materials absorb a large amount of heat in passing from a solid to a liquid state, and then release it when they reverse the change and return to the solid state. They have been packaged in various forms, including tubes and bags that can be mounted in a sunny place. Here they go through their phase change to a liquid during the warm hours of the day and return to a solid, thus releasing heat, during a cooler period.

There is a close relationship between the amount of translucent surface and the volume and surface area of thermal mass. The larger the transparent surfaces, the more thermal mass is needed to absorb the incoming heat. Thermal mass receiving direct sunlight is heated by radiation, which is the fastest means of heat transfer. Thus a sunspace, which has large transparent walls and possibly a transparent roof as well, also requires large areas of thermal mass. The ratio of thermal-mass surface to transparent surface usually should be at least 3 to 1.

The major vehicle for distributing heat within a building beyond a sunspace (if there is one) is convection. Roughly one-third of the solar radiation entering through transparent surfaces heats interior air. This heat is then distributed by convection to all spaces that are open to the heated area. Thermal mass located in all parts of the building in which air is warmed by convection can absorb heat for later release. Although the effectiveness of thermal mass heated by convection may be as little as one-quarter of that heated by radiation, its function is extremely important in keeping the whole interior warm.

The heat storage potential of thermal mass is usually considered in three different time frames. Short-term storage of just a few hours can usually be accomplished by ordinary building materials. Diurnal storage is adequate to keep an interior warm through a 24-hour cycle; that is, the thermal mass absorbs enough heat while the sun is shining for release through the night. This requires some

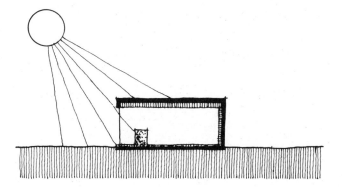

higher-density materials. Diurnal storage is the principal goal of most passive solar design. Beyond that level, thermal-mass requirements can become large and expensive. However, especially in colder climates, buildings are sometimes designed for longer-term storage of several sunless days. For this purpose, solid masonry structures often serve best. For calculation methods, again see Mazria (1979) and Watson and Labs (1983).

Shading

Using solar radiation requires control over the amount admitted. There are times, mostly in winter, when the heat gain should be maximized, and times, mostly in the summer, when it should be minimized, and a great many times in between. To some extent, because the sun passes lower on the horizon in the winter than in the summer, it is possible to design fixed overhangs and other shading elements of a building to allow the sun to shine in during the winter and exclude it in the summer. Movable shading elements, however, can provide much more flexible and responsive control. Overhangs that can be extended in the summer and retracted in the winter or canopies that can be removed entirely in the winter are most effective, especially if they can be adjusted to different positions for fine-tuning the heat gain. A building with movable shading can change with the seasons as the trees do.

The live shading of plants can be even more effective in controlling solar radiation. Here the building connects with the larger landscape that envelopes it. Placed with some care, deciduous trees and vines can allow the sun to shine in during the winter and block it out in the summer. Thus the different responses to solar radiation required in summer and winter suggest that a building's outer shell change with the seasons. Like people, buildings can be dressed differently at different times of year.

Openings

The openings in a structure guide and control the movement of air, thus of heating and cooling. Air movement can be induced by either pressure differences or temperature differences.

The most common condition of interior air movement is cross-ventilation, in which the movement of air is enhanced by the buildup of pressure on the windward side of a building relative to the low-pressure area on the leeward side. Pioneering air-movement studies carried out by Caudill et al. (1951) at Texas A & M University and later by Olgyay (1963) at Princeton provided a good conceptual understanding of air movement within buildings. If openings are located in the walls on the two opposite sides, the difference in pressure causes movement of air between them. If the openings are large and equal in size, the volume of air flowing through will be large and its speed somewhat greater than the wind speed outside. If the outlet is larger than the inlet, the volume of air will be less but its speed greater. If the inlet is larger than the outlet, the flow will tend to dissipate between the two. The placement of the inlet is much more important than that of the outlet. A low inlet placement results in a downward movement of air, while a higher placement causes air to move upward toward the ceiling. An overhang placed above the inlet side increases the pressure and thus the movement of air through the opening.

Partitions placed within the space also have a decisive effect. A partition placed directly across the line of air movement and perpendicular to it dissi-

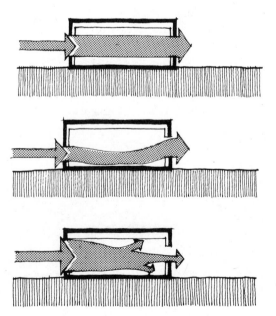

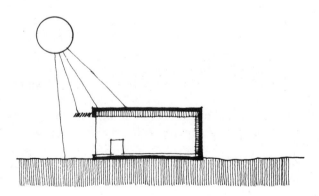

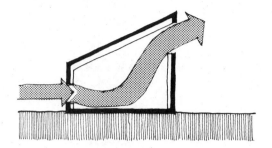

pates the flow, while partitions placed in other positions can guide the movement of air through the space.

The other often-used principle of air movement is that of warm air rising. If inlets are located close to the ground and outlets located high in a structure, the air tends to move from bottom to top. The greater the height difference and the larger the temperature difference, the faster will be the air movement. Heat chimneys are extreme examples of the application of this basic principle. South-facing glass near the upper opening can be used to heat the air at that level and thus to induce more rapid air movement. The high ceilings commonly seen in warm climates follow the same principle.

Cooling Forms

There are a number of architectural forms that use these principles of interior energy flow to induce cooling effects. Among the more effective of these are the following.

Cool Towers

These are large vertical tubes used to cool outdoor or indoor spaces. In the top of the tube, which must be at least 25 feet above ground, is a water-soaked air filter that cools air that passes through it. After cooling, the air, heavier now than the surrounding air, falls to the bottom of the tower, where it flows out through a large opening.

The cool air spreads out from the opening to cool the surrounding space. Experimental cool towers have been installed at the Environmental Research Laboratory in Tucson and have been designed for use in the Urban Oasis Plaza in downtown Phoenix.

Cool Tubes

These are simply long tubes, usually 8 to 24 inches in diameter, buried in the earth and open to the

EXAMPLES OF REGENERATIVE SHELTER

Dispersed throughout this chapter are examples that demonstrate different strategies for controlling energy flow. In each case the strategy is embodied and expressed in the design. Each strategy grows out of the unique set of conditions—topographic, climatic, and human—that exists only in that particular place. Thus we might see here an approach to building that merges shelter with environment. The forms have little to do with fashion and everything to do with land, wind, and sun. They are expressive forms, each different from the others because each of their settings is different from the others.

These observations bring us back to the subject of architecture. Following the strategy of shaping form to manifest process, these forms make visible the intangible dynamics of natural processes according to our late 20th-century understanding. Thus they are shaped by forces quite different from those of conventional architecture, forces that are closer to the primal rhythms of the earth, closer to our source of being. In giving expression to their roles in the natural order of things, they give some hint as to what a truly regenerative architecture might be.

EXAMPLE

■■■

Massive Response to Snow and Ice: The Rocky Mountain Institute

Hunter and Amory Lovins's building in Snowmass, Colorado, a 4300-square-foot structure that houses the offices of their Rocky Mountain Institute as well as their own private residence. Even in the extreme cold of Rocky Mountain winters, the Institute building stays warm with no use of fossil fuels for heating. It accomplishes this primarily through the use of very thick insulation, massive materials for thermal storage, a glass-roofed sunspace to admit solar radiation, and a large array of small energy-efficient devices.

Most strikingly, the Institute demonstrates what can be accomplished with sheer mass of material. The walls are 16 inches thick and composed of two layers of sandstone with a 4-inch layer of polyurethane foam in between. Resting on these walls are 12-by-16-inch oak beams that support 6-by-12-inch oak purlins, which in turn support the 3-by-6-inch cedar roof deck. Covering the deck is a $\frac{5}{8}$-inch rigid insulation board with a vapor barrier and then an 8- to 12-inch thickness of polyurethane insulation, another waterproof membrane, and a porous mat for drainage. There layers are covered by 4 inches of pea gravel, another waterproof layer, and finally 8 to 10 inches of soil. Altogether, this adds up to a 2-foot-thick roof.

Windows are less massive but nevertheless composed of several layers. Between the two sheets of glass is a coated mylar film that reflects infrared radiation back into the building. This film raises the insulation value of the double glazing from R-1.7 to R-4.2. Completing the sandwich between layers of glass is an inert gas called argon, which reduces heat conductivity to one-third that of air.

The sunspace, which covers about a quarter of the building's floor area, has a south-facing glass roof. Where the sloping glass reaches its peak, it has operable ventilators for releasing warm air in case of overheating. The sunspace floor rises in a series of steps like small terraces in which fruit trees and other plants grow. There is also a small fish pond that can produce edible fish.

The sunspace location between the building's office and living wings provides skylighting for most of the building. Areas not skylighted have daylighting from the windows.

Even in the frigid, snow-heavy climate of the Rocky Mountains, this combination of radiation admitting glass and building mass keeps the Institute building warm through the long winters. Actually, the Lovinses claim that it is over 130 percent solar; that is, it provides more than one-quarter again as much heat as needed to keep its occupants warm, even through weeks of cloudy days.

The Rocky Mountain Institute is a showcase of energy-saving technologies, featuring a number of other devices, some common and some experimental. Among the less common are a small clothes-drying room, which features a skylight to admit solar rays that shine on drying clothes suspended on horizontal rods, and five air-to-air heat exchangers, which ventilate the house but also warm outside air when it enters. The devices that are in more common use elsewhere include compact fluorescent light bulbs and on-demand water heaters that heat water as it is actually needed.

The Institute building generates its own electrical power using an array of ten 24-square-foot photovoltaic panels mounted on the roof. The mountings use telescoping brackets, which make it possible to adjust the tilt manually for solar declination. Institute staff members reset the tilt for each of the four seasons. The panels generate an average of about 9 kilowatt-hours per day in the summer and 6 in the winter. This is more than double the power used in the building, though it is considerably less than the amount used in the average American home. Rather than storing electricity, it is sold to the local utility during peak generating periods and bought when power production is too low (Rocky Mountain Institute, 1991).

ROCKY MOUNTAIN INSTITUTE

interior of a structure at one end and to the outside air at the other. As air moves through the tube, pulled from outside to inside either by a fan or by a flow induced by rising warm air, the surrounding earth cools it through its own relatively constant temperature. Since warm air can hold more moisture than cool air, it loses water on the journey through the tube, thus helping to reduce humidity within the structure. Drainage for condensate collecting in the tubes is provided by perforations and an outer layer of gravel or other material around the tube or by sloping the tube downward to the outside end. The diameter and length of the tubes depends on the calculated need for cool air within the structure. Air movement inside cool tubes has been measured as fast as 200 cubic feet per minute.

Thermal Chimneys

These are also small towers, but they work on the corollary convective principle: while cool air falls, warm air rises. If it is tall enough, a vertical tube or hollow shaft will induce a flow of warm air upward from bottom to top. The continuous flow then draws warm air from the space at its base. South-facing glass at the chimney's top is often used to solar-heat the air there and thus induce a more rapid flow. Warm air is continuously replaced by cooler air, which as it is warmed takes its turn moving up

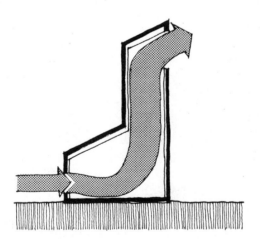

the chimney. The taller the chimney, the greater the volume of flow. The minimum height needed to induce air movement within the chimney is about 25 feet. Heat chimneys are sometimes used in combination with cool tubes to induce an air flow and draw air through the tubes.

Wind Scoops

These also project above buildings, but their purpose is catching the wind rather than the sun. The usual form is a plane which projects at an angle above a hollow shaft. The moving air bounces off the plane surface into the shaft, which conducts it down into the interior of the building. Wind scoops have been most commonly used in India.

Lighting

Although the amount of energy used for lighting is considerably less than the amount used for heating and cooling—about 5 to 10 percent of the energy used for a typical house as compared to 40 to 50 percent typically used for heating and cooling—lighting is still a significant energy user. Lighting is the least-efficient common use of energy: About 95 percent of the energy used in an average lighting system dissipates as heat.

More importantly, the amount and quality of light in the spaces we inhabit seriously affects our sense of well-being. Since most of us spend at least 90 percent of our lives indoors, this makes indoor lighting a most important matter.

Energy used for lighting and for heating and cooling are closely interrelated in complex ways. The more we use daylighting, the less we need electric lighting, but admitting solar light rays means admitting heat energy as well. Most energy codes recognize this relationship but apply it in a highly simplified form by limiting the area of glass to a percentage of the floor area of a building. In California the maximum glass area is 16 percent of the floor area for a residential building. While an architect can transcend this rule by calculating the actual heat loss of a building and showing that it is within acceptable limits, the designers of most buildings, especially tract houses, simply accept the limitation as the easiest way of complying with the code requirement. This has resulted in a great many dark and gloomy houses that have their lights on all day.

Designing for both daylight and thermal energy flow requires that openings serve both purposes. That is, a window should be located so as to guide air movement and provide daylight, and to do both where they will be most effective. The two needs often coincide. South-facing windows can admit more light as well as more heat than windows on other sides of a building. Light coming from above eye level can impart an overall luminosity that is especially beautiful. Thus, the light-flooding character of high windows and skylights can combine with

EXAPMLE

■■

Multiple Energy Paths on a Rainy Hillside:
The Dean Residence

Located on a southwest-facing hillside in the mild but rainy climate of Vashon Island near Seattle, the Dean residence and studio workspace has no need for the massive adaptations appropriate to the Rockies. Rather, it uses the seventh strategy of regenerative design—using multiple pathways—to remain warm under varied weather conditions. The first system is a sunspace, or solarium, incorporated into the structure of the house. While the main body of the house is oriented southwest and northeast in order to fit the slope of the hill, the solarium turns at an angle to face south. Its floor area is about 200 square feet, which is about 7 percent of the floor area of the house, with about 400 square feet of glass. Since the house is heavily insulated, this percentage is enough to keep it warm through fall and spring and on milder winter days but not enough for colder winter days. In this area, winter cloud cover is heavy; solar radiation in December, January, and February is lower than in any other region in the United States. Average radiation on a horizontal surface is 282.6 Btus per day per square foot as compared with 505.5 in Boston, 1045 in San Antonio, or 68.6 in Rapid City, North Dakota. Clearly, the solarium cannot provide effective heating during this period.

The secondary system used in the Dean residence is the masonry heater. Called *Kachelofen* in Germany and Russian stoves in Eastern Europe, masonry heaters have been used for centuries in the colder, grayer climates of Europe. The theory is simple, following the quick absorption–slow release principle. Within the small firebox, wood (or almost any other combustible material) burns very quickly and completely. With complete combustion, air pollution is slight. The firebox is sealed off from the rooms to be heated, though in the Dean residence it has a glass door to make the fire visible. Around the firebox is a massive masonry form several feet high by several feet wide. It is mostly hollow inside, but the interior is divided by baffles into a number of spaces, each a few cubic feet in volume and all open to each other. The firebox releases its heat, which may be as hot as 1200°F, into this collection of internal spaces, where it circulates and in the process is transferred to the thermal mass of brick. After giving up most of their heat, the combustion gases are vented through a chimney. The brick then slowly releases the heat into the surrounding rooms. From a fire that burns for only a short time, the thermal mass can keep the house warm for as long as 24 hours.

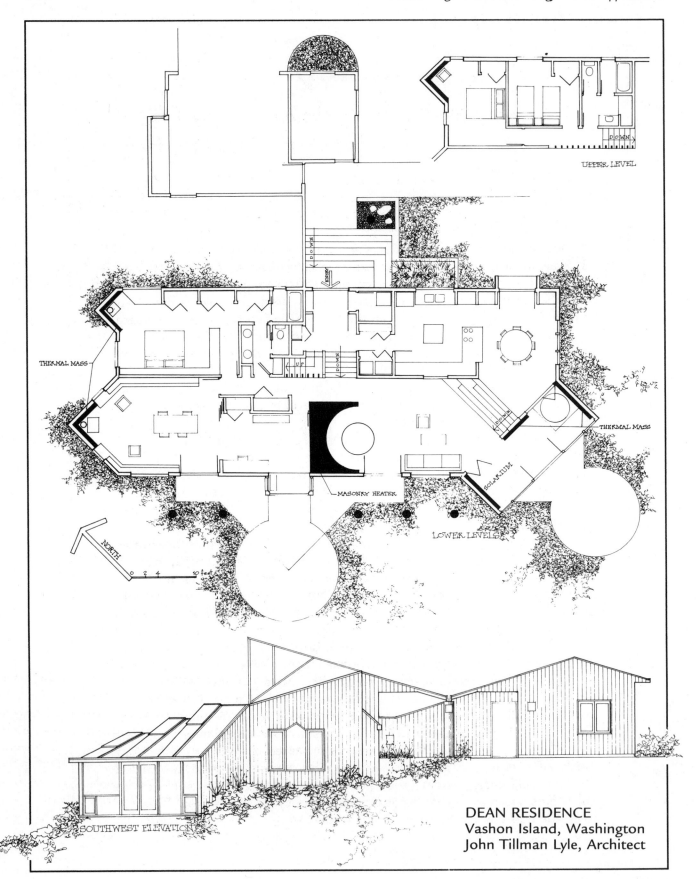

THERMAL MASS

THERMAL MASS

MASONRY HEATER

SOLARIUM

UPPER LEVEL

DOWN

ENTRY

UP

DOWN

DOWN

DOWN

LOWER LEVEL

NORTH

0 2 4   10 feet

SOUTHWEST ELEVATION

DEAN RESIDENCE
Vashon Island, Washington
John Tillman Lyle, Architect

The masonry heater is at the heart of the Dean house, located between the living area and the library with 8-foot-high brick walls facing both of these spaces. From this location its heat can reach every room in the house if the doors are kept open. For days when even more heat is needed, two wood stoves are provided to heat the library and the master bedroom.

On the living-room side the masonry stove forms a semicircular gathering nook that recalls the hearth as the primeval core of home and family. Embedded in another wall of the masonry stove is a cast-iron oven that uses the stove's heat to also do the family's baking during the winter.

Although the sunspace, the masonry heater, and the wood stoves provide more than enough heat, the building code requires a mechanical heating system. A gas-fired forced-air furnace satisfies this requirement.

The thermal mass is the polished concrete floor of the solarium and concentrated near the heat sources at opposite ends of the house in the form of brick walls in the solarium and behind the two wood stoves. The masonry stove itself also serves as a thermal mass, able to absorb heat from other sources when the stove is not in use.

Multiple pathways are most useful if they are flexible enough to work separately or in combination. Thus, in the Dean residence, the three heat sources can be used alone or together. The heat from the masonry stove can be added to the heat from the sunspace on a cold but sunny day, and if it gets even colder, the gas-fired furnace can go on. Note also that the three sources of heat are used in order of energy density. Thus, the lowest-density solar energy is used first, then the higher-density wood, and finally the high-density gas; the last is used only when the first two are inadequate, a condition likely to occur only very rarely. On the coldest of cloudy days, when the solarium may lose more heat than it gains, it can be separated from the rest of the house by insulated panels.

Skylights over the living room, library, and kitchen add to the solar gain. Over the entry is a large south-sloping skylight reaching well above roof height with an opening for venting warm air. Together, even in the gray northwestern winter, these overhead sources keep the house light and airy.

the utility of high openings for venting warm air and inducing convective flow.

The type and placement of lighting fixtures also affects energy use. Lighting layouts that direct light where it is actually needed and minimize overall illumination generally minimize electricity consumption. Light fixtures also vary in their energy consumption. Especially important is the difference between fluorescent and incandescent fixtures; fluorescent fixtures use about one-quarter as much electricity as incandescents to provide the same light level. Using compact fluorescents, which are made to fit fixtures originally designed for incandescents, can reduce energy consumption significantly.

Ecological Roles of Roofs

In conventional design, architects give a great deal of attention to sloping roofs because they are visible and determine much of the projected character of a building. Flat roofs, by contrast, are largely ignored even though most of the roof area in any given modern city is flat. Architect Paul Rudolph once said that no poet ever wrote an ode to a flat roof. Nevertheless, flat roofs constitute a great unused resource, a major problem for maintaining interior comfort zones, and an eyesore for anyone who happens to view them from above.

Ecologically there are good reasons why roof surfaces should be designed to replace the natural processes of the land they cover (see Wells, 1982). These include energy conversion, communities of plants and animals, and collection, filtration, and assimilation of water and other materials. Rooftop design can incorporate all of these. Most interesting and promising is incorporation of roof gardens. The soil, which generally needs to be a foot or so deep, provides an additional layer of insulation, and the plant foliage partially shades the roof. When intensively managed for food production, fruit and vegetable yields can be very high.

The Gaia Institute, which has experimented with rooftop gardens in New York City for several years, has developed a system using greenhouse covers and a lightweight soil employing shredded recycled Styrofoam as a filler. The soil weight is 10 to 20 percent that of natural soils. Institute researchers believe that if this system is used with no space devoted to circulation, the net yield could be 40 to 70 pounds of produce per square foot per year (Walter, 1992). At this rate, each square foot could provide 30 to 50 percent of the vegetables consumed by an average person. This is 30 to 50 times the yield of field crops. While these figures may be optimistic, the potentials of rooftop agriculture are obviously considerable.

Assimilating Indoor Air Pollution

Although it has certainly existed at least since the first Cro-Magnon human brought a burning ember into the cave, we have only recently become concerned about indoor air quality. As long as indoor and outdoor air mingle freely, indoor pollution is just one aspect of the larger problem of air pollution. However, with buildings tightly sealed to conserve energy, indoor pollution has increasingly become an important issue. The EPA recognizes indoor air pollution as a serious health risk (U.S. EPA, 1989). Sources are many. They include building and furnishing materials (especially synthetics);

chemicals used with the building, including cleaners, hair sprays, and deodorants; human biological processes, which emit numerous "bioeffluents"; and the products of combustion.

Ventilation can reduce indoor pollution to harmless levels by flushing indoor air out every 2 to 4 minutes. The ventilating devices mentioned earlier can accomplish this; when windows, skylights, and clerestories (windows in a wall projecting above the roof of a building) are inadequate, whole house fans and ventilators can pull air through the building. However, when the outdoor temperature is very cold, it is virtually impossible for passive heating devices to maintain temperatures within the comfort zone, which raises energy consumption and the cost of operation. Heat exchangers, which use the heat in outgoing interior air to warm incoming cooler air, can reduce loss of warm or cool air but only to some degree. Moreover, air movement only makes indoor air as good as outside air, which in most cities is still unhealthy.

Thinking of the building again as a microcosm of the earth suggests another solution. Plants, the processors of air for the natural ecosystem and for the local landscape, can also process indoor air. It is entirely possible, using a number of common houseplants, to maintain air quality indoors with low ventilation rates, even when outdoor air quality is poor.

Experiments have demonstrated the abilities of various plants requiring low light levels to assimilate a number of airborne chemicals that are common indoor pollutants (Wolverton et al., 1989). These include formaldehyde, xylene, ammonia, acetone, and ethyl and methyl alcohol. The research was carried out by introducing these and other substances into sealed transparent plastic chambers in which the plants were growing.

It is well known that plants take in carbon dioxide while emitting oxygen and water vapor through their leaves. Less widely known is the fact that they also take in a wide variety of other materials through their leaves. These substances move through the plant's internal circulation systems, the xylem and the phloem, to other parts of the plant or to the roots, where they are emitted into the soil. Those substances transported within the plant are diffused and assimilated, while bacteria and other microorganisms break down and assimilate those moved into the soil.

Plants do not take in all chemicals, of course, and they absorb some in amounts large enough to damage or kill the plant. There is much research

■■

Earth Sheltering for a Cold Climate: The Wells House

Malcolm Wells brought 30 years of experience in designing earth-sheltered buildings to the design of his own residence on Cape Cod (Wells, 1982). The structure is long and narrow as energy-efficient buildings often are, but rather than facing south for maximum potential solar gain as most do, the long sides of the Wells house face east and west. This is to fit the topography and take advantage of a view to the east. Thus the house relies very little on solar radiation gain. It relies instead on other devices for controlling energy flow, including earth sheltering, very thick insulation, movement of air, high volume of thermal mass, and seasonal dressing.

About half of the building's roof is covered by 12 to 18 inches of soil, and the walls are buried up to about half their height. Thus it is roughly half encased in the earth. The soil contributes to energy control primarily as insulation since it is not deep enough to have a constant temperature. In addition, the roof insulation is 12 inches thick underneath the layer of earth, and 6-inch Styrofoam sheets line the outside of the retaining walls.

Air movement is one key to the success of the Wells house. By distributing the warm air produced by the oil furnace that heats the north side of the building and by the wood stove that heats the south side, maximum use is made of the available heat. Air is pushed down by small fans through ducts called sniffers, which reach up to the top of the glass ridge of the roof, where hot air collects. The sniffers convey the hot air into a sand bed, which functions as thermal mass beneath the floor. After moving through the sandbed, the air is released back into the house through open slots running around the perimeter of the floor. According to Wells, when the air taken in by the sniffers at the top is at 90°F, the air coming out at the slots is at 70°F. On days that are not so hot, it is also possible to simply allow the hot air to flow out through vents and operable skylights in the ridge.

Thermal mass is provided by the 8-inch thick concrete retaining walls, by the concrete buttresses that support the roof trusses, by the sand bed, and by two concrete slabs, one over and one under the sand bed.

Seasonal dress controls the solar radiation entering the house through the glass ridge that runs the length of the house at its very center. While this glass keeps the interior bright through the winter, its radiation gain is enough to

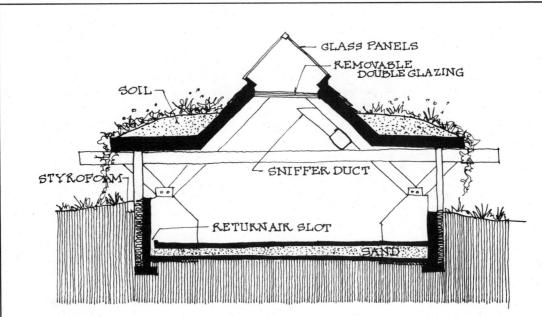

SECTION: WELLS OFFICE—RESIDENCE

contribute only a small amount to heating. The gain is enough, however, to cause overheating in the summer. So Wells attaches canvas covers over the glass each summer, leaving 3-inch openings between panels to allow light to shine into the spaces below. Since the summer sunlight is several times brighter than the winter sun, the amount of light is still quite adequate.

A second task of seasonal dress is the insertion and removal of the translucent plastic panels that divide the glass-enclosed ridge from the space below. In the winter, these form an airlock that reduces heat loss through the glass ridge. They are removed for the summer to allow hot air to rise through the roof vents.

still to do in measuring the abilities of specific plants to deal with specific substances. However, experiments already carried out suggest that a number of common houseplants are highly effective in assimilating pollutants (Wolverton and Wolverton, 1992). These include the following:

- *Chrysalidocarpus lutescens* (Areca palm)
- *Phoenix roebelenii* (miniature date palm)
- *Dieffenbachia* 'Camille' (dumb cane)
- *Dracaena marginata*
- *Nephrolepis obliterata* 'Kimberly Queen' (Kimberly Queen sword fern)
- *Ficus benjamina* (weeping fig)
- *Chlorophytum comosum* 'Vittatum' (spider plant)
- *Rhapis excelsa* (lady palm)
- *Nephrolepis exaltata* 'Bostoniensis' (Boston fern)

Regenerative Qualities of Building Materials

Through most of history, each culture has had only one or two materials available for making buildings. The 20th century is unique in providing hundreds of materials for architects to choose from. However, because materials differ enormously in their ecological roles, the wide choice of materials can cause serious difficulties. This can be true even of materials that serve exactly the same purpose in building. For example, we might enclose a house with wood siding or aluminum siding, either of which will keep the wind and water out and provide a reasonably flat surface to view; they even cost about the same. But the aluminum siding requires over 100 times as much fossil-fuel energy to produce.

Until recently, society demanded of materials only that they serve their purpose with reasonable strength and durability and that they present an attractive appearance and suitable image. The understanding of ecological systems introduces a new set of criteria for choosing materials, which frames considers their value in light of their roles in nature's processes. Among these new criteria are the amount of embedded energy, renewability, reuse potential, and pollution potential.

Embedded Energy

All materials used in building require energy in processing, shaping, treating, and shipping. Those materials not grown or extracted from the earth also require energy for manufacture. The term for this is "embedded energy," and it varies greatly among materials. Although researchers have done considerable work in measuring the embedded energy in building materials, direct comparisons are difficult. This is primarily due to the different units used to specify the quantity of the material.

To aid in preliminary determinations for design purposes, several rough rules of thumb are useful. There is a general, very rough correlation between the cost of a material and its embedded energy. The higher the cost, in general, the greater the embedded energy, though the above example of wood and aluminum siding is clearly an exception. Another study estimated the embedded energy in wood at 639 kilowatt-hours per ton and then calculated the energy in some other common materials in relation to this as follows:

Wood	
Aluminum	126 ×
Brick	4 ×
Concrete	5 ×
Glass	14 ×
Plastic	6 ×
Steel	24 ×

This suggests that materials drawn from locally available, naturally occurring substances requiring little processing are generally least energy-intensive, while those involving manufacturing processes, especially metals, are most energy-intensive.

From the available information, we can see the vague outline of a low-energy building strategy. Many questions remain, however. For example, there is the question of energy consumed in the building process itself. The embedded energy in

concrete would be much greater if we included energy invested in the formwork to get it into place. Steel, on the other hand, might score better because of its ease and speed of placement.

Renewability

The distinction between renewable and nonrenewable resources becomes increasingly important as nonrenewable resources dwindle. However, the distinction also becomes less clear as we use renewable resources at rates beyond their sustainable yield, which is the amount of material that can be harvested without reducing the productive capacity of the resource. The most common renewable building material is wood, but forests with the best building timber are not regenerating at a rate comparable to the pace of logging. The threat of cutting the last stands of ancient coastal redwoods in northern California is the extreme case. This situation renders redwood, for all practical purposes, a nonrenewable resource.

The difficulty is that there are few renewable alternatives currently harvested at renewable levels. Aside from some use of wool and cotton batting in interiors and some cellulose fibers, we build mostly with materials that are dwindling away. One exception is the straw bales that have occasionally been used for building houses in some places.

Another exception is materials shaped from raw earth, such as the mud brick commonly used for at least six thousand years in the Middle East, the adobe used in the American Southwest, and the rammed earth being used occasionally in parts of the United States. As materials that blend into the landscape and make few demands on resources or on natural systems, such materials are most appealing. They are easily used by builders with limited skills. They have high thermal mass and thus tend to maintain narrow temperature ranges. And when their useful life is done, they can melt back into the earth from which they came. Attesting to this are the great mounds of earth in Mesopotamia that were once large cities like Ur or Erech but are now indistinguishable from their natural surroundings except for their mesalike elevation.

The earth materials have serious disadvantages, however. While strong enough in load-bearing capacity, they have no ability to withstand lateral stresses, which means they tend to crumble in an earthquake. This at least partially explains the devastation caused by even relatively mild earthquakes in the Middle East. While steel reinforcement can

■■

Electronic Controls for a Public Building:
The Albany County Airport

For larger buildings in which large numbers of people are involved, situations in which direct feedback and response by individuals is not feasible, electronic and mechanical devices can control solar radiation and air movement. For example, the Albany County Airport in New York features a sloping glass monitor on its roof that extends the length of the terminal building and provides about 40 percent of its lighting and 20 percent of its heating (Rosenfeld and Hafemeister, 1988). Behind the glass in the monitor is a set of insulated louvers that open and close to admit or shut out solar rays. The movement of the louvers is computer-controlled so that when the sun is shining, they open to admit the maximum solar radiation. At night and on cloudy days, they close to minimize the loss of heat through the glass. On very hot days they are turned to reflect the solar rays and prevent the building from overheating. The monitoring and computer control maintain the building's inside temperature within a narrow temperature range, preventing wild swings when outside conditions change. Thus electronics replaces the human mind and muscle that are required to maintain comfort levels in buildings like the Wells residence and studio. Both situations work on the sixth strategy of using information to replace power.

Overall energy consumption in the Albany Airport building is about 25 percent that of the old conventionally designed terminal building. The heating cost is even less—about 20 percent. The cooling cost is a little less than half. In general, it is more difficult to reduce energy consumption for cooling than for heating. The energy reduction for lighting and for operating miscellaneous equipment is about the same as that for heating—roughly 80 percent.

The lighting improvement results from a combination of careful use of daylighting and efficient fixtures. Through the industrial era, the importance of daylight as a light source was virtually ignored; in a great many buildings, daylight was excluded entirely. With careful design, daylight can be well controlled. Some recent buildings like the Albany Airport have demonstrated the dramatic beauty and utility of daylight admitted through skylights, rooftop monitors, and well-placed windows. Much of the light, spacious quality of the airport's internal space is due to the overhead monitor that provides 40 percent of its lighting.

SOLAR COURT
ALBANY AIRPORT

overcome the problem, this is expensive, and some building codes allow no structural value to be assigned to earth materials at all.

Like the land they come from, these materials are also subject to constant erosion. Water wears them away, grain by grain. So they require continuous patching and recoating to prevent their melting back into the earth too soon. Nevertheless, despite these problems, mudbrick adobe structures can last a very long time. The oldest continuously inhabited structure in North America—the Taos Pueblo—is an adobe structure.

Permanence and Reusability

The resource investment in a building material includes the material itself plus the embedded energy involved in its manufacture, preparation transport,

EXAMPLE

■■■

Inner Courtyard as a Heating and Cooling System: The Bateson Building

At least since the time of the earliest cities in Mesopotamia, buildings commonly have been constructed around courtyards in hot climates to provide solar access and air movement. The Bateson Building is an updated set of variations on this ancient theme, applying a range of passive solar devices in relation to the inner courtyard to heat and cool its 276,000 square feet of state offices.

The four-story building covers a square block in the hot, dry urban micro-climate of downtown Sacramento, California, a few blocks from the state capitol building. Its concrete structure is exposed to provide thermal storage for heat generated by people, office machines, and lights as well as for solar heat. The skylights covering the courtyard feature movable louvers on their south faces to admit solar radiation in the winter and screen it out in the summer. Glass areas on the building's south, east, and west sides have similarly controlled shading devices.

In the courtyard, canvas tubes stretch vertically from just above floor level to the roof. Fans mounted near the tubes' bottom ends pull cooler outside air into the courtyard. From there is rises to roof level, where it is vented back to the exterior. This maintains constant air movement in the courtyard. Operable windows on the courtyard sides of the offices allow this air also to move

through the building. During the evening and night and between warm days, fans move cool outside air through all of the building's offices.

Underneath the floor of the courtyard are two concrete containers holding a total of 660 tons of river rock. Outside air is also pumped into these during summer nights and then released into the building during the day. This process is reversed during winter months, with warm air drawn into the rock storages on sunny afternoons and released into the building in the early morning before its occupants arrive for work. Operable louvers protect windows on the east and west sides from direct radiation in the summer. Louvers on the south side are fixed.

Energy consumption in the Bateson Building is less than 15 percent of that of an average conventional office building of the pre-1973 period and less than one-third the maximum consumption allowed by California's state energy code, Title 24. Energy used by the backup cooling and heating systems is negligible, as is that used by equipment. Electricity used by fans for moving air is roughly the same as that of a typical building constructed under the energy code. Most of the energy consumed in the Bateson Building is for lighting (about 66 percent of the total), suggesting that heating and cooling problems have been solved much more effectively than has lighting. Still, use of electricity for lighting is less than half that allowable under Title 24. All work areas are within 40 feet of daylighted windows. The Bateson Building's construction cost was about the same as that of comparable conventional office buildings.

and installation. In the short term these are separate matters from the financial investment measured by the material's dollar cost. Short-term economic biases often make it less expensive initially to use less permanent materials, and to haul those materials to a landfill when they are removed from the building or it is demolished. A large part of the contents of most urban landfills consists of the rubble of demolished buildings.

Longer-term resource concerns favor choosing more permanent materials and reusing materials that are removed. We commonly think of buildings as permanent fixtures of the earth. In fact, like trees, mountains, and other natural features, they are temporary attachments, generally lasting less than a century. A great many building materials have longer lives than buildings. Materials such as bricks, stones, and heavy timbers are often reused. Others, such as glass, doors, and broken concrete, can be reused but rarely are. A truly regenerative building technology will use long-lived materials and reuse them over and over again in building after building over time. The Solar Park at the Center for Regenerative Studies, for example, features paving made from reused concrete (see page 97). Such practices are not new. A great many of the Renaissance churches of the 15th and 16th centuries were built with stones acquired by demolishing Gothic churches of the 11th and 12th centuries.

Question of Density

The three dwelling-workplaces presented as examples of regenerative design (the Rocky Mountain Institute, the Dean residence, and the Wells house) sit in several acres of open land. Such conditions are ideal for experimentation in solar design. The landscape is in place, and there are no other structures around to constrain building orientation and solar access. Landscape and building can work together.

Howard Odum (1976) has argued that such very low density living (less than one person per acre) is the way of the future. As the quality and quantity of available energy decline, there will be a shift in economic advantages toward smaller dispersed units because they can use the land around them to collect and convert solar energy. Higher densities, he believes, necessarily rely on higher-quality energy.

The majority of the American population, and those of many other countries as well, would be pleased with Odum's projection of a low-density fu-

ture. However, there are strong arguments for densities above the single-family-house level. Clustered dwellings are much more efficient in their use of land and can be more efficient in their use of facilities by sharing amenities like swimming pools and play areas. More importantly, if well planned, they can reduce urban distances and bring dwellings closer to places of work, shopping, and schools. Higher densities make walking, bicycling and mass transit much more feasible modes of transportation, thus reducing the use of automobiles and consumption of energy. Even the archetypal suburban city of Los Angeles, faced with traffic approaching gridlock levels and pressing demands to reduce air pollution, has adopted planning policies favoring higher densities.

On a more theoretical level, architect Ralph Knowles (1975) advocates higher-density development on the basis of scientific theory quite different from that applied by Odum. Knowles takes the Schrodinger ratio (which states that the susceptibility of a biological system to environmental stress varies directly with the surface-to-volume ratio) and applies it to buildings. Energy is used to overcome stress. Since clustered buildings sharing party walls achieve much lower surface-to-volume ratios as well as higher densities, this suggests that the higher the density development, in theory, the more energy-efficient the buildings will be.

Buildings clustered tightly together can share half or more of their exterior walls and roofs, thus presenting less than half as much surface for the gain or loss of heat. However, research results on energy consumption are mixed. For example, a study carried out by the Florida Solar Energy Center showed that single-family detached households used almost twice as much energy per dwelling unit as single-family attached households. Calculated on a per-occupant basis, however, the detached houses used only about 50 percent more. When calculated on a per-occupant, per-square-foot basis, energy consumption in the attached units was only slightly lower. This suggests that for conventional buildings, levels of energy consumption may be more closely related to the size of dwellings than to their density.

Size alone, however, is not enough to achieve energy efficiency. Form is also important. Working with the solar-envelope concept, Ralph Knowles has explored design strategies to assure that every building receives adequate solar radiation. The spatial dimensions of the solar envelope are defined by lines drawn between sun and site during peri-

EXAMPLE

■■■

Energy Pathways in a Subdivision: Village Homes

Reconciling the overwhelming preference of most Americans for single-family houses with the need to reduce resource consumption is a key challenge for planning and design. The Village Homes community, designed by architect/developers Judy and Michael Corbett and built in Davis, California, provides a model of suburban energy flow whose attributes could easily be adapted for wider use (Corbett, 1988).

First of all, lots are small, averaging about 3800 square feet, which is enough for an average-sized house and a small private garden. Lots are planned in clusters of eight with each cluster sharing a common area of about one-third of an acre. The whole community of 220 homes shares larger common areas with playing fields, an amphitheater, and community gardens.

The circulation system gives as much emphasis to pedestrian and bicycle paths as to streets; movement within the community is intended to be entirely by foot and bicycle. The streets average 22 feet wide, compared with the standard for the area which is 44 feet. Parking is not directly on the streets but in parking bays provided at intervals along their lengths. This results in less pavement to collect heat during the day in this very warm climate and more area for planting for microclimate control. Most of the trees along the streets and paths are fruit-bearing.

A system of retention swales that weaves through the community collects runoff water for infiltration. Little if any rainwater flows off of the site.

The streets run east and west to allow maximum southward orientation for potential solar-energy use. Most of the houses feature solar water-heating systems, and virtually all use some degree of passive solar heating and cooling. The passive devices range from a few south-facing windows to architect Jim Zanetto's earth-sheltered solar house, which has never used any fossil fuel. Less than 10 percent of the houses have mechanical air conditioning, though summers in Davis usually are very hot.

The solar access of every building is protected by subdivision covenants. Trees are not allowed to shade structures in the wintertime, though they may partially do so during the summer. Studies have shown energy consumption per unit in Village Homes to be less than half that of nearby conventional houses (Morlock, 1990).

The development costs of Village Homes were unusually low as well. The costs of streets, parking bays, bicycle paths, and planting amounted to about $4000 per unit, as compared with about $5000 per unit just for streets in conventional subdivisions during the same period. Resale prices, by comparison, have been higher, generally averaging about 15 percent more than comparable houses in conventional subdivisions.

COMMUNITY GARDENS
VINEYARDS
FRUIT TREES
HOUSES
RECREATION BUILDINGS
COMMERCIAL BUILDINGS
ROADWAYS
WALKING AND
    BICYCLE PATHS

NORTH

0 100 200 FEET

VILLAGE HOMES
DAVIS, CALIFORNIA
After Corbett, 1988

ods when solar radiation is needed. No obstructions are allowed within any building's solar envelope. By means of a series of three-dimensional models, Knowles has shown how building form can vary within the envelope in response to varying solar conditions and orientations. Models made by Knowles and his students have shown that it is possible to provide direct solar access for dwellings even in very tight attached clusters up to at least 72 units per acre (Knowles, 1992). In Knowles's protypical plan at this density, all of the structures are at least two stories in height and most are higher. Knowles believes that as many as 100 dwelling units per acre could share solar access within the envelope (ibid.).

Thus, while Schrodinger's theory does not include an upper size limit, Knowles's work suggests

■■

Regeneration in the Inner City: Proposals for Southeast Los Angeles

For the most part, our cities are unsustainable as they stand, entirely dependent on diminishing sources and degrading sinks. Their future sustainability will depend on how they evolve in dealing with degenerative trends.

Every part of every city is in a continuing state of change. People move away, and new people move in. Buildings become obsolete or deteriorate. Trees and other plants grow and die, and others take their places. Elements of urban infrastructure, especially streets, are hardest to change because they depend on rigidly established public rights-of-way. With strong direction, however, these also can evolve.

Given this ongoing evolutionary flux, it is entirely possible that any city might shift to a regenerative mode of operation over a few decades.

Presented here are a few excerpts from a planning study for the southeast section of the city of Los Angeles, a low-income area with a population roughly 20 percent black and 80 percent Hispanic. The planning work is a joint effort of local residents, the city's planning department, and the 606 Studio (1990).

Though southeast Los Angeles is a medium-density area with mostly single-family houses, it is plagued with economic and environmental problems. Principle issues are the following:

- lack of jobs in the community or within a reasonable distance;
- almost complete dependence on automobiles for transportation;
- air pollution and extreme urban heat;
- lack of access to shopping, schools, and other daily necessities;
- lack of space for recreational activities;
- lack of community identity.

The planning proposals do not advocate sudden or dramatic change, but rather attempt to guide the general processes of urban evolution to begin to address these issues with minimum cost and disruption. The only buildings recommended for demolition are those already deteriorated beyond repair. The urban infrastructure remains in place but evolves in form and function. People are not uprooted but given the power and the means to change their environment. What is proposed is not an ultimate solution but a beginning.

The principal proposals are illustrated in the plans on the facing page. They include the following:

- Establishment of several mixed-use zones for shop–office–light industrial housing complexes.
- Acquisition of available vacant lots for miniparks to be used as recreation/gathering places and as community gardens.
- Redistribution of traffic pattern to allow for:
  - strategic location of stops on light rail lines (which were already under consideration) to connect southeast Los Angeles with other parts of the city;
  - concentration of north-south through traffic on five arterial streets;
  - establishing a system of walkways and bikeways with minimal automobile traffic.
- An urban forestry program to reduce air pollution and urban heat. Trees will be planted by local residents in cooperation with volunteer groups such as the Tree People, primarily in the following locations:
  - along the arterial streets, walkways, and bikeways;
  - in parks and other public lands.
- An aquatic sewage treatment facility to provide irrigation water for the new plantings. This will divert water from an existing city sewage main, treat it in a series of aquacultural ponds, and then pipe it to the areas requiring irrigation water. The treatment facility is located on land already owned by the city and will be designed to serve also as an urban park.

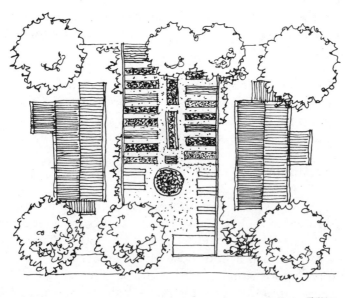

COMMUNITY MINI-GARDEN
After 606 Studio, 1990

0 5 10 FEET

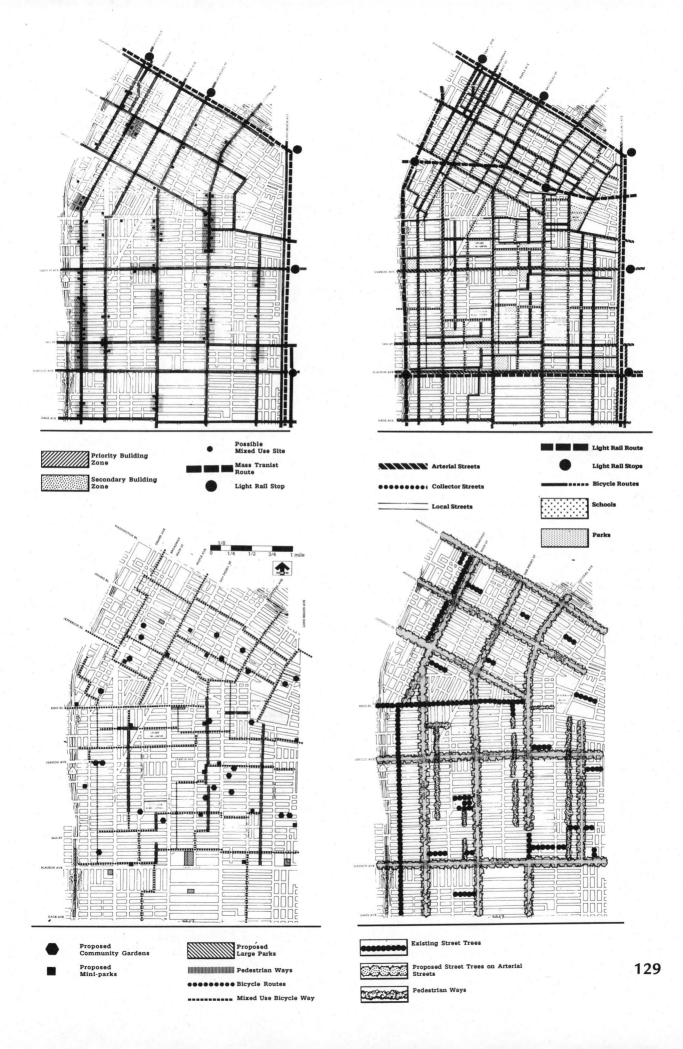

Priority Building Zone

Secondary Building Zone

Possible Mixed Use Site

Mass Transit Route

Light Rail Stop

Arterial Streets

Collector Streets

Local Streets

Light Rail Route

Light Rail Stops

Bicycle Routes

Schools

Parks

Proposed Community Gardens

Proposed Mini-parks

Proposed Large Parks

Pedestrian Ways

Bicycle Routes

Mixed Use Bicycle Way

Existing Street Trees

Proposed Street Trees on Arterial Streets

Pedestrian Ways

129

that a limit does exist, albeit a very high limit; other theorists agree. There are probably both upper and lower limits.

There have been some efforts to determine not only upper and lower limits but to define an optimum density for energy efficiency. The Regional Plan Association (1974) studied the relationship between density and energy consumption in the New York metropolitan area. Their results suggested that per-capita energy consumption decreased up to a density of about 25,000 people per square mile, or roughly 39 people per acre, which amounts to about 13 dwelling units per acre. Then it increased as densities got higher. Thus for that particular place at that particular time, there seems to have been an optimum density.

A major difficulty with general rules concerning urban density, including zoning regulations, is that they fail to deal with specifics of design and especially with the relationship between building and landscape. At any level of density, livability and sustainability require integration of buildings and landscape. Even at the very low density advocated by Odum, if the landscape does not work with buildings in controlling energy flow, energy consumption will be high. This is because additional energy input will be needed to do the work otherwise carried out through the internal natural processes of the landscape. The urban landscape should provide a zone of natural microclimate control around buildings that also provides some biomass, supports a biological community, produces oxygen, absorbs carbon

dioxide, filters the air, and provides for flow and infiltration of water. Such a landscape can form by a continuous green matrix wearing through urban areas.

At 13 units per acre, the density suggested as optimum by the Regional Plan Association study requires attached units. In terms of traditional building forms, it is a townhouse density, and thus considerably higher than most people consider ideal. While numbers of people will undoubtedly be willing to shift to higher-density living under the pressures of rising cost and inconvenience, a great many others will cling to the dream of a single house on a single lot at almost any cost. Adapting the low-density pattern to the inevitable need for energy efficiency will require adjustments both in design and in ways of life. However low the density, the automobile cannot remain the sole means of transport. Community design is integrally linked with circulation systems (as discussed in Chapter 4 and with design of the urban landscape. The space around the single house cannot remain energy-consuming decorative landscape but must become energy-producing working landscape that pays its way in ecological terms.

Energy and Land Use

Among the most entropic effects of profligate energy use in the 20th century is the rigid and wide separation of land uses that characterizes the modern city. This is entirely a 20th-century phenomenon, a byproduct of petroleum. According to one authority, Susan Owens of Cambridge University, over half of the energy use of industrial countries is related to distribution of land uses—that is, to the spatial relationships of residences to places of employment, schools, shopping, and other activities (Flavin and Lenssen, 1990). This has begun to change; a number of urban and suburban developments, like the southeast Los Angeles example, have proposed mixing housing, commercial, business, schools, and even light industrial areas together, bringing all within walking, or at least bicycling, distance. Such patterns offer rich, complex patterns of human interaction, contrasting with the deadly dullness of most single-use residential tracts, business and industrial "parks," and shopping centers of the late Paleotechnic period.

Planning new development for mixed uses is clearly much easier than changing existing patterns. Nevertheless, it is possible to guide evolutionary change within cities to gradually mix uses without cataclysmic disruption. The southeast Los Angeles plan shows how small mixed-use developments can gradually replace old, deteriorated single-use buildings. Simply relaxing some very rigid zoning ordinances would accomplish a great deal in this direction.

The relationship between dwelling and work is changing in other, equally significant ways. Electronic communications make it increasingly possible for at least some people to work at home, as demonstrated by the three examples shown earlier—the Rocky Mountain Institute, the Dean residence, and the Wells house. If the long commute to work is eliminated or minimized, low densities become more reasonable.

Until the beginning of the industrial period, workplace, and dwelling were commonly combined. It was the factory with its need for a massive workforce and then the corporation with its white-collar army that separated them. Commuting trains and then automobiles made the separation feasible. New technology may well support another shift, making possible for at least some people a return to the ancient pattern. Much of the task of communication is already shifting from actual trips to electronics.

The important point to draw from this discussion is that the density of development, while it is a useful statistic and a valuable indicator, is not a basic determinant of energy flow. What really determines the energy flow in a community is the design of the landscape, the circulation system, and the buildings and the pattern of land use. If these are shaped for regenerative patterns of energy flow, densities can vary from those associated with rural living to highly urban ways of life.

Urban Evolution and Future Cities

When we add up all the aspects of human habitat discussed in this chapter, we have a rough sketch for a new kind of city, one that is quite different in form and content from the cities of the present. The city in this sketch, in fact, looks very little like our traditional cities. This suggests a complete reshaping of the urban environment. As our communities grow and as we build new ones, we can apply regenerative principles to achieve sustainability in the new areas if we have the will.

Our existing cities are another issue. Their Paleotechnic forms foreclose some of the options. Nevertheless, cities evolve as do other ecosystems. As old parts wear out, we can replace them with regenerative parts. The southeast Los Angeles example shows some relatively inexpensive and nondisruptive ways of beginning. With sound plans to guide change over time and with decision-making processes that give priority to sustainability, even most degenerative cities might be guided in regenerative directions over a few decades.

In the time frame that we have grown accustomed to, a few decades is a very long time. In this short-term perspective, we tend to think of urban environments as permanent fixtures. Planning regenerative communities will require us to think in more dynamic terms—to think of the human-made environment as ever-changing and to see its buildings as fixtures that are periodically reconstructed and reconnected, perhaps reusing the same materials. Processes of decline and regeneration are part of the urban pattern and thus part of the planning processes.

EXAMPLE

■■

Regeneration of a Building: The Audubon Society Headquarters

While the revitalization of cities will have to encompass whole urban districts such as Southeast Los Angeles in comprehensive ways, the increment of change will often be an individual building. While all buildings will be replaced in time, the unit of time can be very long, sometimes measured in hundreds of years. Considering the energy inbedded in any structure and the difficulties of recycling most building materials, resource conservation requires that the life of a building be extended as long as possible. In recent years, economic concerns have also reinforced the general trend toward remodelling rather than demolishing old buildings and to adaptive re-use.

While old buildings can rarely be remodelled to achieve the same levels of energy and materials efficiency achievable in new buildings, great improvements are possible. Among a considerable number of renovations exploring the possibilities in recent years, the Audubon Society Headquarters in New York City is one of those that stand out as particularly sophisticated in its complex technology.

The Society bought a nine-story 102-year-old office building in Lower Manhattan and asked its architects, the Croxton Collaborative, to use as many means for energy efficiency and environmental amelioration as could pay for themselves in five years or less. The number of technologies meeting this criterion is large, but many of them are not truly regenerative but simply improvements on usual paleotechnic practices. Passive solar heating and cooling are not feasible in this situation for example. The building relies instead on a high efficiency gas fired furnace and chiller. Air intakes are on the roof rather than at ground level to bring in better air, and pumps and fans incorporate feedback devices for precise control of ambient conditions. The system changes the air more than six times per hour, which is 6 times the required rate, and filters out $\frac{4}{5}$ of particulates.

The building uses a number of recycled materials including wallboard made of recycled newsprint, floor tiles of recycled glass, and various horizontal surfaces of recycled plastic. Internal recycling is highly developed by means of chutes running vertically through the building, conveying used materials to a collection center in the lower basement.

The architects paid particular attention to means for reducing energy used for lighting. Fixtures are fluorescent, including compact fluorescent task lights. Most general illumination hangs on pendants from the ceiling to bring it closer to working surfaces. Partitions between work stations are low to share light, and most surfaces are reflective. The top floor features a skylight and clerestories provide light where possible. Dimmers adjust lighting in response to daylight levels.

Though the results of monitoring energy use for the first year were not available at this writing, the Society expects to save about 60 percent of the energy consumed in conventional buildings per unit area. This translates into a saving of roughly a dollar per square foot per year for the 98,000 square foot building for energy alone. Altogether, the cost of the renovation was $142 per square foot or roughly 10 percent more than that of a typical conventional renovation project of similar scope.

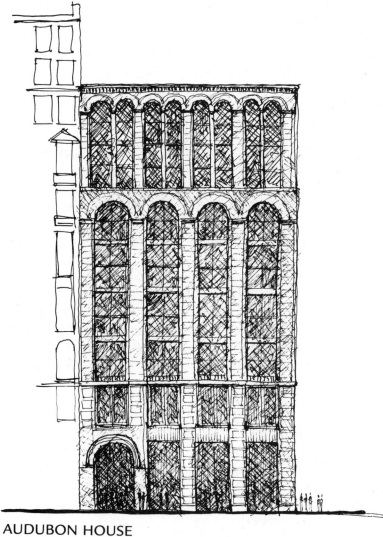

AUDUBON HOUSE

Human Habitat at the Center for Regenerative Studies

Of the Center's total 16-acre land area, the village, which now houses 20 residents and will eventually house 90, also includes teaching and research areas (the workplaces for residents), rests on a site of 2.2 acres. This overall land area includes the landscape in the immediate vicinity of the buildings and circulation routes. This resulted not from any preconceived density target but from design studies matching the number of people to be housed and the facilities required to the specific conditions of the site. Within the 2.2 acres, about one-quarter is planting, one-quarter is circulation space, and about one-half is covered by building.

Although the setting and the circumstances are quite different from those of New York City, it is interesting that the density that emerged from functional considerations for the Center is 41 people per acre, very close to the optimal density derived by the New York Regional Plan Association study. The significance of this is an open question; it may be no more than an intriguing coincidence. If we calculate the overall density of the Center including agricultural areas, the density is about 5.6 people per acre. Since the agricultural lands can provide under optimum circumstances approximately the volume of food consumed by the resident population, this gives some indication of the land area required to meet basic needs. This density is considerably higher than that suggested by Odum, but lower than typical suburban densities of 10 to 20 people per acre.

The landscape within the village area is designed to provide the outer layer of the village environment. Specifically, the plantings will provide for control of solar radiation, water harvesting, and infiltration and productivity.

BUILDING DESIGN

The village buildings accommodate the following functions:

- dwelling space for 90 people, including students and resident and visiting faculty members;

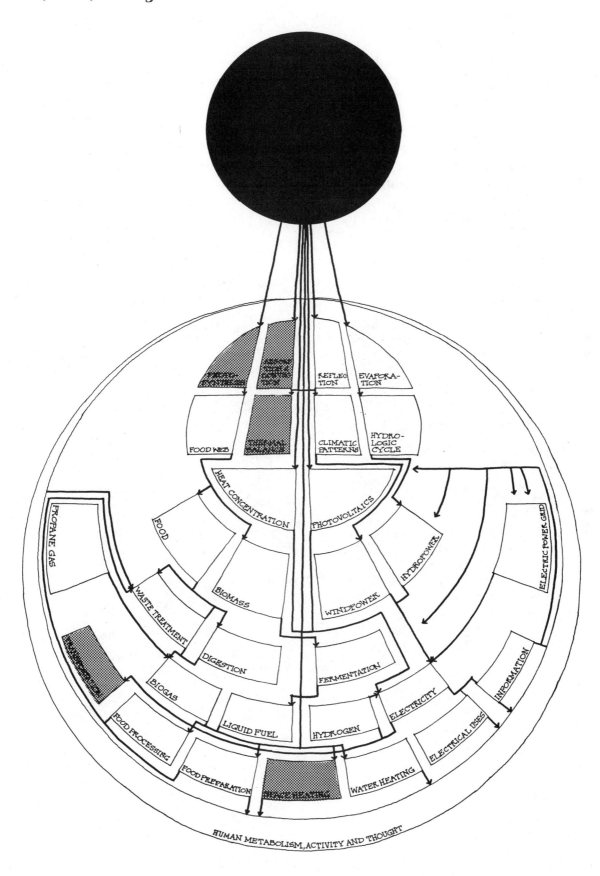

- gathering spaces, both indoors and out, for groups of various sizes;
- the community reception room, a relatively formal space in which members of the Center community present their activities to the outside world;
- dining room and cooking facilities, the symbolic heart of the community where all its members gather for at least one meal each day;
- academic facilities including space for lectures, seminars, a small library, and laboratory work.
- ancillary facilities, which consist of two small service buildings to house tools and farm implements, shops, and work spaces.

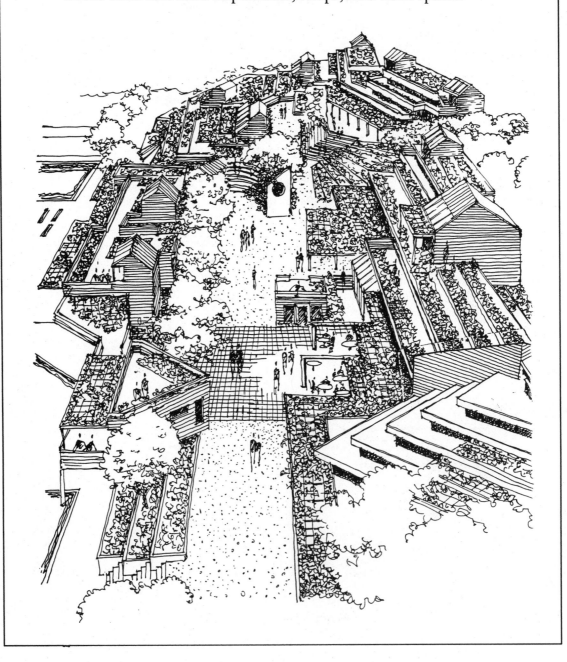

The south-facing hillside site lends itself to any of the three energy-form archetypes described earlier: the building on stilts, the earth-sheltered structure, and the sunspace. All of these are adaptable to the southern California climate, although climatic extremes in this region are not extreme enough to make earth sheltering an optimal solution.

In the interests of both demonstration and research, all three of these basic types will be represented at the Center, with each modified in some ways to suit local climatic conditions. The raised structure is located

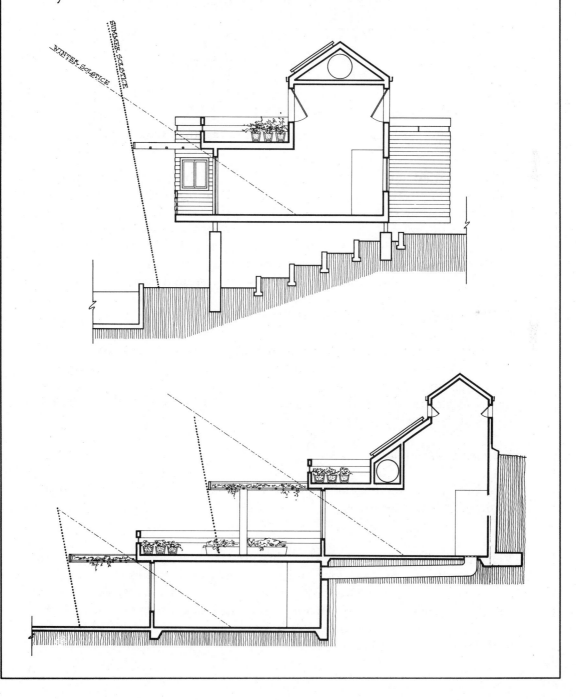

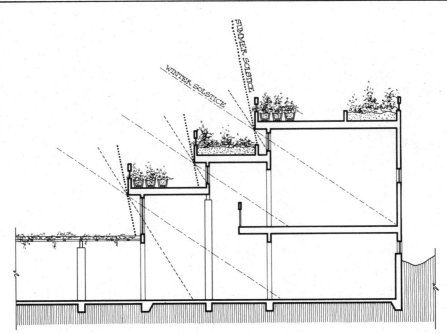

near the valley bottom on the edge of one of the aquacultural ponds, thereby taking advantage of the potential cooling effect of evaporation from the pond's surface. The earth-sheltered forms are located on the lower and middle slopes where the land is steep enough to accommodate their stepped configuration. In this situation, they are only partially earth-sheltered since the upper portions of the north-facing walls are above grade in order to allow for cross-ventilation. The sunspace forms are two stories in height and are sited on the upper slopes.

To reflect their close relationship with the earth, the buildings "step up" the knoll in a series of terraces in the same manner as most of the agricultural lands. The flat roofs serve many of the basic roles of the land surfaces they replace: for collecting rainwater, for collecting energy for water heating (through solar collectors mounted above the roof), for growing plants, and for human activity (mainly as roof decks related to some of the common rooms).

Interior Energy Flow

The buildings are designed to make maximum use of the five basic elements of interior energy flow.

Insulation
Placement of insulation is designed to control heat transfer between the building interior and exterior so as to minimize heat loss in winter and heat gain in summer. However, in this mild climate, extreme levels of insulation are not desirable. Roof insulation has a rating of at least R-30; flat roofs with food-growing areas have the added insulation value of the soil within the planters.

Transparent Surfaces

About 80 percent of the glass surfaces face within 22° of due south, where direct solar radiation can be allowed in when desired. Walls with this orientation are at least 50 percent glass. Glass is single-pane, non-reflective, and nontinted.

In the southern California climate, keeping building interiors cool in the summer is more difficult than keeping them warm in the winter. The potentially most effective strategies for summer cooling are minimizing solar gain during cooling periods, and promoting air flow.

Shading Devices

For minimizing solar gain during the summer, the use of plants as integral parts of the buildings is essential.

Most importantly, plant masses intercept solar radiation on the roofs and on the east and west walls of the buildings. In some places, the roofs will have a layer of soil for planting shallow-rooted flowers and vegetables. In others a system of modular containers will be used. These will be approximately 18 inches square and 10 inches deep, and they will be used for growing plants appropriate for such conditions as well as for starting seedlings for later transplanting. The leaves of these rooftop plants will intercept solar radiation, using much of it for photosynthesis. The soil will provide another layer of insulation, and irrigation water will provide evaporative cooling.

On the east and west ends of the buildings, trellis structures are mounted at a distance of about 4 feet from the building face. Deciduous vines (probably grapes) will grow on these structures, preventing direct radiation reaching building surfaces on hot summer days. During the winter, when they have no leaves and their branches are pruned back, the vines will allow 65 to 80 percent of the radiation to pass through.

Deciduous vines will also grow on outriggers projecting from the south walls of the buildings above the large areas of glass. Like the vertical trellises, these will shade the glass from the summer sun and allow most radiation to pass through and warm the buildings during the winter. On some of the buildings these outriggers will extend farther out to form arbors, shading the sitting areas underneath. In some cases, canopies will be used on the outriggers instead of vines to allow comparisons of their effectiveness in controlling solar radiation.

Finally, productive plants will grow in the sunspaces and behind other south-facing glass, taking advantage of the moderate microclimates created there. These will augment cooling by evapotranspiration from their leaf surfaces and will contribute oxygen to the building interiors while removing carbon dioxide and other gases. In this way they will help alleviate air-quality problems that can develop when buildings are sealed for environmental control.

Thermal Mass

The principal heat storage in all buildings excepting the raised structure is in the concrete floor and the earth underlying it. Most buildings also have some retaining walls backed by solid earth. The ratio of transparent surfaces to thermal surface is between 1 to 3 and 1 to 6. In the sunspace, translucent aquacultural tanks will add to the thermal storage capacity. The raised structure is designed for movable thermal materials, such as bags or tubes of Glauber's salts, to allow for comparative experiments.

Air Movement

All building forms facilitate air movement. Since prevailing breezes generally come from south to southwest, intakes are on the south faces. In some situations earth sheltering does not allow outlet windows in north-facing walls. In such cases, large ducts conduct the air flow from lower to upper levels. All buildings also have areas with high ceilings and outlet vents near the top to draw warm air upward.

In at least one building, earth tubes will also be used for cooling. These are simply long tubes about 8 to 12 inches in diameter buried in the ground. Outside air is drawn through them to take advantage of the relatively low ambient temperatures existing under the earth's surface.

The buildings are also designed for experimentation with various other devices that can be installed and removed easily. These include devices for heat storage and reflection, and fan and duct arrangements for moving air from one place to another.

Energy-performance models calculated for indicate that the buildings will need no additional heating or cooling. According to heat-loss calculations, the design described in this document will maintain the interior climates of all of the buildings within the human comfort zone without use of outside energy sources. To meet local code requirements, however, backup radiant electric heaters will be installed.

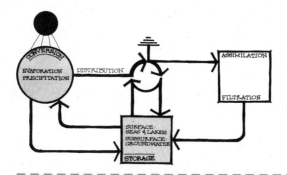

Chapter 6
Water: Going with the Flow

Arthur Jokela, Coauthor

The water cycle is among nature's more elegant and enduring inventions. The basic mechanisms are familiar and, in general outline, deceptively simple. Solar radiation provides the power-evaporating water, mostly from seas and lakes; the water vapor then rises into the atmosphere, forms clouds, and is carried by the wind over the land. It condenses, falls to earth, and flows on and through the land, supplying every living creature before eventually rejoining the seas and lakes to repeat the cycle.

That is the simple outline. The details are complex, always changing and easily altered.

Water Systems and the Water Cycle

Over the last 60,000 years humans have exerted an increasing influence that has often severely altered these long-evolved processes. In the complex web of interactions that comprise an ecosystem, sudden change made for a single purpose usually means severe disruption of processes not directly a part of that purpose.

Human Effects on the Water Flow

Following more or less the sequence in which they developed, we can group the human alterations of the water cycle into four general categories: watershed degradation, crop production, water diversion, and alteration of water chemistry.

Watershed Degradation

Humans first intervened in the water cycle by altering watersheds, and this remains the most important intervention. A watershed, which includes all the land draining into a single stream or river, is the basic land unit of the water cycle. Every watershed is unique, the product of centuries of adaptation and change in response to local conditions. When humans enter this picture, as they do with virtually every watershed on earth, they themselves become part of the process of water flow. Given the human power to reshape the land, they are also agents of change, usually sudden and abrupt change by the standards of geological time. Humans initiate watershed degradation mostly through alteration and removal of vegetation. This began long before re-

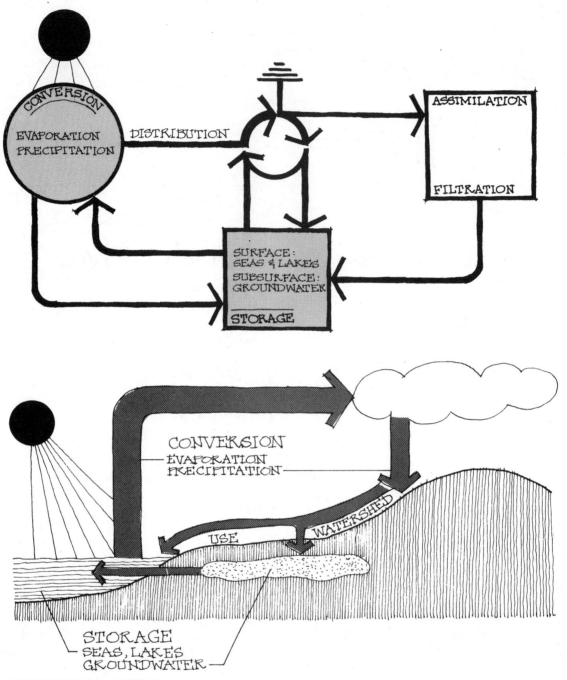

HYDROLOGIC CYCLE

corded history with the use of fire to clear forests. It has accelerated steadily since then, and increased to catastrophic magnitude, especially in most nonindustrial countries, in the last 50 years.

Plants play a multitude of fundamental ecological roles; they provide habitat for other plants and wildlife, use solar energy to create biomass, absorb carbon dioxide and give off oxygen to make the air we breathe, and hold the soil in place. When plant cover is removed, all of these processes are diminished. Among the most immediate effects is erosion. Of the earth's major human-related degenerative processes, soil erosion ranks among the worst.

In a healthy, well-vegetated landscape the plants slow the flow of water, trapping it temporarily on their leaves and branches, releasing it slowly, and providing a detritus layer on the ground into which it can soak. Their roots grasp the soil and prevent its washing away. A healthy landscape absorbs far more water into the ground than flows away on the surface. This water, stored in the soil, brings life to the land.

When plants are gone, erosion increases, and the soil that sustained life is carried to the bottoms of rivers and lakes to restrict their flows and cause flooding and other problems. In some river systems—for example, in the basin of China's Yellow River—immense floods caused by upstream vegetation loss have occurred periodically for centuries. Every year, rains wash tons of silts into the Yellow River, adding about $2\frac{1}{2}$ inches of mud to the river's bottom. One result of increasing volume of runoff in combination with decreasing river-channel capacity is periodic devastating floods. It is believed that as many as seven million people died in the Yellow River flood of 1887; over 3000 villages were flooded.

Most of the world's watersheds, which means most of its landscapes, are in various stages of degradation due to loss of plant cover. It has been estimated that, of the forests that covered over 60 percent of the earth's land surface before humans invented agriculture, less than half remain. The reasons are many, beginning with burning to flush out game and proceeding on to clearing for crops and grazing; cutting timber for fuel, ships, buildings, and paper; and myriad other uses, such as mining and road building.

A second major cause of watershed degradation is overgrazing. About one-quarter of the world's landscape is used as pasture or rangeland (Organization for Economic Cooperation and Development [OECD], 1991). There are no reliable statistics on what portion of this is in degraded condition, but the number is undoubtedly high. About one-quarter of China's grazing lands are degraded by overgrazing, a condition that has contributed considerably to flooding of the Yellow and other rivers (World Resources Institute [WRI], 1988). The amount of land worldwide converted to desert every year, primarily by overgrazing, is roughly 6 million hectares (WCED, 1987).

Crop Production

Just 12,000 years ago, some 50 millennia after learning to control fire, humans learned to cultivate plants and domesticate animals and thus introduced the next vehicle of change in the landscape: agriculture. Baring the soil to grow crops invites erosion even more quickly than does deforestation and overgrazing. The infrastructure associated with agriculture, wells, and small settlements has also contributed to altering the water regime.

As the global forest cover has diminished and rangelands expanded, crop areas have also expanded. About 11 percent of the global landscape is cropland (OECD, 1991). The effects of agriculture on watersheds have expanded with increasing irrigation and the use of chemical fertilizers and pesticides.

Water Diversion

About four thousand years after the first crops appeared in the Zagros Mountains, the first water diversion systems were installed not far from the base of those mountains in the Mesopotamian Valley. Though these early diversions were no more than simple ditches moving water from the Tigris and Euphrates rivers to fields of grain, they changed the world. Within several decades, the earliest cities were growing up on the banks of the irrigation channels (Wittfogel, 1956). The wheel was invented, written communication appeared, and civilization was underway.

Diverting water for irrigation made it possible to grow crops in arid climates, and very soon, thriving farmlands and cities were growing up in the valleys of the Nile, the Indus, and the Yellow River. The technology of water diversion, impoundment, and distribution developed and expanded through the following centuries, and became common practice even in areas of relatively high rainfall. In the 20th century, dams became the most dramatic symbols of industrial power and its ability to overwhelm nature. They came to epitomize the complex and far-reaching effects of industrial technology on natural systems.

Redistributing water for agricultural irrigation or urban use became a key component of the one-way flow system as it developed in the 20th century. The source in most cases is either groundwater pumped from deep wells or a reservoir created by impoundment of a flowing river. Often the places where the water is used are in different watersheds from where it is collected, a situation called inter-basin transfer.

Worldwide, water impoundments are increasing. In 1980 the Global 2000 Report projected that as much as 12,000 cubic kilometers of water would be stored in reservoirs by the year 2000 (Barney, 1980). This was more than three times the amount stored at that time. While comparable figures are not available for the present period, impoundments

■ ■

The Water Resources Plan for Sardinia

As part of a concentrated effort to improve the economy of the Italian island of Sardinia, the engineering staff of the regional water resources agency, Ente Flumendosa, worked in the 1970s and 1980s to develop a plan for exploiting the island's limited water resources. The plan they submitted included over 100 diversion projects, some of them massive in scale. Due mostly to environmental concerns, the plan was not approved by the regional legislature. Ente Flumedosa then contracted with Ambiente Italia, an environmental planning and analysis firm, to carry out an environmental assessment of the plan, including alternatives. Two American consultants, Professor Larry Cantor of the University of Oklahoma and myself, acted as advisors on environmental methodology.

The diagram on page 145 which shows in generic terms the areas affected by constructing a dam, serves as a common basis for initially identifying changes likely to result from any of the proposed projects. It can as well apply to any water-diversion project anywhere.

Since the hydrologic regime functions as a system in which every change brings other changes, it is important to consider the system as a whole. In moving through the system, water moves over the land and within it, with each piece of land along the way playing a different role in the total system. Since the project will affect each of these land areas differently, it is useful to define each of the component land areas with respect to its ecological role. The eight landscapes within a typical hydrologic system are described below:

A. *Area of Impoundment.* This is land area actually covered by the reservoir created by the dam along with its immediate environment. For larger projects there may be two or more reservoirs. The major impact in this part of the system is the actual covering of the land and the resulting disappearance of the terrestrial ecosystem.

B. *Watershed.* This includes all the land draining into the reservoir. While this land is little affected by the impoundment, conditions in the watershed strongly affect the quality and quantity of water in the reservoir. Excessive erosion in the watershed can shorten the reservoir's life through siltation. Thus, effective watershed management to minimize erosion and control runoff is an essential part of a water resources project and should also be part of the environmental analysis.

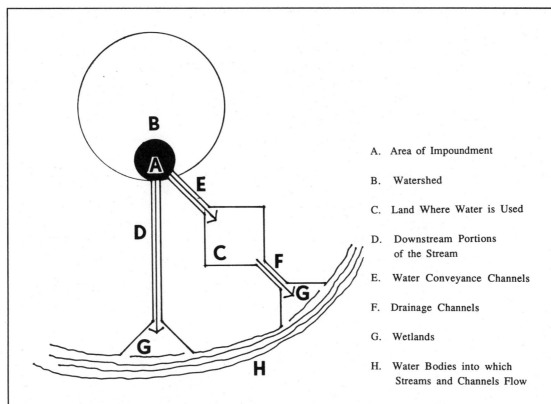

A. Area of Impoundment

B. Watershed

C. Land Where Water is Used

D. Downstream Portions
     of the Stream

E. Water Conveyance Channels

F. Drainage Channels

G. Wetlands

H. Water Bodies into which
     Streams and Channels Flow

WHOLE WATER FLOW SYSTEM AND RELATED LANDS

C.   *Lands Where the Water Is Used.* These are mostly irrigated lands which receive much more water than they would under natural conditions. This can cause a rise in the groundwater table and encourage the growth of species that did not live in this landscape when there was less water. Many of these are pests or disease carriers. In dryer landscapes, increased water usually brings increased deposition of salts, which can build up to the point of inhibiting plant growth.

D.   *Downstream Portions of the Stream.* The stream on which a dam is built will be severely altered in downstream areas. Water flow will be reduced, though it may be increased for short periods. This will alter plant and animal communities within the stream and the riparian communities on its edges. Since flooding will be reduced, floodplain communities will likely be affected. The reduced volume of water may also cause the groundwater table to decline.

E.   *Water Conveyance Channels.* These carry water where little water was present before and can therefore alter communities.

F.   *Drainage Channels for Irrigated Lands.* These also carry much more water than they did in the natural state, which can alter communities as well as raising the groundwater table. If chemical fertilizers and pesticides are used on these irrigated lands, these substances in the drainage water can cause additional problems.

G.   *Wetlands.* Water balances in wetlands are delicate and easily upset by alterations in flow. For coastal wetlands, the balance of fresh and salt water will be altered by the increase or decrease in water quantity, thus tending to alter natural communities and groundwater levels. Wildlife populations are usually especially rich in these areas.

H.   *Water Bodies into Which Streams and Drainage Channels Flow.* These may be rivers or the sea. Their natural communities are often upset by decreases in silt and nutrients resulting from impoundments and by pollutants carried by drainage water from agricultural areas.

I.   *Urban Areas.* Where water is to be used for industrial purposes or to support urban populations, it is important to consider the secondary impacts of those land uses. That is, can this environment support this density of population and human activity and the infrastructure that goes with it?

since 1980 have probably been less than projected, but are still considerable.

Especially where the source is an impoundment, we can summarize the effects of water redistribution very briefly: The portions of the system downstream of impoundment receive a much reduced and usually erratic volume of flow, while the watershed into which the water is carried receives increased amounts. Both the reduction and the increase in water volumes disrupt the ecosystems involved because they drastically change naturally evolved conditions. This brings changes in wildlife species and populations, in erosion and sedimentation rates, in chemical balances (especially those related to salts), in the groundwater table, and in other ecosystem components. In urban areas, changes in the volume of available water can bring population increase or population decline. In the Southern California urban area, the virtually unlimited availability of water diverted from distant watersheds removed the principal limiting factor for growth and allowed the population to grow far beyond the region's carrying capacity in other respects.

Increasing urban concentrations in turn alter the water regime in additional ways. Urbanization replaces plant cover with the hard, impermeable surfaces of roofs and paving. The amount of water absorbed by soil decreases, and the volume of storm-water runoff increases, sometimes severalfold. This increases the incidence of flooding. The Paleotechnic response to the problem of flooding is to move the water out as quickly as possible through concrete pipes and channels, thus completing the destruction of the evolved system of flow.

Alteration of Water Chemistry

Water is the principle vehicle in nature's evolved system for distributing materials. Every material applied to the land is sooner or later carried away by water to streams, rivers, wetlands, lakes, bays, seas, and oceans. In naturally evolved systems, the assimilation capacity of the water regime matches the materials-shedding habits of its landscape environs, so there is little or no surplus of materials to deal with. Agricultural and urban development, especially when carried out in the industrial mode, involve a great many substances introduced in quantities that the water system cannot assimilate. This is what we know as pollution.

Due to intensive use of chemicals and to prevailing cultivation and irrigation practices, agriculture is the greatest polluter of water. Both surface and groundwater in much of the world are badly polluted. In the United States, studies by the U.S. Geological Survey show that the dissolved oxygen, suspended sediments, phosphorus, nitrates, sulfates, and potassium contents of U.S. surface waters have all increased, as have acidity and turbidity, since 1974, in spite of extensive pollution control legislation (Conservation Foundation, 1984). Groundwater quality has correspondingly declined, especially in agricultural areas such as the midwestern states and California's Central Valley.

In addition to applied chemicals, soil salinization also presents serious problems. Especially in the semiarid regions of Africa and the American West, thousands of acres are taken out of production every year due to salinization brought on by overirrigation.

Industrial pollution also remains high, especially in areas of concentrated industrial development like the banks of the lower Mississippi River (the stretch known as Cancer Alley), despite federal laws and advances in pollution control technology.

Urban runoff, laden with petroleum products, lawn fertilizers, pesticides, organic matter, and general debris, has come to be recognized as a major pollution source as well. The EPA has become seriously concerned about urban runoff pollution and in 1990 issued the first regulations attempting to control its quality (U.S. EPA, 1990).

Sewage discharge remains a serious source of water pollution worldwide, even in the United States, where efforts to build adequate treatment plants have been heavily promoted and subsidized for over two decades. Many towns still lack adequate treatment facilities and routinely discharge untreated or partially treated sewage into surface waters. Even in most large cities, modern mechanical treatment plants frequently break down or become overloaded, forcing discharges of raw sewage.

Failure of Paleotechnic Solutions

Through the industrial era, water management practices have accelerated all of these interventions into the hydrologic cycle. Furthermore, response to these issues has generally involved the use of hardware to solve one problem at a time, thus continually expanding the throughput system of flow: Where pollution is a problem, we install pollution control devices. Where flooding is a problem, we build concrete channels to carry the water away more quickly.

There are several difficulties with such solutions. Important among these is their energy intensiveness. Controlling water requires large infusions of energy, as do mechanical pollution control devices. Even more important is the fact that such solutions address only one element enmeshed in a complex web of interacting processes. While a concrete channel may move the water away and solve the flooding problem in that particular place, it fails to deal with the groundwater regime, with the wildlife habitats of stream, wetland, and floodplain, with soil transport, with water supply—even with downstream flooding. These essential components of the ecosystem all become side effects, hardly noticed in the determination to solve one problem. Thus the solution to one problem often creates a number of others, some of them even more serious than the problem being solved.

To provide for ongoing renewal and thus sustainability, it is necessary to deal with the hydrologic system as a whole—that is, with the watershed unit. Whatever approach we take to planning and management, human activity will continue to alter the water regime. The alterations, however, need not be destructive. Within the watershed, in altering water flows we need to understand and apply nature's processes in ways that join into and become integrally part of the natural system. And we need to recognize and work with evolved capacities for distribution, assimilation and storage. In some cases, human alterations can even enhance regenerative qualities. A regenerative water system fosters the ongoing renewal of life as well as the ongoing renewal of the water resource.

Regenerative Water Systems

We face the challenge of providing for human needs while at the same time providing for the needs of other species and maintaining the healthy and sustainable functioning of the system. Accomplishing all of these simultaneously requires that we make full use of the natural processing capacities of the land. In using them well, the principles of natural ecosystems provide guidance.

Ecosystem Structure

Since all living things need it, water is an essential element of the structure of every ecosystem. Its role varies from one system to another. In the desert, where water is present in meager amounts—barely enough to sustain the lives of a few species that require relatively little—water is the limiting factor. If we introduce larger amounts of it, then other species that need more water tend to invade and the structure changes. In an aquatic system, by contrast, water is itself the medium within which the living community exists. If the water is removed, that structure disappears, to be replaced in time by an entirely new one. Thus water is a key factor in the structure of ecosystems. The power to guide the flow of water is the power to shape that structure, especially in arid and semiarid regions.

Ecosystem Function

Of the four major human alterations of water systems listed earlier in the chapter, the first three involve changes in the pattern of flow. Unless the alterations are planned as integral parts of the total system of flow from rainfall back to the sea, they inevitably disrupt ecosystem structures and bring about a degenerative spiral. Among the primary means for giving impetus to regenerative tendencies are those of flow regulation, allowing ample time for filtration and assimilation, and ongoing reuse.

While Paleotechnic hydrologic engineering depends mostly on speeding and simplifying the flow of water, nature's flows generally distribute water at a more leisurely and varied pace. Along its route, water slows down and spreads out in some places to serve meadows and other floodplain communities, to maintain soil moisture, or to be absorbed into underground aquifers for longer term storage. At times it settles into ponds or wetlands to support different communities of species. At other times it may flow rapidly, thus serving species like trout that require fast-moving, well-aerated water. Within the watershed system at any given time, there is water flowing or falling rapidly in some places and moving slowly in others: water spreading out in broad sheets, flowing in networks of channels, sitting in ponds or lakes, or hiding in crannies and crevasses in the depths of the earth. All work together in a kind of dynamic balance. These varied modes of movement make it possible for water to support regenerative processes in myriad ways. Flow systems shaped by humans can follow the same principles. Flows can be varied by applying a range of techniques for guiding the flow, for distributing water, for filtering it, for allowing its absorption and assimilation by various materials and species, and for storing it in surface ponds or subsurface aquifers.

Locational Patterns

In flowing over the land, water follows the ever-varying three-dimensional pattern of topography and soils. Each watershed has a unique set of physical characteristics that distinguish it from all other watersheds. Thus we might consider the earth's water regime as a mosaic of watersheds. This is one of the earth's most fundamental organizing patterns. It is a basis for regional identity and planning as well as a basis for land use and population distribution.

Within each watershed, topography, soils, and plant communities dictate the behavior of water, determining where it spreads or concentrates, whether it pools or soaks into the ground. Thus, regulating water flow is mostly a matter of shaping topography in places where the quality of soils is suitable to the purpose and in relation to human settlement and other activities.

Strategies for Regenerative Water Systems

Most of the general strategies for regenerative design listed in Chapter 3 are important in their specific applications to the design of water systems. The following are especially critical.

Letting Nature Do the Work

While industrial systems of water control rely on concrete and steel, pumps, and other mechanical devices, regenerative systems rely mostly on landform, soil, plants, and biological processes. Paleotechnic technologies for controlling water flow rely heavily on energy inputs which are primarily derived from fossil fuels; water flow and energy flow are inseparable. If carefully fitted to topography and soil, subtle and inexpensive landform alterations such as swales, berms, and depressions can serve to guide or slow the flow of water with little or no energy cost. The roots of trees can hold soil in place better than concrete; unlike concrete, roots do the soil no damage, and they require much less embedded energy. And some kinds of plants, along with their associated microorganisms, can very effectively draw nutrients and even some toxins and heavy metals out of sewage or runoff water. By working with nature in these ways, designing a regenerative water-flow system becomes a matter of providing optimum conditions under which nature can function most effectively.

Matching Means to Ends

In industrial society, water quality has long been a serious and vexing issue. Over two decades after passage of the Federal Water Pollution Control Act in

1972, pollution of rivers and bays by partially treated sewage and urban and agricultural runoff remains a serious problem. In other countries, especially third-world countries, the situation is even worse. As many as three billion people in the world lack access to potable water.

In other situations, water-quality standards are often unnecessarily high, especially those related to the permitted uses of reclaimed water. Customarily, we are required by law to use water of a quality suitable for human consumption to flush our toilets, irrigate our gardens, and even for some industrial processes.

With water, as with energy, quality is expensive. And sometimes, as with nutrient-laden sewage effluent applied to crop irrigation, lower-quality water can be better for a given purpose.

Simultaneous Solutions to Disparate Problems

Since water interacts with all other materials and processes, the opportunities for simultaneous solutions are considerable. For example, the New Alchemy Institute has used the water in translucent tanks for growing fish and as thermal mass in the sunspaces of passive solar buildings (Todd, 1977). Plants used in the process of biological sewage treatment grow at prodigious rates; they can be harvested and used for a variety of purposes, including animal feed and biogas digestion. Among the best means for returning treated water to underground storage are spraying and spreading it over the land, techniques easily combined with crop irrigation.

Prioritizing for Sustainability

Given the present state of technological development and present levels of population, regenerative practices are not capable of accomplishing every task along the path of water flow with the speed and precision that may be required. For a long time to come, we will continue to need concrete dams and channels and mechanical pumps. This means we will also have problems of integrating regenerative and industrial technologies for water management. Decisions will have to be made concerning the appropriate level of technology for any given situation. A prioritizing strategy that favors sustainability will be helpful in guiding these decisions. Thus, if a regenerative practice can do a given job, it should be favored over an industrial practice.

Practices and Technologies for Regenerative Water Management

Since control of water was among the earliest of human interventions in natural systems, the array of techniques for that purpose is vast and varied. And in this area, even more than in others, the distinction between regenerative and degenerative practices is sometimes unclear. It is a new restatement of an ancient distinction, and one with profound philosophical implications. In China two contrasting approaches to managing water have long existed side by side, reflecting the fundamental dichotomy that characterizes every aspect of Chinese culture. On the one hand, there are the Confucians, disciplinarians who follow a code of strict control down a narrow path. In dealing with water, the Confucians prefer to build constricting channels and massive dikes. Their way is to overpower water and move it to their will.

Taoists, by contrast, prefer to let both people and water go their own ways as much as possible. Thus their way with water is to let it spread, giving it gentle guidance as needed.

We can trace the contrasting approaches in China to times before recorded history. One ancient tale, repeated by Joseph Needham (1954), involves the work of an engineer named Kun, who lived in the time of the legendary Emperor Yao. There had been a long period of great floods, and Yao put Kun in charge of controlling the waters. Kun, who was clearly a Confucian, proceeded to build a system of narrow dikes. But the more dikes he built, the higher the waters rose. The penalty for failure being death, the Emperor Yao had him executed and his body dismembered.

Yao himself died soon after, and his successor, Emperor Shun, put Kun's son Yu in charge of flood control. Why Yu chose to accept the position is not explained in the legend, but he wisely adopted a strategy quite different from that of his father. Instead of channeling the rivers, he left their courses exactly as they were but dredged them out to provide capacity for more water. Thus the flood volumes were contained and flooding stopped. Yu went on to several other high offices in the kingdom and in time became a traditional culture-hero.

Despite the implications of the legend, the Confucian school has probably prevailed more often through Chinese history than the Taoist school; the results of this emphasis often have been disastrous in the long run. Though their approach requires

EXAMPLE

Check Dams on the Loess Plateau

In 1957 the Chinese began construction of a dam and hydroelectric plant on the Yellow River at Sen Men Sha with Russian aid. Thirty years later, silts had built up to such levels that water is now allowed to flow straight through the sluice gates during high-water periods, though they remain available for closing during disastrous floods. The turbines work only 7 months out of the year and generate about 20 percent of the electricity planned. What the Chinese learned from this experience is that downstream dams cannot solve flooding problems; rather the solutions lie in their origins upstream, in this case on the loess plateau that drains into the Yellow River. Dams are ineffectual in the lower reaches of dysfunctional watersheds.

Before Chinese farmers began growing crops on the plateau above the dam, the terrain was relatively flat, covered with forests and grasslands. Now it is a badland, carved into a jagged pattern of deep gullies. An average of over 2 inches of soil washes into the river each year. No dam can function for long under such conditions.

Some farmers have been working for 40 years to address the problem in a small way by rebuilding the landscape. Using shovels and wheelbarrows, they work in small groups building check dams across the gullies. The dams are small, constructed of silts brought in by wheelbarrow and compacted by pounding it with stones. Most of the dams are in the range of 15 to 30 feet high with sloping walls. Once the dam is built, silts collect rapidly behind it, creating after a single rainy season a gently sloping area of rich cropland. Water drains through the dam in pipes.

The farmers' efforts may or may not be reconstructing the landscape faster than it is destroyed by erosion. In any case, they are struggling against government policies that emphasize short-term productivity and thus support Paleotechnic endeavors like the dam project. In Mao's era, national food-production policies forced farmers on highly unsuitable lands on the plateau to remove trees and grow grain, thus accelerating the centuries-old process of erosion. Recent changes have allowed the farmers to choose their own crops and farming systems. This has resulted in diversification of crops, especially in the planting of a great many fruit trees to hold the soil in place.

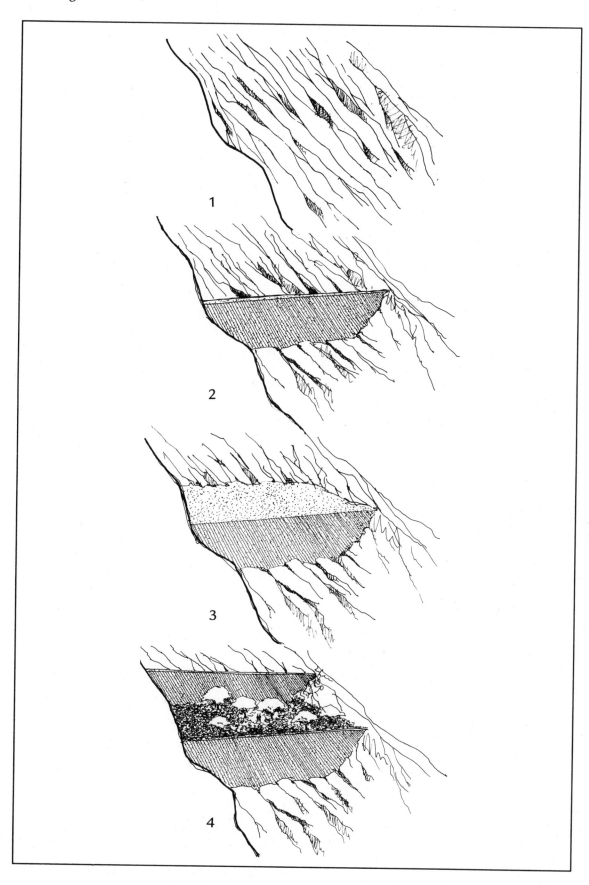

more time and more land, the Taoists often have had their way as well. Which approach was followed in each water resource project seems to have depended on the philosophical orientation of the people in power at the moment. Over time however, according to Needham (1954), whichever approach may have been followed in a project's beginnings, there was an evolutionary tendency for the two ways to merge. Where a stream was forced into a narrow channel, retention basins sometimes appeared in order to absorb the overflowing waters of peak floods. And where Taoist engineers provided broad floodplains, low dikes were often built near the stream's normal course to contain minor floods and allow the use of large areas of the floodplain for growing crops.

While the Chinese, with their particular talent for attaching larger meaning to even the most routine events, have articulated the differences and their significance more clearly than others, virtually every society's approach to water management has fallen into one category or the other. Paleotechnic water management is fundamentally Confucian, while the Neotechnic approach is fundamentally Taoist. Furthermore, the merging tendency still exists.

Basis in Nature

The naturally evolved hydrologic cycle is the organizing system for all human use of water. Water-related practices and technologies must necessarily function within that framework. Achieving sustainability with respect to water use means integrating our water system with the hydrologic cycle in such a way that the dysfunctions discussed earlier no longer exist. A range of practices and technologies are available for accomplishing this.

Following are general descriptions of a number of these. It is not a comprehensive listing but only a sampling intended to convey the general character of water-related regenerative practices and technologies. They are grouped under the headings that suggest means for reversing or stabilizing the four general types of human intervention in the hydrologic cycle:

- protecting the watershed
- controlling agricultural runoff
- reducing water diversions
- controlling water chemistry

Protecting the Watershed

Within the intricate tangle of processes that make up the watershed unit, probably the most pivotally important to the health of the unit as a whole are those that occur soon after the water falls to the earth as rain, before it begins to converge in rivers. Throughout history, degradation of the world's major river systems has usually begun with vegetation loss in the upper reaches of their watersheds.

Watershed regeneration is an immense subject that can easily fill several volumes. Moreover, it is a major global issue that should be near the top of every environment agenda over the next few decades. Given the immensity, complexity, and importance of the subject, we can hardly do more here than sketch a few of the more important techniques involved.

Watershed management usually focuses on specific sets of objectives. Common among these are preservation of the natural community, water yield, timber yield, and support of grazing animals. Where the natural community is the main concern, the purpose of management is simply to preserve and enhance the native vegetation. Where it is timber or water yield or a combination of the two, there are inherent conflicts because each of the two resources depends on the other but in some ways also impedes the other.

Forests, Timber and the Integrity of Watersheds

The roots of trees hold soil in place and thereby help to slow and absorb runoff water. They also pump water out of the soil, up through their trunks and branches to their leaves, where the water is released into the atmosphere through the processes of transpiration and evaporation. If the primary objective is water yield, the land manager prefers to have as few plants, as small and limited in their water requirements, as possible. Where the first priority is timber yield, emphasis is on the maximum number of trees, recognizing that they will consume water and reduce the amount available as runoff. Paleotechnic management often promotes clear-cutting, which means removing all trees in an area, thus maximizing short-term timber production. Since it eliminates transpiration, clear-cutting also maximizes water yield for a very short time. But as the unprotected soils soon begin to wash away, the forest's capacity for regeneration diminishes. Water yields may remain high, but eroded materials carried downstream tend to fill lakes, reservoirs, wet-

CLEAR CUTTING

PATCH CUTTING

THINNING

lands, and bays; raise streambeds; and cause flooding. Since clear-cutting progressively degrades the watershed's capacity to support life, it is a fundamentally degenerative technique.

Regenerative management requires that the goal of watershed sustainability be incorporated in all management programs. This involves leaving some trees in place to protect the soil and foster new growth. The pattern of trees left standing in both age composition and location is important to forest health. In general, there are two basic patterns:

Patch Cutting. In patch cutting, trees are harvested in strips or small areas, each with dimensions of 100 to 300 feet. The harvested patches usually add up to between one-third and one-half of the total forest. Besides reducing transpiration by this amount, in snowfall regions the patches provide places where snow can collect and thus yield more snowmelt water in the spring. The effects on water quality are similar to those of clear-cutting but are much reduced because speed and volume of runoff are interrupted by areas of forest cover.

Thinning. Thinning involves removing single trees in a somewhat uniform pattern that leaves the whole forest less dense. It requires more time and care than clearing and patch cutting and yields less timber, but is more effective in maintaining the quality of both water and forest. The best thinning practices require carefully selecting trees to be cut on the basis of size, health, location, and species mix. This is the basis for the "new forestry" practices instituted by the U.S. Forest Service in some areas in response to widespread opposition to clear-cutting.

These two techniques can be applied on a sustained-yield basis—that is, no more trees are removed than the forest can spare without diminishing its capacity for continuous regeneration. "Sustained yield" is a concept in most areas of natural resource management, particularly important in its application to grazing lands.

Grazing at Carrying-Capacity Levels
This pattern can maintain watershed quality, but it is extremely difficult to carry on over extended periods of time. Throughout history, overgrazing has been a principal cause of landscape degradation as human populations have grown, thus requiring ever more animals to the point where they destroy the vegetation cover. This is particularly a problem in

semiarid grasslands, which are subject to desertification as vegetation is removed. The science of range management is capable of estimating the carrying capacity, which is the number of animals any given land area can support on a sustained yield basis. However, since this number is usually relatively low for exotic animals, the temptation to increase herd sizes beyond this capacity in order to increase short-term yields can be overwhelming.

Controlled Burning
In some situations controlled burning is a useful technique for vegetation control. In fire-adapted communities, such as the California chaparral, burning can destroy invasive exotic species while accelerating regeneration of natives, thus restoring a landscape to its naturally evolved condition. In other communities, burning can repeatedly retard succession; this is commonly done in grasslands devoted to grazing, where managers want to prevent trees from moving in. It also reduces brush and heavy undergrowth as well as returning nutrients quickly to the soil. Burning was the first land management technique, and it may still be the most common one worldwide.

Revegetation
Where topography is severely altered, especially where steep slopes are created as in road cuts or strip mines, natural regeneration may take centuries; human intervention in the form of reseeding quickens the pace severalfold. In these cases the soil cover has often been removed or washed away before revegetation begins. Because natural soil is a scarce commodity, a substitute is needed. Waste materials such a sewage sludge often can provide effective soil substitutes, an example of simultaneous solutions to the disparate problems of soil depletion and waste disposal. We will discuss the subject in more detail in Chapter 8.

In dry landscapes, especially where slopes are steep, effective revegetation requires reshaping the land in subtle ways to promote water retention.

Controlling Agricultural Runoff: Shaping the Land to Hold Water and Soil

Where farms and grazing lands replace the natural cover, the problem of stabilizing both water flow and soil is much more complex, requiring the shaping of a new landscape that merges the utility of human land use with the ongoing functions of natural processes. Following the tenth strategy, land can be shaped to slow the flow, to hasten it, or to stop it altogether.

Perennial Crops

Where large land areas are used for crops, watershed protection is especially difficult. The most ideal agricultural practice for soil protection is the use of perennial plants, with permanent roots to hold the soil in place. Once established, perennial crops do not require soil disturbance. Wes Jackson's Land Institute in Salina, Kansas has long been involved in research to expand the numbers of food-producing perennial species (Jackson, 1980). The number of such species is still small, however, which means the best means in common practice involve ways of shaping the land.

Contour Plowing

It is a simple and rather obvious fact that by plowing along the contours of sloping land and thus keeping the furrows horizontal, it is possible to hold water in the furrows while it soaks into the soil. This minimizes the amount of water flowing off the land while slowing the velocity of flow; at the same time it provides a maximum amount of water for the crops. What it requires is a higher degree of skill on the farmer's part since the form of a hill is more difficult to follow than a straight line. Contour strip cropping, which involves alternating different crops along the contour lines is even more effective.

Contour plowing is an effective technique on slopes up to about 8 percent. Steeper slopes than that require more drastic means like terracing.

Terracing

Carving long steps into the hillsides and using the relatively flat surfaces of the steps for growing crops is an ancient practice seen in every part of the world where food is grown on hills. In some places, like

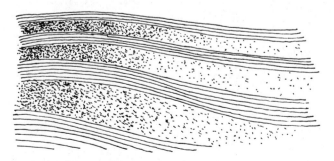

CONTOUR STRIP CROPPING

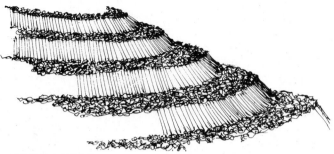

TERRACING

the tea-growing areas in the mountains of Japan or the vineyards on the slopes overlooking the Rhine, terracing techniques have reached a level of sophistication and extraordinary beauty that qualifies them as earth sculpture. Such landscapes have produced high yields for centuries with little loss of soil.

In other places, like some slopes of the Himalayas, terraces have crumbled, baring and eroding the soil and diminishing the crop-growing surface. This is the result of poorly designed, hastily constructed terraces. In regions where populations are growing and the available food-producing land is already producing to capacity, there is a temptation to terrace hillsides that are too steep or that have highly erodible soils. It is tempting as well to increase the steepness of slopes between terraces in order to increase the flat area. All of these actions lead to crumbling away of the terraces and loss of topsoil. In addition to increased erosion the crumbling also means constant need for repair and rebuilding, which drain human energy.

For every soil there is a natural maximum slope at which it is fairly stable, called the angle of repose. For most soils, the angle of repose is approximately two horizontal units to one vertical unit. When unplanted terraces exceed this angle, they erode rapidly. If plants cover the slopes, if their foliage prevents rain or wind from striking the soil directly, and if their roots grasp the soil and hold it in place beneath the surface, then the slope can be steeper. There is still a limit, however, and labor is required to maintain the plant cover.

In India, farmers use deep-rooted native vetiver grass to hold soil in place on sloping land. Planted in dense parallel rows following the contours, the roots and lower stalks of the grass hold back the downhill flow of water long enough for it to soak into the soil. In time, silt trapped behind the grass rows builds up to form narrow terraces that have proven exceptionally fertile. The root system of vetiver grass can extend as deep as 12 feet, which makes it exceptionally effective for erosion control in a variety of situations. It is now used in a number of countries other than India. Its effects on ecosystems outside its native range still need more study, however.

It is also possible to structurally stabilize the slopes of the terraces using stones. In the dry Sahel region of Africa, small farmers commonly place rocks jamming them tightly together in long rows spaced 10 to 30 feet apart on gently sloping land to serve the same purpose as the vetiver grass in India. Such is the pace of soil erosion in this region that it is often possible to harvest crops a year after the rocks are in place. Some cultures have developed intricate techniques for setting the stones in such ways that they lock each other in place, requiring no mortar. Others use bricks or concrete blocks with mortar joints, or poured concrete. Crib walls, which use modular masonry or wood units stacked in a stepping series, have also been developed in recent years. Some of these use units that are open in the middle and thus allow for planting in the wall itself.

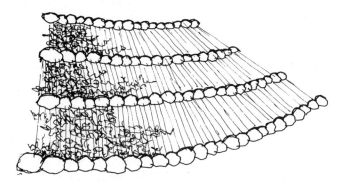

ROCKS ON CONTOURS

Slowing Stream Courses

Where the water flow in a small stream has been hastened by upstream disturbance, it can be useful to slow the course of the water to allow it time to spread and infiltrate. The pattern and pace of water distribution are critical to the health of the watershed. Slowing can also allow time for silts to settle out. If the momentum of a stream is reduced, downstream erosion is also reduced.

CHECK DAMS / The most common means of slowing streams is the check dam, which can be constructed of soil, rocks, woven branches, or other

SECTION: EARTHEN CHECK DAMS

materials. Check dams slow the flow by holding back a small part and allowing most of the water to move over or through. They work best if they do not try to block the flow entirely, as a concrete dam would, but simply hold most of the flow back while allowing a small part to move through. This produces less stress on the structure and makes for a longer life.

Such small dams are especially effective in the intermittent streams of arid and semiarid landscape, where they can stretch the time that water has to do its work. The Native Americans of the southwestern United States used check dams to maximize the water available to their crops during the short rainy seasons. Water trapped behind check dams can be distributed to land on both sides by ditches reaching out and sloping very gently downward along the contours.

Check dams are small, generally 3 to 10 feet high. Dams this size usually have no damaging effects on the larger pattern of water flow or on the environment as a whole. They can be designed to store only the water collecting behind them, to spread the water over a larger area, or to divert it to a small tank, reservoir, or recharge basin. Where check dams are built in streams that are heavily silt-laden, silts are trapped behind the dams and in time build up to form a flat land surface that can be exceptionally fertile.

GABBIONS / One type of check dam that has proven especially useful and long-lived is the gabbion. A gabbion consists of two wire-mesh fences stretched across a stream about 1 to 2 feet apart, with the space between the two screens filled with rocks. When first constructed, gabbions allow much

GABBION CHECK DAMS

of the stream water to flow through, but in time, as debris collects, more water is retained. In a well-aged gabbion the screen and rocks are often hardly visible within a covering of leaves, branches and mud. Silts also build up behind the rocks to form a flat surface as with other types of check dams.

The gabbion principle can also be applied in stabilizing stream banks as well as other applications. For example, in revitalizing riparian zones within Trexler Memorial Park in Allentown, Pennsylvania, the Andropogon design group installed gabbions against eroded stream banks. These provided a supporting matrix for the buildup of soil and colonizing by communities of streamside plants (McCormick, 1991).

Reducing Water Diversion

So overwhelming and far-reaching are the environmental changes brought about by impoundment and redistribution of water that it is essential to establish alternative means for making water available where needed. The first rule, as with energy use and indeed all resources, is to use no more than necessary for any given purpose. In the industrial world and especially in the United States, the extremely wasteful practices of the past provide us with considerable opportunities for using less.

The second avenue is to make more water available in the area where it falls. Here too the practices of the past leave numerous opportunities for improvement. Care is needed to avoid the mistakes of the past. In dealing with water systems, it is best to think not of producing or obtaining water but of borrowing it for temporary use. Where to borrow water from the hydrologic cycle, and where and in what condition to return it, are crucial questions in maintaining the integrity of the whole water-flow process.

In focusing on the dramatic engineering feats involved in Paleotechnic practices of redistributing water over the landscape, planners often overlook the potentials for using water available on a given piece of land. They also commonly ignore or undervalue the available means for conserving water through efficient practices and technologies and thus overestimate the volumes of water needed for both agricultural and urban uses. Such oversights have led to the construction of water-diversion projects far larger than actually needed, including some not needed at all. Following is a brief discussion of some techniques for making on-site water available for use in rural and urban settings and for achieving maximum efficiency in the use of water in agricultural irrigation.

Water Harvesting

Even in dry climates, minimal and subtle alterations in landforms and vegetation can guide water into places where it can be stored or used to grow crops. Among the most ancient techniques for accomplishing this are the catchment devices developed over 2000 years ago by the Nabateans. These devices were a means for making the most of the meager rainfall in the arid hills of the Negev Desert and the Arabian Peninsula (Evanari and Koller, 1956). The catchment device consisted of two parts: a watershed and a growing area. Water falling in the watershed, which was 17 to 30 times the size of the growing area, flowed through a series of natural channels and streams. These brought the water to a flatter valley, where a human-made system of broad channels crossed at intervals by dikes made by piles of rock held the water back to supply crops growing in the floodplain. Although modern-day reconstructions have demonstrated the effectiveness of this technique, it is probably too limited in scale to have widespread contemporary application. Furthermore, the loess soils of this area tend to harden and become almost impermeable when wet, thus making the volume of runoff comparatively high. Nevertheless, the general principle of carefully guiding water, from where it falls to where it can be used, is applicable anywhere.

KEYLINING / Bill Yeomans, an Australian farmer, pioneered the keyline technique on his own farm, demonstrating that it could provide large volumes of water even in a relatively dry landscape and that

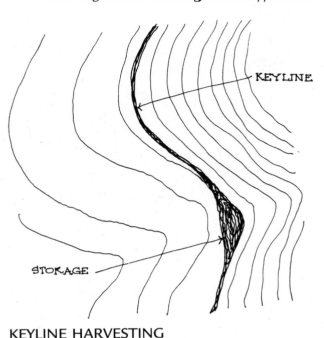

KEYLINE HARVESTING

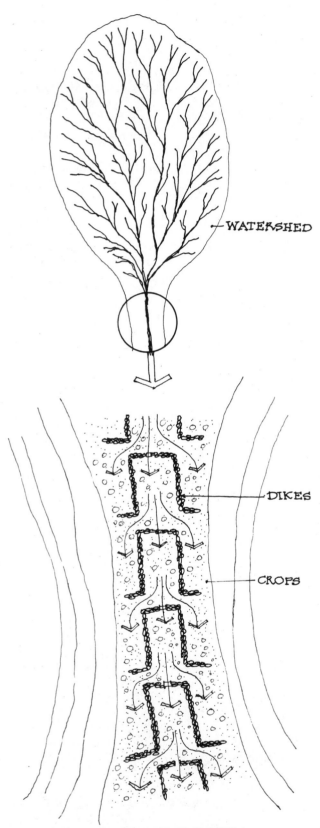

NABATEAN CATCHMENT SYSTEM
After Envanari and Koller, 1956

the water in turn could provide high crop yields if combined with tillage techniques that minimally disturb the soil.

The keyline of a hillside is that line where the slope visibly becomes less steep. We can easily see it on most slopes. It is usually somewhat closer to the base than to the peak of the hill. Within a stream or drainage channel, the profile of the stream shifts from convex to concave at a point on the keyline, which is the keypoint (Mollison, 1988). On that line, water can easily be trapped by minor changes in landform—a small ditch or reservoir, for example. Once trapped, the water can be guided slowly and distributed to ponds along the keyline, always using the guiding capacity of the landform and the energy of gravity. As with the Nabatean system, endless variations on the keyline technique are possible, following the principle of minimal disturbance. On one 758-acre (307-hectare) hillside, Yeomans developed a keyline system that included 16 small reservoirs fed by channels on the keyline; these collected both rainfall and irrigation runoff water.

At its most extreme, water harvesting can mean covering an area of land with an impervious surface such as a plastic sheet or nonporous asphalt and catching the water as it runs off. In this way, hardly any water is lost to soil or evaporation. However, the land so covered is killed; in the Paleotechnic tradition of emphasizing productivity to the exclusion of other goals, all processes other than water collection abruptly cease. The soil is dead, there is no photosynthesis, no wildlife, no succession or evolution. Nevertheless, in urban settings, where impermeable surfaces like play courts, plazas, and the roofs of buildings serve other purposes, such water harvesting is useful.

On land that is otherwise alive and productive, it is best to practice water harvesting in concert with other processes. Subtle variations in landform can guide water to retention basins, dry wells, or tanks, where it can be stored. Shallow swales are among the devices useful for this purpose; to increase water yield, they can be covered with an impervious material such as clay.

While such techniques can be applied on a small scale to irrigate a single field or a few trees, they can also be applied to organizing larger basins, called microcatchments, for collecting and using runoff. Carefully located plantings, like the Indian vetiver grass mentioned earlier, can also contribute to trapping and holding water. In using plants, there is always a tradeoff between water conserved and water lost to evapotranspiration. This means it is important to select plants carefully for adaptation to the local water regime. Plants that evolved in dry climates, for example, generally have low evapotranspiration rates.

Combinations of water-harvesting techniques that include small storage reservoirs can provide yields high enough to serve as effective alternatives to large impoundment projects. The Environmental Defense Fund has analyzed such a plan as an alternative to the massive proposed dam in India, finding it just as effective and about half as costly (Postel, 1989).

Urbanization and Runoff Water

Especially in urban areas, techniques for holding water in the area where it falls as rain provide an alternative pattern of distribution to storm drainage systems, which speed it away. Storm drainage systems are expensive and energy-intensive; they create a need for even larger structures downstream, and they usually make the water unavailable for further use.

Some flood-control jurisdictions in the United States have adopted "zero runoff" policies, requiring that the volume of runoff from a piece of land in its developed state be no greater than the volume in its natural state. The Maryland Stormwater Man-

agement Act, for example, states that its "primary goal is to maintain after development as nearly as possible the predevelopment runoff characteristics" (Stormwater Management Division, 1984, p. 1-1). Some of the means for accomplishing such a goal are the following.

DETENTION BASINS / These are like large bowls set in the landscape to hold water temporarily during heavy rainfall and release it slowly for some time after the rain ceases. Where space is limited, detention basins can also be installed underground. Usually a detention basin features an overflow pipe to carry the water away when it reaches a level near the basin's capacity. While detention basins spread the water flow over longer periods and thus reduce the need for flood-control structures, they are not truly regenerative in the sense that they do not necessarily make water available for recharge and reuse. It is important that detention systems be planned on a watershed basis so that flows are distributed through time. Otherwise, several detention basins might delay flows for equal periods, then discharge simultaneously into a common stream. This does not reduce flooding but simply delays, and it some cases increases, it (Ferguson, 1991).

INFILTRATION BASINS / Sometimes called retention basing, infiltration basins are, like detention basins, large bowls in the land surface. Rather than holding water to release it, however, they hold water for infiltration into the ground where it is stored for future use. The Maryland Stormwater Management Standards define a retention or infiltration basin as "a water impoundment made by constructing a dam or an embankment or by excavating a pit or dugout in or down to relatively permeable soils" (Stormwater Management Division, 1984, p. 3-2). The more permeable the soil, the faster the infiltration process and the smaller the basin can be for a given area of land drained. Soils with infiltration rates of less than 27 inches per hour are usually not suitable for infiltration basins.

The functions of detention and retention are sometimes combined in a single basin by providing an outlet above the bottom. Above the outlet is a detention basin, below it a retention basin. This device is especially useful in flood-prone areas.

The surfaces of both detention and retention basins are usually covered with plant materials, although they can also be lined with rock or gravel.

EXAMPLE

Earthworks Park

The storm-water retention system in the town of Kent in upper Washington State came about in an unusual way, and the results are unusual as well. The Seattle Art Museum sponsored an exhibition exploring the possibilities of earth sculpture, and one of the sites was the mouth of a canyon that runs through the center of Kent. For this site, artist Herbert Bayer designed a series of large earth sculptures that also serves as a recreation area and an infiltration basin.

A stream called Mill Creek runs along the canyon floor with a rich mix of riparian plants growing on its banks up to the base of the canyon walls. A canopy of tall deciduous trees shades the stream and the flatland on both its sides. All this remains in its natural state up to about 1000 feet before the canyon opens out into the town center of Kent. In this thousand feet is Bayer's earth sculpture/infiltration basin. It includes several small wetlands reaching out from the edges of the stream and two large ponds also fed by the stream. One of these is circular with a doughnut-shaped island that seems to float inside. Ducks particularly like to play in the protected area of the inner pond. The second pond is larger and forms a swimming hole for children.

Except for streamside vegetation, which remains along Mill Creek's edges, the ground is covered in turf. It is heavily used for picnics, sunbathing, and games. There is also a system of winding walkways and bridges and an amphitheater at the base of the canyon wall on one side. Altogether, it is a splendid blend of art, play, and ecological function; it has much to tell us about what the future can look like.

EXAMPLE

■■

Arroyo Seco

Runoff water and snowmelt flowing from the slopes of the San Gabriel Mountains on the edge of the southern California conurbation are concentrated in a series of streams and washes at the base of the mountains. From there the water moves over the heavily populated basin through concrete channels that were once free-flowing rivers to the sea. Above the city of Pasadena, mountain runoff water collects in the Devil's Gate Reservoir before being concentrated in a concrete channel that passes through a much broader natural canyon called the Arroyo Seco. Along its journey through the Arroyo Seco, the channel collects additional runoff water from the surrounding city of Pasadena. Then it moves on to join the wider, deeper concrete channel that now encases the Los Angeles River, through which it flows to the Pacific Ocean.

The concrete channel within a natural channel was built during the 1930s. Since then, the Arroyo landscape has deteriorated, but it still serves as a linear park through the city. It is a uniquely quiet green environment, separated by steep canyon walls from urban activity, but extensively used only by a few special interest groups for activities like archery.

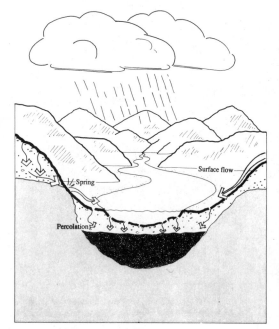

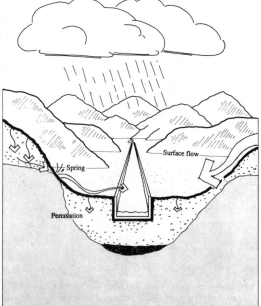

WATER FLOW: HISTORIC   WATER FLOW: PRESENT

Due mostly to concern for the degraded natural communities and the sporadic use of the park, the city of Pasadena commissioned the 606 Studio to develop a master plan for the lower portion of the Arroyo Seco. Professor Roland Ross of California State University in Los Angeles had carried out detailed studies of the plant species on the site, documenting the loss of native species and proliferation of exotics over time after the channel's construction.

The key fact that emerged from analyses of Ross's work and other studies was the fundamental importance of water as the controlling element in the Arroyo's ecology. The concrete channel had severely altered the water regime of the Arroyo Seco by curtailing the occasional overflows that covered the canyon floor and by cutting off percolation to soil and underground storage (606 Studio, 1988a). These changes then reduced the diversity of plant communities by eliminating species that required the occasional flood or whose roots tapped into the groundwater. Since the animal community is directly dependant on the plant community, the loss of plants brought about a reduction in animal populations. The overall result was a badly degraded ecosystem. The lack of water, and the diminished natural community resulted in reduced human use of the Arroyo as well.

Had this degradation of the Arroyo landscape been the necessary result of protecting the surrounding urban areas from flooding, then we might say it was justified. However, such was not the case. The Studio's hydrologic studies showed that the walls of the Arroyo were more than high enough to contain any flood that might occur. The narrow concrete channel within the much larger natural channel was unnecessary. As is typical of such massive projects, the Los Angeles flood-control system was concerned with general abstract issues without consideration for specific landscapes. Instead, the same standard solution to the flooding problem was applied along the entire length of the river.

The first step in restabilizing a viable natural community is to restore the natural system of water flow, the key processes of assimilation, filtration and storage. This means removing the concrete channel and reestablishing the stream. Unfortunately, at the lower end of the portion of the Arroyo that carves through Pasadena is a small group of houses sitting on the Arroyo flow.

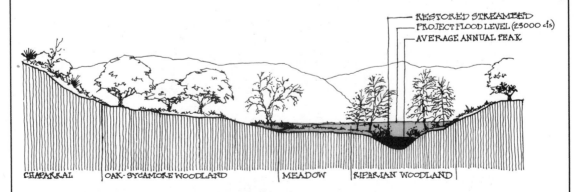

SECTION: THROUGH THE ARROYO SECO
After 606 Studio, 1988

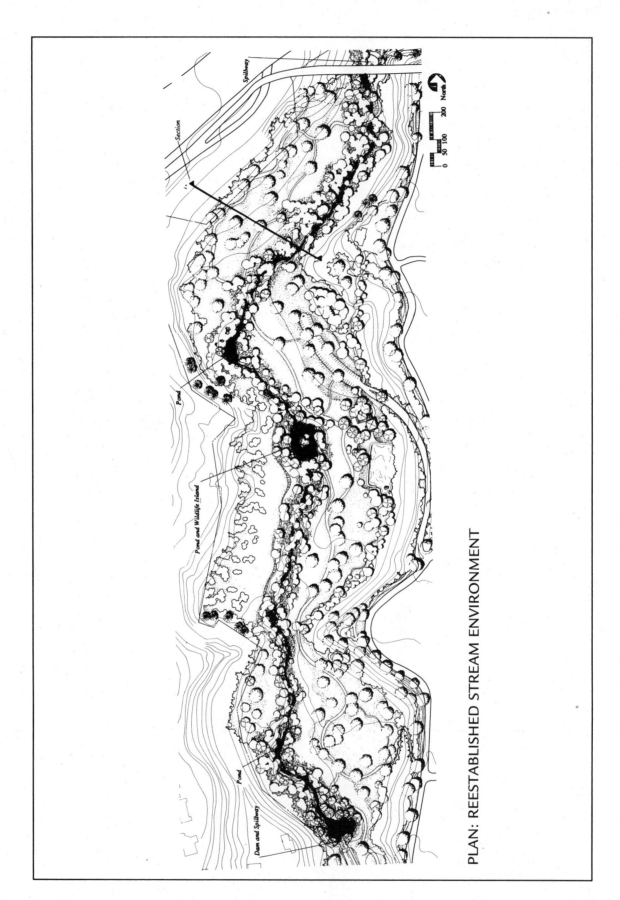

PLAN: REESTABLISHED STREAM ENVIRONMENT

164

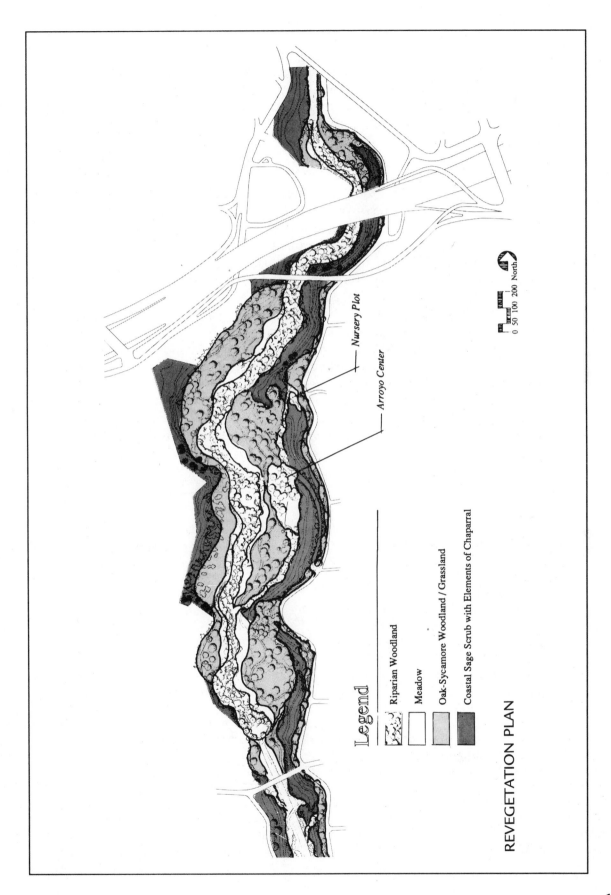

Legend

Riparian Woodland

Meadow

Oak-Sycamore Woodland / Grassland

Coastal Sage Scrub with Elements of Chaparral

Nursery Plot

Arroyo Center

0 50 100 100 200 North

REVEGETATION PLAN

These were built after the channel; thus are bad decisions compounded and rendered permanent. To protect these houses, it will be necessary to build an earthen dam about 8 feet high upstream from them and then return the water to the channel below the dam. After that the concrete channel will continue until it has passed the houses.

The earthen dam will hold back floodwaters and convert the Arroyo into a giant infiltration basin (see section). This will serve to reduce the danger of downstream flooding and thus allow more options in redesigning the flood-control system between the Arroyo Seco and the Pacific Ocean. It also means that the Arroyo's recreational areas will have to be designed for periodic flooding. The recreation areas will be many and diverse, but generally quiet, including areas for fishing, hiking, games, picnicking, and nature study and interpretation. There will also be sizable areas of wildlife reserve where humans are not invited in order to leave the wildlife undisturbed.

The stream course itself, while it will be returned to its natural function, need not be a faithful restoration of the original. Rather, it will have large and small ponds along the way for fishing, recreation, and wildlife habitat. The pond edges will be complex in form to maximize the all-important pond-edge habitat. The native plant communities of the riparian edge, valley floor, and slopes are being reestablished by a cooperative effort of local environmental groups (see plan and section). In its new form, the Arroyo Seco will support a richer, more numerous and diverse natural community than even it did before the channel was constructed.

POROUS PAVING / Since impermeable paving is a major contributor to increases in urban runoff, paving surfaces that allow water to soak into the ground can contribute to stabilizing the water table. Gravel and unit pavers with soil or sand in the joints can accomplish this, as can concrete paving units with open cells in which plants can grow. Some composition paving materials also allow some portion of the water on their surfaces to soak through. Porous asphalt is inexpensive although toxic to soils.

ROOFTOP COLLECTION / Conventionally, the roofs of building are designed to shed water as quickly as possible. While this does help to minimize leaks, it also increases the volume of water to be absorbed by the land around the building. Alternatively, if water can be held on the rooftop, it can be released slowly. Water stored on a rooftop can also serve as insulation and as thermal storage for passive solar heating.

CISTERNS / Tanks placed in the basement or underground for storing water collected on rooftops are called cisterns. They have long been used in dry climates, where it is important to collect every available drop of water.

DRY WELLS / Water can also be directed by downspouts from a rooftop into rock-filled pits called dry wells. After collecting in the spaces around the rocks, the water then soaks slowly into the ground as it does in a retention basin. Dry wells are typically 3 to 12 feet deep. They are especially useful where ground area is limited and where water concentrates, as, for example, at the base of downspouts.

SWALES / On gently sloping land, water can be intercepted in swales. These are shallow ditches that run parallel to the contours, collecting and directing its flow for infiltration without concentrating it in amounts that can cause erosion. It is important that the swale surfaces be covered by materials, such as plants or rocks, that both protect the soil from erosion and allow water to move through and into the soil surface. Swales hold water only for brief periods following a rain or irrigation application. Small check dams, 6 to 24 inches high, can hold the water back for longer periods. Even without check dams, most of the water flowing into swales soaks into the soil. Where flood control is important, swales connect to basins, streams, or other collecting elements of a flow network. Swales can also be used adjacent to roads and other paved surfaces.

Irrigation Techniques

Globally, about 70 percent of water use is for crops (Postel, 1989). In the United States the figure is about 83 percent (Rogers, 1985). In California about 85 percent of the water moved through the state's massive delivery system goes to farms. Globally, about one-third of the world's crops are produced on the 17 percent of farmland that is irrigated (Postel, 1989). In the United States the figure is about one-third on the irrigated 14 percent (Day and Horner, 1987).

Clearly, water and agriculture are inseparable. As with other resources that support agriculture, water resources are stretched beyond their sustainable capacity. About 24 percent of the water used for irrigation is drawn from groundwater storage (Rogers, 1985), and less then half of that is returned after use. In 1983, groundwater levels under about one-third of the irrigated farmlands in the United States dropped between 6 inches and 5 feet (Frederick, 1991). There is no reason to believe figures for more recent years are less. The capacity of surface sources is under equal stress.

All of the techniques described so far in this chapter can help reduce amounts of water used in irrigation. Most of them, however, are more readily applicable on relatively small farms, whereas in the United States most agricultural production is on farms measured in thousands of acres.

Due largely to water prices that are far lower than the cost of delivery, irrigation practices worldwide are highly wasteful. Although the efficiency of irrigation technology has improved dramatically in recent decades, most farmers have no financial incentives to install improved equipment. This is an economic issue involving government policy, and we will return to it in Chapter 11. Meanwhile, the remainder of this section on irrigation techniques describes some of the technological improvements available for reducing water use. Experience has shown that applying even one or two of them can reduce water consumption by 25 to 30 percent. Shifting an entire irrigation system to the most water-efficient technologies can reduce consumption per unit area by more than 50 percent (Rogers, 1985).

The benefits of efficient water use extend far beyond water saving. Most of the environmental impacts of irrigation increase disproportionately as the amount of water applied increases beyond the amount actually used by the plants at which the water is directed. Salinization is caused mostly by the evaporation of standing water; chemical pesticides and fertilizers are carried to streams and rivers by water that is unused by plants running off the land; erosion is accelerated by excessive runoff. Thus the goal of improved irrigation technology is to deliver water to the roots of the plants it serves with as little as possible going anywhere else.

UNDERGROUND IRRIGATION / Water can be distributed to crops through a system of perforated subsurface pipes. These bring water to the plants where they need it—in their root systems. Furthermore, there is no evaporation loss because the water is never exposed above the ground surface.

DRIP IRRIGATION / Water is distributed through a surface system of flexible tubing with small emitters placed along its length adjacent to the plants to be watered. The emitters release water slowly so that it is absorbed into the soil before it can evaporate. In general, drip irrigation works for large plants, mostly trees and shrubs, and is not easily adaptable to grains or vegetables. Drip emitters can also be part of an underground system, making them even more efficient.

BUBBLERS / These are installed on the pipes of a conventional irrigation system. However, rather than spraying the water into the air, as conventional irrigation heads do, they release it in a steady stream that drops to the ground. There it can be held in small basins to soak into the soil, or it can be guided through small furrows.

The same principle can be applied to the massive irrigation systems that water dozens of acres in a slow sweep. The process is called "low-energy precision application." Instead of sprinkler heads that spray water into the air, vertical tubes attached to the water-delivery arms carry water directly to the ground where it is needed. This eliminates evaporation loss and avoids watering large areas of soil where water cannot reach the plants.

TENSIOMETERS AND CONTROLLERS / To deliver water when it is actually needed, that is, when the soil is not already saturated, sophisticated devices for timing the periods of watering clocks are in common use. More precise in matching application to need are devices called tensiometers, which measure the moisture content of soil. When moisture falls below a certain level, a signal from the tensiometer triggers the controller to begin applying water.

The major disadvantage of all these improvements in irrigation technology is their cost. Since they are more expensive than conventional devices, farmers have little incentive to use them as long as the cost of water is kept artificially low.

CONTROLLED FLOODING / At the other end of the technology spectrum, less costly than full irrigation systems and more applicable in nonindustrialized countries, are the wide range of devices for guiding the flow of water. Water harvesting and flow-slowing techniques mentioned earlier are typical of these. Flood-recession agriculture is an even more ancient practice, dating back to the earliest farming in the Nile Valley. Water that periodically covers a floodplain is temporarily trapped by subtle changes in landform. Crops are then planted in the saturated soil. Through careful control, the amount of water evaporating or running off the land can be minimized. However, while cost-effective, controlled flooding is far less efficient in delivering water where it is needed than are underground or drip systems or electronic controls.

Controlling Water Chemistry

Of the four major sources of water pollution, the two largest—agriculture and industry—can only be controlled effectively at the source, before the pollu-

tants they produce enter the water-flow system. Water supplies will only be protected from agricultural chemicals when applications of fertilizers and pesticides are reduced to assimilable levels. Chapter 7 deals with some alternatives to fertilizer and pesticide use. Eventually, most industrial pollutants can also be eliminated from processes of production as well. Those that cannot be eliminated must be taken out of the water before reaching the larger water-flow system.

Water from the third source—urban runoff—is best treated by filtration and assimilation integrated with the water-flow system. The simplest, most cost-effective means for accomplishing this treatment are those used in nature for the same purpose: green plants and microorganisms. These have the ability to assimilate most of the materials carried in water and to use them in growth processes or break them down into harmless substances.

Living Filters

Runoff pollution presents a problem for all devices designed to cause surface water to infiltrate the ground. After flowing over urban surfaces, runoff water is usually laden with grease, oil, organic matter, and other debris. Some studies have shown it to be lower in quality than secondary sewage effluent. This is especially true of the water running off during the first few minutes of a storm. After that, surfaces are cleaner and less material washes off. In flowing through a landscape planted in turf and dense ground covers, materials suspended in water tend to be assimilated by the landscape. They settle out or attach themselves to leaves or roots along the way. There microorganisms attack and decompose them into substances that are assimilated by soils and plants. Some organic materials are directly taken up by plants. Thus, if urban runoff collected on hard surfaces is introduced into the green land-

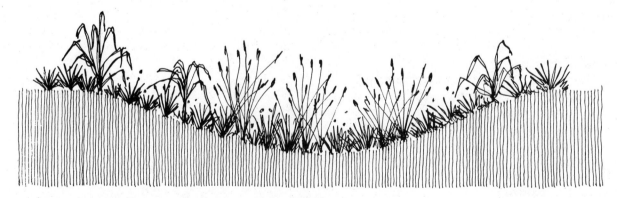

WETLAND TREATMENT FOR RUNOFF WATER

EXAMPLE

Shop Creek Wetlands

The Cherry Creek Reservoir is a large lake standing on the southeast edge of Denver, Colorado. The lake was formed by an earthen dam built to hold back floodwaters and protect the urban area. The reservoir is surrounded by a park that is mostly a more-or-less natural prairie landscape, though parts of it are intensively used by the urban population on weekends.

In the 1970s, suburbs began spreading over the landscape upstream from the park. Shop Creek, which is one of several small streams feeding the reservoir, became badly polluted with silts eroding from construction sites, with the usual debris and oily substances found in urban runoff, and with eroded soils from the park itself. Landscape architect William Wenk worked with park officials to design a water retention and treatment system that fits gently into the natural landscape of the park, controls flooding, removes silts and chemical pollutants from the water, and provides large areas of rich wildlife habitat.

In Wenk's design, immediately after the water in Shop Creek flows from the adjoining residential area into the park, a sizable pond retained by a small

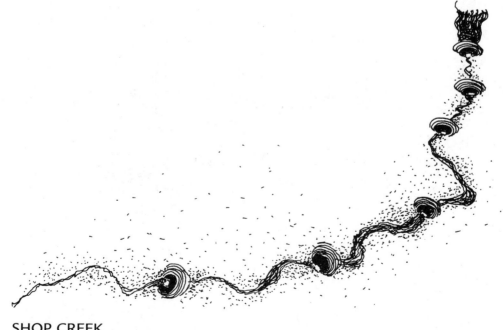

SHOP CREEK

dam collects it. Here, while the water stands relatively still, most of its load of silts and suspended particles settle to the bottom. The pond's bottom will have to be cleaned out periodically, but as yet nobody knows how often.

From the pond the water flows through a series of five additional small dams or drop structures. Each of these provides a similar sequence of flow. The dam stops the water at grade, but a culvert with its intake well below the water level conducts the flow through the dam to a pool several feet lower on the other side. The culvert's outlet is below the pool's water surface, so that when the water flows out, it erupts in a bubbling white foam that provides aeration. When the water leaves the small, roughly circular pool, it flows into a shallow marsh filled with cattails, bulrushes, and other wetland plants, and with frogs, turtles, birds, and small mammals as well. At the other end of the marsh, about a hundred yards farther on, another dam holds the water back and begins the sequence again. During flood conditions the water flows over the tops of dams to allow for faster movement.

The dams and the marshes give an extraordinary sense of blending of human design with the natural landscape. They are free-flowing, somewhat semicircular forms joining low, rounded knolls on either side of the creek. The construction material is soil cement, a mix of native soil and cement, built up in layers like one slab laid on top of another. Each slab has a rough edge and is somewhat smaller than the one underneath so the form rises from the earth in a series of steps.

After moving through five repetitions of the sequence, laboratory tests have confirmed that the water is somewhat higher in quality than that in the reservoir; that is, it meets the "fishable and swimmable" standards of the EPA.

DROP STRUCTURE
SHOP CREEK

scape to flow for some distance overland, it is soon treated to a high level of quality. Swales and infiltration basins can work in this way.

For larger volumes of water or water that is more polluted, wetland species such as reeds and bulrushes are especially effective water purifiers. In natural systems, wetlands function as water treatment centers at critical junctions in the water distribution process. It is possible to introduce wetlands shaped by humans, using the same plant species, into urban drainage systems to serve the same purpose. These can be relatively small since it is essential only for the first few minutes' runoff to flow through them; storm waters tend to carry away pollutants collected on the surface soon after the rain starts to fall. If larger volumes overflow after that, their pollution levels are usually insignificant.

At the Leach Botanical Garden in Portland, Oregon, water draining from a parking lot flows into a 10,000-square-foot wetland created by excavating a bowl-shaped depression and planting it in a mix of wetland plants, including reedgrass (*Calamagrostis*) and cattails (*Typha*). From the wetland the water moves through a grassy swale and then cascades down a hillside for aeration. Along the way some of the water soaks into the ground to make its way to groundwater storage. The rest flows eventually into Johnson Creek, which was once a salmon run but whose aquatic life was largely destroyed by Portland's urban pollution. Portland's planners hope that a series of projects similar to this will restore water quality and perhaps the salmon (Trank, 1992).

Also effective for dealing with runoff pollution are vegetative filter strips of grass. Such strips slow overland water flow and remove suspended materials by filtration, absorption, and gravity sedimentation. To be effective, the vegetation structure must be dense at ground level.

Reusing Wastewater

The almost universal practice of discharging waste-laden water after human use into larger natural water bodies has two sets of effects. One set involves deterioration of quality in the receiving water. The other involves loss of resources, both the wastewater itself and the potentially useful residual materials it carries, from further human use. Both kinds of effects are seriously damaging; both play major parts in the spiral of degeneration worldwide.

Regenerative practices deal with both sets of effects simultaneously by using biological processes to assimilate the potential pollutants, and thus to produce water of usable quality. Thus both the water and the materials carried by it are returned to ecosystemic function, and receiving waters are spared pollution.

In Chapter 8 we will further discuss regenerative processes for waste treatment. Here we will describe some of the processes for returning treated water to the cycle of use. Since treated wastewater is the largest potential source for augmenting present supplies, recycling it is an extremely important subject.

GROUNDWATER RECHARGE / Given present sewage treatment technologies, authorities on the subject agree that the best means for reuse is to percolate the effluent into underground storage after advanced treatment and store it there for later recovery by wells. In the process of percolating, the effluent moves through the porous soils and rock of the vadose zone—the section between the land surface and the water table—which filters out remaining suspended solids, pathogenic organisms, nutrients, and heavy metals. A number of carefully controlled studies have shown this filtering to be highly effective in protecting groundwater.

The Los Angeles County Sanitation Districts have used this method for a number of years, returning each year as much as 37,700 acre-feet of treated effluent to aquifers, where it mixes with water already there. A long-term health-effects study compared the quality of water in aquifers receiving treated wastewater with that of aquifers recharged only by runoff and found no difference (Nellor et al., 1984).

In this situation the water moves from the treatment plant into spreading grounds, where it flows in sheets over the land surface and then soaks into the soil. However, the water can perform other roles as it spreads over the land. At some cost in water consumption, it can provide irrigation water for plants, in both agricultural and urban landscapes, and it can provide water for wildlife habitat. It can also be used to maintain the viability of ecosystems such as streams and wetlands that have been deprived of their water supplies by other urban functions.

LANDSCAPE IRRIGATION WITH RECLAIMED WATER / In the dry western states, sewage effluent is commonly used to irrigate parks and golf courses. Water for the irrigated portions of the vast Griffith

Park in Los Angeles comes from the nearby Glendale Treatment Plant. Water not used for irrigation is released by the treatment plant into the nearby Los Angeles River flood-control channel. Since the channel has an earthen bottom, the steady supply of water supports a profusion of wetland plants, which has in turn made the channel prime bird habitat.

A number of golf courses, cemeteries, and other public landscapes in the Los Angeles urban region receive treated effluent, as do many in the Phoenix and Tucson areas. In Pomona, on the eastern edge of the Los Angeles conurbation, the campus of California State Polytechnic University (Cal Poly), including its extensive agricultural fields, has been irrigated with effluent piped from the nearby Pomona treatment plant since 1966. This water undergoes advanced carbon filtration and is close to potable standards. In this area the demand for sewage effluent to be used for irrigation is considerably greater than the treatment plant can supply.

AGRICULTURAL IRRIGATION WITH RECLAIMED WATER / For watering crops, using treated effluent still carrying some dissolved nitrogen and potassium is particularly appealing because it completes the circle of nutrient flow. Some of the nutrients removed from agricultural soils and shipped to consumers in the form of crops can make their way back in the water to be reassimilated by the landscape. However, there are two difficulties that present barriers to the extensive use of effluent for crop irrigation. The first relates to geography, the second to potential health problems.

Geographically, sewage treatment plants are usually located in urban areas far from farms where the water might be used. The cost of piping the water to the farms is usually prohibitive. The city of San Francisco, for example, studied the cost of a pipeline to carry water from its treatment plants to the nearest sizable agricultural areas and found it too expensive to compete with other sources available in those areas. However, if the pricing structure of water changes in the future to more accurately reflect is real cost, the balance could tip in the direction of reclaimed water. Meanwhile, there are potentials in cities for increasing urban agriculture, either by growing crops intensively on rooftops otherwise unused or by planting derelict land within the city. This is further discussed in Chapter 7.

As for health effects of using reclaimed water, the level of risk is not clear, though almost certainly minimal. While there have been documented cases of cattle dying of nitrate poisoning after drinking sewage effluent, these incidents involved untreated sewage. Researchers have conducted numerous studies of the effects of reclaimed water use on humans for as long as 40 years and have found no indications of ill effects. A study in Monterey County, California, monitored the effects of irrigating vegetable crops with treated effluent for ten years and found no ill effects (Postel, 1989). Based on experience up to that time, Congress built inducements for agricultural use of effluent into the Water Pollution Control Act. Thus, such use is a matter of national policy. The EPA has water-quality standards for reclaimed water use on both food and nonfood crops. Among the most critical parameter is the coliform bacteria count. The maximum is 23 per 100 millimeters, which is met fairly easily by both conventional and natural treatment systems.

WATER FOR WILDLIFE / Water is an essential ingredient for wildlife habitat. In general, the more water there is in a landscape, the larger and more diverse is the wildlife community. Especially in drier climates, water is often the limiting factor in wildlife areas. When water is added, both populations and species diversity increase dramatically.

The value of adding water in arid landscapes is sometimes questionable because it can make conditions favorable for exotic species that might then have competitive advantages over native ones. This can then disrupt whole ecosystems. However, in most regions, human activity has severely reduced the amount of water available to wildlife. In California's Central Valley, for example, where millions of acres of mechanized agriculture now spread over the flat landscape, large patches of wetland once provided feasting areas for birds on their annual migration routes and for other birds and animals that lived there year round. Wetlands created there are now using treated wastewater simply to restore a part of the wildlife resource that once existed. It is not an uncommon situation.

The potentials for using wastewater in different ways to shape a variety of habitats are many. Small ponds can attract birds in multitudes, especially in urban areas. In Los Angeles a pit excavated as a source of fill material for a nearby road-building project collected rainwater during the winter wet season. Its surface area was less than 10 acres. Birds appeared almost instantaneously to cover its surface. The builders had planned to refill the pit, but when they began to do so, wildlife protection groups insisted that it must be preserved; after some controversy it was.

■■■

Etiwanda-Day Canyon Community Plan

The site of the future Etiwanda-Day Canyon Community covers 3600 acres (roughly 1440 hectares) at the base of the San Bernardino Mountains about 50 miles east of the city of Los Angeles. Until a few years ago, this was productive agricultural land, covered with vineyards and fruit trees. The vines and trees are gone now, victims of rising land values and the high price of imported water for irrigation.

Suburban tracts are rapidly covering the landscape all around the site. In their use of land and other resources, these tracts follow the pattern that prevailed in this region for more than a century, with water systems typical of the once-through, source-to-use-to-sink pattern. Water comes from two source landscapes: the small streams that collect water from the slopes of the adjacent San Bernardino Mountains, and the Colorado River more than 200 miles away. After a single use in suburban homes, the wastewater moves to a distant regional treatment plant and from there through the Santa Ana River system to the Pacific Ocean. Water that falls within these communities as rain, as well as much of the water flowing into the valley through mountain streams and irrigation runoff, collects in flood-control channels and moves through them to the river and the ocean as well.

The new community plan prepared by the 606 Studio for the Etiwanda–Day Canyon area takes a very different approach (606 Studio, 1986). It centers on a water-flow system that relies entirely on water flowing onto the site from the adjacent mountains, avoids importing water from the Colorado River, redistributes treated wastewater from an on-site treatment plant, and uses the aquifer that underlies the site as its primary storage medium. In addition, the plan takes advantage of this flow system to support large agricultural areas that form an open-space network within the community.

Through the late winter, spring, and early summer, water pours out of the mountains through Etiwanda Canyon onto the site. At the base of the canyon, instead of being carried away in a concrete channel, it will be trapped in a series of infiltration basins that also serve as wildlife habitat and recreation areas. After percolating through the basins into underground storage, it will be available for use in the community's 3000 homes and commercial area. Following its use in the community, the wastewater will flow to a small treatment plant located in the lower part of the Etiwanda-Day Canyon community, where it will be treated to an advanced stage beyond the secondary level. Then

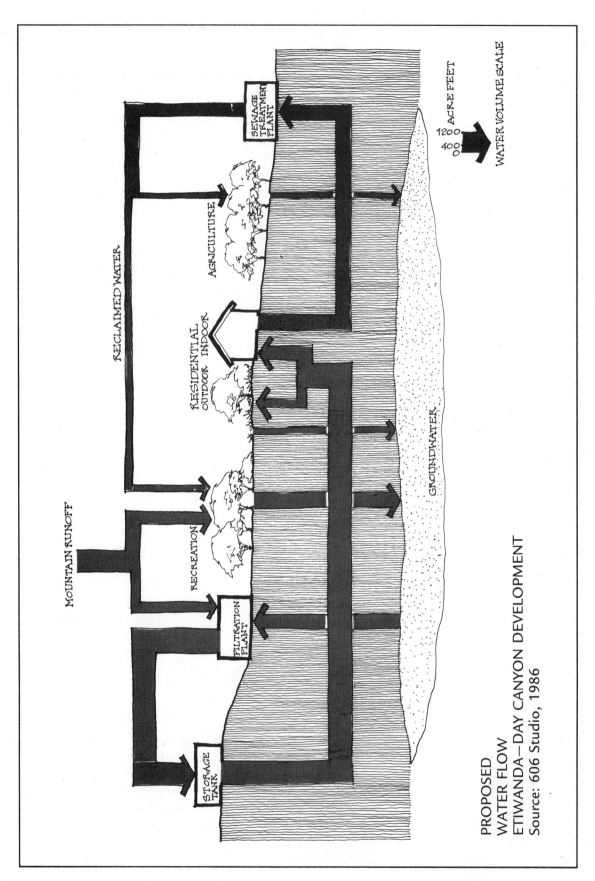

PROPOSED
WATER FLOW
ETIWANDA–DAY CANYON DEVELOPMENT
Source: 606 Studio, 1986

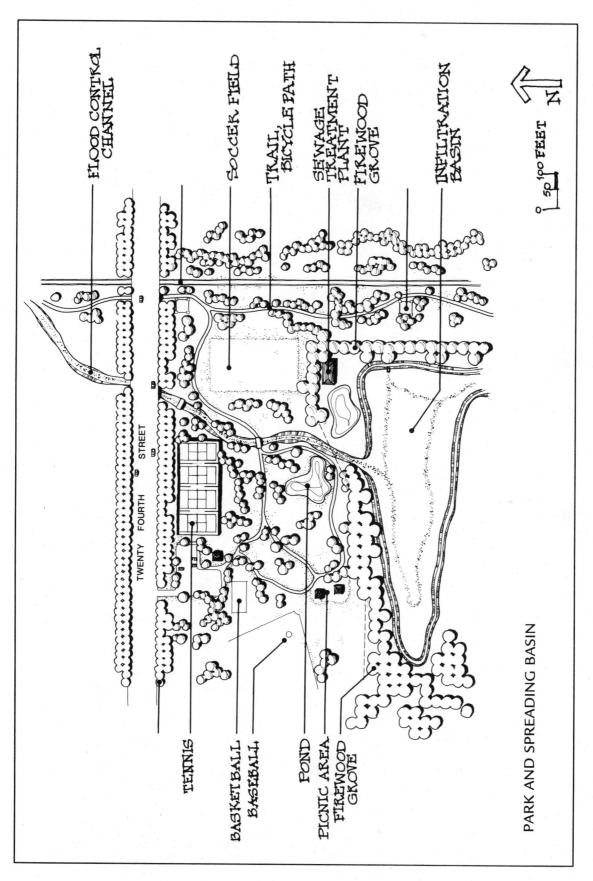

FLOOD CONTROL CHANNEL

SOCCER FIELD

TRAIL; BICYCLE PATH

SEWAGE TREATMENT PLANT

FIREWOOD GROVE

INFILTRATION BASIN

N

0 50 100 FEET

TWENTY FOURTH STREET

TENNIS

BASKETBALL

BASEBALL

POND

PICNIC AREA

FIREWOOD GROVE

PARK AND SPREADING BASIN

175

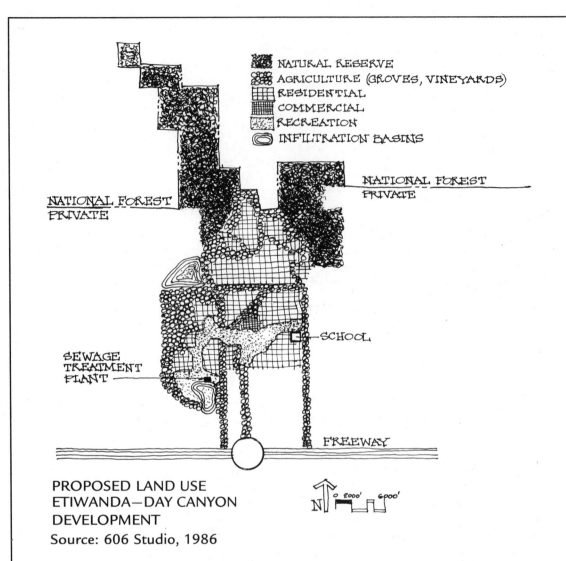

Legend:
- NATURAL RESERVE
- AGRICULTURE (GROVES, VINEYARDS)
- RESIDENTIAL
- COMMERCIAL
- RECREATION
- INFILTRATION BASINS

NATIONAL FOREST
PRIVATE

NATIONAL FOREST
PRIVATE

SCHOOL

SEWAGE
TREATMENT
PLANT

FREEWAY

N   0 2000'   6000'

PROPOSED LAND USE
ETIWANDA—DAY CANYON
DEVELOPMENT
Source: 606 Studio, 1986

it will be conveyed to agricultural and recreational areas within the community and distributed over the landscape as irrigation water.

The agricultural areas are a combination of citrus groves and vineyards, along with some other fruit trees and a few eucalyptus groves grown for firewood. These will cool the air in the hot summers as explained in Chapter 5 and produce food and fuel as well. The availability of low-cost reclaimed water will make these areas economically feasible again. Along with recreational areas, including a golf course, the agricultural areas form a continuous system of green space woven through the community fabric. They also form a giant sponge, soaking up the treated wastewater and using it to support the growth of plants or filtering it through the soil it to underground storage. The cycling process will be almost continuous: Water lost to the system through evaporation and other outward pathways will be replaced by water flowing in through the mountains and the canyon. Preliminary calculations show a balanced water budget. The monetary budget is also balanced; most of the green space

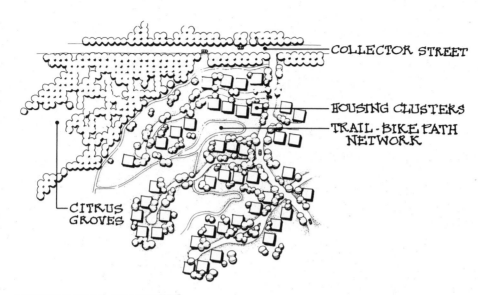

COLLECTOR STREET

HOUSING CLUSTERS

TRAIL-BIKE PATH NETWORK

CITRUS GROVES

RESIDENTIAL CLUSTERS

is already in public ownership. Developers will dedicate the rest during the development process without economic cost to either themselves or the public. Food and energy production will pay the cost of management.

The plan for the Etiwanda-Day Canyon community also provides for reducing internal consumption of energy and materials in a number of other ways. A system of pedestrian and bicycle ways gives alternatives to the automobile, for example, and site planning encourages solar heating and cooling in the buildings.

Live streams can provide even richer habitat. It has become commonplace for flood-control channels and water-diversion projects to leave natural streams dried up and lifeless. Where treated effluent is available, it can often be used to restore the life of a stream. It sometimes happens, in fact, that sufficient treated water is available to supply a larger stream than existed naturally or even to create one that flows year round rather than seasonally. This then raises one of the difficult and profoundly important questions related to human ecosystems. In such cases, humans have the power to improve on nature in the sense of making an ecosystem richer and more diverse than it would naturally be. However, this clearly constitutes tampering with nature's evolving order and might well bring about other changes in other places that might be damaging, perhaps seriously so. While we can develop analytical predictions based on cause and effect, we well know that the effects of altering ecosystems are often unpredictable. Our understanding of the intricate inner workings of ecosystems is far from perfect.

On balance, considering the massive changes already wrought by humans on natural systems, it seems that efforts to improve on nature where we think we can are usually well justified. However, it also seems that we have an obligation to predict as accurately as we can the behavior of the new system. Ecosystem design is an emerging art that will be surrounded by such difficult issues for decades to come.

Possibilities for creating richer-than-natural habitats exist to a still greater extent in constructed wetlands. As in California's Central Valley, vast areas of wetlands have been lost almost everywhere in the world. While natural wetlands are among nature's richest environments, wetlands created with wastewater can be even richer. Nutrients dissolved in the water can stimulate the growth of more diverse communities. By careful design, constructed wetlands can incorporate the best qualities of natural wetlands. For example, research has shown that the surface composition of the most productive freshwater wetlands generally includes about half water and half land area (Weller, 1987). Relatively few natural wetlands have that land–water ratio, but it can be designed into a constructed wetland. Nevertheless, questions concerning the desirability of such human control remain. Is it possible that the wide variation in land–water ratios represents some strategy of nature? By designing all constructed wetlands using the ideal ratio, might we be limiting the diversity of available habitat and perhaps limiting in some way the utility of the aggregated wetlands? Might we be bringing on some future disaster?

As with other uses of treated effluent, water quality is an important issue when water is used for habitat. While quality standards need not be nearly as high as for human consumption or even agricultural irrigation, water with certain constituents can have disastrous effects on wildlife. Several serious incidents have dramatically underscored this fact in recent years. The widespread malformations and deaths among bird populations at the Kesterson Wildlife Refuge in California showed that even naturally occurring substances in large amounts can be poisons. In this case, the culprit was selenium, a nonmetallic element that had been concentrated far above natural levels in the agricultural runoff that provided water for the reserve.

More commonly, the constituents of wastewater that can be dangerous to wildlife include heavy metals and a range of toxic substances. Plants can take up metals but are usually not seriously affected. However, animals then eat the plants and the metals along with them. Thus, the metals can work their way up through the food chain and collect in the bodies of some animals with lethal effect.

The level of quality required for each use of water is different and can be defined with some accuracy. As in the case of energy, the higher the quality, the higher the cost. This suggests that it is unwise to use water of a higher quality than needed. Using treated wastewater where its quality is high enough for the purpose also helps to reduce the demand for an increasingly scarce resource.

A Natural-Human Water Cycle

Without drastic reductions in population there is no way we can ever return to the naturally evolved water cycle as it functioned before human intervention. However, continuing our present degenerative practices in managing water will ultimately lead to serious shortages and universal pollution. The only hopeful alternative seems to be even more intensive management. We cannot avoid altering watersheds, growing crops, diverting water, and even altering water chemistry. As this chapter has shown, there are a great many regenerative means for accomplishing all of these actions, but all of them require more thought than the degenerative alternatives. It seems certain that we will find it necessary to devote more time and skill to planning, design, engineering, and management of water resources in the future.

CASE STUDY
■■

Water Management at the Center for Regenerative Studies

In the semiarid southern California climate, water is often the most limiting factor for supporting life. This is true of both natural and human ecosystems. Here virtually all agriculture is irrigated, and cities depend on water imported from considerable distances. Both of these are common situations in areas with low levels of rainfall. Some similar areas experience serious difficulties in providing water in adequate amounts. Many nonindustrial nations in arid and semiarid zones have populations that have grown well beyond the capacities of their watersheds. Even in many regions with relatively wet climates, shortage of water has emerged as a serious problem.

For these reasons, water management is among the major issues addressed by the Center for Regenerative Studies. Its infrastructure will provide for a wide range of water uses. Efficient use and recycling of water and the interrelationships between water and other resources are important subjects of education and research.

Due to an unusual topographic condition, virtually the only drainage water entering the site is that which falls on the site itself. For this reason, the amount of runoff water is quite small. Nevertheless, a number of devices will be applied to maximize its use. Especially important is the shaping of the hillsides to hold water, direct it to plants, and minimize erosion. Landform techniques are directly related to topographic conditions. Five distinct topographic zones occur on the site, as shown on the map.

The valley, which slopes less than 10 percent and where water naturally settles, is devoted to water-related uses. These include aquaculture and sewage treatment, irrigation for rice paddies and other crops needing large amounts of water, water for the main reservoir, and other uses functionally related to these.

The knolltops, which form the dominant visual features of the site, are gently rounded with brows that slope less than 10 percent. They are ideally suited for contour plowing and grain production.

The bases of the knolls are also relatively flat where they spread out into the valleys. They are well suited to intensive vegetable production and the rectilinear planting beds that are preferred for most intensive methods.

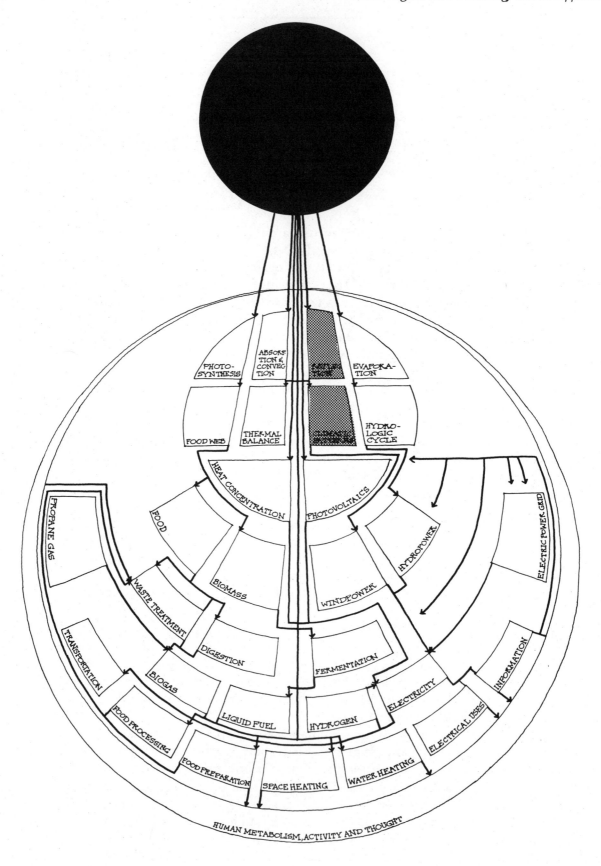

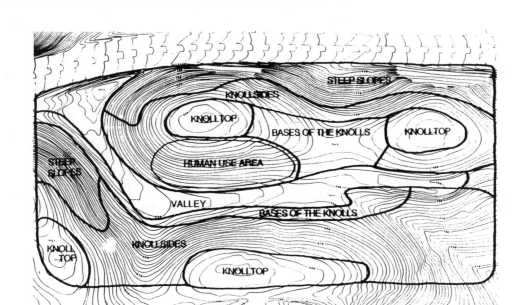

The knollsides are those areas between the bases and tops of the knolls with
   slopes varying from 10 to 35 percent. They will require terracing to be
   used for food production.
The steep slopes, those over 35 percent, are best stabilized by planting perennial vegetation. These slopes will remain in their natural forms. They will
   be covered by trees, shrubs, and ground covers selected for their productive uses as well as their soil-holding capacity.

These agricultural areas will trap and use rainwater where it falls.
Water not used directly, including runoff from paved surfaces, will be
directed to retention basins, which will hold it for infiltration to underground storage. Rooftop planting beds will use water falling in the roofs
of buildings with the surplus collected by gutters, scuppers, and downspouts for storage in cisterns for later domestic use.

Besides rainfall, there are two other sources of water: the domestic
supply and treated sewage effluent.

The domestic water from the Pomona Water District will provide
water for human consumption inside the buildings. After use, this water
will be directed into an aquacultural treatment system. From there it will
flow into a reservoir and later be used for irrigation.

Treated sewage effluent will be supplied by the Pomona Water Reclamation Plant. A pipe from this plant is already in place near the site, and
the water is now used to irrigate plantings on the landfill. The Center
will use it for aquaculture and irrigation. Before being used in aquaculture, this water will require additional treatment to reduce its ammonia
content.

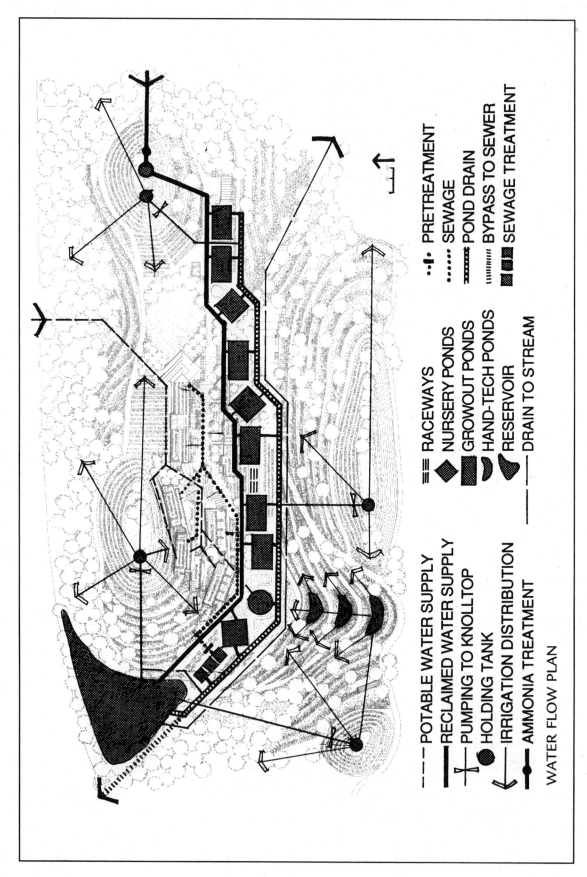

WATER FLOW PLAN

POTABLE WATER SUPPLY
RECLAIMED WATER SUPPLY
PUMPING TO KNOLLTOP
HOLDING TANK
IRRIGATION DISTRIBUTION
AMMONIA TREATMENT

RACEWAYS
NURSERY PONDS
GROWOUT PONDS
HAND-TECH PONDS
RESERVOIR
DRAIN TO STREAM

PRETREATMENT
SEWAGE
POND DRAIN
BYPASS TO SEWER
SEWAGE TREATMENT

182

RECLAIMED WATER:

    Maximum Inflow = 100 G.P.M.
    Average Inflow = 72 G.P.M.

    Minimum Detention Times for Aquaculture:
        Raceways - 2.8 hours
        Nursery Ponds - 7 days
        Growout Ponds - 7 days

    Irrigation Demand = 15-50 G.P.M./Acre

POTABLE WATER:

    Maximum Inflow = 9000 G.P.D.
    Average Inflow = 3600 G.P.D.

    Detention Times for Sewage System
        First Pond - 2-3 days
        Second and Third Ponds - 2 days

    Average Outflow to Stream = 30 G.P.M.

    G.P.M. = Gallons per Minute

WATER DATA

These three sources—rainwater, domestic water, and treated effluent—provide a wide range of possible subjects for experimentation and demonstration of varied levels of quality for different purposes. The general water data on this page show approximate quantities of water needed for various purposes. The Los Angeles County Sanitation Districts provide both potable and reclaimed water to the site under the terms of its agreement with Cal Poly.

The valley functions as a highly controlled human-made river at the core of the water-flow system. The open tanks store water to be used to grow fish and aquatic plants. A supply line along the north side of the valley links all of the tanks with the water sources. A drain line on the south side links them with the reservoir at the lowest point on the site in its northwest corner. The reservoir serves as a holding tank. The drain-line will connect with pipes to carry water to the storage tanks on the knolltops for distribution into the irrigation system. Solar electric pumps will carry the water up. Water not needed for irrigation on-site (which will at times amount to as much as half of the volume of flow) will go back to the southeast border of the site, where it will be conveyed to other irrigated areas.

AQUACULTURE

As manifested in its focal position along the central valleys of the site, aquaculture plays a pivotal role in the ecosystem. The plan calls for rapid development of both the facilities and the program to engage in appropriate aquacultural research as soon as possible. This will meet a growing need for improvement in aquacultural technologies. This need is currently most obvious in the nonindustrial world, but it is likely to increase in developed nations as well.

The three aquaculture ponds in the hand-tech areas are varied in size. They will be used for growing fish such as carp and tilapia that are particularly important in providing protein for nonindustrial societies. Water pumped from the reservoir will fill the ponds, which will also serve as holding tanks for irrigation water distributed to cultivated areas on the adjacent terraces.

The ponds along the valley bottom are designed for highly controlled research and can be used to grow a wide variety of freshwater species. In the ultimate stage there will be three nursery ponds, each with an area of 2500 square feet, and six growout ponds (where fish grow to harvestable size), each with an area of 2800 square feet.

The reservoir at the west end of the site will be used for research and demonstrations in cage culture and farm pond management. Cage culture involves the growing of fish in wire-mesh containers within larger bodies of water; it has widespread potential application in the growing numbers of human-made lakes and water-supply reservoirs in many parts of the world. Aquatic plants raised in net enclosures within the reservoir pond can provide fish food, forage for terrestrial animals, and compost materials.

IRRIGATION

While the Center includes areas for both irrigated agriculture and dry farming, high levels of productivity in this region require some irrigation. Education and research will focus on means of irrigation that are the most economical and effective and least damaging to the soil and environment. Flood, sprinkler, drip, and underground irrigation may each be appropriate under certain conditions.

Especially in the hand-tech area, cost and simplicity are major concerns and may require some compromises in efficiency. Test plots will permit comparisons of varied devices under varied conditions. This is especially important at a time when increasing areas of the world's agricultural lands are being irrigated and new devices are appearing regularly.

The availability of water of varied levels of quality also presents opportunities for research. Ongoing and impending water shortages in many parts of the world suggest that we are likely to see far more water recycling in the very near future. Education and research in this area will be increasingly important. Research questions will involve the matching of irrigation devices to soils and water quality as well as to cultural and economic circumstances.

Various techniques for automated control of the irrigation systems are also of particular interest. Clocks and feedback devices such as tensiometers promise much improved efficiency in water use. Centralized computer monitoring of irrigation may prove very effective. Technologies like these will be limited to the multitechnology area because they are not applicable now for the nonindustrial areas of the world. Comparisons of performance in this and the hand-tech area will be most instructive.

WATER AND AGRICULTURE

The percentage of water use devoted to agriculture—about 70 percent globally—makes it clear that water and agriculture are intertwined. The fact that the Center's water-flow system relates mostly to agricultural uses underscores and manifests this close relationship. Virtually every decision and task on a farm relates to water. This means that the next chapter, which mostly concerns agriculture, is in many ways a continuation of this one.

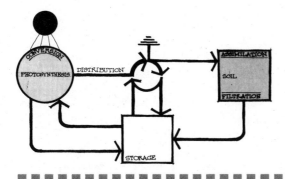

Chapter 7
Growth, Form, and Productivity

Dean Freudenberger and Victor Wegrzyn, Coauthors

Reduced to essentials, agriculture biologically combines energy, nutrients, water and air in the context of microbial activity of the soil in the photosynthetic conversion process to produce plant-based food and fiber. Until the 20th century, the energy came directly from the sun, nutrients came from regenerative processes in the plant and soil system, water came from the clouds, and the air was unpolluted. Industrialization during the 20th century changed all that.

The Fatal Flaws of Paleotechnic Agriculture

Resource Consumption

Energy Use
Energy for the initial conversion process of photosynthesis still comes from the sun, but the industrial agriculture of the Paleotechnic era heavily invests and expends fossil-fuel energy as well. This contributes to food production several ways. The most important of these are petroleum for driving tractors and other farm machinery, and petroleum and natural gas as feedstocks for producing chemical fertilizers and pesticides. With some justification, modern agriculture has been called a process for converting petroleum into food. The conversion, however, is not particularly efficient. Amory Lovins and his colleagues at the Rocky Mountain Institute have calculated that U.S. agriculture uses about 2 calories of energy for each calorie produced (Lovins and Lovins, 1982). For some crops the ratio is much higher. For cauliflower it is about 5 to 1 and for lettuce about 3 to 1. For most grains it is lower: for rice about 0.4 to 1 and for corn 0.3 to 1. Some studies have indicated much higher returns on energy invested (for example, Geyer et al., 1986). By any measure, however, Paleotechnic agriculture compares unfavorably in energy efficiency with much preindustrial agriculture. Consider, for example, the 0.06-to-1 ratio of energy investment to food calories routinely achieved by one typical community of rainforest milpa farmers (Rappoport, 1971).

A major achievement of Paleotechnic agriculture lies in substituting chemicals, machines (capital), and fossil-fuel energy for labor. This has dramatically reduced the need for people living and working on farms. In 1930 about 25 percent of the American labor force lived on farms; in 1990 the figure was less than 3 percent. Actual hours of human labor invested in food growing declined by more than 92 percent between 1920 and 1970 (Grossman, 1978). Not coincidentally, use of petroleum and petroleum products in agriculture multiplied during this period, especially during the years after World War II. In 1950 the equivalent of 276 million barrels of oil were used on farms worldwide. In 1985 the total was 1903 million barrels (Brown, 1987).

Water Use

The increase in water use has been equally dramatic. While irrigated agriculture has been practiced for nearly 6000 years, irrigated lands included only a small fraction of the world's croplands until the middle of the 20th century. Since then, irrigation projects have multiplied, and the amount of water consumed per acre is high. There are about 58 million acres of irrigated farmland in the United States (Brown, 1987), and the average water application rate is nearly 3 acre-feet per acre of crop. Most of this water evaporates or transpires; only about 45 percent finds its way back into the terrestrial water-flow system. By contrast, most water used for nonirrigation purposes is not consumed but only used and returned to the system, albeit often polluted. Altogether, about 83 percent of water consumption (not use) in the United States is for agricultural irrigation (Rogers, 1985).

Water use in turn involves energy use. For example, it requires energy to draw water up from underground storage or move it uphill when the source is surface water. Between 1950 and 1985, fossil-fuel use for irrigation increased worldwide approximately sixfold (Brown, 1987).

Agriculture and Society

No longer is agricultural production the employer of most workers and the bedrock of economy and society, although estimates indicate that as many as 20 percent of the jobs in California are directly related to the food system from farm to table. Now agriculture is a key supplier on the source side of the one-way system of materials and energy flow, providing food to a mostly urban population, which duly converts it to waste and moves it on to the nearest large body of water or landfill. The movement is fast and enormous in volume. There is no

denying that the agricultural industry accomplishes this task in more than adequate volume and at low cost. By the measure of volume of food produced per human hour of labor, American agriculture is the world's most productive, and that of the other industrialized nations is not much less. Abundant inexpensive food is a great asset to any economy, and the agricultural industry seems to have achieved this, at least in industrialized nations. However, there are a number of costs inherent in this system that are not paid by consumers in the supermarket.

High Cost of Productivity

Weighing against the impressive productivity that industrial agriculture has achieved by substituting fossil fuels for human energy are its negative consequences in terms of resources, environmental health, food quality, food security, and an unraveling social fabric.

We well know the fossil fuels that drive modern agriculture, indeed, which make it possible, will soon run short, increase in cost, and one day run out. Long before they run out, scarcity will drive the price of fossil-fuel energy to a level that might make food produced by modern technology too valuable to eat—at least for most people.

Since water is continually replenished, it will not diminish over time and then entirely disappear as fossil fuels will, but it may nevertheless run short in both quality and quantity. Given the present level of water resource exploitation, many authorities have predicted serious shortages over widespread areas during the next few decades.

Loss of Soil Quality

Among the other serious environmental effects of industrialized agriculture is its effect on soils. In growing food with applied chemicals, we replace the organic life of the soil with inorganic materials that, over time, usually degrade soil quality.

In addition to the deteriorating soil quality brought on by machines and chemical use, such as compaction and loss of humus, erosion losses are increasingly widespread. How seriously erosion losses will affect food production over the next few decades is a matter of disagreement among authorities on the subject. The U.S. Soil Conservation Service calculates the amount of any given soil that can be eroded away in a year without seriously affecting that soil's ability to produce in the future. This figure, called the loss tolerance or T-value, is actually considerably higher than the rate at which natural processes create new soil, and thus does not represent a true measure of sustainability. Even by this measure, America's best soils are washing away. The average loss tolerance (T-value) for prairie soils under cultivation is about 5 tons per acre. The actual average water erosion rate that occurs is 4.8 tons per acre, and wind erosion averages 3.3 tons per acre. Thus the total annual average erosion loss is 8.1 tons per acre (Conservation Foundation, 1987). This considerably exceeds what is tolerable for sustainable productivity.

The cost of erosion is high. According to one estimate, the annual economic loss due to erosion in the United States is $2.5 billion in lost productivity and $6 billion in off-site damage (Runge, 1986). About 69.5 million acres, or about 17 percent of U.S. cropland, are losing soil at a rate greater than three times the T-value (ibid.). On grazing lands, especially the public lands of the western states, the erosion rates are even higher. Studies indicate that 3 to 4 percent of U.S. public and private grazing lands are in excellent condition and another 29 to 30 percent in good condition. The rest (about 67 percent) are fair, poor, or worse. (U.S. Department of the Interior, n.d.a.; Society for Range Management, 1989).

Environmental Pollution

Agriculture is responsible for more pollutants in U.S. surface and groundwater than all other industries combined. The pollutants are mostly chemical fertilizers and pesticides. In the Midwest at least half of all rural well water is contaminated to some degree with nitrates from fertilizers. The pesticide problem is surprising when we consider that while pesticide use has increased 15-fold since World War II, the rate of crop loss to pests has remained about the same (Kowalski, 1978). However, even naturally occurring chemicals can become pollutants when they are brought into dangerous levels of concentration by agricultural irrigation. An example is the concentration of naturally deposited selenium in agricultural runoff in California's Central Valley. As described in Chapter 6, the selenium laden-water drained into the Kesterson Wildlife Reserve, and caused widespread malformations in wild birds.

Loss of Biodiversity

The genetic base of seed varieties available to farmers has narrowed enormously as industrial agriculture expanded. Selection of crop varieties for resistance to certain diseases and pests and responsiveness to fertilizer inputs has resulted in the discarding and disregard for valuable exotic germplasm. Genetic diversity provides buffering against sudden outbreaks of pest species, diseases, and other evolving and unforeseen environmental conditions, such as climatic change. The biodiversity essential for sustainability has been seriously impaired by designing varieties for monocropping. The same is true of livestock. In the short term (decades) this increases productivity, but in the long term (generations) it presents a high risk.

Wildlife populations have been greatly diminished by the expansion of agricultural lands as well. Industrial agriculture spreads out to cover the landscape without regard for natural communities or habitats. Of the 215 million acres of fresh- and saltwater wetlands that once existed in the United States, about 125 million have been destroyed, mostly filled for cropland (Conservation Foundation, 1987). Wetlands are among nature's richest, naturally productive environments, home to a great diversity of fish and bird species. These natural wetlands actually produced several times as much total biomass per unit time as the croplands that replaced them, despite fossil-fuel use, though much of the natural production was not directly usable by humans.

Social Structure

From the time when most of the human population began depending on agriculture for its food supply until the 20th century, most people around the world worked on farms and lived in small towns or rural areas. Rural life was the foundation of most societies, which were solidly connected with nature. Industrialization began moving large numbers of people off the farm into the city in the 18th century. The movement accelerated through the 19th century, grew to tidal-wave dimensions during the Depression, and continues today. As agriculture became an industry, capital requirements became so great that more farmland is owned by absentee landlords (usually corporations) than by farmers. U.S. production agriculture is a tenant-based system. With declining farm populations and declining farmer ownership, the rural communities that once were society's solid anchor—the social structure of yeoman farmers that Thomas Jefferson once envisioned—began to disintegrate.

As small towns lost population, cities grew, usually in larger numbers than they could absorb. Though they escaped the harsh rigors of farm labor, most of the rural migrants to cities were ill-prepared for urban life, especially for urban employment. Unemployment became endemic, along with epidemics of urban ills such as crime, gangs, drugs, and family disintegration that can be at least partly traced to rural decline. Not only were cities forced to absorb more people faster than they could assimilate, they had lost the strong counterbalance of rural values, centered in the family and rooted in the land.

Global Agricultural Decline

In other parts of the industrialized world, the situation with respect to agriculture is much the same, as Norwegian professor Magne Brun (1991) writes in his report *Countryside in Transition:*

> The latter half of this century has brought about one of the most radical transitional processes known in the history of rural Europe. Rapid urban and industrial growth in conjunction with expansive development of transportation, rationalization and mechanization of agriculture, and decline and dereliction in those rural zones which have lagged behind and ended up in a marginal position—these are the important key words in describing this process (p. 2).

In the third world the situation is much worse. Small farmers rarely have money to buy tractors or gasoline even when they are available. Chemical fertilizers and pesticides are equally costly though they are often indiscriminately applied on the large cash-crop farms.

Nevertheless, most third-world governments continue to promote industrial agricultural development, perceiving it as the only way to reverse their economic decline. Some governments, including those of Columbia, Ecuador, Egypt, Ghana, Honduras, and Indonesia, have subsidized 50 to 70 percent of the cost of chemicals, which has strained national budgets (World Bank, 1988). This pattern is largely a result of decades of indebtedness to lenders in the industrialized world, as desperate third-world countries took to agricultural production as a means of generating revenue to pay the interest on their debts.

Soil loss and pollution are even more serious problems in third-world countries. In Africa and South America, erosion is occurring on agricultural lands almost nine times faster than in Europe (Dover and Talbot, 1989). Even after paying the costs in resources and environmental deterioration, third-world agriculture is failing to feed the growing populations adequately. The Food and Agriculture Organization of the United Nations has predicted that 64 countries in the third world will not be able to feed their people in the first decade of the 21st century; 29 of these are in Africa (ibid.). Many are in tropical regions with soils that are thin and poor, often with low rainfall, and with management problems the industrial nations have hardly begun to understand.

Searching for a Regenerative Agriculture

Clearly, by most measures other than productivity per hour of labor, industrial agriculture is a degenerative process. Recognition of its incipient failure has stimulated a considerable amount of thinking and experimentation among farmers, researchers, and other concerned people and to some degree within government agencies. Dean Freudenberger (1988), a professor of social ethics at the Luther Northwestern Theological Seminary who spent 25 years as an agricultural missionary in Africa, calls regenerative agriculture "the agenda for the twenty-first century" and defines it as an agriculture that "produces in a way that enhances the physical and biological environment which at the same time brings greater dignity and welfare to the producing community" (p. 8).

Terminology abounds. Before the terms "sustainable" and "alternative" came into widespread use, there was "organic" or "natural" agriculture. More recently, the terms "agroforestry" and "agroecology" have entered the vocabulary. Some farmers prefer to call it "sensible" or "practical" agriculture. Though each term has somewhat different connotations, farmers and researchers involved with the subject seem to agree with the National Research Council (1989) that the pressing need is for an agriculture more thoroughly integrated with natural processes. This is essentially an application of the first strategy of regenerative design: letting nature do the work. Most also agree that closer relationships with the human community are vitally important.

Very briefly then, we might summarize the goals for a regenerative agriculture as including:

- A capacity for self-renewal;
- reasonable levels of productivity within the sustainable capacities of available energy, soil, and water;
- beneficial integration with the larger ecosystem including the human community;
- profitability as measured by accounting methods that include ecological and social costs as

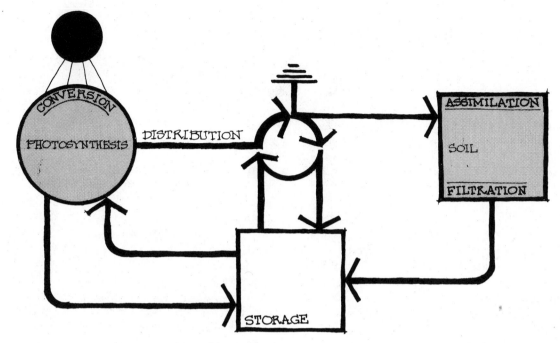

well as the internal costs included in conventional accounting;

- careful management of the landscape including the microbiotic community within the soil.

Thinking of a crop production area as an ecosystem casts it in a perspective somewhat different from that of an outdoor factory. Consider what it means to grow crops following the modes of ecosystemic order.

Structure: Interactive Diversity

In nature, different species within a landscape aid each other in providing conditions for life such as nutrients, water, microclimate, protection from pests, and population control, thus forming a community. Industrial agriculture uses chemical inputs—mostly fossil-fuel-based—to replace such stabilizing interactions. Regenerative agriculture applies the ecosystemic principle of interactive diversity, incorporating varied crop and animal species into agro-ecological communities. Such communities naturally incorporate ongoing regenerative processes that provide soil fertility and protection from pests and thus can avoid use of chemical fertilizers and pesticides.

Function: Ongoing Reuse

By making optimum use of solar radiation and by internally recycling nutrients, regenerative agriculture can establish sustainable patterns of energy and material flow. This involves the continuous recyc-

ling of organic waste materials and the use of nitrogen-fixing plants, as well as many other plants and animals.

Location: Adaptive Fit

The earth's surface varies greatly in its ability to support agriculture. Soils, slope conditions, climate, infrastructure, population concentrations—all of these differ from one place to another even within a small region. Some combinations of these conditions are suitable for one cropping system, some for another, some for none at all. Regenerative agriculture responds to these varied conditions in its use of land. It is well within our technical capability to analyze the suitability of any piece of land for any use and thus to shape suitable and sustainable patterns of land use.

Practices and Technologies for a Regenerative Agriculture

In terms of practice and technology, regenerative agriculture is both an advance beyond the recent past and a recovery of the best traditions of the 12,000-year-old mainstream of agricultural evolution. In its radically different way of using energy materials, mechanization, capital, and all the changes stemming from those, industrial agriculture made an abrupt break with the historical path. Most of the diverse agricultural experiences of the past seemed to have become irrelevant to the present. In the light of experience gained over the last half century, it is now clear there are important lessons to be learned and values to be recovered from the past. The emergence of a regenerative perspective can reestablish connections with a rich and varied history; not only is historical experience relevant, it is useful. Preindustrial agriculture was regionally varied, having developed by adaptations to local conditions of topography, soil, and climate. Knowledge gained from it can be useful in the modern context.

As it did with the design of buildings and cities, industrialization overrode all the factors of climate and landscape that produced regional differences and in their place imposed systematic uniformity. With the demise of industrial agriculture, regenerative agriculture will again adapt to local conditions and become integrally part of evolved local ecosystems. This will be the basis for research and development for sustainability. There is much to be learned from other times and places, but the appropriate practices and technologies for any region are the product of that region's climate, landscape, and human culture.

It is important to remember that we can learn from mistakes of the past as well as from its successes. While much preindustrial agriculture was successful, there were some dramatic failures. The historical archives provide numerous examples of agricultural societies that failed. The most common reason for failure was allowing populations to outgrow the productive capacities of their soil. Lowdermilk (1978) estimated that, since its beginning, agriculture has destroyed half of the earth's arable soil resources. Much of this was due to overexpansion of populations that overly exploited their soil base. When soil quality is diminished, land and society decline together in a degenerative spiral. This is another of history's basic lessons: keep population in balance with the land's capacity to produce.

Agricultural Ecosystems: The Example of the Chinampas

For history's other lessons, we need to look at the specific mechanisms of some historical examples. When we consider some agricultural systems once regarded as primitive from the perspective of industrial technology, we can see surprising levels of subtlety and sophistication. An example is the raised-bed agriculture of ancient Mexico. Some examples have been restored in the Xochimilco Gardens near Mexico City.

The raised beds in this case are rectangular islands, called "chinampas" by the Aztecs and built up above water level in low-lying marshy areas. Such agricultural techniques are also found in several parts of Asia. The Aztecs used sophisticated techniques in constructing their chinampas. They built the retaining walls defining the edges with posts and interwoven branches and then planted willow trees to help hold them in place. This technique required relatively little labor and was flexible in responding to varying conditions; trimming of the willows also provided some wood for other purposes.

The posts and woven branches formed a porous frame that the Aztecs then filled with soil dug from the canals between chinampas. Then the Aztecs planted their crops, which included several polycultures. Among these were the squash-beans-maize complex, which was widely used by many Indian tribes in North and Central America. Also commonly planted on chinampas were the more complex amaranth-bean-cassava-maize-pepper complex and a number of food-producing trees and shrubs.

Periodically, the Aztec farmers dredged the sediments from the bottoms of the canals and added them to the tops of the chinampas. This served the dual purpose of keeping the canals clear for the flow of water and continuously replenishing the crop-growing areas with nutrient-rich soils. In recent reconstructions of chinampa systems, farmers and researchers have allowed water hyacinth (*Eichornia crasipes*) to grow on the surfaces of the canals. The hyacinths grow rapidly and in the process draw nutrients from the canal water. The hyacinths are harvested and then either composted to provide a soil supplement or fed to some of the animals kept in small corrals on the chinampas. These animals, which include chickens, ducks, and pigs, form an essential part of the system, providing protein for the farmers and nutrients in the form of manure for the crops as well as consuming agricultural wastes. Fish grown in the canals as another source of protein also eat mosquito larvae and thus help to control malaria.

Applications of Ecosystemic Principles

The chinampas illustrate the agricultural applications of the principles of ecosystemic order with rare clarity and directness. The species structure of the chinampa system is diverse in its inclusion of a number of complementary annual species along

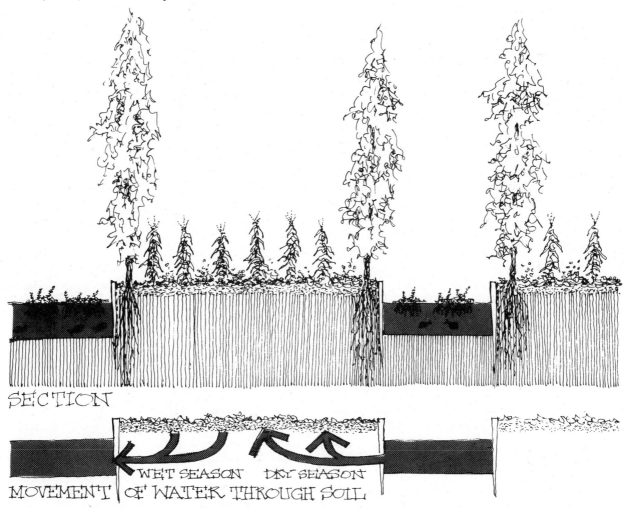

SECTION: CHINAMPAS

with several perennial trees and shrubs and both riparian (willow) and aquatic (water hyacinth) species. Terrestrial animals and fish are also critically important, interactive components of the system.

Functionally, the chinampa system cycles over-time nutrients and water with no need for inputs or outputs of either. Nutrients for plant growth come from canal sediments and animal manure, while animals are fed waste and surplus from agricultural production. The energy inputs come from the sun and from human metabolism fed by the food grown here with no need for additional inputs.

Water moves continuously through the chinampa system as part of the larger pattern of water flow, feeding the crops along the way but losing no more water to their consumption than would be the case if the natural community were still there.

Locationally, the chinampas are situated on low-lying flat landscapes where they can draw on nature's patterns. In these places, water and nutri-

ents are brought to the chinampas by the processes of nature.

Recent Advances

While there exist few contemporary examples with the richness and complexity of the chinampas, re-generative agriculture has continued its evolution and development up to the present. Despite the predominance of industrial agriculture, philosophically committed thinkers on the subject like Rudolph Steiner in Germany, Masanobu Fukuoka and Mokichi Okada in Japan, and Louis Bromfield and J. I. Rodale in the United States have developed their own advanced variations on ancient agricultural themes.

The period since the appearance of *The Silent Spring* (Carson, 1964) has been especially fertile with new ideas and experiments despite the lack of financial support from government and foundations.

The work of the Rodale Research Center in Emmaus, Pennsylvania and the publications of its companion Rodale Press have demonstrated the practical potentials of chemical-free farming and its applications within the mainstream of American agriculture. In a more radical vein, Bill Mollison and his Permaculture Institute, which is based in New Zealand, have worked on a broad range of regenerative techniques and disseminated them widely through publications and short courses. Equally radical and effective for a number of years was the work of the New Alchemy Institute on Cape Cod, Massachusetts, which explored a range of connections between agriculture and other basic life-support processes. Wes Jackson and his Land Institute have spent years studying the Kansas prairie as a model for a perennial agriculture.

At the same time, a number of working farmers who stubbornly refused to adopt chemical methods for reasons of their own have demonstrated the viability of nonchemical agriculture and have contributed to the science as well.

John Vogelsberg and his brother, for example, were skeptical when they returned from World War II and found other farmers near their family farm in Iowa using chemical fertilizers and pesticides on their fields. They decided to try the new chemicals on a few acres of neighboring rented land. They compared the yields with those of the 860-acre family farm where their father and his forefathers had been farming since 1875 and where no chemicals were used. For three years the yields were about the same. So why use chemicals? Even though chemicals were cheap then and all of the neighbors had begun using them wholeheartedly, the Vogelsbergs concluded they were not worth the trouble.

In the 1960s the word "organic" came into widespread use to describe chemical-free farming and gardening, but John Vogelsberg doesn't use it. To him these are just "good farming practices." Year after year, his yields have been about the same as those of his chemical-using neighbors. Economically the difference is just the cost of chemicals, but since the 1970s that has been an increasingly significant difference. By the mid-1980s, it amounted to as much as $30,000, which could make the difference between a good year and a bad year on the farm.

While the Vogelsberg farm is organic in the chemical-free sense, it is also regenerative to some degree in the broader sense. As a human ecosystem, it works in a sustainable way, planting diverse species, rotating crops, and spreading animal manure over the fields.

Making these changes is not an easy matter for most farmers. Agriculture exists in social, economic, and governmental contexts that offer strong inducements to farm in one way or another. Right now the inducements forcefully favor industrial agriculture. This will have to change before a widespread swing to regenerative practices can occur. Nevertheless, change is happening.

Scattered about the country is a surprising number of farms similar to that of the Vogelsbergs. While the details vary widely according to regional climate, soil, and topography, the overall patterns are similar: diverse combinations of crops and animals continuously cycling nutrients back into well-cared-for soils. In some parts of the country there are whole communities of farmers following the same pattern, most notably the highly successful Amish communities of Pennsylvania and Ohio.

Methods for Regenerative Agriculture

Altogether the methods of regenerative agriculture are as diverse as their sources. Some derive from the long and globally varied experiences of traditional and indigenous agriculture. There are the experiments and devout teachings of dedicated people like Steiner, Okada, Fukuoka, Rodale, and Mollison. There is the evolved wisdom of practical farmers like Vogelsberg and many farmers' grassroots organizations. Tying all these together and providing a firm basis are the principles revealed by modern science, especially those of ecology. A truly ecologically based agriculture does not exist in practice. Even with our long historical experience, there is a great deal of research still to be done. A science of agroecology is emerging (Altieri, 1987; Gliessman, 1990), but putting it into operation, especially within the contemporary economic context, will require a great deal more knowledge. Nevertheless, we can perceive at least five reasonably clear, though intertwined, major directions of change:

1. protecting and revitalizing the soil
2. planting for polycultural diversity
3. strategic pest control
4. interactive roles of animals
5. integrated farming systems

Within each of these general directions, there are numbers of specific practices and technologies for practical application. In this section, we discuss a few of the more common practices under each heading, representing the current state of the art.

Protecting and Revitalizing the Soil

Sustainability in agriculture depends on the health of the landscape, the stability of the farm operation, and the vitality of the farming community. The three are essential and inextricably interrelated. The foundation for landscape health is the soil. Sustaining soil quality is essential for sustaining landscape, farm, and community.

In the United States and other countries where industrial agriculture is widely practiced, tillage practices and the use of chemical fertilizers and pesticides are progressively diminishing soil quality in many places. Current conventional tillage has a long history, extending back several centuries before the time of Christ to northern Europe. The early farmers of that region invented the moldboard plow to cope with the dark, heavy soils that were kept moist by frequent rainfall. With this plow they developed the system of turning up parallel furrows and dropping their seeds in the furrows, thus producing crops that grew in long rows. Fertilized with manure from the cows and pigs that were an integral part of their farming system, this plowing-and-row-cropping technique proved both productive and sustainable. The farming regions of northern Europe are still prosperous today.

Since it was so successful there, the row-cropping system spread to other parts of Europe. After the discovery of the Americas, it was widely applied there as well, and during the period of colonization it was carried to Africa and Asia by European settlers. In most of these areas it proved less successful than in northern Europe. Where rainfall was extremely heavy or where sparse soils were thin and poor in organic matter, plowing and row cropping usually proved disastrous. Wes Jackson has called tillage agriculture "a global disease."

Cultivation reduces soil quality in three ways (Cox and Atkins, 1979). The first is the decline in microbial activity and thus in organic matter brought on by disturbance (Stinner and Blair, 1990). In rich, moist soils where the organic content may be over 15 percent, this may not be so critical. In drier regions or in tropical soils, where the organic content is often less than 5 percent, it can lead to virtual sterility.

The second effect is a deterioration over time of soil structure, which results in a reduced ability to hold both minerals and water. The third is an increased susceptibility to wind and water erosion due to long exposure of loose unprotected soil surfaces.

Despite these problems, largely because it proved easily adaptable to use of machinery and chemicals, row cropping has become the prevalent system over most of the world. However, it is not the only system. Especially in the tropics, a great many agricultural systems that evolved in relation to local soils, climate, and culture still survive and even thrive. Many of these depend on shifting cultivation, or the successive clearing and planting of forested areas, which are allowed to return to their natural vegetation cover after producing crops for a few years. Most involve planting seeds in more or less random patterns rather than in rows. A common technique is simply to punch a hole in the ground with a stick and push the seeds in. Another is to toss out handfuls of seeds and allow them to fall where they may—the ancient technique of broadcasting. Most also feature polycultures or multicropping—that is, diverse combinations of plants—rather than single species planted over large areas. All are adapted to specific local conditions.

A number of agricultural experimenters have developed contemporary versions of preindustrial indigenous techniques.

Random Broadcast

Among the prominent contemporary advocates of broadcasting is Masanobu Fukuoka, the Japanese advocate of natural farming whose simple practices (Fukuoka, 1978) have attracted both agricultural researchers and dedicated followers. In his field on the island of Shikoku, Fukuoka grows rice in the summer and wheat and barley in the winter. In May, about 2 weeks before harvesting the wheat and barley, which he grows in separate fields, he broadcasts rice seed over the almost mature plants. Then after harvesting and threshing the grain, he spreads the wheat and barley straw over the fields. In the fall he plants the wheat and barley seed in the same way, spreading seeds over the maturing rice and later, after harvesting, spreading rice straw over them. Fukuoka claims to get about the same yields as his neighbors, who spend large amounts of money on chemical fertilizers and pesticides.

Fukuoka's techniques for rebuilding poor soils are also instructive. For a barren red-clay soil, for example, he recommends planting pine and cedar with a ground cover of clover and alfalfa. As the leguminous ground covers enrich the soil, by fixing nitrogen on which other plants can feed, weeds and shrubs appear and regeneration is underway. It often happens, he says, that within 10 years the top 4 inches of soil are enriched.

Mulch

In Fukuoka's system, as in others that avoid tillage, covering the fields with the residue from the last crop is an essential part of the process. There it provides a mulch, or protective layer, preventing the sun's rays and drops of rain from striking the soil directly. Most natural systems provide similar kinds of protection for the soil in the form of a layer of decomposing organic matter. Under the protective layer, the soil retains its moisture far better than if exposed. Moisture retention is essential to the health of soil organisms, including both earthworms and microbes.

While crop residues are the most convenient mulches for large-scale agriculture, there are a great many other materials that make effective mulches. For high-value speciality crops like strawberries, plastic sheeting is often used. Various kinds of fabric, including old sheets, are also useful. Even newspapers have served the purpose. Thicker mulches formed of loosely packed materials with air spaces are generally best. Among these are materials like crushed bark or shells or corn husks. Mulches are especially important in regions where water is scarce because they help to minimize evaporation loss.

Deep Cultivation

Deep cultivation involves complete digging up and loosening of the soil. While a number of traditional agricultural systems have used similar techniques, the originator of deep-cultivation techniques in modern times was Rudolph Steiner. Like Fukuoka, he was a thinker who used agriculture as a means of giving concrete form to his thoughts. Steiner used raised beds with soil loosened and cultivated to their full depth of about 12 inches and no chemicals. On this basis he developed the intensive vegetable-growing systems that he called biodynamic. Alan Chadwick, one of Steiner's students, combined the biodynamic method with the French intensive method, which calls for growing vegetables in animal manure. Chadwick's French intensive/biodynamic system uses raised beds 12 inches deep and 3 to 6 feet wide. Between beds are narrow pathways for walking and wheeling implements. The beds contain a rich mixture of native soil and either manure or compost. Depending on the original soil texture, the manure or compost can constitute 25 to 75 percent of the soil, which is thoroughly cultivated and loosened in the mixing process. Bone meal, wood ash, and manure are then added to the top layer of the soil mixture, and vegetable seeds are planted close together.

The French intensive/biodynamic method is highly productive in terms of resource use. John Jeavons (1974) claims, apparently with justification, that it produces four times the quantity of food on the same area of land as conventional agriculture,

EXAMPLE

Produce Gardens

Supplying salad vegetables to a number of high-quality restaurants in Los Angeles and a number of other cities as far away as Boston, Produce Gardens grows more than 50 varieties of lettuce along with 25 other vegetables. The gardens cover 3 acres in the right-of-way beneath power lines owned by the Los Angeles Department of Water and Power in the Los Angeles suburb of Tarzana.

The produce grows in deeply cultivated beds, with plants closely spaced, using no chemical fertilizers or pesticides and no machinery. In the mild southern California climate, both planting and harvesting are year-round operations, which makes it possible to maintain a workforce of 10 people all year full-time in addition to the owners, who are husband and wife. Netting suspended over the growing areas protects the plants from birds.

The owners estimate the productivity of their 3 acres as being about four times that of vegetable growers on larger farms outside the city. Their methods make it possible to supply a market that demands consistent quality, reliable quantity, and freshness with no hint of chemicals.

using one-half the water and 1 percent of the fossil-fuel energy. However, the labor requirement is considerable. This is a method suitable only for small, intensively managed plots.

Potential Applications

Since these techniques, with the exception of deep cultivation, all evolved to fit particular natural and cultural conditions, they cannot be easily transferred from one context to another. Nevertheless, there are certain common underlying concepts such as random patterns and minimum soil disturbance that might well be widely applied. As they stand, however, all of these systems are highly labor-intensive, and they do not adapt readily to the use of farm machinery. In the present marketplace they are too expensive. They are much better adapted to small-scale subsistence farming than to the demands of large-scale production agriculture. While they can be effective on small urban or suburban farms even in industrial countries, they are unlikely under present circumstances to have a major role in producing the huge quantities of food needed for the huge populations of the 21st century.

Conservation Tillage Techniques

Recognizing this, and recognizing as well that conventional tillage is unsustainable on most soils, farmers have developed a number of minimum-till, or conservation tillage, techniques. These are capable of reducing the damage done by conventional tillage but are at the same time adaptable to large-scale farm operations. Minimum-tillage techniques are defined as those that leave a minimum of 30 percent of crop residues covering the soil.

NO-TILLAGE / Rather than planting into a prepared seedbed, no-till farming calls for planting into sod, stubble, or crop residue. The only soil disturbance is that caused by a device on the planter that cuts a slot into which the seed is dropped. Usually, crop stubble remains in place as a mulch.

No-till systems have proven effective in maintaining organic content, and reducing water loss and erosion. One study showed that no-tillage farming reduced runoff by 86.3 to 98.7 percent and soil erosion by 96.7 to 100 percent (National Research Council [NRC], 1989). Time and cost are also reduced since the use of farm machinery is much less than for conventional tillage.

The major disadvantage, however, is a most important one. Crop residues left in place can provide an ideal environment for some pests, and more weeds tend to survive and grow when their life cycles are not disturbed by tillage. This can increase the need for chemical pesticides. No-till farms are often more dependent on chemicals than conventional-till farms.

CHISEL PLOWING / Of the several conservation tillage techniques, the most common uses a chisel plow to cut a narrow slit in the soil, mixing crop residues into the opening. Thus nutrients and water can make their way to deeper levels.

Chisel plowing also reduces erosion but not as much as no-tillage. Studies suggest reductions of 30 to 50 percent compared with conventional tillage. The ability of chisel plowing to allow water and nutrients to penetrate without extensive soil disturbance makes it an effective technique for rehabilitation of disturbed soils.

RIDGE TILLAGE / A second conservation tillage technique that reduces erosion without increasing pests is to till ridge tops only for planting in the spring. This creates a seedbed on the ridge top while pushing the crop residue into the valleys between ridges, where it helps to hold soil moisture and reduce erosion. Weed seeds also tend to concentrate in the valleys; when they do sprout, they are easily controlled by cultivation.

While these and other minimum-till systems have significant advantages over conventional tillage, they are less than ideal. Most involve some level of soil degradation, and no-tillage, which minimizes soil degradation, involves high levels of pesticide use. Thus, minimum-till techniques are not truly sustainable.

At best, they are effective interim measures that farmers can apply to slow soil degradation until they are able to implement truly regenerative systems.

Wes Jackson is exploring one kind of truly regenerative agricultural system at his Land Institute in Kansas. Jackson envisions an agriculture for the plains based on herbaceous perennial polycultures. The structure of his polycultures replicates the natural shortgrass ecosystems of the plains. Jackson's key strategy is the second strategy of regenerative design—using nature as model and context. Since the plant species are perennial, there is no tillage, no annual planting involved. Turning this concept into a successful agricultural system, however, depends on perennial species producing a high yield of edible seeds (Jackson, 1980). This remains an unknown.

In any case, virtually all regenerative agriculture systems—past, present, and future—are polycultures; that is, they are diverse, interactive combinations of species in contrast with the monocultures of industrial agriculture.

Planting for Polycultural Diversity

The structures of natural ecosystems involve groups of plants and animals growing together in close proximity, forming communities held together by complex interactions among species. As an example of the third strategy—aggregating, not isolating, functions—each species helps to provide for the needs of the others. The diversity of species and the network of interactions contribute to the health, stability, and longevity of the community as a whole.

Using chemicals instead to provide for the needs of plants, industrial agriculture eschewed the ecological community concept and replaced it with monocultures—vast areas of a single crop species. The concept of plant and animal community interaction provides a useful means of providing for the needs of plants and animals within the system without using chemicals. Polycultures, or groups of species, can be designed according to the general principles of natural ecosystems to form agroecosystems that are analogs of evolved ecosystems.

Guilds

A community of species devised by humans is called a guild. Generally a guild is formed around a central species of plants or animals. Ideally each member of a guild provides some needs of at least one other member. Among the needs provided for are

- *Pest Control.* Some plants repel pests that prey on other plants, and some animals prey on pests. Simply intermixing the individuals of different species can spread and diffuse, and thus reduce, the pest population.
- *Microclimate Control.* Trees or high shrubs can provide shade for lower-growing plants. Plants with dense foliage can shelter others from the wind or fend off rain or snow.
- *Providing Nutrients.* As discussed earlier, some leguminous plants support fixation of atmospheric nitrogen in the soil, which then becomes available to other plants.
- *Soil Preparation.* The roots of some larger plants can both loosen soil and hold it in place for the benefit of smaller plants.
- *Physical Support.* Taller plants can provide poles and frames on which other plants, especially vines, can grow.
- *Processing and Assimilation of Materials.* Soil organisms such as earthworms and various microorganisms are members of the guild as well, and are essential for maintaining soil health.

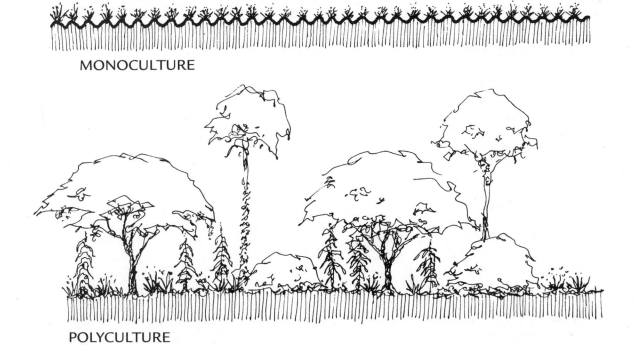

MONOCULTURE

POLYCULTURE

EXAGMPLE

■■

CET Model Farm

The Centro de Educacion y Technologia (CET) of Chile has instituted a program for aiding peasants in establishing small farms that can provide year-round food for their families (Altieri and Anderson, 1986). Several model farms a half hectare in size demonstrate the principles and methods of intensive mixed farming. Farmers from various parts of the country live on these farms for periods of time and participate in the various phases of operation and management. Then they return to their communities to apply what they have learned and teach it to their neighbors.

The demonstration farms follow a basic model designed to function in Chile's coastal region, which has a Mediterranean climate—semiarid with wet winters and long dry summers. The model includes vegetables, forage and row crops, fruit trees, and several species of farm animals. Vegetables grow mostly in intensively cultivated raised beds located adjacent to the small farmhouse. Beehives and chicken coops are also near the house; cows and pigs are farther away, as is a compost pile. A row of fruit trees forms a buffer between all of these and the road.

Bordering this intensively managed complex is a cluster of six approximately equal rectangular fields separated by fences, one field for each year in the rotational program. The rotation includes more vegetables, legumes, cereals, and forage plants with combinations designed for crop diversity and continuous soil regeneration as well as high yields.

Though the land area is small, productivity is high, with the vegetable beds yielding as much as 83 kilograms each month and the field yielding about 6 tons of food per year. Animal manure and legumes provide for ongoing soil regeneration.

Guilds can also provide economic benefits by supplying other crops in case one is weeded out by an infestation, or in case of a bad market for one or two crops. Guilds can provide higher overall productivity by fully using several environmental levels. And in community farming, they can provide a varied diet.

In North America the most common guild, or polyculture, has long been the squash-beans-maize complex grown by many Indian tribes. The seeds of squash, beans, and maize are sown together. As the cornstalks shoot upward, bean vines wind around them and thus can move upward into the sunlight as well. The leguminous beans help provide nutrients for squash and corn by fixing nitrogen. Squash plants spread over the ground at the bases of the corn and bean plants, covering and protecting the soil and limiting the growth of weeds.

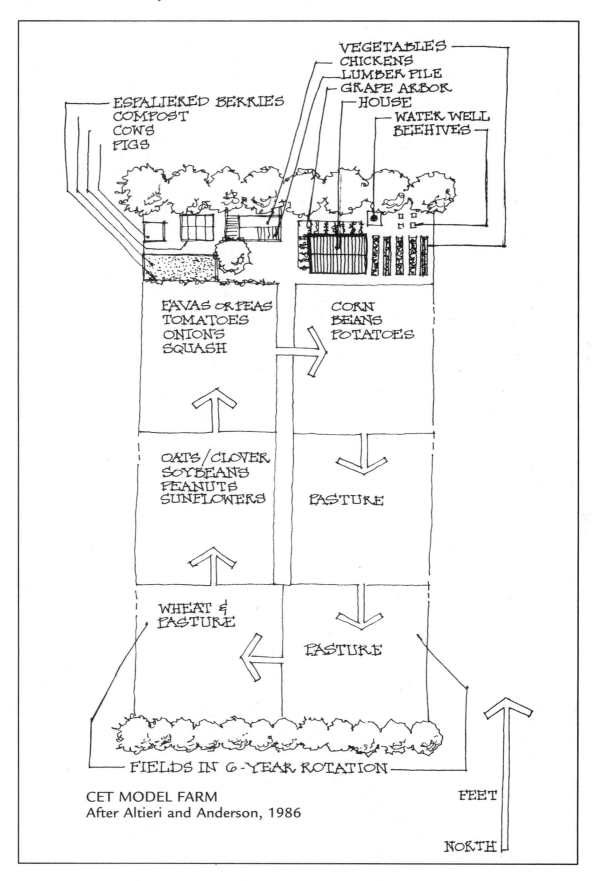

ESPALIERED BERRIES
COMPOST
COWS
FIGS

VEGETABLES
CHICKENS
LUMBER PILE
GRAPE ARBOR
HOUSE
WATER WELL
BEEHIVES

FAVAS OR PEAS
TOMATOES
ONIONS
SQUASH

CORN
BEANS
POTATOES

OATS/CLOVER
SOYBEANS
PEANUTS
SUNFLOWERS

PASTURE

WHEAT &
PASTURE

PASTURE

FIELDS IN 6-YEAR ROTATION

CET MODEL FARM
After Altieri and Anderson, 1986

FEET

NORTH

This is the simplest of polycultures. Some traditional examples are far more complex, especially in the tropics where some of the most successful agroecosystems follow the structural principles of the highly diverse, multilayered rainforest. For a region in Africa, Bede Okigbo devised a complex guild system that features different polycultural combinations of species for each topographic condition and for each season of the year. Some species overlap in time and space, creating a highly interactive and dynamic landscape (Okigbo, 1989).

Agroforestry

These complex tropical guilds are layered vertically; trees are included at the highest level and sometimes at one or two levels below that.

This principle is at work in indigenous farming systems in many parts of the world. In Java, for example, villages sit in the middle of spreading rice fields. Farmers earn their living growing rice but also grow the food for their families within the small spaces of the villages. They make the most of the small spaces by using a complex layered system. At ground level are root crops such as the sweet potato. At the next level up are plants that reach well above ground, like corn and cassava. Just slightly above those are the branches of fruit trees like mango and ranbutan. At the highest level, as in the region Huetar Atlantica, are coconuts. Vines like passion fruit wind up the trunks of the trees and mingle at the top with their branches. To observers, these village gardens look like the natural rainforest, stands of which still exist nearby (Soemarwoto, 1975).

The comparison between the village gardens and the rice fields that spread out around them in instructive. Most strikingly, while pests present serious problems in the rice monoculture, there are virtually no pests in the village gardens. This is almost certainly due to the mix of species. Moreover, the

INDONESIAN POLYCULTURE

gardens are considerably more productive. The farmers reportedly derive more income from the village gardens than from the rice fields (ibid.).

The advantages of agroforestry, which means all farming systems that include trees, are increasingly understood in other parts of the world as well—even in the industrialized countries. In addition to their obvious contributions of food or fiber, they can provide firewood and materials for small construction, habitat for birds that can aid in pest control and shelter from sun, wind, and rain. Their roots help to hold the soil in place, and they often survive extreme weather conditions that kill smaller plants. On the larger scale, they help to reduce air pollution, absorb carbon dioxide, and produce oxygen. They contribute leaves for mulch and compost and also help to keep soils loose for rainfall retention. They also pump moisture back into the atmosphere and thus help to maintain overall humidity levels.

Moreover, in at least some situations, the inclusion of trees in an agricultural system increases productivity. In one experiment, fields with acacia trees produced more grain, required shorter fallow periods, and supported more farm animals than fields planted in monocultures of grain (NRC, 1983). In Senegal, agricultural systems combining annual crops, trees, and livestock have supported as many as 60 people per hectare (about 24 per acre) (Dover and Talbot, 1989).

ALLEY CROPPING / Up to now, agroforestry has been primarily practiced in the tropics on a relatively small scale. However, there is no reason why the concept could not be applied on a larger scale in temperate zones, even in the mechanized agriculture of the industrial countries. Alley cropping offers one approach. In alley-cropping systems, rows of trees are planted far enough apart to allow for row crops between rows of trees. In Ohio, researchers have planted rows of the leguminous Siberian pea shrub (*Caragona arborescens*) 15 meters apart, providing windbreak and wildlife habitat. Between the rows of the large shrub are rows of corn and wheat.

Strip-cropping and Intercropping
As with agroforestry, most polyculture systems so far have been used in small-scale subsistence agriculture. The easiest means for applying the polyculture concept at larger scales are strip-cropping and intercropping, which involve alternating rows of different crops. The difference is that the strips in strip-cropping are wide enough for independent cultivation while intercropping rows may require special equipment. Stinner and Blair (1990) recommend alternating strips of a leguminous crop like alfalfa with a nonlegume such as corn. Tomatoes might grow in rows between rows of squash or beans for example. Intercropping potatoes and mustard plants, for example, considerably reduces nematode populations because the mustard gives off toxins. Alternating rows of okra, tomatoes, ginger and mung beans helps to reduce leaf spot for reasons not entirely understood.

Crop Rotation
Planting a sequence of different crops in a given field is an ancient practice that achieves polycultural diversity through time. Rotation sequences follow 2- to 5-year cycles, occasionally longer. The possible sequences are almost unlimited, but they often include a leguminous crop to introduce nitrogen into the soil. A typical rotation might include corn, soybeans, and alfalfa. The advantages of rotation in terms of increased productivity, pest control, and soil health are well established. Yields of wheat following legumes in a rotation, for example, are commonly 10 to 20 percent higher than those in comparable, continuously cropped fields.

Strategic Pest Control

The first rule of pest control within a regenerative agricultural system is to learn to live with acceptable levels of pest populations and manage them. A lesson learned during the most extreme years of chemical pesticide use was that a pest species is never entirely eliminated; when populations are reduced to minimal levels, they are likely soon to come back larger than ever. With pest populations at manageable levels, crop losses are generally at acceptable levels. This applies to both insects and weeds. Most regenerative farmers tolerate some weed populations. Basicly, is a matter of seeking optimal levels for multiple functions, the fourth strategy. Fukuoka sometimes calls his method "farming among the weeds."

Integrated Pest Management
The strategy that has developed to reduce pesticide use in conventional farming, called integrated pest management (IPM), involves three basic steps. The first is to establish a tolerance threshold or a maximum level of pest predation that a farmer can tolerate. Thus it is important to recognize that pests cannot be eradicated, and if they could, eradicating

EXAMPLE

Kirschenmann Farm

Located in central North Dakota near the town of Windsor, the Kirschenmann family has operated its farm without using chemicals since 1976, when Fred Kirschenmann took over its management. Large for a family farm, especially an organic family farm, it covers 3100 acres.

The farm's single most important operating principle is crop diversity. Among the crops are buckwheat, flax, millet, rye, soybeans, and wheat, all grown in small fields that form a patchwork quilt on the prairie. The diversity has economic as well as ecological value, spreading the risks and providing what Kirschenmann calls his insurance. Crops shift yearly in these fields following a 3-, 4-, and 5-year schedule. The crop rotation serves to limit populations of pests that cannot multiply annually. Each fall the Kirschenmanns also plant cover crops that they plow back into the soil to fertilize it in the spring.

The farm's main source of nutrients is manure from its 100 head of cattle. Spreading is done with a tractor and spreader. The Kirschenmann farm has a full complement of machinery, including six tractors and two combines and all the implements that go with them. The equipment is relatively light; there is no four-wheel-drive tractor, for example, because the soil is looser, less compacted, than that of conventional farms.

Economically, the Kirschenmann farm is a very stable operation. Its products bring premium prices because they are entitled to the "organic" label. Not having to buy chemicals also saves considerable money. Neighboring farms of similar size invest $30,000 to $50,000 each year in chemicals, usually borrowing this money in the spring along with money to buy seeds and gasoline. For several years, Kirschenmann has not borrowed money in the spring.

This level of ecological sustainability and financial stability was not achieved quickly, however. Kirschenmann reports that his first year of operation as a regenerative farm was easy and profitable, mostly due to very favorable weather. For the next 2 years, however, yields were poor, and there was some concern that the shift toward regenerative farming might not work. The fourth year was much better, as was the fifth and the years since.

them would not be desirable. A farm is an ecosystem that includes many species, some of which consume a small portion of the crops. The NRC (1989) defines the threshold level as being "when the predicted value of the impending crop damage exceeds the cost of controlling the pest" (p. 208).

The next step involves applying the perception-and-feedback strategy, or what IPM proponents call scouting. This is a matter of observing pest populations and determining when they reach the threshold level. After that the farmer can consider a whole range of agricultural techniques that can help to keep populations below that level. These include diversifying crops, using genetically resistant strains, introducing predator species, choosing various tillage practices, leaving residues, using pheromones (to prevent mating), using pest-repelling species (allelopathy), releasing sterile males, precisely managing water and fertilizer, adjusting times of planting and harvesting, and using bacterial insecticides.

Finally, there is the technique used in theory as a last resort: applying pesticides directed at specific pests in carefully controlled amounts. Control is important to minimize pesticide use and especially to minimize the amount that is not consumed by the pest and goes elsewhere to cause damage.

Practiced as intended, IPM has the potential to virtually eliminate pesticide use except perhaps for emergency situations.

Among the practices mentioned above that have proven to be most effective in reducing pest populations to manageable levels are the following:

DIVERSIFICATION / The diversified systems described earlier all apply the strategy of letting nature do the work of population control. This happens in several ways. By simply spreading the individuals of a species farther apart, crop diversification spreads the populations of pest species and thus slows their multiplication. Creating a community of crops also creates a community of pests, and the species within a community tend to keep each other's populations within limits. Furthermore, the tendency of some species to repel others can be used by design. Marigolds, mustard, and *Crotalaria,* for example, all are believed to repel nematodes. Crop rotation removes the food supply of specialized pest species, thus periodically decimating their populations.

GENETIC RESISTANCE / Plant geneticists have had considerable success in building resistance to a number of pests into the genes of cultivars for some crops. Some plant diseases have been almost elimi-

nated by building resistance, and predation by insects and mites has been much reduced in others. This is another fertile area for research.

INTRODUCTION AND AUGMENTATION OF NATURAL ENEMIES / The most common example is introduction of ladybug beetles to eat the aphids in vegetable gardens. Other examples abound. Since the Australian vedalia beetle was successfully introduced into California citrus groves in the late 19th century to prey on the cottony cushion scale insect, about 70 insect pests have been controlled in the United States by introduced parasites and predators (NRC, 1989).

Interactive Roles of Animals

Until the predominance of industrial farming, animals were an integral part of most agricultural systems. They supplied food for the farmers and sometimes for sale in the form of milk, cheese, eggs, meat, and honey. They also consumed wastes and crops inedible for humans. Most importantly, they were the major means of recycling nutrients back to the soil and the crops. As chemical fertilizer became a nutrient source, industrial agriculture took animals off the integrated farm and, following the industrial-era strategy of disintegration and concentration, moved them into more specialized operations such as dairies, feedlots, and vast ranches. Some of the functions that made animals important parts of the farm system now in concentrated numbers create problems. Cattle crowded in dairies or feedlots, for example, produce enormous quantities of manure. The same is true of chicken farms. In quantities that can be assimilated by the landscape, animal manure is an important means of returning nutrients to the soil. In amounts larger than that, it becomes a potential pollutant, difficult to use effectively, difficult even to dispose of. In a number of places, nitrates leaching through the soil from dairies, feedlots, and chicken farms have become major sources of water pollution.

To understand both the complex roles of animals in agriculture and some of the problems that arise when they are removed from the agricultural system, consider the water buffalo of Sri Lanka (Dover and Talbot, 1989). In that country, water buffalo once provided power for plowing and also for threshing grain. In the years following World War II, the buffalo were largely replaced by tractors, which was economically efficient because the tractors saved at least 8 worker-days per acre every year.

However, the farmer now had to purchase several things once supplied at no cost by the buffalo. No longer was nature doing the work. Among these were gasoline for the tractor at wildly fluctuating prices, chemical fertilizer to replace the buffalo dung and urine that once fertilized the fields, and milk for the family. Furthermore, tractors compacted the soils and in some places soil structures began to break down.

Most of the ponds used as buffalo wallows that once punctuated the rice fields were removed because tractors do not wallow. With the ponds went the fish that once inhabited them, including the 300 to 400 pounds of edible fish once harvested from each acre of pond each year. Also gone were the fish that once preyed on mosquito larvae. After the ponds were drained, frequent insecticide sprayings became necessary to keep the mosquitos, and thus malaria, under control. Gone also were the rat snakes that bred in the wallows and preyed on rodent populations, which in turn ate the rice as it matured and burrowed through the paddy dikes, causing water-control problems. Another species that once bred in the ponds and is now disappearing is a small lizard that eats the burrowing crabs whose digging destroys the levees that form the channels needed to bring the water to the rice fields.

Whether the tractors are worth the price or not and whether the tractor-based system can be sustained or not are questions not yet answered with any degree of certainty. Certainly, the tractors displaced human labor, thus contributing to unemployment and poverty. Without question it is a less diverse, more fragile system than the buffalo provided and less sustainable in the longer time frame.

As illustrated in this story, animals have a variety of roles to play in regenerative agriculture. Among the more important are the following.

Consuming the Surplus

Pigs and chickens are especially useful in the assimilation function, consuming materials that are produced on farms as byproducts that otherwise have no use. Chickens, ducks, and geese can graze on weeds and can also be fed household wastes. Pigs thrive on household wastes. Cows and horses can graze in pastures where clovers, vetch, and other leguminous crops grow in rotations to enrich the soil.

Manure as a Source of Nutrients

On the highly stable and productive farms of northern Europe, where agriculture has been sustained for several thousand years, a common, highly visible feature on every farm is the manure pile. The pile is continuously replenished by the farm's animals, which are pampered like children and which often spend winters in immaculately clean quarters on the ground floor of the farmhouse. Seasonally, farmers spread the manure over the fields.

Other farming systems have other ways of returning nutrients to the soil through the capacities of animals to convert food into fertilizer. Among the devices often used in nonindustrial countries are the various animal tractor systems. The chicken tractor consists of a small wire-mesh pen within which a flock of chickens is confined for a period ranging from 3 or 4 weeks to several months. The chickens eat the weeds and scratch the ground, all the while spreading their manure over the soil. When the chickens are moved to the next plot to begin their work anew, grain and vegetable seeds are spread over the well-prepared ground. Sometimes vines grow on the fencing, and trees can also grow within.

Pig tractor systems are similar in operation but are used on larger farms. The fenced area for pigs covers usually 1 to 5 acres. Mollison (1988) recommends using a pig tractor to develop pasture for milk cows using chicory, dandelion, clover, various grasses, and other forbs. The pigs can eat waste products from the dairy to constitute a continuously regenerating system.

Endless variations are possible on the basic animal tractor system to fit local climate, landscape, and culture. In the Canary Islands, for example, milk goats are tethered to prepare the land for growing fruit trees.

Farm Work

Before mechanization, heavy farm work like plowing and threshing was done mostly by animals; in many places in the third world it still is. In some areas where animals have given way to tractors, as in Sri Lanka, there are several good reasons to regret the change. Even in the industrial countries there are a considerable number of tasks that might be carried out by draft animals.

Game Ranching

Cattle and other ruminants such as sheep and goats graze on about half the world's lands, and most of those lands are in a degraded state. This is due partially to animal species (especially cattle) being introduced onto lands not naturally suited to support

EXAMPLE

Hopcraft Game Ranch

Among the successful experiments in game ranching—no longer just an experiment but a now successful commercial venture—is the 20,000-acre natural ranch operated by David Hopcraft on the Athi Kapiti plains in Kenya, some 25 miles from Nairobi. Having grown up on his family's cattle ranch in Kenya, Hopcraft has seen firsthand how cattle devouring the African grasslands leads to the latter drying up and eroding away, with starvation the end result.

Hopcraft undertook his first experiment with support from the National Science Foundation. He fenced in a 300-acre plot of dry grassland in Kenya, divided it down the middle, and stocked one side with cattle and the other side with native gazelle. The cattle side he operated according to accepted ranching practice. The gazelle side he managed according to a system of culling that kept the herd at a more or less constant level and the vegetation intact—essentially sustained-yield management.

At the end of 3 years Hopcraft added up the results and they were startling. The gazelle side had produced 14.6 pounds of lean meat per acre per year, while the cattle side had produced only 7.9 pounds. The grass cover and climax vegetation within the cattle enclosure had been significantly reduced, while the vegetation in the gazelle enclosure was essentially unchanged. Financially, the gazelle side produced a net profit three times that of the cattle side (Hopcraft, 1975).

Given these results, Hopcraft next acquired his 20,000-acre ranch on the Athi Kahiti plains. The research aspects of his operation were supported this time by the Lilly Foundation, and the results have been similar to those on the smaller plot (Hopcraft, 1980).

Fourteen animal species roam free on the 20,000 acres, and four of these are regularly harvested: Thompson's gazelle, Grant's gazelle, Coke's hartebeest, and wildebeest. About 40 percent of the animal population is harvested each year; even with this off-take the numbers increased by about 12 percent over the first 3 years (Stelfox et al., 1984).

them, and partially to overloading the land with larger numbers of animals than it can support (that is, to exceeding its carrying capacity).

One means for adding to protein production without excessive concentration or overgrazing is the technique of game ranching, which follows the strategy of letting nature do the work by harvesting some species within a natural ecosystem on an organized sustained-yield basis. Generally, the most promising species for this purpose are the large herbivores, which exist in large numbers in some ecosystems, generally far more numerous than carnivores. Many of them are well suited for human consumption. Examples are the buffalo of the American plains, the pronghorn antelope of the West, and many antelope species in Africa. The standing crop of large herbivores in the African savannah has been estimated as about 500 kilograms per hectare, which is about the same as that of cattle grazing in the pastures of the same region (Stelfox et al., 1984). Thus, for the same yield, game ranching keeps the naturally evolving ecosystem in functioning order, with no problems of excessive concentrations or difficulties with supplying quantities of inputs or disposing of outputs (Hopcraft, 1980). Deer ranching is approaching sheep ranching in pounds of meat produced in New Zealand. A number of successful game ranches are operating in various parts of the world, demonstrating potentials for revitalized ecosystems in landscapes degraded by overgrazing.

As with most means of harvesting renewable resources, game ranching has been subject to a number of abuses. Especially on elk ranches in western states, ranchers have been found luring free animals through their gates and increasing herd sizes beyond their carrying capacity.

Aquaculture

In some parts of Asia, especially in China, aquaculture is an essential part of the agricultural system. This makes particularly good sense when we consider both the extraordinary productivity and the waste assimilation capacities of fish ponds. A given area of an aquacultural pond is several times more productive—as many as 20 times more productive—than the same area planted in crops. When we consider that what is produced is high-quality protein, the difference becomes especially important. Moreover, the nutrient inputs can come from materials that might otherwise be wastes.

The productivity of aquaculture is partly due to the fact that water supports the weight of its inhabitants, allowing them to use more energy for biomass production and growth than land animals, which must invest a larger portion of their available energy for resisting gravity and moving about in search of food. Furthermore, a pond has the capacity to support a complete food chain in a small area. Microorganisms can consume waste materials thrown in a pond and are in turn consumed by longer microorganisms and small fish, which are consumed by larger fish that can be harvested to be consumed by humans.

This active food chain functions on several levels occupying the full depth of a pond. The high-efficiency spread throughout the depth of a pond yields large amounts of high protein biomass for harvesting. In systems where different species occupy distinct levels, productivity can be even higher. The polyculture principle applies in fish ponds as to crops. William McLarney (1976) attributes much of the success of Chinese aquaculture to their ability to fill all the niches with species usable by humans: plankton feeders, bottom feeders, algae feeders, and predators. On a relatively simple level, according to McLarney, tilapia have been stocked in catfish ponds in some instances in the southern United States to feed on algae near the surface while the catfish scavenge on materials falling to the bottom. The two species do not interfere with each other, and both provide good, tasty food. The results of introducing tilapia are considerable increases in productivity, including greater numbers of catfish. A third species could be stocked for the level in between these two, possibly a predator that would eat some of the tilapia young, thus allowing more food for the healthier survivors to grow faster.

Integrated Farming Systems

To some extent, establishing a regenerative agriculture is a matter of reassembling structures dismantled by industrial agriculture—the strategy of aggregating, not disaggregating—such as relationships between animals and crops or between cover crops and food crops. In doing this we begin to think of farms as integrated systems—agroecosystems— rather than as specialized production units. The possibilities for integrative operation are considerable. The different parts within a regenerative farm can interact in a number of ways, as do the species within a polyculture.

Agriculture/Aquaculture

Probably the best example of system integration is integrated agriculture/aquaculture, which has been

EXAMPLE

An Integrated Farm in Nepal

The Fishery Development Section of the Department of Agriculture in Nepal selected a small farm 14 kilometers from the capital city of Kathmandu for a case-study project in integrated agriculture/aquaculture. The purpose was to develop guidelines for management and production methods (Rajbanshi, 1980).

The farm covers about 1 hectare, with roughly half this area on a lower plain adjacent to a stream and the other half on a higher terrace several meters above the level of the stream. The case-study project included 2 years of operation. During the first (baseline) year the farmer grew local cereal varieties. For the second year, with guidance from the Fishery Development staff, he added fish ponds stocked with carp and covering about a quarter of his land. He also added ducks and pigs and grew higher-yielding varieties of cereal.

Even though the amount of labor decreased by 39 percent from the first year to the second, both the total yield of the farm and its profits increased dramatically. Crop yields went up by 56 percent, and net profits increased by 183 percent. These increases occurred despite the fact that the farmer limited the numbers of pigs and ducks to considerably less than the actual capacity. He has since increased both the numbers of animals and his own profits, though this increase was not monitored closely enough for accurate quantification. Researchers also reported a considerable improvement in the farm family's diet due to the protein available from ducks, pigs, and fish.

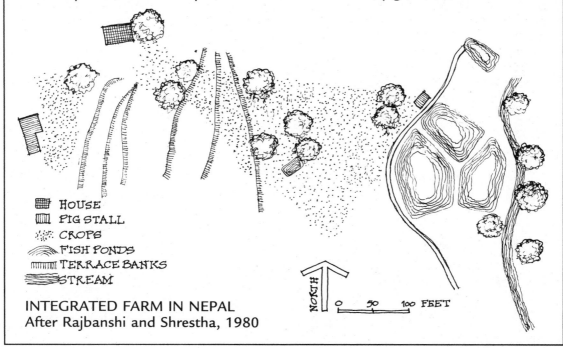

HOUSE
PIG STALL
CROPS
FISH PONDS
TERRACE BANKS
STREAM

NORTH   0   50   100   FEET

INTEGRATED FARM IN NEPAL
After Rajbanshi and Shrestha, 1980

practiced in various forms for thousands of years in China and which has been further refined by modern experimentation. The basic concept is an expansion of the functions of the basic aquacultural pond on both the input and output sides. On the input side, animal manure enriches the pond food web, which on the output side, the pond water, enriched by both animal manure and fish wastes, is highly effective for irrigation.

Once in the pond, manure can make its way into the food web in three ways. The first is at the very bottom of the web's primary production: as a source of nutrients and minerals used in photosynthesis to produce phytoplankton, which in turn become food for zooplankton, which in turn are eaten by higher organisms. The second way is by sinking into the sediments on the bottom of a pond, to be taken up by heterotrophic microorganisms, which might also become food for zooplankton or might be consumed directly by some fish. In the third way the manure could be consumed directly by fish. However, manure is a poor fish food, usually shunned. Thus the first two models are far more important.

While manure from almost any animal can be used in such systems, pigs, chickens, and ducks are most commonly used. In most of Asia but not in China, pigs and ducks are commonly raised in pens resting above the fish ponds with openings in their floors to allow both urine and manure to fall directly into the pond. In Thailand one system, illustrated below, uses a pig pen over the fish pond with a chicken coop over that. The pigs then feed on chicken feces which drop from above and in turn contribute their feces to the pond below.

Researchers have studied both the nutrient values of animal manure and the productivity of manure-fed ponds in a number of contexts. Manure has proven consistently rich in the essential nutrients nitrogen, phosphorus, and potassium and adequate in the necessary trace elements. Urine has even higher nutrient content. Thus, both are effective in nutrient recycling. However, the manure is low in available energy and protein, which accounts for its low food value when directly consumed by fish.

The productivity of manure-fed ponds is high compared to other means for producing protein, but the yields per unit area are only about half those of ponds fed with prepared, fossil-fuel-derived feeding pellets. However, the operating cost for the manure-fed ponds is less than half as much. A study in the United States showed a cost of about $0.41 per kilogram of fish in the pellet-fed ponds compared with a range of $0.02 to $0.21 per kilogram in manure-fed ponds (Delmondo, 1980).

Almost unlimited variations on the integrated agriculture/aquaculture theme are possible. The traditional Chinese method, practiced for centuries, involves collecting and composting pig manure. The compost is then both spread over fields and dropped into fish ponds. The average yield of Chinese fish ponds is very high—about 3 tons per hectare per year (Schroeder, 1980).

In the central plains of Thailand, the system of pond and crop rotation shown in the section below is sometimes used. This involves two identical plots, each with a series of parallel ridges with water channels in between (Delmondo, 1980). Each year, the farmer floods one of the plots for fish production while vegetable crops grow on the ridges of the other. Water in the channels between ridges of the plot with crops is used for both irrigation and fish production. On a higher ridge between the two plots is an animal house with chickens on the top level and pigs on the lower level.

In some other parts of Asia, the rice paddy-fish culture is common. In this system, fish (usually carp and sometimes tilapia) grow in the water of rice paddies with the rice. Fry are introduced early in the

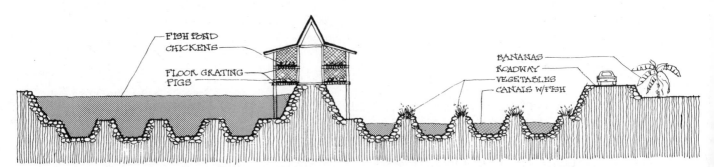

INTEGRATED AGRICULTURE/AQUACULTURE SYSTEM IN THAILAND WITH POND ROTATION
After Delmendo, 1980

growing season and grow to edible size for harvesting when the paddies are drained in the fall. Research in the Philippines has shown fish yields of about 100 to 200 kilograms per hectare per year and rice yields of about the same as nearby rice paddies without fish (Huat and Tan, 1980). No fish feeds or fertilizers were used. The fish fed on naturally produced algae, and the rice was fertilized by fish manure.

Rice culture is the simplest way of using the nutrient-rich water from fish ponds for food crops. There are, however, other ways. One of these is simply to draw the water from the pond through channels of pipes and then distribute it through flood or sprinkler irrigation systems.

While such aquaculture/agriculture systems are the best examples of complete operational integration, there are numerous other examples of efficiencies gained through simultaneous solution to dissimilar problems in agriculture. Two techniques pioneered by the New Alchemy Institute illustrate the point.

Composting Greenhouse

The heat given off by the composting process can be put to beneficial use. The New Alchemy Institute incorporated a composting bed into the north wall of a greenhouse and directed its surplus heat to raise growing temperatures.

Aquaculture Thermal Mass

The New Alchemy Institute has also put to good use the heat-storage potential in the water of aquacultural ponds by locating them in solar-heated buildings (Seale and Wolfe, 1981). The tanks made of translucent plastic, 5 feet in diameter and about 5 feet high, are especially useful for this purpose. Located in the direct path of solar radiation during the day, they can collect a great deal of heat while the sun is shining for release at night. The heat also stimulates the biological activity within the tank, thus increasing fish productivity.

Diversity of Agroecosystems

The most striking characteristics of the examples of regenerative agriculture given throughout the chapter is their seeming dissimilarity, their striking diversity in size, form, and even methods. This underscores the fact that while industrial technology in agriculture seems to drive farms into ever larger mechanized and monocultural units that are essen-

tially the same everywhere, the range and variety of regenerative techniques suggest the potentials of diverse types of farming units. Some regenerative technologies are suitable for use on large farms geared to mass production, but many are not. Regenerative systems can thrive in a number of contexts where industrial technology cannot. Context is all-important; landscape, climate, economics, and culture determine what system will work in a given setting, and these are endlessly diverse. Thus we can expect a diversity of forms and roles emerging for agriculture as regenerative practices and technologies come into wider use.

Since most of the world's arable land is already producing crops and since a major part of that production is in the industrial mode, achieving such a regenerative diversity will require transition. Shifting the land from chemical and fossil-fuel-intensive farming to regenerative farming can take time. Like Fred Kirschenmann (see the example on page 204), many farmers who made the change have reported that it took 2 to 4 years to achieve adequate yields under the new system. The transition can take longer, often up to 6 to 10 years. Especially for systems such as Fukuoka's that rely less on management and more on natural processes, the transition can be longer still. Such systems are commonly very labor-intensive in the early years, with the labor requirement becoming gradually less as the land and its processes adapt to the new regime.

Agriculture in Nonindustrial Countries

Probably the most immediate need for regenerative agriculture is in the nonindustrial countries of Africa, Asia, and Central and South America. The standardized methods of industrial agriculture, transplanted into the tropical world during the period of colonization, have consistently failed to fit local conditions in nonindustrial countries. According to Miguel Altieri and Kat Anderson, "the major technological problem that development projects constantly face is that global recommendations prove to be seriously unfit for the highly localized heterogeneity of peasant farms" (p. 31). As a result, soils and social fabric have degenerated in tandem, in many areas to the point of desperation. Petroleum and chemicals are usually too expensive even if they could help to solve the problems. Regenerative methods offer hope because they work within local resource bases, they fit local conditions, and they are suited to labor-intensive economics. The examples in Chile and Nepal (pages 200 and 209) illustrate some of the potential. They also illustrate some of the dramatic differences between methods appropriate within two different contexts.

The farms in both of these examples are based on traditional agricultural systems, evolved over the course of centuries, with carefully calibrated infusions from other cultures as well as from modern science. The infusions are designed to fit the local landscape and culture and to integrate with traditional practices.

Urban Agriculture

Producing food in cities is an important and widespread activity, though hardly a dominant force in global agriculture. A 1981 study by the Gallup Organization for the National Association for Gardening indicated that about 38 million households in the United States, or about half of the total number, grew food of some sort. Some of these had sizable vegetable gardens, and others probably had only a pot or two. Some gardeners have plots in community gardens. Altogether, their food-growing areas were estimated to cover a total of about 1.7 million acres. Among the reasons given for vegetable gardening were saving money, having fresh chemical-free food, engaging in healthy activity, and the satisfaction gained from working the soil.

In addition to these hobby gardeners, there exist in cities surprising numbers of intensively cultivated, highly productive commercial urban farms like the Produce Gardens example. Since food production cannot pay the cost of urban land, these farms usually exist on otherwise unused plots such as those beneath power lines, in floodplains, and within rights-of-way. Like Produce Farms (page 197), they commonly produce specialty crops that they can deliver fresh to restaurants and markets.

A third type of urban agriculture includes the part-time farmers who often thrive around the edges of cities. Their farms are usually small, rarely more than a few acres, which is not enough to support a family but enough to provide significant supplements to salaries earned at city jobs. In the United States the number of part-time farmers is about 50 percent greater than the number of full-time farmers, and most of the former are within metropolitan areas (Smith, 1987). As with the urban vegetable gardeners and small urban farms, their methods are intensive, minimally mechanized, and highly productive. They usually produce high-value crops and sell through farmer's markets, roadside stands, and pick-your-own programs. Often they

also process their own produce, making products like jam, sauerkraut, and cider.

Regenerative techniques are well suited and easily adapted to all these forms of urban agriculture, both because for the most part they are inherently intensive and because they make little use of chemicals or heavy machinery, which are ill suited to cities. Regenerative methods also can make good use of a range of urban resources, such as reclaimed water and sewage sludge. Urban agriculture can potentially provide part-time and temporary jobs for the urban unemployed and underemployed. It can even benefit from the heat island effect, which results in longer growing seasons.

As fossil-energy supplies wane, especially if governments allow the price of petroleum to reach levels that match its cost, all these factors could become far more important than they have been in the past. If the cost of transporting food also rises, that could give a market advantage to food grown in around cities. Food grown within cities tends to have far lower rates of spoilage before reaching the market (Meier, 1972). Altogether, it is not hard to imagine that urban agriculture might grow in the 21st century from playing a minor role in the food production system to major one.

Already in some countries urban agriculture makes major contributions to food supplies. The allotment gardens on the edges of some European cities provide their gardeners with considerable amounts of food. Small farms growing fruits and vegetables also form highly productive green rings around many European cities, sometimes fertilized with sewage sludge. In Asia a number of cities grow enough vegetables within the city limits to feed their entire populations. In some cities, such as Beijing, vegetables seem to grow year-round on every vacant sliver of land in semi-cylindrical, plastic-covered greenhouses. Given the amounts of open land available, this is at least theoretically possible in a number of U.S. cities, including Los Angeles, where urban agriculture could provide a market for the enormous quantities of treated wastewater that could be available. In New York the potentials of rooftop vegetable gardens have been demonstrated by the Gaia Institute proposals described in Chapter 5.

The Family Farm

Until the mid-20th century, family farms produced most of the world's food, and in most of the world they still do. In the United States, however, their numbers have declined as farming corporations have gathered more and more land into ever-larger holdings. Nevertheless, though reduced in numbers and pressured by the industrially driven economies of scale, a great many family farms still thrive. Some family farms like those of the Amish have shown that it is possible to resist the pressures and still thrive.

Much larger than the Amish farms and closer to the agricultural mainstream are those like the Kirschenmann and Vogelsberg farms described earlier. These and a great many others that have at least partially rejected the use of chemicals are in the usual size range of American family farms. This is generally between 600 and 1200 acres, though the Kirschenmann farm is much larger than that, because of its location in the dry region of North Dakota. These farms operate in the context of the conventional economy and social structure. In embarking on this course, these farmers have set themselves apart and become simultaneously bearers of traditional farming and pioneers in regenerative practices. In the 1980s increasing numbers of farmers followed the pioneers in adopting regenerative ways; within a few years, chemical agriculture may be practiced on only a small minority of family farms.

Corporate farms have not been so quick to change. Few have even experimented with regenerative practices, though some of the practices described in this chapter are clearly adaptable to large-scale farming. Given the failure of corporate farming to prepare for a most uncertain future, its long-range future is in doubt.

Reintegrating Animals

Given the severely degenerative effects of industrial livestock practices, ranging from desertification in Africa to rainforest loss in Central America to groundwater pollution in Europe and the United States, regenerative means for livestock management seem likely to assume increasing importance. Mixed-farming practices as seen on the Kirschenmann and Vogelsberg farms point in one important direction. By reintegrating animals and crops, they turn the urine and manure that are major problems and pollutants on feedlots into resources. However, the capacities of farms to reabsorb animals is limited, as is their capacity to produce animal protein. David Pimentel (1980) has estimated that producing eggs, milk, and meat in the United States without feed grain would reduce the energy cost of pro-

ducing these items by 60 percent, but it would produce only half as much food. Shifts in diet—that is, eating more grains and less meat—could make up much of the difference if present dietary trends continue.

Given the steady deterioration of grazing lands worldwide, it seems inevitable that at some point, sooner or later, it will be necessary to reduce the sizes of herds on grazing lands to sustainable levels. However, this will mean a reduction in the amount of food produced. The yields achieved by David Hopcraft suggest that game ranching may offer a promising alternative, not only for Africa but for other regions of the world where overgrazing is a problem. The American West is an important example. Much of this land has topography, climate, and indigenous species similar to those of Kenya. Over time the degraded grazing lands might be returned to health, and various species of deer, antelope, elk, and bison might be selectively harvested. There are reasons to believe the protein yield would be higher than those from the present herds of cattle and sheep.

The game-ranching concept might have application on the Great Plains as well. Some part of Pimentel's scenario might be put into practice, and a portion of the lands now producing grains for animal feed could be taken out of production. The native grasses might be reestablished and utilized by the herds of bison like those that once grazed on them. Over time we might restore natural communities to much of this land. Much of this could at the same time produce food for humans. In fact, a number of bison ranches have already been established.

Thus we might see the process of establishing regenerative livestock management as a matter of reintegrating animals into agroecosystems on the one hand and natural ecosystems on the other. This is already suggesting a decisive step in returning the global landscape to a healthy state.

The Uncertain Future

Of all regenerative practices and technologies, those related to agriculture are most enmeshed in uncertainty. This chapter includes a great many techniques that have proven effective under certain circumstances. The circumstances of the global landscape are enormously varied, however, and the Paleotechnic dream of a universally applicable, increasingly productive, industrially based agricultural technology is dying a slow, hard death. Achieving a broad range of fully regenerative agricultural techniques remains a goal for research, but as yet only a tiny portion of agricultural research is addressing this problem. Even if such a range of techniques were now available, there would still be the problem of integrating them into our economic and social systems. This presents an even greater challenge than technological development. There is, for example, the problem of markets. The present system seeks to adapt cropping systems to produce what the markets demand, but regenerative agriculture requires that crops be selected to fit local conditions and that they fit into the patterns of agroecological community structure. Since markets may not exist right now for some well-adapted, useful, and nutritious crops, we will inevitably face the problem in some places of adapting markets to ecological circumstances rather than the reverse.

Meanwhile, the world's population continues to grow. Each day's population growth requires already overstressed agricultural lands to feed more people. The capacity of these lands to feed even the present population on a sustainable basis is open to question. It is a desperately serious question deserving far more attention than it has yet received.

CASE STUDY

Regenerative Agriculture at the Center for Regenerative Studies

The agricultural areas of the Center for Regenerative Studies provide a setting for exploring and applying the principles of regenerative agriculture. Plans for the Center's operation include various practices for protecting and revitalizing the soil, for polycultural diversity, for natural pest control, for incorporating animals, and for integrated farming systems.

Though the site is small in contrast with the scale of most conventional agricultural production, its range of topographic and microclimatic conditions permit the demonstration of a wide variety of agricultural practices and techniques. Programs emphasize practices that conserve resources even though they may require higher levels of management and labor than conventional practices. They integrate educational and research efforts toward a common goal: food production systems that function in the self-renewing ways of natural ecosystems. Practices that protect and enhance the soil, that reduce energy consumption and the use of fossil-fuel-derived fertilizers and other chemicals, that maximize multiple-use potential and recycling, and that reduce water use—all these receive particular attention. To the greatest extent possible, all materials, including those normally considered as wastes, will recycle within the system.

Most important is optimizing biological diversity, following the ecological principle that stability is best developed through a diverse range of interactions among heterogeneous species selected for specific site conditions. Plantings have been adapted to the climatic and topographic conditions of the site as a whole and to specific locations within it.

An array of agricultural systems and practices will be included, beginning with a few and expanding over time, with potential applications in both industrialized and nonindustrialized countries. Given the location in an urbanizing area, the Center emphasize practices suitable for food production under urban conditions and at the urban-rural interface. Since integration with the community is also an important goal of the Center, growing food consumed by the resident population will be important. While projections indicate that at times more food will be grown on the site than can be consumed by the community, students' dietary habits suggest that some food items will probably have to be brought in and surplus quantities of others will have to be exported.

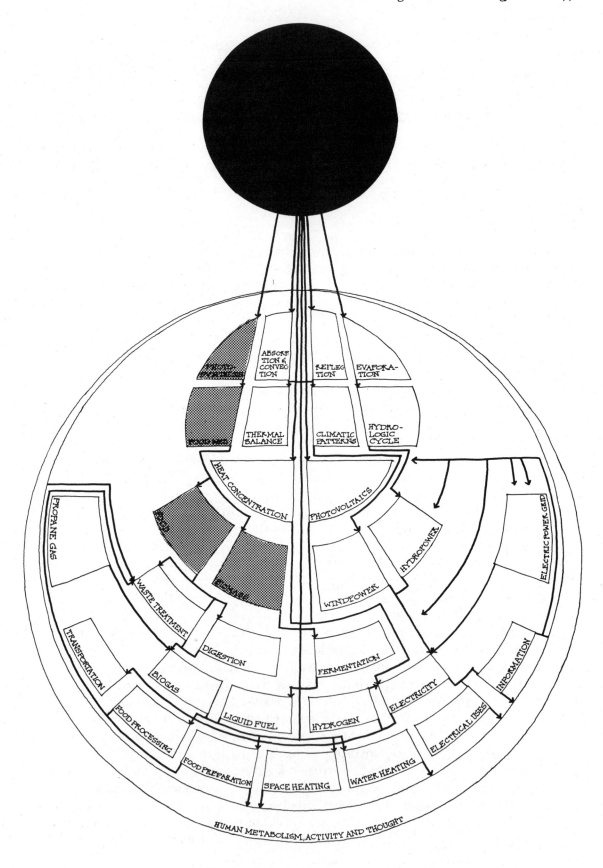

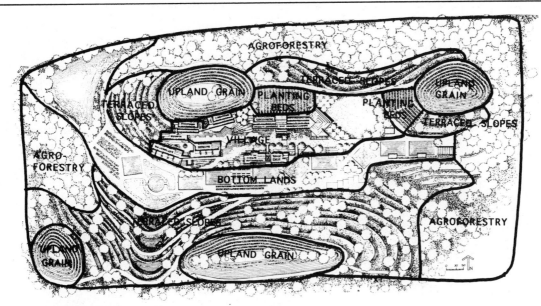

LAND USE

Topography and other local conditions determine relationships between biotic productivity and landscape. Within the six types of production areas, specific practices eventually will include the following:

THE VALLEY:
Bottomlands
(2.4 acres)

1. Integrated agriculture/aquaculture/livestock production as a fundamental means of recycling nutrients in animal wastes. This system is a key integrating element and is explained in detail in the Case Study in Chapter 6. Among the livestock included will be:
   - goats for meat and milk;
   - cattle, both beef and dairy;
   - domestic poultry, quail, and other game birds; ducks used for weed control;
   - beehives for honey production as well as for pollination of adjacent crops.
2. Paddy rice growing in the bottomland area near aquacultural ponds.
3. Productive aquatic plants growing in the fish ponds and in beds adjacent to them; these can include water spinach, water chestnuts, watercress, taro, and duck potato.

BASES OF KNOLLS:
Planting beds
(0.4 acres)

4. Diversified vegetable production, including:
   - French intensive cultivation in raised beds;
   - market gardens with mixed vegetables;
   - both dry land and irrigated systems;
   - greenhouses, cold frames, and other means of extending the growing season.

KNOLLSIDES:

5. Polycultures, including various combinations of species intermixed and occupying different vertical layers. Mixtures of different crop species will be devised to:
   - buffer against plant disease;
   - modify specific conditions of microclimate such as air movement, humidity, light, and temperature where desirable;
   - establish biological control of insect pests;
   - make use of allelopathy for weed control.

6. Forage crops and waste plant biomass (called green manure), with particular emphasis on:
   - leguminous and grass cover crops, green manures, undersowings, and living mulches;
   - model crop-rotation systems;
   - green-crop confinement systems.
   Areas for pasture and dry-land range production are located on lands immediately west of the Center. Activities in these areas can be operated in conjunction with the Center.

STEEP SLOPES:
Agroforestry
(5.1 acres)

7. Trees for fuel wood and for fruits and nuts will be interplanted in different patterns and densities with various perennial and annual crop species. Trees will also be used for living fences, windbreaks, shade, animal forage production, construction materials, implement making, oils, and soil retention, especially on steeper slopes.

KNOLL TOPS:
Upland Grain
(2.4 acres)

8. Diverse grain crops, especially barley, wheat, corn, and oats, will be grown on upper knolltop areas of the site. These include:
   - interplanting such as corn and beans;
   - small grains and rotation systems such as cereals and legumes;
   - root crops;
   - various economic plants for marketing.

HUMAN USE AREA:
The Village
(2.2 acres)

9. Plants with high esthetic quality that also serve other purposes such as food production and environmental control.

10. Productive trees useful in urban situations, including citrus, deciduous, and tropical fruit trees.

11. Rooftop plantings, including herbs, various shallow-rooted vegetables, container plants, and seedlings to be replanted in other locations.

ALL AREAS:

12. Pest control systems for small-scale IPM, including:
    - repellent plants;
    - allelopathy;
    - trap crops such as alfalfa strips;
    - habitat for beneficial insects.
    Preventative pest control systems using these and other methods will be used secondarily under careful controls only when necessary.

13. Composting and use of composted material, including animal manure, plant trimmings and waste, and refuse from dwelling areas and the kitchen.

14. Propagation and growing seedlings.

15. Winter vegetable production.

Most of these practices will be applied in both the 4 acre hand-technology (hand-tech) and multitechnology (multitech) areas, but the hand-tech operation (see the plan on page 220) will emphasize a diverse mix of species, intensive and efficient use of the land, and integration of crop production with aquaculture and livestock. Since this area will simulate conditions that exist in many nonindustrial countries, only widely available tools will be used. Fossil-fuel-derived products and other materials that are unavailable or expensive in those countries will be excluded. Particular attention will be given to labor-intensive techniques to gain high yields of varied nutritional benefit while sustaining ecologi-

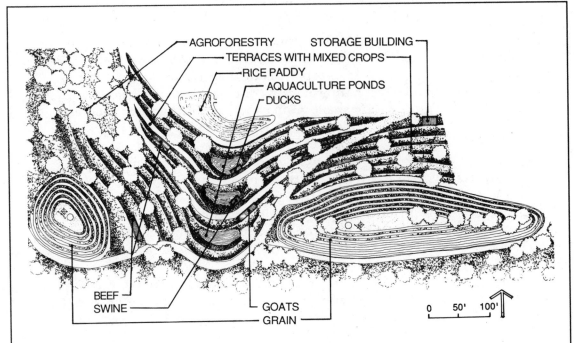

AGROFORESTRY   STORAGE BUILDING
TERRACES WITH MIXED CROPS
RICE PADDY
AQUACULTURE PONDS
DUCKS

BEEF
SWINE   GOATS
GRAIN

0   50'   100'

HAND-TECH AREA

cal integrity. There will also be exploration and demonstration of means for restoring ecological function and productive capacity to lands degraded by misuse, accomplished through various techniques for slope stabilization and soil enhancement.

The overall goals and guiding principles for the multitech area are the same, but the technological means are not limited. Within the principle of minimal use of nonrenewable resources, appropriate technological means at hand may be tried. Many applications require electronic monitoring and controls, and other electronic devices are possible. Fossil-fuel-derived materials will be used sparingly and only for tasks not effectively accomplished by other means.

Plantings in the village emphasize species especially useful in urban situations and other areas for producing food and other usable materials. At the same time, plants will serve other important roles: providing shade and other microclimate controls, spatial definition, visual quality, and soil stabilization. It is also important that plants used in this area be adaptable to urban conditions, including air pollution, constriction of root areas, and pruning. The Center has begun to develop a database of such plants.

ANIMALS

The Center's plans include small numbers of animals kept for milk and meat as well as for research and demonstration of the roles animals play in agroecosystems. Recycling of nutrients in animal wastes is of particular interest, as is the feeding of animals with various crops and crop residues.

The hand-tech area will include pens for beef, swine, and goats. At least one platform house for swine will stand over a fish pond in order to experiment with the recycling of manure through the pond ecosystem.

Beef, swine, and goats will also be maintained in the multitech area in close proximity to composting and methane digestion facilities. Platforms for ducks and swine will stand over two of the fish ponds.

AQUACULTURE

As manifested in its focal position along the central valleys of the site, aquaculture plays a pivotal role in the ecosystem. The plan calls for rapid development of both the facilities and the program to engage in appropriate aquacultural research as soon as possible. This research will meet a growing need for improvement in aquacultural technologies. This need is currently most obvious in the nonindustrial world, but it is likely to increase in developed nations as well.

The three aquacultural ponds in the hand-tech areas are varied in size. They will be used for growing fish, such as carp and tilapia, that are particularly important in providing protein for nonindustrial societies. Water pumped from the reservoir will fill the ponds, which will also serve as holding tanks for irrigation water distributed to cultivated areas on the adjacent terraces.

The ponds along the valley bottom are designed for highly controlled research and can be used to grow a wide variety of freshwater species. In the ultimate stage there will be three nursery ponds, each with an area of 2500 square feet, and six growout ponds (where fish grow to harvestable size), each with an area of 2800 square feet. The growout ponds are identical so that trials can be replicated in two or more of them at a time. All ponds are lined to prevent leakage. There will also be a small hatchery in the solar greenhouse consisting of five 100-liter hatching jars, two tanks each 4 feet by 8 feet, and two 2-by-10-foot raceway tanks (through which water moves very rapidly) with biofilters. These provide ideal conditions for the development of recently hatched fish (which are called fry). A second group of raceway tanks will be located outdoors in the valley.

A number of solar silos and other types of small tanks will also be located in various places on the site: in the greenhouses and sunspaces, along the edges of the valley, and on the knolltops. Solar silos are translucent plastic tanks 5 feet in diameter by 5 feet tall. Large water surfaces exposed to solar radiation can be highly productive of the plant biomass on which fish feed. The size of these tanks makes it possible to place them in various locations where they can serve dual purposes. For example, those on the knolltops can store the water pumped for later irrigation use, and those in sunspaces and greenhouses provide thermal storage.

The reservoir at the west end of the site will accommodate research and demonstrations in cage culture and farm pond management. Cage culture involves growing fish in wire-mesh containers within larger bodies of water; it has widespread potential application in the growing numbers of human-made lakes and water-supply reservoirs in many parts of the world. Aquatic plants can also grow in net enclosures within the reservoir pond to provide fish food, forage for terrestrial animals, and compost materials.

The importance of aquaculture in the Center's ecosystem lies partly in its ability to produce large amounts of protein in a small area. The growout ponds can provide more than enough protein for the ultimate population of over 90 residents. In practice, of course, residents will want a more varied diet, and much of the fish produced will be used for other purposes. Nevertheless, the intensive productivity is important in serving the basic purpose of the Center.

However, the roles of waste processing and recycling may be as important as productivity. Both animal wastes and feed plants will be introduced into the ponds to provide nutrients for the growth of organisms at the base of the food chain, which eventually produces the organisms eaten by the fish. Animal wastes are particularly effective in this respect. The plan calls for locating a pen for six pigs over one pond and a house for about 25 ducks over another. The wastes from these animals will then drop directly into the ponds. This is an ancient and highly successful practice common in several parts of Asia. However, monitoring water quality is essential, since bacterial concentration must be kept low to meet health standards.

On the output side, pond water enriched with fish wastes provides nutrient-laden irrigation water. Using such water can almost eliminate the need for artificial fertilizers. For use in irrigating food crops, the California Environmental Health Criteria for reclaimed water require a coliform count of less than 23 per 100 milliliters. The output water from the ponds should have coliform counts well below this level.

RESEARCH

Recognizing that we still know relatively little about regenerative agricultural practices and therefore that the systems proposed here will probably function in imperfect and experimental ways for some time to come, the food production areas will continuously focus on a number of complex basic questions:

- How can we define the sustainable capacity for production given that the carrying capacity of a land area may be determined by a number of factors, including its abilities to supply the materials needed for growth and to absorb wastes?
- To what degree can we define and make use of the many interactions among species?
- How can we maximize our use of on-site energy?
- Can we shape economic and social practices and policies that are congruent with the complexity of regenerative systems?
- What are the most effective management techniques for dealing with the complexity of integrated regenerative systems?
- How can a small organization devoted to regenerative practices manage its relationships within the larger context of social, economic, and political institutions so as to encourage cooperation, stimulate evolutionary change, and minimize conflict?
- What behavioral limitations and demands do regenerative agricultural systems place on those who work and live with them?

Within each of these broad questions are many more specific ones. The Center is addressing these issues, using the landscape described here as a medium. All research at the Center follows a basic set of ethical guidelines. The work must fall within the definition of regenerative systems, and its purpose must be to benefit both human society as a whole and the natural community.

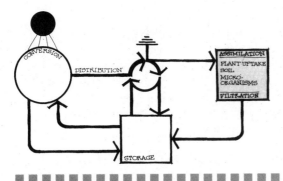

Chapter 8
Waste as a Resource

Much of our difficulty with waste is embedded in the word itself. Waste is defined as material considered worthless and thrown away after use. In this sense it is a human invention, essential to the one-way flows of the throughput system; this definition depends on the assumption that energy and materials, having once served our immediate purposes, can simply cease to exist in any functional sense.

The laws of thermodynamics tell us otherwise. Energy continuously degrades and materials change form and state, but they are not destroyed and they do not disappear. In the functional order of natural ecosystems, materials are always reused. Natural processes have evolved a number of ways of accomplishing this on various time scales. In quantities matched to the evolved capacities of the landscape, materials are reintroduced after use into the processes of assimilation, filtration, storage, and production to continue their roles in nature's cycles. When the chemical composition of the waste materials is such that nature has not evolved a means of reprocessing them, or when their quantities are beyond the processing capacity of the landscape, then the sink side of the flow equation develops a serious problem of pollution or overload.

Waste in the Paleotechnic Environment

Throughout the Paleotechnic period and especially during the last half of the 20th century, both overloading of sinks and introducing unassimilable materials into them have become regular, ongoing occurrences. There are several reasons for this. The populations of cities have multiplied, increasing the concentrations of people and thus of their wastes. Especially in the industrial nations, increasing levels of consumption have meant increasing amounts of waste produced per person. In the United States each person produces 50,000 pounds of waste each year and almost 20,000 gallons of sewage.

The preferred method in the United States for dealing with solid waste (or trash) in recent decades has been to bury it in landfills, which is the municipal equivalent of sweeping dirt under the rug; in Europe, incineration has been more common. Both have serious difficulties.

Landfill Problems

Historically, municipal landfills have been responsible for a great deal of soil and groundwater pollution. About 20 percent of the sites in the EPA's Superfund cleanup programs are municipal landfills. However, most of these are old sites. The technology of landfilling has improved considerably over the past few decades, but the improvements have been mostly palliative. Sealing the bottoms of landfills has reduced the chances of wastes getting into groundwater, at least temporarily. The heavy plastic liners now being used are expected to last at least 30 years. Decomposition processes, by contrast, are likely to go on for hundreds of years. Thus we might expect a plague of leaking landfills in the 21st century.

Effective drainage systems on the surfaces of finished landfills have reduced infiltration of water into the buried trash and thus the danger of chemicals being leached through the trash levels and through or around the sealed bottom. Problems with rodents, birds, odors, and blowing debris have been reduced to manageable levels by sanitary filling, that is, by covering each day's trash deposits with a layer of soil. Somewhat more regenerative in character are the methane collection systems that draw off the gases escaping from decomposition processes. These consist of networks of pipes buried in the layers of trash, which collect the methane as it is generated and convey it to boilers where it is burned to make steam. In most cases the steam is then used to generate electricity, which is fed into the electrical grid.

Such technological improvements have rendered landfilling a relatively harmless means for dealing with nontoxic, nonhazardous wastes. With methane collection, a small portion of the energy embedded in trash is returned for reuse. Even with these improvements, however, landfills remain a degenerative way of dealing with waste; they are a means for wasting waste. Material discarded and consigned to a landfill is effectively removed from the realm of human use. The materials, many of them nonrenewable, and the energy embedded within them, are no longer in the economy. Most of these materials are in fact reusable by some means.

Landfills do not facilitate nature's recycling processes either. Decomposition of buried trash is extremely slow. A number of researchers have dug up materials long ago deposited in landfills and found them hardly changed since the day they were covered over. Finding 30-year-old newspapers that are still readable and food items like hot dogs that are still recognizable is fairly common. Certain microorganisms are needed to decompose these materials and make their components available for reorganiz-

ing into new forms. The dry, anaerobic conditions inside a landfill provide a poor environment for them. Thus within a landfill, nature's continuous regeneration is slowed virtually to a standstill. In terms of ecological function, landfills provide not assimilation but storage.

Incineration

Trash burning, which is commonly practiced in many cities in Europe and in a few in the United States, has appealing short-term advantages. It comes closer than any other technology to simply making waste disappear, and this makes it attractive within the Paleotechnic ethos.

A second advantage is that, like methane collection, burning can recover some of the energy imbedded in waste materials by using the heat to generate electricity.

The disadvantages of burning, on the other hand, are numerous. Even with the best pollution control equipment, incinerators release into the air considerable volumes of carbon monoxide, sulfur and nitrogen dioxides, dioxin (which is extremely toxic even in minute quantities), and numerous metals, including lead and mercury. The fluidized bed gasifier being tested by the Southern California Edison Company, discussed in Chapter 4, may be a pollution-free incineration technology, but we will not know that for sure for some time.

With burning, groundwater contamination also remains a problem. Incineration does not make the trash entirely disappear. At least 25 percent of the original weight and 10 percent of the original volume remain in the form of an ash residue that still must be disposed of, usually by landfilling. This ash still contains in concentrated form a considerable amount of the dangerous materials that were in the trash before burning, especially metals actually released in the burning process.

Moreover, incinerators are costly devices. For each ton of burning capacity per day, the cost has been estimated at $100,000 to $150,000, which is several times the capital cost of materials recovery systems.

Furthermore, incinerators, like landfills, fail to make use of the potential utility that remains in a great deal of the material considered as waste.

For some public officials and even for some citizens groups who oppose landfills and incinerators in their own environs, exporting trash also has the appeal of seeming disappearance. In Los Angeles there have been several proposals to ship it to the desert. For a great many people, the austere, sparsely vegetated, and almost unpopulated landscape of the desert is a wasteland and thus a suitable place for urban refuse. This has made it a likely location for facilities that would not be acceptable in cities, such as coal-fired generating stations. It sometimes happens that desert towns with economies as sparse as their landscape are quite willing to accept the exported urban pollution for a price. The effects on the fragile natural systems of the desert, however, can be considerably more damaging than they are in the more resilient urban environs.

In eastern U.S. cities, where lack of landfill space has been an even more pressing problem than in western cities, exporting garbage has been an even more enticing solution. Philadelphia exports trash to eastern Ohio and northern Virginia. The famous garbage barge Mobro dramatized both the problem and some of the difficulties with the export solution: It wandered about the world for 55 days in 1988 searching for a place to dump its cargo of urban refuse from New York and eventually ended the journey where it began. Eastern cities nevertheless routinely propose exporting trash to nonindustrial countries in South America and Africa. Whether intentionally or not, they provide a fitting metaphor for the relationship between the industrial and nonindustrial worlds.

Sewage Treatment

Since Thomas Crapper invented the water closet in the 19th century, the prevailing means for dealing with human excrement in the United States and Europe has been to mix it with water in that device and then convey the mixture through underground pipes to the nearest sizable body of water, usually a river or bay. Along the way a highly mechanized sewage treatment plant separates the solids from the liquids. That is, after conventional treatment, the sewage is still there, though in different form.

As long as populations are small and dispersed in relation to the volume of water, rivers and bays can assimilate and dilute the nutrients and other materials in the sewage. However, at some point, as cities grow, the volume of nutrients and other materials becomes too great for the assimilative capacities of the water bodies, resulting in an excessive buildup of nutrients and other pollutants. This has happened in waters around most of the world's cities. Since the 1960s, Congress has tried repeatedly to solve the water pollution problem in the United States through a series of Water Quality Control

acts. It is now illegal to dump treated sewage water into a body of water if the quality is lower than what is already there. Nevertheless, in 1991, 19 years after amendments to the Clean Water Act established this requirement, over 2000 beaches were reportedly closed along U.S. coasts due to sewage pollution (Stammer, 1992).

In response to this requirement, many sewage plants have added a secondary level of treatment involving mechanical and biological devices to break down the organic solids still remaining in the water after primary screening. Some have also added various forms of advanced treatment to remove other specific materials.

Nevertheless, despite hundreds of billions of dollars spent on treatment plants, pollution problems persist in the rivers and bays where cities dump their sewage, especially the larger ones. The cities of Los Angeles and New York provide cases in point. Both concentrate their sewage in gigantic mechanical treatment plants. Los Angeles has only one, the Hyperion plant, which treats the sewage produced by over 3 million residents and discharges the water into Santa Monica Bay. New York has two, one discharging into the Hudson River, the other into the East River.

When it is working properly, the Hyperion plant treats enough sewage each day to fill the Rose Bowl twice. After primary screening, about one-quarter of this receives secondary treatment. These processes separate the water from the solid matter, which is called sludge. After secondary treatment, the water moves into Santa Monica Bay. When the plant is not working properly or when it is overloaded, raw sewage goes into the Bay as well. Since the 1970s, pollution of the bay has been looming ever larger as an environmental and political issue. Bacteria in the water attack the organic residues and, since the amount of these residues is so large, use the oxygen in the water faster than it can be replaced. Deprived of oxygen, a number of sensitive species in the bay die away. At the same time, toxic hydrogen sulfides produced in the decomposition process make the ocean bottom a lifeless place in some areas. The once prodigious and diverse fish population is now much diminished. Bottom feeders like the white croaker are especially affected; fishermen often pull them from the water with rotting fins and parasitic diseases. Large predatory fish like the white sea bass, which were abundant just a few years ago, are scarce now, and studies have found exceptionally high levels of toxic chemicals in virtually all fish taken from the bay.

After being separated out in the treatment process, the sludge is much more difficult to deal with than the liquid. At one time the Hyperion plant dumped sludge into the bay as well. But in the mid-1970s the EPA ordered this practice stopped because it violated the Clean Water Act. After years of delays, postponed deadlines, and general avoidance of the issue by city officials, environmental groups obtained a court order forcing Los Angeles to comply with the law. The Hyperion plant stopped dumping sludge into Santa Monica Bay in 1988.

Soon after the initial EPA order, a group of engineering consultants studying the sludge disposal problem recommended burning it and using the heat produced to generate electrical power. This recommendation was accepted, and the sludge incinerator was substantially completed in 1988 at a cost of over $400 million. However, its operation was plagued by fires and breakdowns; it never functioned as expected and will probably never burn more than a small portion of Hyperion's sludge.

Since 1988, with the incinerator not working, most of Los Angeles' sludge has gone into landfills. A portion has been hauled to the Mojave Desert in freight cars and used as a soil supplement for crops. Several proposals for shipping it even farther away have been considered. One scheme would have had about one-third of Hyperion's sludge loaded on ships and hauled to Guatemala, a quintessentially Paleotechnic proposal, but this proved too expensive.

While the situation in New York differs in detail, the pattern is much the same. Instead of a bay, the partially treated water goes into both the Hudson and the East rivers. As for sludge, for decades the city dumped it in the Ambrose Bight 12 miles offshore. When pollution problems became obvious there, barges were sent 90 miles farther out, where the water is much deeper and organisms more dispersed. It is an environment more capable of assimilating the large input of foreign material. The effects of the new dumping area are as yet unknown.

Besides municipal solid waste and sewage there are other waste issues that bear examination. At least as pressing as these are the problems of industrial wastes discharged into land, air, and water. While pollution control devices have much reduced the amount of industrial pollution in the United States, the state of some waterways like the lower reaches of the Mississippi River attest that industrial waste is still a problem. In most other countries, industrial pollution is much worse.

Disposal and Degeneration

These few examples are typical of the means of dealing with waste that have become more or less standard practice during the industrial period. As generally practiced, all of them are degenerative processes, not only because they result in pollution but because they do not contribute to the earth's processes of renewal and rebirth. They do not recognize the resource value of waste. Not being regenerative, they are essentially degenerative.

As the term "waste disposal" implies, all of our conventional means of dealing with wastes address only one disaggregated part of the larger issue of material flow through human ecosystems. To dispose of waste—to get it out of sight, thus out of mind—is only part of the job that is needed. The other equally essential part is to emulate nature's ability to assimilate the material into use or the natural processes that support life. Practices that accomplish this are regenerative.

Any of the three means of "disposal" discussed above can be regenerative if practiced in quantities that the sinks can assimilate. Burning is a regenerative process if the heat energy can be put to use, if valuable resources are not destroyed by the burning, if the byproducts do not pollute the air, and if the ash can reenter nature's processes without doing damage. Burial can be regenerative if conditions within the burial place are such that either materials are stored for future reuse or if decay and renewal continue on.

By thinking of landfills in a more realistic way, not as places where trash can disappear but as places where materials are stored for reuse, we might integrate them into a regenerative urban ecology. Following the ninth strategy, we might regard landfills as storage areas where discarded materials are held until we can find ways to reuse them. With only minor changes, we might design landfills as warehouses, or perhaps mines, for maximum preservation. Especially if we maintain our present consumption patterns and keep the throughput system in operation, landfills may become the most productive mines of the 21st century.

At the other extreme, we might design them for rapid decomposition. By introducing some water in carefully controlled quantities, we might convert landfills into giant biogas digesters. With more complete decomposition, the methane gas yields could be much higher than those of present methane recovery systems, and the residue could be mined as needed to provide a rich fertilizer. Thus, by one means or the other, landfills could return waste materials to the ongoing processes of reuse.

Introducing treated sewage into bodies of water can be environmentally benign in suitable quantities. Water can absorb some quantities of some materials, especially nutrients, without harm and sometimes with benefit. Research has demonstrated that both fresh- and saltwater environments can make use of nutrient inputs to enrich the processes of life and biotic production—up to a point. Even the export of wastes can be regenerative, if they reenter the ecosystem at the end of the journey and if their contributions outweigh the energy cost of transporting them.

There are other ways of dealing with waste, most of them much better. When we consider the purposes of waste management as going beyond disposal to focus on reassimilation, then there are numerous means of accomplishing the task, with less cost and far greater social and ecological benefit. If we put our major emphasis on reassimilation rather than disposal, then pollution will either disappear or become a minor problem.

Practices and Technologies for Materials Regeneration

Among the most serious difficulties with waste management in the industrial nations is the immense quantities of materials to be dealt with. The industrial economies' high emphasis on productivity necessarily results in large volumes of waste. This is the essence of the throughput system. Given that the capacity of any environment—land or water—to assimilate waste is limited, large quantities create a basic conflict.

Regenerative design applies the first strategy described in Chapter 3—letting nature do the work—to increase the assimilative capacity of land and water. At the same time, thoughtful design can make more land available by multiple functions; that is, land used for processing wastes can often be used also for other purposes. However, these strategies can accomplish only so much. Regenerative goals make it clear that the volume of waste to be processed should be limited by the capacity of the environment to assimilate it.

Waste in Other Cultures

The success of industrial sewage systems in achieving their overriding goal, the control of disease vectors, has made it easy to assume that the western industrial way is the only way. In fact, there are numerous, radically different ways of dealing with sewage in operation in other cultures. In China the excrement of a household, called night soil, is still left near the door in buckets to be collected during the night in some areas. In these places collectors take it to nearby farms where it is used as fertilizer. While this system does not provide the same protection from the spread of disease that western pipe-and-water systems do, it does have the advantage of returning nutrients to the soil. Whatever its shortcomings, it is regenerative. For obvious reasons, however, farmers find it objectionable and many have turned to other sources of fertilizer in recent years. In some parts of Japan, the night soil is stored in tanks in many cities and periodically collected by trucks that pump it from the holding tanks into their own tanks. This somewhat more sanitary process also returns the nutrients to the soil in nearby agricultural fields (Pradt, 1971).

Solid-waste practices are not so varied simply because few societies outside of contemporary western industrial societies have produced enough material goods to present serious problems in their disposal. Solid-waste issues were born of the one-way flow system and the extraordinary effectiveness of industrial technology in speeding the flow and thus the quantity of material collecting in the sinks at flow's end. In addition to reducing the volume of material by various means, regenerative practices can return these materials to the processes of natural and human ecosystems by two fundamentally different means: reuse and environmental reassimilation. There are two kinds of reuse: direct reuse and mechanical recycling.

Direct Reuse

In industrial societies, the low cost of material goods often causes them to be discarded long before their usefulness is exhausted. In the reuse of these goods there is enormous potential for slowing the flow and thus for reducing both resource use and waste. Varied means for accomplishing this have appeared spontaneously, most of them operating outside the mainstream of the market economy. Among the examples are garage sales, flea markets, swap meets, junkyards, and thrift stores. In some third-world cities like Mexico City, small entrepreneurs have made a business of collecting usable items after they have been dumped in landfills and then reselling them. In cities like Los Angeles, complex underground economies have developed among ethnic minorities, dealing in secondhand goods, often on the basis of barter or credit. Thrift stores, usually operated for particular charities, also serve to keep reusable goods in circulation. Many of these do especially brisk business in clothing, furniture, and children's toys.

The sales volume of all of these combined is still minuscule in comparison with that of mainstream retailers. Nevertheless, they demonstrate that a reuse marketing network does function effectively even with no institutional incentives. Should social forces move away from one-way flows—should materials become suddenly less available or more expensive, for example, or the cost of disposal abruptly increase—then the importance of the reuse markets could become much greater. Each recession foreshadows such a trend, when thrift store and secondhand sales increase while those of conventional retailers decrease. A trend toward more durable, longer-lasting goods might also give impetus to this market.

Besides personal items, there are a great many materials commonly used on a large scale in industrial societies that might be reused to a far greater extent than they presently are. Prominent among these are building materials, as discussed in Chapter 5, and containers, especially metal and plastic food and beverage containers.

Mechanical Recycling

As compared to reuse, mechanical recycling requires the reshaping or remanufacturing of an old material into new form and thus involves energy use. Most of the items in the typical waste stream of an industrial society not suitable for reuse are suitable for recycling, through either mechanical or biological processes.

The composition of household trash varies considerably by region, by season, and even by district within a single city. The National Solid Wastes Management Association estimates the composition of household trash on a national basis as follows:

Paper	40%
Food	17%
Yard waste	13%
Glass	9%
Metals	9%
Wood	3%
Miscellaneous organics	3%
Plastics	2%
Rubber and leather	2%
Textiles	2%

While all of these categories are recyclable by some means, the value of recycling is greater for some than others. Recycling metals is especially important because of the nonrenewable materials and the energy used in manufacturing them. Making a can from recycled aluminum requires only about one-third the energy needed to make one from new aluminum. The ratio for steel is about two-thirds. The energy ratio for glass is roughly the same as for steel. However, the raw materials for glass are far more common than for aluminum or steel.

While the recycling of metals and glass became common practice in the 1980s and is increasing with growing government incentives, plastic recycling is still difficult and limited in its effectiveness. Most plastics are recycled into products far less valuable than those from which the material came. Low-grade packing and building materials are common uses.

The recycling potential of paper is limited by the fact that fibers are weakened with each remanufacture. Thus, with each recycling paper becomes weaker, lower in quality, and eventually loses its usefulness entirely. At that point, it can be biologically recycled, or composted.

As recycling becomes more common, the processes for it are increasingly superimposed on existing community structures which so far have evolved with no concern for such matters. However, to be truly effective, recycling will have to become an integral part of the community. Recycling centers, composting sites, and separation facilities can become important activity nodes. Building design can also facilitate recycling. The renovated Audubon Society Headquarters described in Chapter 5 features chutes running vertically through its nine stories for carrying used materials to a recycling center in the lower basement. There are separate chutes for aluminum, glass, organic materials, paper, and plastics. The Society's goal is to recycle 79 percent of the materials that enter the building.

As they become integral parts of our culture, recycling processes affect the built environment in myriad ways. With recycling, materials often be-

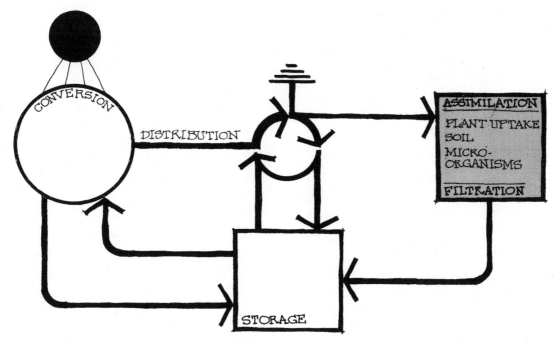

come far more diverse in their uses than the specific functions of their first generation. Consider automobile tires for example. The best second-generation function of tires is retreading and reuse. They may be retreaded a second and perhaps a third and fourth time as well, but eventually they become too worn for their original purpose. Then they can spread out into the environment. Without changing form, tires can become bumpers on boat docks or loading docks or crash barriers or swings on playgrounds. They are sometimes sunk in the ocean as artificial reefs or to support growth of crustaceans such as mussels. By cutting them up, it is possible to shape paving blocks, stair treads, or, commonly in nonindustrial countries, soles for sandals. Ground into crumbs, tire rubber makes an excellent roadbed or mulch for agricultural or sports fields. Tires crumbs can also be mixed with asphalt to make RUMAC, which is quieter, more resilient, holds more heat, and lasts twice as long as asphalt alone. Finally, tires can be decomposed by pyrolysis to yield fuel oil. While it is true that the economy has difficulty absorbing some of these products and tires continue piling up as waste, it seems almost certain that repeated and diverse recycling pathways will soon bring dramatic change to both the economy and the landscape.

Biological Reassimilation

Biological reassimilation differs from reuse in that it follows the first strategy, letting nature do the work, by drawing on natural processes of decomposition to reintegrate materials into the landscape. Filtration and reassimilation of materials depend on the decomposing activity of countless bacteria and other microbes working unseen in our environment. Though we are hardly aware of them most of the time, these microbes account for most of the earth's biological activity. We can make use of their efforts in a number of ways, three of which are especially important: composting, natural sewage treatment, and bioremediation. These technologies are extremely significant for the future, likely to develop in effectiveness and sophistication.

Composting

The composting process biologically decomposes organic material under controlled conditions. The product is a loosely structured soillike material that can be handled, stored, and applied to the land as a beneficial soil amendment without adversely affecting the environment. In some areas, compost can provide at least a partial antidote to prevalent conditions of soil degradation.

Important to the utility of compost is its very low, virtually nonexistent health risk. In the composting process, the activity of bacteria in decomposition causes the material to heat up. The high temperature kills pathogens and insect larvae in the mixture as well as most weed seeds (Hornick et al., 1979).

Most organic materials can be composted, though some decompose faster than others. A mass

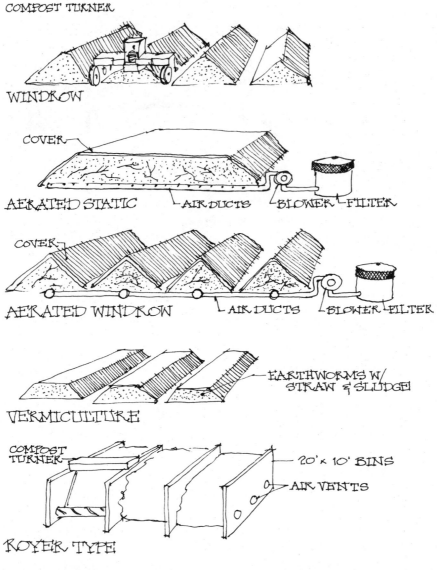

COMPOST TURNER

WINDROW

COVER

AERATED STATIC — AIR DUCTS — BLOWER — FILTER

COVER

AERATED WINDROW — AIR DUCTS — BLOWER — FILTER

VERMICULTURE — EARTHWORMS W/ STRAW & SLUDGE

COMPOST TURNER — 20' x 10' BINS — AIR VENTS

ROYER TYPE

**LARGE SCALE
COMPOSTING METHODS**
Source: 606 Studio, 1988

of organic material can be organized for composting in any number of ways. Piles and rows are common forms. For small operations on the scale of a backyard, it is common practice to load the organic material into a bin with openings in the sides for air movement. Since composting is an aerobic process involving a community of bacteria, fungi and other microorganisms, providing for air movement is essential. There are several means for accomplishing this, ranging from periodically turning small piles and bins by hand, to forced-air devices, to large machines that move between the rows of large composting operations, turning the material mechanically.

Composting can also be accomplished in large containers which provide optimum conditions and also control odors.

Under optimum conditions the composting process generally takes from 3 weeks to 2 months, though the period can be as short as 12 days.

GREENWASTE COMPOST / The principal ingredient of solid-waste compost is plant trimmings, also called greenwaste. According to the chart on page 230, greenwaste makes up about 13 percent of the solid-waste volume in the United States. Actually, in many cities, especially less densely built cities in the

South and West, the percentage is much higher, usually over 20 percent. In Los Angeles County the figure is 35.6 percent.

For composting in a reasonably short time, greenwaste is ground to the point where all of the wood chips are less than 1 inch in their largest dimension. Other materials in the solid waste, including food, leather, and low-grade paper, can be ground up at the same time. Some commercial machines are capable of grinding the entire volume of solid waste for composting. The resulting material, however, has limited application since it is laced with particles of glass, metal, and plastic, which are very slowly reassimilated into the environment.

Compost made from organic materials, by contrast, makes an excellent mulch for either the urban landscape or agriculture. It is low in nutrient content, however, and thus does not qualify to be termed a fertilizer (Golueke, 1977).

The cost of composting greenwaste and other organic materials is considerably lower than disposing of them by either incineration or landfilling. Although the resulting compost material is useful, its market value is negligible.

SLUDGE COMPOST / Composting is also an effective means for treating sewage sludge and returning its materials to ecological processes. Because of the higher risk of pathogens, the EPA requires that sludge composting processes achieve a temperature level of 131°F for a period of 5 to 15 days, depending on the method used. After this treatment the compost is considered safe for human handling and application in public spaces.

The nutrient content of sludge compost is considerably higher than that of solid-waste compost, but still not usually high enough to qualify for the fertilizer label. Nevertheless, it is a most useful soil amendment and is used in a number of cities in parks, golf courses, and other public landscapes. It has proven highly effective in forest applications (Johnson, 1987), and it does have some market value for landscape application. The Los Angeles County Sanitation Districts sells sludge compost to the Kellogg Supply Company, which has been bagging and selling the material in large quantities for use in home gardens since 1926.

However, there are several materials often found in sewage sludge that can limit its use. Metals, in particular, are common components of sewage collected in areas with industrial plants, and composting does not affect them. Among the metals identified as potential hazards are cadmium, copper, nickel, and zinc. The EPA establishes maximum application rates to food-chain crops for all of these metals, and these rates usually determine the amount of sludge compost that can be applied to an agricultural landscape. Of the four regulated metals, cadmium is often the most limiting because it is commonly present in industrial sewage and because of the very low tolerance level for cadmium established by the EPA. While there is no indication that cadmium harms plants, they do take it up from the soil and it is highly toxic to animals. Thus cadmium can work its way up through the food chain and cause widespread deaths among wildlife populations.

Because of its density and high moisture content, sludge is mixed with a bulking agent such as sawdust, straw, rice hulls, or wood chips before composting. This raises the possibility of using ground-up compostable components of solid waste as a bulking agent.

CO-COMPOST / When sewage sludge and solid waste (primarily greenwaste) are composted together, the product is called co-compost, and it has several advantages over compost made from either material separately. The sludge provides a higher nutrient content, while the greenwaste provides bulk and looser texture. Co-composting simultaneously solves two of the most difficult solid-waste problems and at the same time provides an organic material useful for maintaining and rebuilding soils in almost any situation.

The 606 Studio developed for the city of Los Angeles a plan for co-composting sewage sludge from the Hyperion treatment plant and from greenwaste collected from various parts of the city (606 Studio, 1988b). Application sites were the many degraded landscapes within the city and around its edges, including deforested slopes, construction sites, landfills, abandoned farms, mines, and quarries. A surprising fact that came to light was that a major portion of the urban and exurban landscape was severely degraded in the sense of having lost the natural regenerative capacity of its soils and the plant communities they support. Co-compost provides the raw material for the soil-rebuilding process.

COMPOSTING TOILETS / These devices eliminate the need for a collection system by applying the composting process at the smallest scale, that of the individual toilet. Composting toilets incorporate a large chamber into which the excrement drops,

EXAPLE

■■

Sludge Use in Seattle

In 1973 the Municipality of Metropolitan Seattle (called Metro) began applying sewage sludge to the University of Washington's Charles Lathrop Pack Demonstration Forest. Since it was part of a reforestation research project carried out by the university's College of Forestry, the results have been carefully monitored for effects on trees and soils as well as for potential health effects and financial costs.

Initial applications were on clear-cut areas, where it was found that sludge stimulated growth to the point of becoming the victim of its own success. Plants and grasses grew so fast that the profusion attracted inordinate numbers of animals that eat young trees. Thus it was hard to maintain continuous growth, and the experiment was shifted to established forests. For application the researchers developed a pumping vehicle that could spray a mixture of 13 percent water and 87 percent sludge a distance of 150 feet. There the results showed tree diameter increases that were at least 50 percent greater than those in the control group to which sludge was not applied. Studies also indicated that there are no risks to public health or to the environment in such uses of sludge, provided that established management practices are followed.

Partly due to the success of forest applications, Metro later developed a sludge management plan that included a number of other uses. Among these were application to other forests, improvement of degraded soils, and production of compost. Significantly, an economic analysis showed that forest and other land applications cost one-quarter to one-third as much as other alternatives, even when the cost of buying the land is included. The difference was mostly in initial capital investment.

Under the plan, Metro has used sludge fertilizer on a number of landscapes, including city parks, college campuses, and an airport. It has also been used for regeneration of a strip-mine site and a landfill. In addition, composted sludge is sold as a mulch and soil amendment under the name GroCo.

turning into compost over a period of time. The material, which is essentially the same as that produced in the sludge composting process, is periodically removed for use in pots or gardens.

The large size of the composting chamber presents problems in fitting these toilets into architectural plans, especially since the chamber is almost the height of a full floor level under the seat of the toilet. Some models use heating and air circulation devices to make possible a reduced chamber size, but this involves energy consumption.

Aquatic Sewage Treatment

Since the 1960s, researchers have developed an array of treatment systems that use the capacities of both plants and microorganisms to process sewage without using the elaborate, energy-intensive, often-unreliable mechanical devices used in industrial sewage plants. That is, they let nature do the work of sewage treatment. Essentially, these systems replicate and intensify the processes of nature in organic recycling. They simultaneously filter the water and assimilate the solids into living organisms. They use water as a medium and treat sewage as it comes from the conventional collection systems.

The essential point concerning natural treatment systems is that they are landscapes in their basic character and operation, while the conventional treatment systems of the industrial period are basically machines. This is a fundamental difference with far-reaching implications that transcend the technological distinction to involve the design of environment, the shaping of cities, and even the character of societies. We will return to this point in Chapters 9 and 10.

Before entering a natural treatment process, the solids are separated out of the water by settling or screening. The treatment systems fall into three general types: aquacultural ponds, wetlands, and root-zone beds, all of which have certain characteristics in common. The sewage water travels slowly among the roots and stems of aquatic plants, which take up some nutrients and other materials from the water in the process of supporting their own growth. However, the bulk of the work is done by bacteria and other microorganisms living on the roots and stems. Plants and microorganisms are capable of taking almost any materials out of the water, including nutrients, metals, and pathogens. The degree of treatment depends on the time; given enough time, natural systems can produce water suitable for human consumption from the densest raw sewage.

In natural treatment systems the limiting factor is usually biological oxygen demand, or the oxygen content of the water. The oxygenating activity of aquatic plants is important in maintaining oxygen levels as many of the plants take in oxygen through their leaves and release it through their roots. The oxygen-rich environment at the roots supports a rich microbial community that is very effective in the treatment process: bacteria, fungi, filter feeders, detritivores, and their predators.

AQUACULTURAL POND TREATMENT / In aquacultural pond systems, the sewage water flows through a series of ponds with floating aquatic plants. Such a system can treat raw sewage or can accept water already treated up to a primary or secondary stage. Although a number of floating plants such as duckweed (*Lemna* spp., *Wolfia* spp., *Spirodela*) and water fern (*Azolia* spp.) are sometimes included, the most common by far in sewage treatment is the water hyacinth (*Eichhornia crassipes*). This is mostly due to their high growth rate. The productivity of a pond populated with water hyacinths has been estimated at 154 tons of biomass per acre per year. While this frenetic level of biomass production supports rapid nutrient uptake from the water, it also imposes a need for frequent harvesting. If not harvested, the plants simply fall back into the water as they die to decompose, thus returning the materials they took out. Fortunately, the harvested hyacinths are useful in two important ways. They make an excellent, protein-rich animal feed, and they can be digested to produce methane gas and a residue useful as fertilizer. Estimated energy value of the gas produced is roughly the equivalent of 120 gallons of petroleum per acre per year.

Water hyacinths have two major disadvantages: Being tropical plants, they are easily killed by freezing, and when released into lakes or reservoirs, they multiply rapidly and tend to completely dominate the environment. In a short time they can eliminate other species and even cause a water body to dry up.

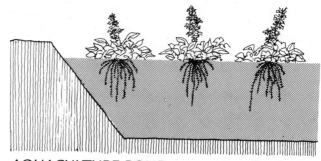

AQUACULTURE POND

EXAMPLE

■■

Tijuana River Valley

The Tijuana River Valley lies adjacent to the border between the United States and Mexico on the American side. The watershed of the Tijuana River stretches out to the east, straddling the border. More than 80 percent of it lies in Mexico.

The difficulty began when the Mexicans built the Rodriguez Dam, which impounded the river in the mountains to supply water for the border city of Tijuana. Since the dam was in the lower part of the watershed, it reduced the flow of water to a trickle, leaving only a limited amount available for irrigating the farms in the valley on the U.S. side.

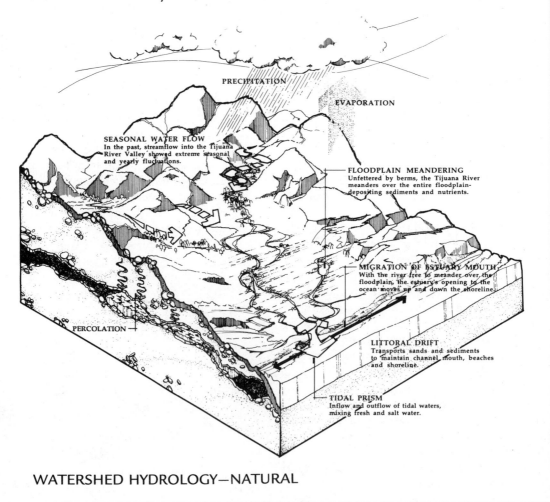

PRECIPITATION

EVAPORATION

SEASONAL WATER FLOW
In the past, streamflow into the Tijuana River Valley showed extreme seasonal and yearly fluctuations.

FLOODPLAIN MEANDERING
Unfettered by berms, the Tijuana River meanders over the entire floodplain-depositing sediments and nutrients.

MIGRATION OF ESTUARY MOUTH
With the river free to meander over the floodplain, the estuary's opening to the ocean moves up and down the shoreline.

PERCOLATION

LITTORAL DRIFT
Transports sands and sediments to maintain channel mouth, beaches and shoreline.

TIDAL PRISM
Inflow and outflow of tidal waters, mixing fresh and salt water.

WATERSHED HYDROLOGY—NATURAL

However, as Tijuana grew, the amount of water flowing into the United States gradually increased. Water diverted from the river to the city was coming back again as Tijuana sewage. The Mexicans eventually built a treatment plant to treat the sewage before releasing it into the river, but that has proved to be only a partial solution. The treatment plant often fails to function. Even when it is working, most of the water in the river comes from uncontrolled residential development in several canyons near the border. These areas have no sewage system at all; the material simply flows through the drainage ways that lead down to the river.

Thus most of the water in the river is raw or partially treated sewage, which crosses the border, moves through the valley, and then enters the Tijuana National Estuarine Research Reserve, a network of estuarine channels at the river's mouth. The Tijuana Reserve is the only coastal wetland in southern California that is still in a reasonably natural state (except for its water quality) and an important habitat for migratory birds.

After moving through the estuary, the water flows out into the Pacific Ocean. Then it is picked up by the northerly littoral drift, and much of it washes up on the serenely beautiful beaches that stretch between the city of

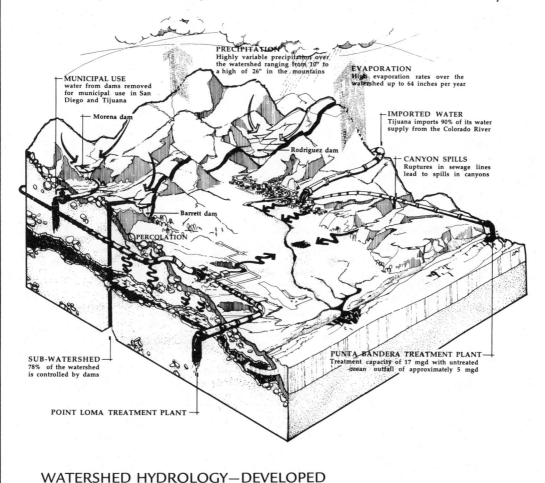

WATERSHED HYDROLOGY—DEVELOPED

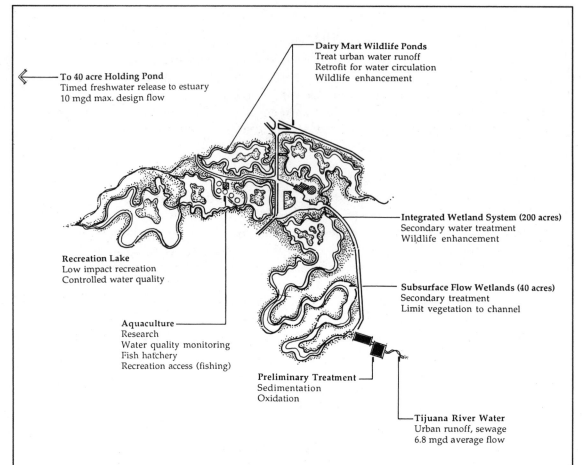

To 40 acre Holding Pond
Timed freshwater release to estuary
10 mgd max. design flow

Dairy Mart Wildlife Ponds
Treat urban water runoff
Retrofit for water circulation
Wildlife enhancement

Integrated Wetland System (200 acres)
Secondary water treatment
Wildlife enhancement

Recreation Lake
Low impact recreation
Controlled water quality

Subsurface Flow Wetlands (40 acres)
Secondary treatment
Limit vegetation to channel

Aquaculture
Research
Water quality monitoring
Fish hatchery
Recreation access (fishing)

Preliminary Treatment
Sedimentation
Oxidation

Tijuana River Water
Urban runoff, sewage
6.8 mgd average flow

WETLAND WATER TREATMENT CONCEPT

San Diego and the border. In recent years these beaches have often been closed for long periods due to the pollution. Tijuana sewage has become an increasingly volatile international issue.

In 1989 the San Diego County Department of Parks commissioned the 606 Studio planning research group to make recommendations for new recreation areas in the border area and, at the same time, to look for solutions to the sewage problem (606 Studio, 1989).

The group designed a pond and wetlands treatment system. In this proposed scheme, after primary screening and perhaps secondary treatment, the sewage water will move slowly through a long lagoon in which most suspended solids settle to the bottom, where they will be attacked by bacteria. After that, it will move through a series of ponds and wetlands where various species of aquatic plants and microorganisms will take up nutrients and other materials dissolved in the water. Upon reaching the end of the journey through the ponds and wetlands, the water will be clean enough for release into the estuary and, finally, into the ocean, where it will do no harm to the beaches.

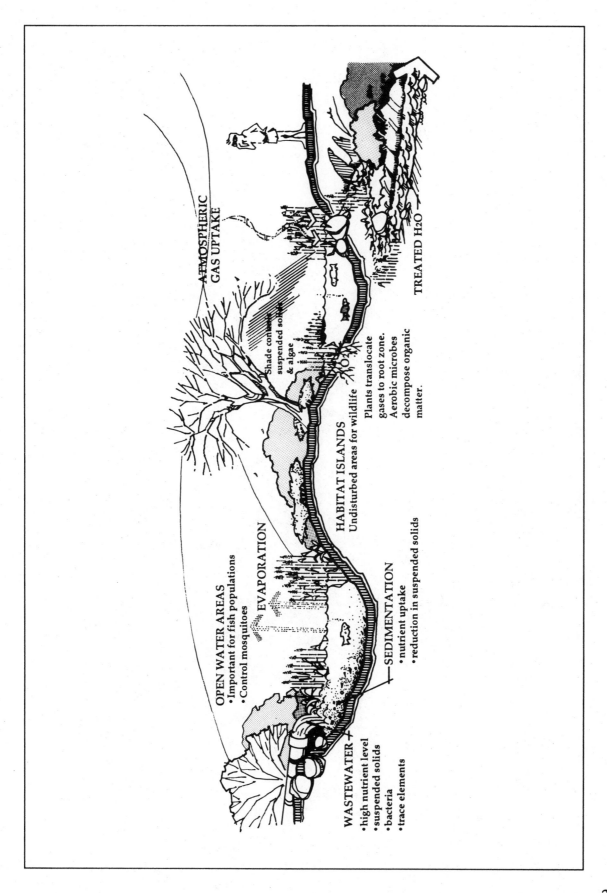

ATMOSPHERIC GAS UPTAKE

TREATED H₂O

Shade controls suspended solids & algae

HABITAT ISLANDS
Undisturbed areas for wildlife

Plants translocate gases to root zone. Aerobic microbes decompose organic matter.

OPEN WATER AREAS
• Important for fish populations
• Control mosquitoes

EVAPORATION

SEDIMENTATION
• nutrient uptake
• reduction in suspended solids

WASTEWATER
• high nutrient level
• suspended solids
• bacteria
• trace elements

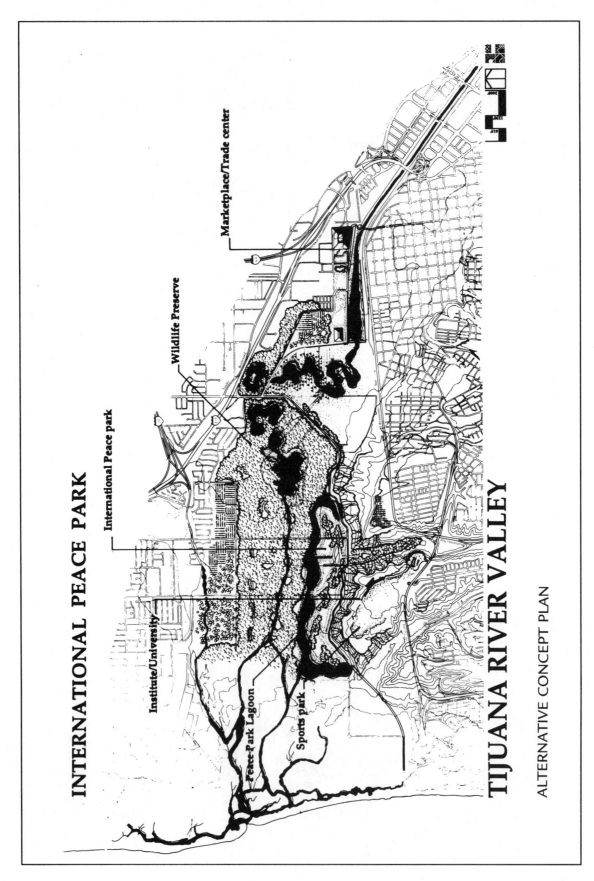

INTERNATIONAL PEACE PARK

International Peace park

Wildlife Preserve

Marketplace/Trade center

Institute/University

Peace-Park Lagoon

Sports park

TIJUANA RIVER VALLEY

ALTERNATIVE CONCEPT PLAN

The treated water can also be used to irrigate the farms that still occupy much of the river valley and future recreation areas. Much of the water applied to the land will eventually soak through the soil into underground storage, thus helping the aquifer underlying the valley to resist saltwater intrusion.

What the Tijuana River Valley plan can accomplish is the establishment of a new ecosystem that combines urban and natural processes. It is functionally analogous to the natural system in that it provides for a balanced system of energy and material flows. Moreover, the water treatment system can become an integral part of an international park straddling the border providing wildlife habitat, irrigation water, visual delight and a variety of recreational experiences.

Duckweed is increasingly used in both aquaculture and wetland systems due to its extremely fast growth rate (Hillman and Culley, 1978). Floating on the water surface, the tiny duckweed leaves can double their numbers in as little as 4 days. They have a high protein and fat content and are rich in nutrients, making them an exceptional animal food (ibid.). They are also somewhat more cold-tolerant than the water hyacinth.

Aquacultural ponds are highly effective in taking up nitrogen from the sewage water and processing it through ammonia volatilization, nitrification, and denitrification. Plants can also remove phosphorus, potassium, sulfur, calcium, and other minerals (Wolverton, 1979). They are effective as well in removing metals by precipitation and by adsorption on plant roots and substrate. Suspended solids are taken out in the same way. Like most other treatment processes, aquacultural systems are much less effective in removing phosphorus. They rarely achieve more than 50 percent phosphorous removal.

The form of aquacultural ponds is important to their functioning. Good water and plant distribution assures that both oxygen and biotic activity are spread more or less evenly throughout the volume of the pond. Anaerobic conditions and their related odors can occur in oxygen-poor areas. This is a problem in long, narrow ponds with influent points at a narrow end (Tchobanoglous et al., 1987). In such cases, most of the biotic activity usually occurs at the intake end, leaving downstream areas short of oxygen. For this reason, the best shape for aquacultural ponds is roughly square with several influent points at intervals along the input edge to insure even water distribution.

The area of aquacultural ponds needed to treat sewage in a given situation depends on the volume of sewage and the retention time in the ponds. The Texas Department of Health (1979) recommends 0.2 million gallons per day per acre with a mean depth of 3 feet. Usually the treatment system involves a series of three or four ponds with the water held in each pond for 2 to 4 days.

Two problems that can occur in aquacultural ponds are excessive algae growth and mosquito breeding. Keeping the pond surface shaded by plant growth usually controls algae. Fish, such as koi or goldfish, that feed on algae can also grow in the ponds. These fish also eat mosquito larvae, though most effective in reducing mosquito populations to hardly noticeable levels are mosquito fish (*Gambusia*).

WETLAND TREATMENT / Wetlands serve a water-cleansing function within natural systems, and the same processes can treat human wastes. It is generally not feasible to use natural wetlands for treat-

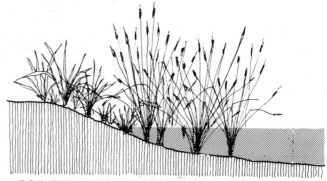

CONSTRUCTED WETLAND

EXAMPLE

Arcata Marsh and Wildlife Sanctuary

Arcata is a town of about 15,000 people located on the northern California coast. For decades its sewage was piped into an oxidation pond for a few days and then moved on to the Pacific Ocean. The federal Water Pollution Control Act of 1972 rendered this treatment system clearly inadequate. Some form of secondary treatment would have to be added, and the conventional technologies were very expensive. So in the late 1970s, Arcata developed a small pilot wetland system to function between the oxidation pond and ocean release. The results showed that the wetland could provide advanced treatment with capital and maintenance costs considerably lower than those of a mechanized secondary treatment system. On the basis of those results, the city developed its present system.

This system begins with primary settling after which 2 to 3 million gallons of sewage move into three oxidation ponds each day and an equal amount moves out. After that, a 5.3-acre intermediate marsh, planted mostly with the hardstem bulrush (*Scirpus acutus*), reduces suspended solids. Mosquito fish control mosquito populations. Chlorination and dechlorination follow the intermediate marsh; then the water moves into the 154-acre Arcata Marsh and Wildlife Sanctuary and from there into Humboldt Bay. In this marsh, cattails grow along with bulrushes, and duckweed covers much of the surface. Analyses required by the state to maintain the facility's permit to discharge into the bay show that the water moving into the bay meets the standards for secondary treatment. Studies have shown that refinements in the design of the marsh could improve the treatment to the level of standards for advanced treatment.

As important as sewage treatment in the Arcata Marsh is the combination of other functions that it supports. Wildlife habitat is varied and extensive. This is due partly to the inherently diverse character of land-water interactions in a wetland and partly due to the way in which this inherent quality was further augmented by design. In its final grading the levels of the marsh bottom were varied to provide conditions for a range of marsh plants that grow at different levels of submergence. These plants in turn provide conditions for a range of microbes, mollusks, fish, and birds. Over 220 bird species have been recorded here, many of them migratory species that stop over on their journey along the Pacific flyway.

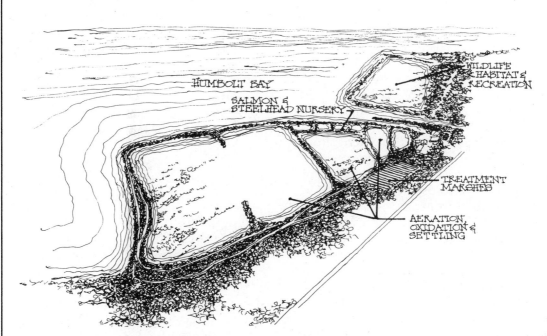

ARCATA MARSH TREATMENT SYSTEM

Researchers have also established a fish hatchery in the lagoon. Salmon fry are imprinted to return here as adults to lay their own eggs.

The recreational value of the marsh has been proven as well. Over 100,000 people visit the area each year. Most of these are from the city of Arcata, since the marsh has become a local focal point, but many are tourists. A significant increase in the number of tourists visiting Arcata has been documented by the city.

ment purposes because the quality standards established by the federal Water Pollution Control Act for water discharged into natural bodies are considerably higher than the quality of most sewage. Nevertheless, it is possible to construct wetlands for that purpose. In addition to their cleansing function, constructed wetlands can provide wildlife habitat.

Wetlands are among nature's most biologically productive landscapes, rich in species from detritivores to birds of prey. Wetlands are also among the landscapes most ravaged by the expansion of human habitat. More than half of the wetlands in the United States have been lost to urbanization and agriculture since the first Europeans arrived. However, newly constructed wetlands can incorporate all of the habitat qualities of natural wetlands.

Indeed, by knowledgeable design they can enhance and augment habitat value. Constructed wetlands can help to replace at least a small part of the wetlands lost, while processing urban sewage to a level of quality suitable for reuse.

Before being introduced into a wetland system, sewage goes through primary screening or settling and usually spends time in an oxidation pond as well. In contrast, with aquacultural ponds, wetlands function best in the form of long, narrow channels less than 2 feet deep with rooted aquatic plants growing in dense stands in the channel bottoms. The plants most used include bulrushes (*Scirpus* spp.), cattails (*Typha* spp.), reeds (*Phragmites* spp.), rushes (*Juncus* spp.), and sedges (*Carex* spp.). All of these act as small oxygen pumps, drawing oxygen in through their leaves and releasing it through their roots. This provides an aerobic environment for the microcommunities that live on their roots and stems on the channel bottom.

Each of these aquatic plants provide conditions for certain microorganisms by secreting through its roots substances that meet their needs. The microorganism communities then live on the roots and stems, consuming the nutrients in the sewage water. They also take up other chemicals in the water, including pollutants from industrial and agricultural sources, and break them down into simpler compounds that the plants can then use. Wetlands treatment has proven effective in dealing with industrial effluents. In Martinez, California, a constructed wetland successfully treats process water laden with hydrocarbons flowing from the adjacent oil refinery.

Research has shown wetland treatment to be most effective in reducing biological oxygen demand, nitrogen, suspended solids, metals, trace organics, and pathogens. Bulrushes seem to be the most effective plants for nitrogen removal. In experiments at the Santee plant in San Diego, bulrushes removed 94 percent of nitrogen from the sewage water compared with 78 percent for reeds and 28 percent for cattails (Gersberg et al., 1985). The processes for removing metals, suspended solids, and phosphorus are essentially the same as those in aquacultural systems; the effectiveness is also similar.

An important advantage of wetland systems is that they can function in colder climates with some freezing, though long freezing periods can seriously reduce oxygen levels in the water.

ROOTZONE TREATMENT / Also called vegetated submerged bed treatment, subsurface treatment, rock-reed filter, and by other names as well, rootzone treatment is similar to wetland treatment. While wetlands can treat even very large quantities

of sewage, rootzone systems are generally more appropriate for smaller volumes, typically less than 100,000 gallons per day. Rootzone treatment employs a porous bed of large-grain material, usually gravel but sometimes sand, through which the water flows. In general, the coarser the texture of the medium, the faster the water flows and the larger the bed must be. Finer textures also require wider ponds.

Rootzone systems require somewhat closer control than aquacultural or wetland systems. The water level is ideally maintained just below the top surface of the medium, while the bottom is sealed to prevent percolation. The roots of the plants grow within the spaces provided by the porous medium, forming a kind of web through which the water filters. Thus the microbe communities have direct access to the water with its load of nutrients and other materials. They consume nutrients and break down various chemical compounds as in wetlands, but the process is more effective because of this continuous contact.

Scientists at the University of Goettingen and the Max Planck Institute pioneered the development of rootzone systems beginning in the early 1960s. Since then a number of rootzone systems have been built in Germany, other parts of Europe, and in the Mideast and Asia. Several towns in the southern United States have also built rootzone systems in preference to conventional treatment plants, primarily because of the former's much lower cost. The town of Benton, Louisiana, has used a combination of oxidation pond and rock-reed rootzone system to treat all of its sewage since 1986 and has never failed to meet strict EPA standards for discharge into the nearby Red River. A number of the systems now working are associated with industrial plants, serving specifically to treat water polluted by industrial processes before it is returned to lakes or rivers. One example is a large textile plant in Germany.

BROADER APPLICATION / Aquatic treatment concepts are not limited to municipal or industrial facilities but can be applied in myriad ways at any scale in any situation where purer water or a richer aquatic environment is desirable. Water in a polluted stream, for example, might be diverted through a series of wetlands for treatment and then returned to the stream. A series of ponds and wetlands located at strategic points in a city's drainage system could treat urban runoff to a level suitable for return to natural waterways.

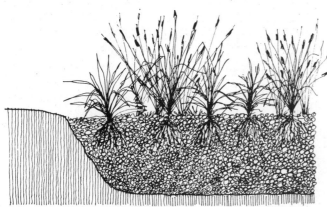

ROCK—REED FILTER

EXAGMPLE

■ ■

Crowley Sewage Treatment Plant

Crowley is a town of 18,000 people located in southern Louisiana. When the town's 30-year-old mechanical treatment plant, which had functioned sporadically and unreliably for several years, seemed on the verge of final breakdown, the town council received an estimate of $5 to $6 million for a complete overhaul. The town is surrounded by marshlands, which are among nature's best filtering systems, and Mayor Robert Estre, who had been fishing in the marshes all his life knew them well. He also knew Crowley's treatment plant from long experience, and he had little confidence in it, even if refurbished. He was intrigued by the water-purifying capacity of the marshes; water flowed in on one side murky and discolored, and flowed out on the other clear and odorless. Wondering if a sewage treatment system could be engineered to work in the same way as the marshes, he discovered the work of B. C. Wolverton, a pioneer in natural sewage treatment. Wolverton suggested a combination of wetland and rootzone system. Estre persuaded the council to accept the idea. Wolverton worked with engineers Charles Mader and Frederick Trahan of Mader-Miers Engineering to develop the design. The cost of the new natural system was about the same as that of overhauling the old plant.

The process they designed begins with about 2.5 million gallons per day of raw sewage flowing into the oxidation pond that covers more than half of the

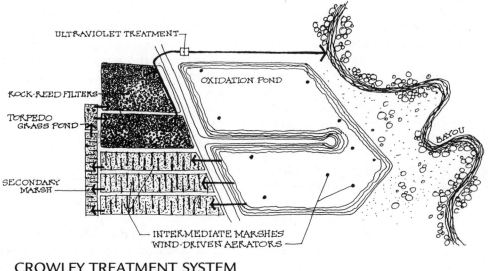

CROWLEY TREATMENT SYSTEM

facility's 178 acres. Ten wind-driven aerators, activated by probes that detect oxygen depletion, keep oxygen content at acceptable levels. Water stays in the oxidation pond 50 to 60 days and then moves through the intermediate marshes, where operators believe the major work of water treatment is accomplished. There are three of these marshes, rectangular in form, operating independently in parallel. Each has rows of giant bulrushes reaching out perpendicularly to its edges to work like a series of baffles through which the water meanders. The water surface is covered with duckweed, which kills any algae that may appear by shading it out. The dead algae then drop to the bottom to become food for the bulrushes.

After about 3 days in the intermediate marshes, the water moves into the secondary marsh, which is similar in design to the intermediate marshes but somewhat larger than any one of them. The water stays here 1 day and then moves quickly through a pond planted with torpedo grass, which filters out any materials suspended or floating in it, including remnants of duckweed.

One end of this pond is aerated by two more wind-driven aerators, which add oxygen before the water goes into a rock-reed filter. There are actually two filters that work in parallel, both about 18 inches deep and filled with limestone rocks 1 to 4 inches in their largest dimension. A variety of aquatic plants grow in rocks with the dominant type being bulrushes. Retention time in the filter is 1 day, after which the water goes through ultraviolet radiation for disinfection and a final aeration before being discharged into a nearby bayou.

The Crowley sewage treatment plant is a beautiful and tranquil place, with geometric forms that are clearly of human devising. Nevertheless, it is a rich landscape that recalls the nearby natural marshes. There are no odors other than those of a productive natural marsh.

Aquatic treatment systems in all their forms are among the best and clearest examples of regenerative technologies. They are in themselves complex ecosystems which naturally do the work that human society needs done. They can treat water to any level of quality. They do not need the concrete and steel structures or the machinery, the pumps and pipes of conventional industrial treatment. They can work at any scale and are not subject to the breakdowns that plague mechanized treatment systems. They do not use fossil fuels or pollute the air. Finally, they cost far less than do mechanized systems.

The main disadvantage of aquatic systems is that they occupy more land than mechanized systems. In urban areas this can present serious problems. However, in this respect too, aquatic systems are quintessentially regenerative in that they in-

corporate all of the processing capabilities of the landscape: assimilation, filtering, storage, and production. They are also integrally related to other life-support processes. Besides supplying clean water for any number of uses, they can provide biomass for energy conversion and fertilizer for food production and food for animals, both domestic and wild.

Land Sewage Treatment
There are three basic types of land treatment systems that use terrestrial biological and physical processes rather than aquatic processes to treat sewage water: slow-rate treatment, overland flow, and rapid infiltration. All of these involve spreading water over the land, but each accomplishes the treatment process in a somewhat different way.

EXAMPLE

Denham Springs Treatment Plant

The plant in Denham Springs, Louisiana, is several years older than the Crowley plant and has reached a more mature state. The process is simpler here, consisting only of an oxidation pond, a rock-reed filter, and a sprinkler aeration system. The marshes and the torpedo-grass pond at Crowley were added partly in response to problems experienced in the Denham Springs filters with clogging by organic matter.

In its mature state, the Denham Springs plant looks like a water garden with its giant marsh plants and the many species of birds that float in its waters and dig around its edges. The water is teeming with turtles, frogs, and fish. All these have moved into the area without human encouragement, suggesting the enormous potentials these treatment plants have for biotic production and wildlife habitat.

SLOW-RATE TREATMENT / The most common land-based system is slow-rate treatment, which has been practiced since the 16th century. It involves distributing the water over the landscape to be taken up by plants or filtered through the soil to underground storage. This may involve spreading the water in thin sheets or shallow channels, or it may use an irrigation system. The latter might be of any type, but for purposes of conserving energy and water, it is ideally a drip or subsurface system.

Since infiltration through the soil to the groundwater is presently the most effective means of making sewage effluent available again for human use, slow-rate treatment is commonly used with varied levels of pretreatment. At the very least, primary screening or settling is necessary before land application. Oxidation ponds are commonly used as the primary treatment because they also provide storage capacity for water awaiting land application. Often, slow-rate treatment serves as a final step of soil filtration following secondary or even advanced treatment. Where the irrigation system applies effluent to human food crops, secondary treatment is required. In such cases, land treatment can be coupled with some form of aquatic treatment.

The landscape for sewage treatment may serve any number of other purposes as well. In the San Jacinto Wildlife Area, described elsewhere in the chapter, the water increases habitat diversity in a number of ways while it percolates into the soil. In cities, slow-rate systems commonly irrigate parks, golf courses, and other urban landscapes. In forest applications the water stimulates tree growth. Agricultural applications are most common, with crops varying according to local suitability and the purpose of the system.

Where the maximum level of water treatment is most important, crops are usually selected for their capacity to take up nitrogen. In the western states, alfalfa is commonly grown in land treatment systems because of its high nitrogen uptake rate. The evapotranspiration, or water consumption rate, of the plants is also an important concern, especially in dry climates.

Evaporation loss also presents serious problems. Among the largest systems is that of Muskegon County, Michigan, which irrigates over 5000 acres with a center pivot system. Such devices employ long arms that rotate around a central pivot point on wheels, showering water on crops as they go. Though often used, center pivotal systems lose a great deal of water to evaporation and consume considerable energy in their operation. A somewhat simpler slow-rate system in Bakersfield, California, applies the water to crops through a ridge-and-furrow flooding system, which also incurs high evaporation losses by having the water sit on the surface for periods of time. Seattle's slow-rate system distributes water by sprinklers in a forested area, also with considerable evaporation loss.

OVERLAND FLOW / In natural landscapes, water is often cleaned when it flows for some distance over a grass-covered slope. Overland flow systems use the same principle, releasing water at the upper level of a slope, usually through sprinklers or perforated pipes, and allowing it to flow in a more or less even sheet over a grassy surface. Actually, the roots of the grass taking up some of the water, but most of it filters through the lower stems of the grass and the detritus and thatch lying just above the top of the soil. The degree of treatment depends mostly on the length of the slope, which is usually between 100 and 200 feet long.

Because they are designed to recover the water rather than return it underground, the soils in the slopes are compacted or underlain by an impermeable layer. Usually less than 8 percent of the water is collected at the bottom of the slope for reuse or return to a water body.

Following primary screening or settling, overland flow systems are capable of secondary or advanced secondary treatment. They are especially effective in removing biological oxygen demand, suspended solids, and nitrogen.

SEPTIC SYSTEMS / Septic systems use an enclosed tank for settling out solids followed by distribution of the water into a series of perforated pipes buried under the surface of the soil. In the past they were considered appropriate only for single houses on large areas of land. The field area that the pipes occupy is large in itself, and health regulations usually require that the lots occupied by houses using septic systems be much larger than the field itself in order to avoid concentrating effluents. Septic systems also have a reputation for unreliability because individual homeowners find them difficult to maintain. Furthermore, there is the disadvantage that the settling tank requires pumping out periodically. A service truck usually performs this service and thus there is still the sludge to be dealt with.

However, research begun in the 1970s suggests that these limitations are surmountable. Septic systems may well have an important place among re-

EXAMPLE
■■■

San Jacinto Wildlife Area

The Wildlife Area covers an area of 4669 acres on the edge of the southern California metropolitan region. On one side is a large reservoir called Lake Perris, but a low range of hills separates the lake from the wildlife area. On the other sides, housing tracts are expanding and will soon crowd up to the wildlife area's boundaries.

Until a few years ago the wildlife area was marginal farmland. Now it is covered by scrubby vegetation. The San Jacinto River, which flows through it, carries little water now due to upstream impoundments. In fact, despite the adjacent lake there is little water in the whole area. Though this is now a dry region, water was probably once abundant. Judging from what is known of the landscape before European settlers arrived, there were at one time numerous vernal pools holding water from the winter rains until late July or August and supporting a rich plant cover and bright arrays of wildflowers. These were plowed over when the land was leveled for farming.

The wildlife area exists because part of it is ideal habitat of the Stephens kangaroo rat, a species on the Threatened Species list. The kangaroo rat requires only the water in the plants it eats, but most other species native to this area are drawn to landscapes with water. Without water the wildlife area has very limited habitat value except for the kangaroo rat. With more water, as it once had, it could be a diverse and lively habitat again.

A short distance away there exists a source of water: The Hemet–San Jacinto Wastewater Reclamation Facility has no use for the secondary effluent it produces. A plan developed by the 606 Studio (1988) proposes to pipe this water to the site and then treat it to an advanced stage using a pond-and-wetland system. This process will feed the water through a series of ponds and narrow channels, which themselves will serve as wildlife habitat. When the water emerges from them, it will be high enough in quality for use in recreational ponds, for percolation to underground storage, or for release into the San Jacinto River. Thus the land of the wildlife area will not only serve the wildlife populations but also play a pivotal role in the larger water-flow system, processing water for storage and later reuse. The aquifer recharge role will be especially important because the water table in this area has been dropping at a rate of about 6 feet per year.

After treatment in the wetland process, the water will be used in several ways to create a diverse range of wildlife habitat. It will flow through shallow

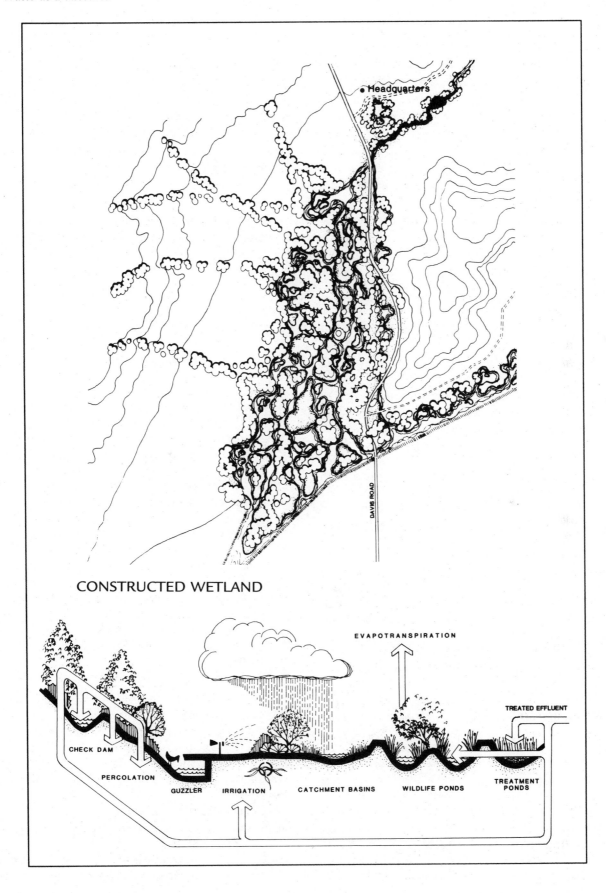

CONSTRUCTED WETLAND

channels to fill ponds on other parts of the site. Some of these will be vernal ponds like those that were here before the farms, filled only in the winter and early spring and allowed to go dry in later summer.

Some of the water will feed a temporary irrigation system used for 2 or 3 years after replanting to help reestablish the native plant communities. Part of the water will be piped up the hillsides using solar pumps and released into the streambeds to create live streams. Check dams along the stream courses will slow and spread the water periodically to enrich the riparian vegetation and provide some standing water.

Altogether, when this water-flow system is in full operation, it will probably support a diversity of wildlife species and population levels even higher than that which existed before the land was first cultivated. It is a marriage of city and nature: Urban resources and processes join natural processes to create a richer natural community.

---

generative treatment technologies. For a small system serving a cluster of dwellings or a community, they can be followed by natural treatment, such as aquacultural ponds or wetlands. The following are other means of further treatment.

LOW-PRESSURE DISTRIBUTION SYSTEMS / For the first stage of treatment, the low-pressure system uses a settling tank like that of a conventional system. From there a pump conveys the effluent in carefully measured amounts into the distribution system, which, as in a conventional system, consists of perforated pipes buried in the ground. However, there are major differences between low-pressure and conventional distribution devices. The pipes are smaller, closer together (3 to 5 feet apart compared with 8 to 10), and closer to the surface (1 or 2 feet deep compared with 3 to 5) than conventional systems. These differences, combined with the better-regulated flow, allow for more even water distribution (Jewel, 1980). The placement near the soil surface, where air is circulating, also encourages aerobic decomposition, which is faster than the anaerobic decomposition occurring at lower levels.

Together, these differences provide for more reliable treatment in a land area that can be as small as one-fifth of that needed for a conventional system. More significantly, they make water and nutrients more available to the roots of plants, and thus become media of regeneration. Perhaps even more importantly than that, low-pressure systems can conveniently serve more than one house. They can be designed for clusters of buildings, which makes

them feasible at densities suitable for urban and suburban situations.

Neutralizing Pollution

All of the technologies mentioned so far can be long-term components of human ecosystems, integrated into the processes of daily life and operational elements of the life-support infrastructure. In contrast, the pollution-neutralizing technologies are designed to deal with specific situations that would not exist in a truly regenerative world. However, since we do not live in such a world and probably will not for some time (if ever), technologies for inexpensively rendering intensive levels of pollution harmless are important. Such technologies are likely to become more important as we undertake the revitalization of the millions of acres of polluted land left in the wake of the industrial era. They are emerging from research laboratories and becoming available. Among the more promising are bioremediation and solar detoxification.

BIOREMEDIATION / Among nature's ways of dealing with problems of potential pollution are bacteria and fungi that dwell in the soil and devour whatever materials may come to be there, even those toxic to other species. Using this process to deal with toxic or hazardous waste is called bioremediation.

In nature, toxic and hazardous materials generally occur at very low concentrations. Humans tend to concentrate materials more; nevertheless, the decomposing microorganisms can deal with materials deposited by humans, such as spoiled food buried

■■■

Westchem Cleanup

In April 1987, a warehouse belonging to Westchem Agricultural Chemicals in Minot, North Dakota, caught fire. Water used in fighting the fire spread toxic chemicals, including 2,4-D and MCPA, over the landscape, where they quickly soaked into the soil. The first cleanup proposal was the usual solution: to dig the soil up and haul it to a landfill. But the company's general manager proposed trying bioremediation instead.

A team from the Ecova Corporation began work the following June. Their first task was to analyze the contaminated soil to determine what microorganisms might consume it. Then they studied the soil on the site to see if such a creature existed there. It turned out there was a bacterium that appeared suitable for the task. Next the workers excavated a shallow treatment bed on the site, 5 acres in area and lined with clay to prevent leaching of contaminants. Then the crew began transporting contaminated soil to the treatment bed and mixing in populations of bacteria. They also added nutrients, oxygen, and water to stimulate bacterial growth.

Progress, however, was still too slow, so the soil had to be treated in large tanks called bioreactors. The workers screened the contaminated soil to take out rocks and debris, loaded it into the tanks, and added bacteria and water. Then the tanks churned the mixture while air and nutrients were continuously injected. This worked quickly enough. The bacteria consumed the chemicals at a frenetic pace and converted them into harmless gases, mostly carbon dioxide.

After emerging from the reactors, the soil was returned to its original place with the chemicals now removed. Even with the added cost of the bioreactor process, the cost of the whole operation was far less than the cost of hauling the soil to a landfill. More significantly, the soil was kept in use and no toxic materials were deposited in the landfill to cause future problems.

in a pit or even toxics—up to a point. When the concentrations become too great, as in a landfill or a chemical spill, the job becomes more than the microorganisms can accomplish, at least in the time needed by humans.

Scientists have learned to speed up microbial activity in some situations by providing concentrated materials like water, oxygen, and nutrients. Often the microbes needed to deal with a particular substance are already in the soil where the pollution occurs, and stimulation is all that they need. An early example of using this principle is the stimulation of microbes to devour 130,000 gallons of gasoline spilled into a water-supply reservoir in Ambler, Pennsylvania. By providing nutrients and oxygen, microbial action was hastened enough to bring the concentration of petroleum in the water down to safe drinking levels. It was estimated that without stimulating microbial activity, the task would have taken at least 50 years.

Sometimes, especially in the case of chemicals invented by humans, microbes have to be brought in for a specific task. For example, laboratories have been working to find bacteria to deal with widespread pollution by polychlorobiphenyls (PCBs). Microbes have been hauled from laboratory to site for this task with partial success.

William Frankenberger and Ulrich Karlson found naturally occurring fungi in the soil of the Kesterson National Wildlife Refuge that were capable of devouring the selenium that had been disastrously concentrated there. By plowing up the land, irrigating it, and adding fruit pectin and fertilizer, they stimulated the fungal activity to a level that will bring selenium concentrations down to acceptable levels within about 5 years. After eating the selenium, the fungi release it into the atmosphere as a harmless gas.

Genetic engineering can potentially provide microorganisms for processing particular materials. The bacteria mentioned in Chapter 4, for example, developed for converting cellulose to ethanol, can deal with a wide range of organic waste materials including some sludges. This may be another fertile field for scientific invention.

SOLAR DETOXIFICATION / When a stream flows through the direct sunlight of an open meadow, its waters are cleansed of some chemicals by light rays that trigger photolytic chemical reactions. Processes of solar detoxification apply the same principle to break down a number of toxic or hazardous chemicals. The quantum effect of high-energy photons in combination with the thermal effect of infrared photons breaks the chemical bonds of a number of dangerous residuals including most industrial solvents, dioxins and PCBs, leaving harmless elements and compounds.

Exploring the means for accomplishing this, with emphases on water and gas detoxification, has become a major area for technology development in the U.S. Department of Energy's solar industrial Program.

Solar treatment of contaminated water uses technical means similar to those of other water-heating applications. Inexpensive and highly effective are long mirrored troughs that focus reflected solar rays on a pipe that carries the water. In a system designed for a pilot plant to treat polluted groundwater at the Lawrence Livermore Laboratory in California, the pipe is made of transparent glass with a porous and transparent matrix carrying catalyst particles on its inner surface. An extraction well pulls the water up from underground. After that it

moves through a series of such pipes, all with reflected photons bombarding the chemicals carried with it. The clean water that results can then move on to other uses or back into underground storage.

Of a number of potential applications of gasphase solar detoxification, two of the more promising are destruction of dangerous compounds existing in soils and destruction of those in concentrated chemical waste. For these targets, a photolytic process can concentrate a large area of the solar spectrum to heat and break down volatile molecules in the soil or to vaporize chemical wastes. Temperatures in the range of 700°C to 1100°C are required for this. Experiments have proven the process effective for a number of chemicals such as chlorinated solvents, aromatics, and polynuclear aromatics.

Systems for Waste Regeneration

The range of regenerative approaches to waste management suggests a far greater diversity of means than is the case with mechanized treatment systems. Following the 12th strategy—prioritizing for sustainability—we can pose a simple order of preferences for applying a range of means. For solid waste, a strategy of prioritizing for sustainability suggests an obvious order of preference. Most important is using less material, and the current habits of Western societies afford enormous potential for using less. For materials that are used, the best practice is direct reuse followed by recycling. For organic materials, biological reassimilation is next in order of preference, and burning for energy after that. For materials resistant to all of these, landfilling is a last resort that should rarely be necessary.

Sewage is somewhat more complex. Since regenerative technologies function in close concert with natural processes, each has a range of local environmental conditions within which it works best. A water-processing system that works well on one soil type or geological structure may not work at all on another. Thus within a regional system, there might be a great many different technologies in operation, each responding to local conditions, but each playing its part in the larger whole.

Furthermore, as is the case with other areas of application, regenerative technologies for waste management do not exhibit the same economies of scale usually associated with industrial technologies. While few sewage treatment technologies can operate at the scale of a single family residence, almost all of them can function very effectively at the scale of a cluster of houses or a small community. Most can also deal with very large quantities of sewage.

This diversity and flexibility suggests decentralizing and diversifying processes that might ultimately reshape existing highly centralized treatment systems as well as shaping new ones in developing landscapes.

The city of Los Angeles is a case in point. The city's gigantic Hyperion treatment plant is seriously overloaded. This results in periodic spills of raw sewage into Santa Monica Bay, which add to the partially treated sewage regularly discharged into the bay. Malfunctions sometimes make large discharges unavoidable. Even when the treatment system is functioning well, heavy rains often flood the system, pushing raw sewage along with storm water into the bay. The city has commissioned several engineering studies to determine what are the best means for expanding the plant. It may be that this is not the best question. Perhaps the city should ask instead how it can best deal with its sewage. Or better, it might ask how the sewage might be turned into a resource. These questions could give rise to a virtually unlimited number of solutions that could draw a great many benefits from the water and nutrients in the sewage.

One proposal, for example, called for using the reclaimed water for recreation areas and community gardens in the severely depressed southeast section of Los Angeles. Under this proposal, which is one component of the multifaceted plan for this area described in Chapter 5, water would be drawn from a sewer main passing near a piece of land owned by the city. The city would build a small primary treatment plant on its land to provide screening and grit removal. Then the water would be fed into a series of aquacultural ponds using water hyacinths to bring it to an advanced level of treatment. After the last treatment pond, the water would flow into a small lake to form the centerpiece of a neighborhood park. Local residents could use the lake for boating and fishing. Water would also be conveyed from the lake to nearby community vegetable gardens and to other areas needing landscape irrigation. Thus the problem sewage might be converted into a community asset, serving the deprived people of a problem neighborhood, at a cost considerably less than that of treating the sewage at Hyperion.

The same approach might be applied in every neighborhood in the city. The technology and the landscape would be different in each place, but in each locale, the treated water would make a contribution to the quality of the local environment, providing visual and recreational amenities and wildlife habitat. For a city that imports its water from over 200 miles away, this could have considerable value.

The massive network of pipes, a distribution system working in reverse, leading to the Hyperion plant would then function in a much more flexible and useful way. With sewage being put in and taken out at many locations, it would bear an operational similarity to the electrical transmission grid discussed in Chapter 4. The Hyperion plant would still serve its established purpose at the end of the line for water not put to better use elsewhere. Thus we can see the intriguing possibilities for the linear distribution systems of the Paleotechnic period to evolve into flexible networks for the Neotechnic.

In new communities it is possible to build regenerative processes into the landscape from the very beginning. Treatment ponds can be integrated into subdivision design (Oswald et al., 1966). Consider again the example of the design for the Etiwanda-Day Canyon community given as an example in Chapter 6. A small treatment plant will process the sewage from this community of 3600 people. The treated water will then irrigate the landscape, consisting mostly of trees that produce fruit and firewood. Water not used by the plants will soak through the land into subsurface storage. Thus a circular flow will replace the one-way flow by using the capacities of the landscape for assimilation, filtration, productivity, and storage. The distribution and redistribution network becomes part of the community's infrastructure. From the aquifer, the community can draw the water up again to supply domestic needs, where the circuit begins again.

The Etiwanda-Day Canyon example shows how regenerative processes can reenter the urban fabric and give meaning and substance to the urban landscape. They can also provide economic support converting greenspace from an economic liability to an asset, from a luxury into a necessity. Giving visible expression to the ecological processes can give the cities of the next millennium forms quite different from those of the past.

Since most of the means for waste regeneration occur within the landscape, they can provide a functional, economic basis for the greenspace that is so desperately needed anyway for its amenity value. The biological processes that form the basis for Neotechnic waste management are far more compatible with human habitat than the physical processes that were the basis of Paleotechnic waste management.

Waste Management at the Center
for Regenerative Studies

Except in emergencies, there will be no waste pickups at the Center. Materials produced there or brought in will be reused in some way, except in cases of emergency or serious difficulty.

Materials brought into the Center for common use—not including private possessions—will be inventoried and assessed for their durability and their reuse or recycling potential. Where choices are available, items with the best reassimilation potential will be selected. This includes packaging and containers as well as the items themselves. Those with low potential that are nevertheless essential will become subjects for study and research to find substitutes or means for reuse or recycling.

REUSE

The Center will hold periodic garage sales to sell both common and private items that are no longer used. Reusable items not sold will be donated to local thrift stores. When the Center needs new items, members will shop in local thrift stores before buying anything new.

RECYCLING

Recyclable materials that cannot be dealt with internally will be collected and taken to a nearby recycling facility. This will include paper, metals, glass, and plastics. Kitchen scraps and other food items will be fed to animals. Agricultural wastes, including plant trimmings and other organic matter, will be returned to the soil directly or digested for biogas. Animal manure will also go to the biogas digester. The solid residue of the digestion process will be used as a fertilizer.

Kitchen wastes that cannot be fed to animals, along with agricultural wastes that cannot be returned directly to the soil or digested, will go to the compost bins. Compost will be used as a mulch and soil amendment.

Items for which reuse and recycling are extremely difficult, such as used batteries, oil sludge, and some laminated plastics, will become subjects for research to find substitutes or means of reassimilation.

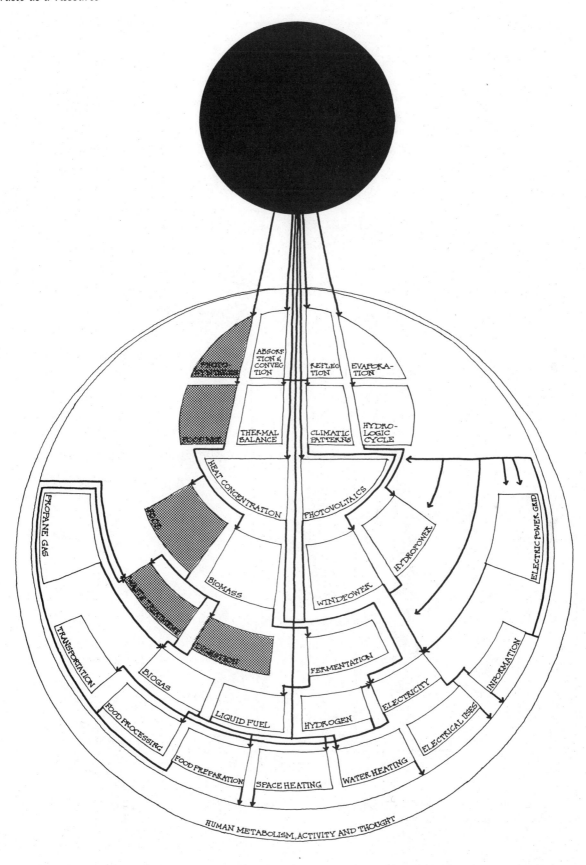

SEWAGE TREATMENT

Since the Center's purposes include development and testing of regenerative technologies, the sewage treatment system involves three of the
basic natural processing systems functioning in parallel. The aquaculture system, the surface-flow wetland system, and the rootzone system,
will operate side-by-side with plumbing that permits them to be used

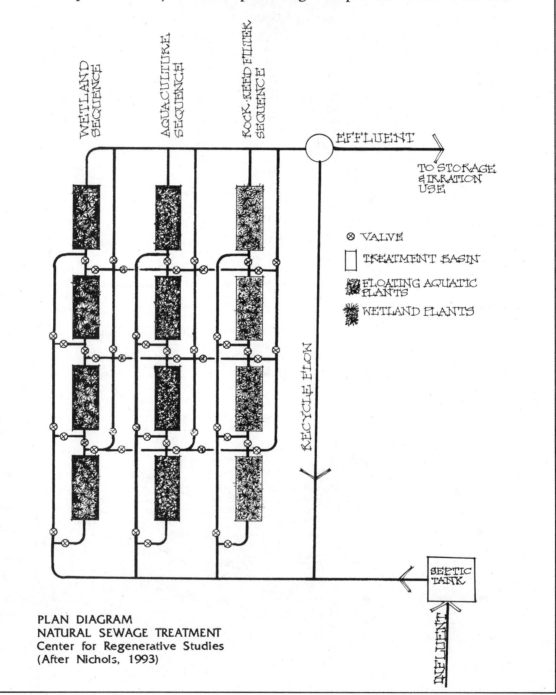

PLAN DIAGRAM
NATURAL SEWAGE TREATMENT
Center for Regenerative Studies
(After Nichols, 1993)

simultaneously or alternately, in combination or (conceivably) in sequence. This will provide the flexibility needed to test the effectiveness of all three systems according to various parameters, and to compare their performance.

A septic tank will accomplish the first stage of treatment, producing an effluent with $\frac{2}{3}$ lower solids content and $\frac{1}{3}$ reduction in organics (Nichols, 1993). The sludge will be removed from the tank periodically and composted for use as a soil amendment.

The effluent from the septic tank can move into any of the three treatment sequences. The minimum treatment objective for all three is to achieve at least the quality levels required for secondary treatment by the Clean Water Act of 1972. While this level is adequate for irrigation use, the systems are actually designed to achieve biological oxygen demand and suspended solids levels of ≤ 20 milligrams per liter (mg/L). This is 10 mg/L lower than required.

Because the Center uses a number of devices to reduce water use, including low-flow showerheads and toilets, the design is based on an estimated influent volume of 55 gallons per person per day rather than the usual 100 gallons per day.

Each of the three systems is divided into a series of four compartments or basins. This will prevent short-circuiting and facilitate even patterns of flow. It will also make it possible to easily move effluent from one system to another, to isolate one or more basing for controlled experiments, and to close a basin for maintenance or in case of disease. All basins will have plastic liners with concrete sides.

The dimensions of the basins used for the three systems vary according to the conditions required (Nichols, 1993). While all will be identical in length (31 feet) in order to fit the area available, the widths vary. The surface width of the aquaculture system will be 10 feet, that of the surface-flow wetland system 17.5 feet, and the rootzone system 16.75 feet. This gives some notions of the relative land areas required for the three types.

Their depths will also vary. The basins for the aquaculture system will allow for 3 feet of water with one foot of freeboard. The basins for the wetland system will be 4 feet in depth with one foot of soil on the bottom for plant roots, two feet of water and one foot of freeboard. The rootzone system will provide a two foot depth for sand or gravel media and one foot of freeboard.

The problem of aeration is one of several that involved difficult tradeoffs. Maintaining aerobic conditions is important for several reasons, among which are the facts that anaerobic conditions create odors and provide an unlivable environment for mosquito fish which eat mosquito larvae and thus prevent mosquito infestation. Assuring aerobic conditions through natural flows required larger basin sizes than would otherwise be needed. The alternative is to use aerators, but these use some electrical power. The decision was to use a small aerator in each basin of the wetland and aquaculture systems because the advantages of avoiding objectionable conditions and achieving smaller basin size outweigh the rather minor amount of electricity consumed.

An important difference in the three systems involves biomass harvesting. The wetland plants used in the wetland and rootzone systems grow relatively slowly and will have to be harvested no more than once each year and perhaps as seldom as every 5 years. This requires minimal maintenance time. The water hyacinths to be used in the aquaculture system, in contrast, will have to be harvested almost continually. This will require a considerable amount of labor, but the labor investment is more than offset by the fact that the harvested plants make an excellent animal feed and can also be digested to produce biogas.

III

■■■■■■■■■■■■■■■■■■■■■■■■■■

Implementation and Its Implications

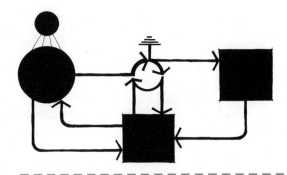

Chapter 9
Regenerative Systems
in the Social Fabric

So emeshed is technology within society that the relationship between the two seems incomprehensible. Does one beget the other? People create, operate, and maintain machinery and therefore must ultimately control it. But do they?

Since the early years of the Industrial Revolution, there has existed a pervasive feeling that technology is actually in command, or at least ever threatening to take command. Books, plays, and film from *Frankenstein* to *Terminator* bring to the surface a current that runs deep in contemporary culture. The tones are dark, bordering on despair. There is nothing we fear more than our own destructive tendencies, especially when those tendencies are powered by advanced technology. Yet the dark current seems to have no effect on the common craving for the products of technology.

In recent years this ambivalence has been most visibly acted out in the environmental arena; and the outcome remains far from certain. The degenerative trajectory of industrial technology has proven extremely persistent, especially in the industrialized countries. Paleotechnic practices that are unsustainable from the longer perspective may work quite

effectively in the short term. Often they are extremely profitable for those who control them. In the nonindustrial world the predominant ambition is generally to enter the Paleotechnic world without concern for its trajectory of decline. This is one of the strange tragedies of the late 20th century.

If we take the optimistic view that humanity will indeed prevail against the odds and gain control over technology and thus over our own destiny, we can expect that the character of the new technological base will have a strong influence in shaping the emerging society and the culture. If the general shift to regenerative technology and sustainable development that we have glimpsed from several perspectives so far in this book does indeed grow into a dominant direction of change, then regenerative systems will eventually reshape the Neotechnic landscape and play a major role in shaping Neotechnic society. Exactly what this means no one can predict with any confidence. Visions of the future offered by fiction writers by and large have been pessimistic. With a few exceptions like Callenback's *Ecotopia* (1975), the imaginative literature that explores the future has focused much more on the

263

likely outcomes of staying on the industrial-Paleotechnic path than on the possibilities of a regenerative-Neotechnic future.

Without resort to a crystal ball, however, and without even exerting a great deal of imagination, we can see in the descriptions of the last five chapters a few important characteristics patterns that have strong implications for society and culture.

Scale and Social Structure

The first of these involves scale of operation. Industrial technologies, as mentioned in Chapter 4 with respect to energy, are generally characterized by considerable economies of scale and therefore tend to grow continuously in organization as well as in physical size. We can see examples of this tendency in, for example, ever larger farms, supertankers, corporations, office buildings, sewage treatment plants, and universities. Regenerative technologies, in contrast, vary greatly in scale because they must be responsive to given biotic communities. In its implications for social organization, this is an important difference—perhaps the single most important difference between the two approaches. A great many of the social ills associated with industrial technology, along with its environmental ills, arise from sheer size. As Wendell Berry (1977) sees it, "the aim of bigness implies not one aim that is not socially or culturally destructive" (p. 41).

Massive industrial facilities employ masses of people, reducing most to more or less mechanical roles and rendering all beholden to monolithic organizational structures. This also tends to concentrate power and resources among a very small number of people nominally in control of the organizations. Those in control can then play with the organizations and all their human and nonhuman components like chips at the gambling table. This has been demonstrated in recent years by short-sighted corporate acquisitions, junk-bond schemes, and savings-and-loan manipulations.

Max Weber (1927) pointed out that the identifying characteristic of industrial society is rationalized administration. Whether a bureaucratic structure is capitalist or socialist, it features hierarchical organizational forms that are essentially the same: massive and rigid administrative structures to control massive and rigid technological systems, with the whole apparatus geared to production.

Lewis Mumford (1966) takes the somewhat different view that large-scale organizational structure preceded mechanical structure by several hundred years and indeed made the vast machine of industry possible. Whichever came first, there is little doubt that the mechanical structure of industry and the rigid hierarchy of organization are two legs of the same body.

In capitalist societies, corporate organizations tend to beget large government to provide control and counterbalance, and large government in its turn exhibits many of the same tendencies, especially in its massive hierarchical bureaucracy. Large organizations of both types tend to develop their own sets of purposes.

Corporations, by the rules of incorporation, are primarily concerned with making profits for shareholders. In recent years, shareholders have increasingly sought short-term profits in preference to long-term stability. Their motives have little to do with the well-being of their employees or that of the general public.

John Galbraith (1975) has pointed out that over the past half century, corporate management hierarchies, which he calls the "technostructure," have taken control of the larger corporations and shaped them to their own purposes. The first purpose is to achieve short-term profits and thus keep the shareholders satisfied and uncritical of management. The second, larger, and more compelling purpose is growth, which makes it possible to continuously create new positions within the hierarchy to assure advancement, career development, and ever higher salaries. Without the need for profits, governmental technostructures have much the same compulsion to grow for much the same reasons.

This drive to grow has provided much of the impetus for the throughput economy and its one-way flows. It also has much to do with otherwise unexplainable resistance to ecological protection and development, with the vast dimensions of the most powerful corporations in the industrial world, with the reduction of most employees to insignificant roles, and with the exclusion of much of the population from any economic role at all.

According to Galbraith's analysis, the greatest threat to the power of a corporation's technostructure is its employees, who benefit from the organization far less than management. For this reason, managers are usually inclined to replace workers with machines, which are more docile, when the necessary technology becomes available. The very threat of being replaced by machines tends to reduce any inclination on the part of the work force to challenge the power of the technostructure. Thus, much of the population is reduced to powerless positions in vast organizations and other large segments of society are excluded from productive work entirely.

Galbraith also points out that private technostructures tend to develop close alliances with governmental technostructures and thus to gain strong influence in governmental decisions. Not surprisingly, they tend to use this influence to promote programs that benefit themselves and to oppose programs that do not. Among the latter very often are those that increase environmental safeguards; make changes in consumption patterns; and encourage use of smaller-scale technology, land-use controls, social welfare, and equitable distribution of income. Their success in limiting such programs certainly has much to do with government's failure to deal adequately with the environmental resource crisis and with the growing numbers of people living in poverty. This, combined with the exclusion of large segments of the population from employment, has a close relationship with the drug abuse, rampant crime, unemployment, mistrust of government, and general sense of alienation that characterize the late 20th century.

In facilitating the exercise of power and diminishing the roles of most people, the technostructure inhibits the flow of information. Power moves vertically downward through the well-defined channels of the hierarchy. The complex interacting lines of communication needed for broad participation and information flow are weak or nonexistent. They do not respond so readily to power unsupported by information. By their very nature they follow the sixth strategy for regenerative systems: using information to replace power. Since regenerative systems work in continuous interaction with both people and natural processes, they require a great deal of cultural as well as scientific information for both

design and management. Through their use of information, they suggest a shift in the scale and organization of society's support functions. They also suggest an eventual breakdown of hierarchical organization and a far broader participation in decisions. The shift seems to be already well underway. Horizontal networks linked by microcomputer are becoming common even within large organizations.

Because they generally lack economies of scale and because they function in close concert with the landscape, regenerative technologies have functional patterns quite different from those of industrial systems. As discussed in earlier chapters, regenerative systems generally rely heavily on continuous infusions of information. In the managerial as in the physical sense, information replaces power. Thus they require complex, interactive networks of information flow rather than hierarchical structures of

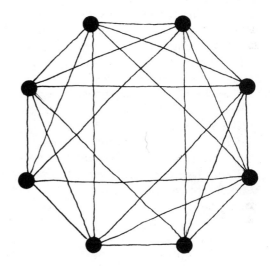

power transmission. As also discussed earlier, regenerative technologies vary considerably in scale of operation. Most are modular. That is, they function in small, discrete units, and any number of units can be assembled to provide the needed capacity. Given that any number of modular units can function efficiently, there are distinct advantages in decentralization and local operation if only in savings of transportation and transmission costs. As electronic communication media become more sophisticated and less expensive, it becomes increasingly more efficient to move information rather than materials over long distances.

Some regenerative technologies are necessarily localized, inseparable from the community and its development. Water retention, solar heating and cooling, and most means for waste recycling func-

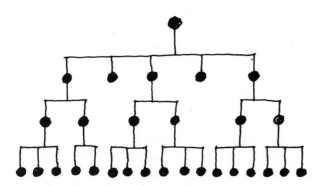

tion best at smaller, local scales. As shown in Chapter 8, local treatment facilities lend themselves to integration within the overall pattern of development.

All of these factors suggest that a small scale of operation will give rise to communities in which much of their life-support systems are integral parts of the local landscape. Managing energy and water flow, recycling wastes—even to some degree growing food—can all become community responsibilities. Thus the community functions as an ecosystem, cementing connections between people, their technologies, and the landscape. Studies of social interactions within one apartment complex in Berlin that features a wetland sewage treatment system in its common space showed measurably greater social cohesion than existed in comparable complexes (Legewie, 1993). This set of relationships engenders a sense of place. We might expect that bringing business, shopping, and schools into closer proximity with residential areas, which will ultimately be essential to reducing energy consumption and air pollution, will also help in strengthening human relationships within communities.

Operating locally and at a smaller scale, regenerative technologies lend themselves to greater community control. This can help to refocus local identity through shared responsibilities of management. In the 20 years since the first residents moved in, Village Homes (see pages 125 and 126) has developed a much stronger sense of social cohesion than neighboring subdivisions. Perhaps not coincidentally, resale values are also perceived as higher, though supportive data are lacking (Morlock, 1990).

We might expect reduction in scale of agricultural operations to have similar effects on rural communities. Especially in the United States, but to some degree in other countries as well, industrialization of agriculture has been widely blamed for the disintegration of rural communities. Farmers who borrow heavily to buy farm equipment and more land on which to use it and then borrow more each year to buy diesel oil and chemicals, are easily nudged into bankruptcy in years when crops are poor or prices low. As their farms are absorbed into vast agricultural corporations, rural regions lose the citizens who provide their solidity, continuity, and economic base; gone, then, are the yeoman farmers envisioned by Thomas Jefferson as the backbone of the nation. Replacing them are more and bigger machines, more chemicals, seasonal labor, and greater indebtedness. Cash flow moves to distant cities along with the one-time farmers, who usually have

few skills to offer in the urban economy. Rural towns fade away while cities grow beyond control, a common pattern in both industrial and nonindustrial countries. Like corporate and governmental bureaucracies, farms and cities are caught in a spiral of uncontrolled growth with no means for responding to negative feedback.

Regenerative agriculture, though hardly a panacea, offers a direction for change that can shift the pattern of interactions between agriculture and society. While there probably do exist some economies of scale for various types of regenerative agricultural operations in various locations, the range of scales is broad indeed. The examples in Chapter 7 range from the 3-acre Produce Gardens in Los Angeles to the 3100-acre Kirschenmann farm in Kansas to the 20,000-acre Hopcraft game ranch in Kenya. Adequate farms in nonindustrial countries are often as small as 1 or 2 acres as shown by the examples in Chile and Nepal. Each of these is viable for its own purpose in its own context.

Particularly important for the future of the rural landscape in the United States is the promise of regenerative techniques for the family farm. The Kirschenmann and Vogelsburg farms and many other similar operations in every part of the United States demonstrate the viability of family-size regenerative farms. While regenerative farms can probably be much larger—up to the several-thousand-acre spreads of most corporate farms—there are no apparent economies of scale to give such large operations an advantage. Indeed, the experience with regenerative agriculture up to this point suggests it will require more careful and intensive management —that is, a quality of thought of the sort that a dedicated farmer with many years' experience on the same land can give—but not necessarily more labor. If this turns out to be correct in the light of further experience, then it probably constitutes a distinct advantage for the family-size farm over corporate operations. In this case we might hope for a rural renaissance as people return to the country and begin to rebuild a vital economy and healthy soils.

It is important also to recognize the influences of the larger context. In the cases of energy, water, and waste, earlier chapters showed that local facilities will probably always operate as parts of larger networks. While the reasons to expect—and hope for—decentralizing trends in the entire spectrum of life-support infrastructure are compelling, the extreme of complete independence for discrete units is hardly more desirable than centralization. Interdependence provides important advantages, in being able to borrow and trade, for example. Different elements of a larger network can provide emergency backup for each other, and they can balance out disparities in resources. Shared storages for resources such as water can increase security. The electrical grid—with its ability to supply or collect energy at any point, to use potential energy wherever it exists within the network, and at the same time to supply concentrated power where it may be needed—is probably the best example of potentially effective relationships between the network and the units within it. It is a relationship of symbiosis rather than dependence. Such a network offers a promising alternative to centralized structures, and a much more flexible, diverse, and effective means for maintaining security. Such physical networks correspond in basic structure to the information and decision networks that can make them function.

Participation

It became obvious in the early years of the Industrial Revolution that the new technology—massive in scale, polluting, and to most eyes ugly—was incompatible with the daily lives of people. Technology then moved out of sight and has mostly stayed out of sight ever since. While this removed a source of discomfort from the visible landscape, it also separated people from some fundamental aspects of their lives. Wendell Berry (1977) put it this way: "The community disintegrates because it loses the necessary understanding, forms and enactments of the relations among materials and processes, principle and actions, ideals and realities . . ." (p. 21).

Reality was constructed within a narrow domain of experience. Electricity became something that comes from a plug in the wall, water from a faucet, and food from a supermarket; sewage goes into a toilet and garbage into cans. Within this limited experience, it is difficult to think about the larger world in which the plug, the faucet, and the toilet are connected to complex processes within vast landscapes on which all depend but few ever see. The true dimensions of the environment are hard to grasp, and the dilemma surrounding it is hard to comprehend when it is so removed from experience.

As they reenter the community, regenerative technologies can bring all of these functions back into the realm of daily life and experience. Being part of the community, these technologies can come under the control of the community, and this means direct participation in decisions.

Among the major social trends of the last half of the 20th century has been the movement toward broader participation in governmental decisions, especially decisions concerning the environment. Daniel Bell (1973) believes this desire for participation in governmental decisions to be one of the defining characteristics of the postindustrial period: "in Western political systems, the axial problem is the relation between the desire for popular participation and bureaucracy" (p. 115). In recent years, people have persistently demanded roles in the decisions that determine the quality of life; in fact, the National Environmental Policy Act (NEPA) and other laws make public participation a legal requirement, though it is rarely fully realized.

Broad participation, like interdisciplinary teams, is a means for expanding the information base for regenerative design. Herman Daly and John Cobb (1980) have pointed out that the effectiveness of the market in guiding some aspects of the economic structure lies in its ability to bring together vast quantities of information in orderly and positive ways. Since regenerative systems, like market-based economic systems, are inherently information-rich, they require means for assembling and ordering large amounts of information. With some improvement in their mechanics, participatory processes might serve this purpose. In this case we might expect to see them beginning to replace the power-intensive hierarchical administrative structures of the Paleotechnic era. Bell (1973) predicted that conflicts between participatory and hierarchical decision-making processes would characterize the early decades of the postindustrial era. There are reasons to believe we are making a transition in both public and private organizational structures from rigid vertical hierarchies to more flexible network-like structures that can facilitate flows of information in all directions. A number of the more forward-looking corporations (TRW, for example) have initiated moves in this direction. For some time, however, the emerging networks are likely to be superimposed on the established hierarchies, and it is likely to be an uncomfortable juxtaposition. Regenerative support systems are unlikely to be fully operational until the transition is complete (see for example Toffler, 1992).

Programs for public participation have had varied success. In general, the smaller the project and the more closely related it is to a local population, the more active the participation. Proposals to site incinerators and landfills, even shopping malls, in residential neighborhoods often bring crowds of people to public meetings. The profusion of NIMBY ("not in my backyard") movements in recent years has made highly visible people's concerns for their local environs. Larger projects in more distant locations, even those with major environmental implications, usually fail to stir as much interest except among large environmental groups. Locally based community issues often stimulate positive participation and imaginative visions of the future. The workshop process, which came into wide use in the 1970s, involves large numbers of community members in suggesting and exploring planning alternatives. In a group of six Florida coastal cities, for example, landscape architect Lloyd Vogt and workshop director Jim Burns held a series of workshops in which hundreds of members of the communities envisioned the future. Working with the designers, they then translated their visions of the urban future into concrete plans that gave expression to shared visions. Whether or not those visions eventually become reality, such efforts have almost invariably been notably successful in fostering a sense of community. Success depends on the skill and sensitivity of the workshop director, or facilitator, who guides the complex interactive process. Confrontation, deadlock, and disintegration are always possible. Avoiding them and guiding the process in positive and creative directions requires particular abilities that until recently were not often associated with planning and design. Sally Woodbridge (1989) believes that in "taking participation beyond the stage of attending public meetings and serving on committees, community designers have given activism a new, creative dimension" (p. 81).

In light of such experience with participatory planning, we can expect regenerative technologies to engender more active and more effective participation. With many systems functioning locally at smaller scales, they are likely to stimulate local interest. Since regenerative technologies are more diverse, they can offer more alternatives with varying levels of cost and environmental effects. Thus, rather than dividing those people involved into proponents and opponents, regenerative technologies tend to fuel debate among varied options. A desire to devise better solutions can replace the aura of negativism often surrounding environmental causes.

How far the trend toward public participation will reach beyond environmental issues is hard to predict. Even if it is confined to environmental matters, we might see widespread participation in planning as a large step away from complete reliance on local representatives and toward a more participatory form of democracy.

It is not unreasonable to expect that regenerative systems, given their smaller scale of operation, their tendency to work with participatory rather than hierarchical organizational structures, their community interactions, and their decentralizing tendencies, will tend to foster more equitable distribution of wealth and greater social justice. This may be as true of relationships among nations as of relationships among groups and individuals.

Whatever its social and political benefits, however, we cannot assume that public participation necessarily leads to regenerative planning. Though the environmental preferences of an established resident population within a project area are more likely to be ecologically benign than those of a developer motivated by profit or of a governmental bureaucracy, they are not necessarily always guided by ecological understanding. In California, for example, suburban residents have persistently resisted all forms of cluster development even when clustering allowed large areas of land to remain open. Clustering means higher densities at least in some places, which involves apartments and condominiums. This directly challenges the long-standing, almost universal preference for living in a single house on its own piece of land amid other people who live the same way. The sources of this preference are deep, entangled in conflicting emotions. Probably there are connotations of economic and social class. There may also be an element of nostalgia for an agrarian past, real or imagined. One often hears the desire for a "rural atmosphere," even where the reality is a suburban tract. Even deeper seems to be the territorial instinct, a need for control of one's own domain in an often incomprehensible, sometimes threatening urban world.

Planners know very well that large-lot subdivisions waste land, increase automobile use (thereby raising gasoline consumption and air pollution), make public transportation difficult, fracture wildlife habitat, and bring numerous other environmental ills. They also make housing more expensive and thus exclude many of those most in need of shelter. Nevertheless, the taste for large lots persists; it is invariably clearly expressed by an articulate majority at workshops and public hearings. Such contradictions are extremely hard to deal with because so many invisible factors enter into these preferences, and few of them are accessible to rational argument.

Nevertheless, we might guess that if people really understood the ecological significance of such decisions, they might be more amenable to solutions based on natural processes. Furthermore, as the ecological and social roles of the local landscape become greater, the attachment to a single lot and house might expand to include the larger place and community. We might imagine attitudes shifting from the emphasis on total ownership and control to an emphasis on holding the community landscape in trust for the community good. Such an attitude necessarily involves connections beyond the community extending to include the earth in an ecological and social understanding that we can only accomplish through education. Thomas Jefferson wrote: "I know no safe depository of the ultimate powers of society but the people themselves; and if we think them not enlightened enough to exercise their control with a wholesome discretion, the remedy is not to take it from them, but to inform their discretion by education."

Education as the Motive Force

Perhaps we should ask the fundamental question in this way: How do we educate the mind in nature? While Paleotechnic culture invests enormous faith in scientific information, especially in numerical data, it makes few demands on its citizens to understand that information. Technology is considered the realm of experts qualified by their specialized training to make decisions concerning technical support systems for the society. The technical experts are generally closely aligned with the hierarchy of control. However, in recent years, faith in experts has declined dramatically. Because expertise is necessarily narrowly focused, it blocks out a great many concerns peripheral to its boundaries but nevertheless intimately connected to the concerns within the boundaries. For example, flood-control engineers are rarely concerned with watershed protection, even though the condition of the watershed largely determines the volume and quality of floodwaters. Similarly, the designer of a coal-fired power plant usually knows little about the environmental effects of strip mining. As the interconnections among all these systems become clearer, the need for areas of expertise to merge together likewise becomes obvious. The need for information expands and becomes more essential to decision-making processes.

As development projects come under greater public scrutiny and as public participation in planning and design becomes more common, such a general common ground of ecological understanding becomes necessary not only for those professionally concerned but for everyone. It has often happened in recent years, especially in the United States, that political leaders lacked adequate understanding of basic natural processes to make responsible decisions on those subjects. If the decision-making base does indeed grow larger with public participation, the need for knowledge will grow greater as well. It will be necessary not only for politicians but for everyone who aspires to participation to have a broad, though not necessarily a deep, comprehension of basic natural processes and their interactions with technology and society.

Inevitably, this places yet another demand on an already beleaguered and overstressed educational structure. The pace of intellectual evolution is faster than the pace of institutional change, and schools are prime examples. School and university curricula evolved to their present state during the Paleotechnic era in response to the needs of an industrial society. Much of their form and some of their content, especially the rigidity of lines between disciplines and of administrative structures, is obsolete in the light of emerging understanding. What is needed is basic changes in our ways of thinking about the world and the roles of humans within it. Educating the professionals, the technical experts, the political leaders, and the knowledgeable citizenry in the ways of thinking needed to implement the Neotechnic age will involve greater emphasis on at least five areas of understanding.

1. The Ecosystem as a Matrix for Comprehending the Natural and Social World

Since 1970, basic ecological principles have been widely incorporated into school curricula to the point where ecological understanding is now widespread, at least among younger people within the society. However, it usually has been treated as a separate unit of subject matter added onto other subjects. Some biology texts include ecological principles as a chapter added at the end. This probably reflects the learning sequence of the textbook's authors, but it does not reflect the reality of the natural world, and it leaves the social world out entirely. The development of ecological understanding is not simply another subject to be learned but a fundamental change in the way we comprehend and view the world. Ecology is not just another new discipline. Its basic organizing concept, the ecosystem, is a comprehensive matrix within which other scientific and social disciplines can fit. The ecosystem is the fundamental order of life on earth as we currently understand it. Once fully grasped, the ecosystem also provides a context for understanding environmental issues and for communicating and working with others, as well as for deeper knowledge of particular subjects. Thus a basic understanding of ecosystems and how they work should play a key role in the early years of education.

2. Connections with Everyday Life

The great vitality of ecological understanding lies in its usefulness in everyday life. It is not abstract knowledge but an integral part of daily experience. This requires that it be taught largely through experience. Students, especially in elementary schools, need to dig in the dirt, make plants grow, and adjust tracking mirrors to the angle of the sun. Thus they can regain the direct contact with nature lost in Paleotechnic society. Soil, plants, and solar energy become part of their inner being. Direct experience is by far the most memorable means of learning, especially since the student must eventually use what is learned.

In conveying the basics of applied ecology and regenerative systems, two of the basic roles of the educator are to provide the experience and to make it meaningful. Dewey (1916) writes: "To learn from experience is to make a backward and forward connection between what we do to things and what we enjoy or suffer from things in consequence" (p. 140). Experience, he continues, is not cognition. Most importantly for the educational process, "it includes cognition in the degree in which it is cumulative, or amounts to something or has meaning" (ibid.). Thus both experience and cognitive understanding are essential to environmental education.

3. Complexities and Possibilities

Ecological understanding and the regenerative systems that grow out of it are not inert facts or theories but a vital, dynamic network of connections that we can view and use in innumerable ways. The possibilities for reinterpretation and new connections are unlimited, which means that expression and interpretation are essential. Possibilities require exploration and discussion. Even children in early primary grades can apply simple modeling and simulation techniques to explore and compare alterna-

tives. Ecological principles offer complex, often contradictory guidance, especially in their application to design of the human environment. Experience and understanding are applied to daily activity and to the design and management of environment—but not in a direct linear mode. It is important for students to understand that the world is incomprehensibly complex and always changing.

4. Analysis and Creativity

While science is usually taught as an analytical activity, applying the principles of ecology and regenerative systems requires creative thinking. When seeing the world in this perspective, nothing is certain, numbers are approximations, and possibilities are many. Ideas are at least as important as analyses. Thus both the right and left hemispheres of the brain come into play. This means that ecological education should do far more than is usually done in school to stimulate creative thinking. Regenerative design and the related educational processes have the potential to bridge the chasm between art and science. Environmental education and especially learning processes for regenerative thinking should embrace both art and science. For a more complete treatment of this topic, see my earlier book *Design for Human Ecosystems* (Lyle, 1985b).

5. The Fundamental Relationship between Place and Process

Paleotechnic education tends to focus on products, treating them as if they were frozen in time. From the ecological perspective, in contrast, all that exists is process; every physical object exists at a point in the ongoing trajectory of change. Each object and each person has a history and a future of growth, forming and decomposing, that are more important than its form at this instant. We can only understand nature and the human environment in the context of past and future. Ecosystems, including cities, are ever changing, not static, and planning and design are means for guiding the processes of change. The same is true of other parts of the human environment.

The emphasis in ecological education is necessarily on natural processes and their time dimensions in relation to human culture in specific places. To really understand these, students have to observe not just objects but transitions. Ideally, they become involved with particular places as they change through the course of seasons and years. Place is the constant setting for change as well as the setting for human activity, culture, interaction, and attachment to the landscape. To understand the earth's larger processes, it is necessary first to understand those occurring in one place.

David Orr (1989) calls the study of place the "fundamental organizing concept for education" (p. 4), and draws a distinction between residents and inhabitants. Residents are transient occupants who form no connections with place and no knowledge of its processes. Inhabitants are "part of a complex order that strives for harmony between human demands and ecological processes" (ibid., p. 5). Thus the place of education and the students' relationship with it are all important.

Relationships with Land

A central task of ecological education, at least for the next several decades, is to change our society's shared mental model of nature and the earth from the mechanical conception that has shaped our world-view since the Renaissance to the ecological conception. This is a monumental task involving ethics along with art and science. The relationship with nature and landscape resides in the soul of a culture.

Roderick Nash and a number of others have characterized the environmental dilemma as a moral crisis. Nash (1989) believes our moral perspective is growing every broader and more inclusive, gradually coming to include every living creature.

Among the first to articulate an ethic including more than humans were Albert Schweitzer and Aldo Leopold. Schweitzer (1933) insisted that we can behave in an ethical way only when all life is sacred to us, including the life of animals and plants as well as humans. Aldo Leopold also made a strong plea for respect for all life, but in calling for a new ethical sense, he focused on the land, which provides sustenance for all life. Land, in this sense, is the sum total of places. The connections with land are extensions of the connections with place. Leopold (1949) proposed a new land ethic that "changes the role of *Homo sapiens* from conqueror of the land community to plain member and citizen of it" (p. 240). He summarized his ethical position in a brief statement that might well serve as the moral basis for regenerative design: "A thing is right when it tends to preserve the integrity, stability and beauty of the biotic community. It is wrong when it tends otherwise" (ibid., p. 240).

As Leopold observed, land-use policies and practices based entirely on economic self-interest usually "tend otherwise" and thus are not ecologically viable. They ignore fundamental natural processes, and so are neither regenerative nor sustainable. The processes continuously carried on in the landscape, supporting all life and indispensable to our existence, are not necessarily profitable, and they are easily overridden—obliterated and replaced—by what our land-use policies irrationally designate as "highest and best use." Carried to its logical extreme, this way of determining the use of land could eventually replace all support functions with more profitable ones and thus leave the world financially wealthy but unpopulated.

This strange contradiction pervades our attitudes and behavior toward the landscape. Missing is the sense of buildings and cities, and indeed ourselves, as parts of the earth's ongoing process—that is, the sense of the profound meanings of landscape. The failure of planning in particular results largely from society's commonly accepted concept of land as commodity rather than as life-giving process, extending through time.

The view of land as a source of private wealth has a long history in Western culture. Both capitalist and Marxist doctrines define land as an economic resource, tacitly denying its larger values. Until banking developed during the Renaissance, land was the only truly dependable source of both wealth and power. During the industrial period the importance of land in generating wealth was diminished somewhat by the rising importance of capital and labor. Thorstein Veblen (1921) called land one of the three "factors of production," the other two being labor and capital; for Veblen the three factors of production represented the three classes of income, which were rent, wages, and profits. More recently, the speculative value of land has far surpassed its rent value. The increase in land speculation has multiplied the difficulties of establishing sustainable patterns of land use, driving land prices in many places up to levels that can only be paid through intense exploitation.

The view of land as commodity is not universally shared. It stands in stark contrast to the relationship with land and with nature in general of most tribal cultures. Shawnee Chief Tecumseh protested government sales of tribal lands to Governor W. H. Harrison in 1805. The Indians, he said, were united:

. . . in claiming common and equal right in the land, as was at first, and should be now—for it was never divided, but belongs to all. No tribe has the right to sell, even to each other, much less to strangers. . . Sell a country! Why not sell the air, the great sea, as well as the earth? Did not the Great Spirit make them all for the use of his children? (Turner, 1974).

There are some signs that as the industrial period winds down, Western attitudes toward land may be moving closer to those of Chief Tecumseh and farther from those of Veblen. The Wilderness Act, wetlands and endangered-species protection, coastal-zone management measures, even certain aspects of NEPA, are among the examples.

Inseparable from environmental ethics is the problem of land ownership. Clearly, where land is privately owned, especially in a capitalist economy, it is easy to consider land as commodity. Increasing recognition of the conflict between land as commodity and land as ecosystem on which all depend has played a part in the trend away from the absolute rights of property owners and toward more concern for the common good.

However, the opposite extreme of collective ownership does not work very well either. Several countries in Eastern Europe seem to have created the greatest environmental disasters of the 20th century under communist regimes with common ownership. The collective farms of the communist states were notoriously inefficient; small private farms in the same regions were invariably far better managed, more productive, and more sustainable. Public land and urban spaces are usually difficult to maintain. In most Western cities they are increasingly covered in graffiti. As Garrett Hardin (1963) has shown, lands owned by nobody or by everybody tend to be exploited and abused by everybody. Experience with regenerative farming practice suggests that farmers who own their land are much more willing to exert the care and attention needed for sustainability than farmers who rent their land. This is equally true for urban dwellings and suburban lots and gardens.

Present trends suggest that we may be evolving toward a system of land tenure that recognizes the rights of both the general public and private owner. It will be a delicate balance, a merging of traditional concepts of land tenure that have proven too rigid, with concepts of shared responsibility, and it is still in the distant future. Present practices strongly favor private property, often to the serious detriment of public and environment.

Regenerative Systems and Social Evolution

Throughout this chapter, I have pointed out some of the critical points of connection between technology and society and explored the implications of regenerative systems for society at these points. It seems clear that as technology and society continue to evolve in tandem, profound changes are in store. Regenerative technology cannot simply be superimposed on Paleotechnic culture. If culture is to survive and thrive, some of society's basic institutions, including the structures of government and business, the educational system, and land-tenure practices, will have to evolve rapidly. Tension and conflicts will probably surround the evolutionary process, and the abstract rigidities of our legal system will not be able to deal with them. Processes of evolutionary change and conflict resolution will have to become part of the social structure.

CASE STUDY

■■■

The Learning Environment at the Center for Regenerative Studies

Among the institutions of contemporary society, the university, with its diverse range of expertise and its spirit of inquiry, seems to offer a unique setting for exploring the technological, esthetic, social, and political meanings of regenerative future. Bell (1973) called the university the primary institution of the postindustrial era. However, he does not take into account the fact that the late-20th-century university is a product of the Paleotechnic period, rigidly organized according to academic disciplines, each enclosed by boundaries that are crossed only at great risk. The university has also developed a hierarchical administrative technostructure that parallels corporate structure and has similar motivations. Despite the counterbalancing effect of its information-oriented faculty, the university technostructure can slip abruptly into authoritarian ways. It is in many respects beholden to conventional industrial technology and institutional habits. Boards of trustees are usually drawn from a narrow segment of society heavily committed to Paleotechnic order. In some disciplines—for example, agriculture and some areas of engineering—research and educational grants come largely from industry. Conflicts between efforts to move the university into uncharted territory and its tendencies to inhibit change in many ways model conflicts within the larger society.

Thus, the Center for Regenerative Studies is in some ways like a kidney, or perhaps bone marrow, being transplanted in a human body, or like a new child in the schoolroom. It has to deal with strong tendencies toward rejection. On the other hand, fascination with new ideas, especially those that offer hope for the future, is a uniquely human habit that is especially vigorous in universities. The birth pangs of the Center involved ongoing tension between these tendencies along with varied, sometimes subtle interactions among the many participants and their diverse points of view. The long and complex process of realization is instructive and is itself an important part of the Center's learning and research.

DESIGN PROCESS

The Center for Regenerative Studies grew out of my initial concept followed by several years of study, exploration of technical ideas, and discussion among students and faculty members. When the design team was formed, it built upon concepts already shaped by broad informal participation. The key characteristics of the design team (described in the Case Study for Chapter 2) were its interdisciplinary composition; its highly interactive, network mode of operation; and its loosely supportive but independent relationship with the university's corporate structure. From its beginning the Center was conceived as an integral part of the university but one that would operate in a different, more interdisciplinary mode. As a network, it grew as the design process developed, eventually drawing on the knowledge of a wide range of people scattered over the United States and in other countries.

In this setting, environment and curriculum are inseparable; the environment is the teacher. John Dewey (1916) wrote that "we never educate directly, but indirectly by means of the environment. Whether we permit chance environments to do the work, or whether we design environments for the purpose makes a great difference" (p. 19). Faculty members are part of the environment, and the curriculum provides direction and organization. Living within the Center is a totally integrated learning experience. Design is an ongoing process in which students and faculty participate.

Reorganization

The interdisciplinary team published its proposal and preliminary design for the Center (then called the Institute) in a descriptive report (Lyle et al., 1987). Based on this, several private foundations contributed grant funds for its construction. At this point, the university president, at that time a man with a strong commitment to hierarchical management, used his power to recast its organization in the mold of the university's existing corporate structure.

The original design team was dismissed. Design and curriculum were divided into separate activities. Design development became the responsibility of a committee appointed by and answering to the president. Six of the seven members were university administrators, selected not for knowledge or interest but for their roles in the hierarchy. The seventh was the director of the original design team (myself). The committee chairman was the Dean of the College of Environmental Design. This committee was allowed no funds for further research or design, which meant that no conceptual development took place. The president further decided that final design development and construction drawings would be done by private consultants.

At the same time, the university provost, who was closely attuned to the Center's nature and purpose, appointed a committee of five faculty members to shape the curriculum. This group was formed in the mold of the original design team, and included two members of that group. One of these was myself as chairman. The others on the curriculum committee were faculty members selected for their knowledge of and commitment to the subject matter. This committee then formed an advisory group that included all of the original design team members. It also scheduled a series of seminars that would provide a forum for student participation in shaping the learning process. Thus, while the design development committee took on a hierarchical bureaucratic form, the curriculum committee retained the interactive form that had characterized the Center's development from its beginning. The contrasting organization, operation, and results of the two committees provide useful insights.

With the design development committee, the stage was set for acting out the conflicts between information-rich participatory decision making and power-rich bureaucracy. It was a classic example of the struggles predicted by Bell as characteristic of the postindustrial era. In practice, the contrasting composition of the two committees turned out to be an enlightening, though unintentional and sometimes discouraging, experiment in institutional change.

The new design development committee had difficulties from its inception. These did not derive from any lack of support for the Center; all of the committee members, especially the chairman, were strong supporters. Rather, the problems derived from the absence of the information-based common ground on which the original team had stood; that is, the committee lacked commitment and experience with the principles associated with regenerative thinking. Lacking this basic commitment, other concerns tended to take precedence. Usually these concerns reflected conventional practice and administrative convenience. For example, there were concentrated efforts to remove the rooftop food-growing areas because they were unknown in conventional agricultural practice and uncommon in building practice. Furthermore, they seemed to present maintenance problems. The dining commons was almost removed even though the original design team had considered it a key unifying element for the community. The reason had to do with operational difficulties associated with food preparation at so small a scale.

Furthermore, the risk of liability presented a major difficulty. Any departure from the most conservative or standard practice is commonly viewed as a liability risk and many of the university's administrators viewed any level of risk as unacceptable. This was clearly in conflict with the center's experimental and integrative purposes. Altogether, in the light of this committee's experience, it became easy to see how administrative decisions that are ecologically and socially destructive can be made on the basis of criteria that are quite rational in their own limited terms. In the case of the Center, such decisions threatened for a time to seriously compromise its integrity and function.

The university president also adhered to the university system's standard practices in hiring design consultants and retained private firms to complete the design and construction documents: architect Betsey Dougherty of Dougherty and Dougherty, and landscape architect Ronald Izumita of the Peridian Group. While the consultants were highly capable professionals who supported the Center's purposes, they lacked the knowledge and experience gained through the intense research and design efforts that has been going on for more than 10 years. Avenues for moving the rich fund of information vested in the original design team and its successors into this critical final phase of the design process were extremely limited. That is, the rigid hierarchical structure continued to inadvertently block the flow of information.

With the members of the university's design development committee in disagreement, and the consultants struggling to adhere to the original design concepts while at the same time adapting to a number of changed conditions without adequate information, the work for a time bogged down completely. While the hierarchical administrative structure was undeniably effective in dealing with standardized procedures and routine situations, it proved incapable of providing the information flow required for a new, unconventional, and technically and socially complex project.

Eventually, there was a change in university administration. A new president, Bob Suzuki, took office, and he approved the request of the committee's chairman to reconstitute the design committee's membership. The reconstituted committee was smaller. It included a second member drawn from the original design team and only those administrators with responsibilities for specific aspects of the Center's operation. The committee chairman also changed its way of working. To replace the periodic one- to two-hour meetings, he began a series of half-day work sessions with the consultants. The cooperative spirit was regained to at least an adequate degree, and the design work was completed with results that followed reasonably closely the original concept design while taking into account conditions added later for various reasons. However, the committee's rigid, administratively oriented format did not allow for full exploration of many unconventional aspects of regenerative design. This meant that some design features had to be compromised or abandoned and others, such as the sewage treatment system, postponed to later phases.

Curriculum Development

The work of the curriculum committee progressed in a quite different way, working interactively with the advisory group and the seminars. The five committee members acted as instructors for the seminars, discussing educational approaches as well as technical material with the students, soliciting both ideas and feedback, trying different readings and having the students articulate their thoughts in writing. After the first exploratory year, the seminars constituted trial runs of courses to be taught within the Center curriculum. Thus curriculum design became a participatory process with a rich communication network for flows of information.

Learning Sequence
The curriculum that evolved out of this situation is uniquely suited to the unconventional subject matter but fits neatly within the university's curricular structure. Students take courses or series of courses in which the various aspects of regenerative systems are integrated; that is, the subject matter is not divided into separate disciplines. The core sequence is for students living in the Center who take one five-unit course each quarter for 2 years. In the first year, students learn by following instructions and examples; in the second year they take responsibility for leadership and development. The sequence progresses as follows:

FOLLOWING
1. Basic Principles
2. Basic Applications
3. Confidence in Applications

LEADING
4. Managing People and Technology
5. Improving and Inventing
6. Designing Workable Systems

There is also a parallel track for students who are unable to live at the Center. Students in this sequence also use the Center's facilities, share some courses with residents, and follow the same general progression. In both tracks the learning sequence carries the student to a level at which the creative shaping of systems is possible. This does not, however, imply great depth of understanding of any one technological area. For depth and expertise in specific disciplines, the regenerative studies program combines with curricula of certain existing departments (engineering, biology, and plant and soil science, for example) to form joint majors that can combine breadth of ecological thinking with depth of scientific and technological expertise.

Each course includes lectures, laboratories, and seminars: lectures to impart information, laboratories for actual experience in working with regenerative systems, and seminars for discussing the meaning of what students are doing and learning and for dealing with specific questions. The laboratories are at the heart of the learning-by-doing process: Here students carry out the operational tasks at the Center such as growing food, generating energy, and managing wastes. Interdisciplinary teams of faculty members participate in all courses.

Importance of Organizational Structure

The contrast between the two organizational modes is instructive. The participatory mode of the curriculum committee was clearly far more successful in giving operational substance to the Center's purpose. The administratively based hierarchical mode of the design development committee was far more difficult in operation and less successful in serving the Center's purpose although it did eventually succeed in getting construction underway. Some argue construction would never have begun had the participatory, networking mode been applied through the contract documents phase. In some ways, this committee's work constituted a kind of odyssey of obstacles to the Center's basic ideas. We might see their purpose as obstruction, but it seems more accurate to see it as an attempt to adhere to organizational habits that had proven workable, if not ideal, in the past. The need for assurance that the new organ is indeed worthy probably played a part as well. In this respect, the scenario played out by this committee is likely to be played out many times in the transition to a more regenerative society. The immune system has its purpose. The process of challenge, discussion, conflict and accommodation is all important. The Center's basic concepts, as well as its design and technology, were severely challenged and tested. Partly as a result of the challenges and conflicts a number of people were involved in shaping the institute who otherwise would not have been, and in most cases, their contributions, even those given from a quite different perspective, were useful. This compensated in some respects for the loss in information flow and resulting compromises. Creative interaction among the people involved in any development effort is essential for success, and this is likely to become even more true in the future. In the processes of its development as in its physical form, the Center seems to be a microcosm of the larger world. Where participation is based on common understanding and agreement, the development process is generally smooth and highly productive. But situations in which regenerative approaches meet established paleotechnic ways in serious conflict will probably be more common, and their outcomes will often be more important for the future.

REINFORCEMENT OF SOCIAL RELATIONSHIPS

In the operation of the Center, as in its design, the network for interaction and exchange of information is a fundamentally important factor. The design of the Village attempts to build the setting for such a network into the physical environment.

The buildings accommodate groupings of various sizes to facilitate different levels of communication. The basic unit is the sleeping room for two students designed to permit various furniture arrangements, including division into two semiprivate spaces by the use of a divider. Three or four such rooms form a suite for six or eight students who

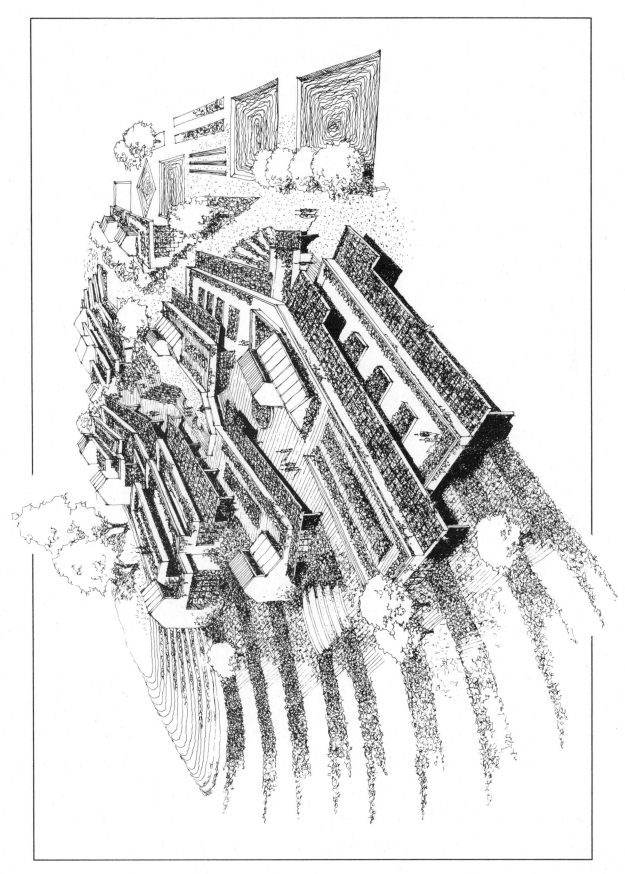

share a bathroom and an access corridor. In some buildings the interior spaces will be left undivided to allow occupants to arrange interior partitions to suit themselves. The spaces in each suite also have close access to a common room that also is easily accessible from a major circulation route and thereby available to other residents as well. The common rooms, while identified with particular groups, are in no sense private. As a group, these rooms can be organized in various ways for specialized purposes. For example, one might become a quiet study room and another a recreation area or computer room.

Each building contains two such suites, accommodating six or eight rooms, or a grouping of 12 to 16 students. Finally, the entire community shares the reception room/kitchen/dining room complex, which is located adjacent to common outdoor spaces and has panoramic views of the campus and the San Gabriel Mountains beyond. To underscore the central role of these three spaces in the community, forms very different and more dramatic than those of the residential buildings distinguish the structure containing them.

Outdoor spaces also accommodate groups of various sizes. The greensward to the east of the dining room is a casual outdoor recreation space for the entire community. Sitting and lying on the grass and tossing frisbees will probably be common activities here. Three amphitheaters are located for both formal and informal gatherings of various sizes. Several other small spaces accommodate groups for four to eight students. All are connected by the central circulation/communication spine—the pedestrian roadway.

In terms of overall organization, the major outdoor community spaces are organized in a sequence of public to private orientation. The first community space that one moves into after entering the Center from the eastern side is the plaza. The reception room and the entry to the kitchen and dining room face onto this relatively formal space, as do the classroom, the offices, and a small laundry–lounge. It is partly shaded by grape arbors extending out from the building to the north. The next space in the sequence is defined by residential buildings on its north and south sides and is more private but still relatively formal. To the west of that space, one enters a complex of smaller, more private, more irregular spaces among the hillside residential units. These will be intimate in character and designed for small groups.

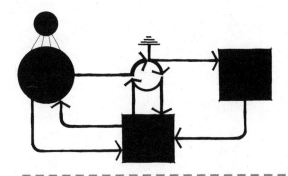

Chapter 10
Garden Communities
in Gaia's Garden

Since we have come to view the earth as a complex, interacting whole, perhaps even as a single organism in the sense of the Gaia hypothesis, but certainly as a global ecosystem, the planning framework for regenerative systems necessarily encompasses the whole earth. Though we can easily imagine a day when our planning horizon takes in other planets, perhaps even other stars, the whole earth is the largest unit for which we can envision specific policies, programs, and plans, at least for the time being.

Some natural systems are global in scope; that is, they cannot be broken down into local parts or areas. The composition of the atmosphere is joined into a single system by the worldwide patterns of air movement. The atmosphere is shared by everybody everywhere, though the acts that alter it have local origins. Thus the buildup of greenhouse gases and depletion of the ozone layer are global issues; dealing with them requires global cooperation and global design. In this sense, planning is a matter of policy initiatives, such as international agreements to limit carbon dioxide emissions, which means reducing the burning of carbon-based fuels.

Other issues are global in scope even though their immediate effects are more local. Examples are populations of migratory wildlife species. Some species, for example, can only be saved by global agreement. Filling a coastal wetland in California can threaten species that spend their summers in Alaska and their winters in Central America, even though they may spend only a day or two in the wetland on route between home ranges.

Other systems within the global complex are defined by regions. The system of water circulation is organized by watersheds, which are regional in scale. Under natural conditions, once water reaches the ground, it moves out of its watershed only to return to the sea or the atmosphere. This neat geographic definition makes the watershed an appropriate unit for designing water systems and for dealing with water-borne pollutants. Since a great many ecological and economic concerns converge in the flow of water and the materials carried by water, the watershed unit is generally an appropriate unit for regional landscape planning.

Where pollutants are carried from the watershed into the sea, however, the scale of concern increases to include other lands bordering the sea. The nations bordering the Mediterranean, for example, formed a consortium to deal with the severe pollution caused by the intense concentrations of cities, industries, and agricultural lands draining into it. Similar kinds of cooperation are needed among countries bordering rivers, such as the Danube, that carry polluted water draining from all of them. Acid precipitation also crosses borders, following the winds with no concern for political distinctions. Such situations give rise to the need for design on a scale between that of the whole earth and that of the region. This we might call the subcontinental scale.

Planning at these large scales of the whole earth, the subcontinent, and the region is broad and very general, expressed primarily in terms of policy and more rarely in terms of specific programs. The institutions that might exert some planning and management authority at these scales are recent in origin and still searching for effective means.

At the global scale, the United Nations Environment Program (UNEP) and the United Nations Educational, Scientific, and Cultural Organization (UNESCO) are active but lack legal authority. They have been useful in assembling global databases such as UNEP's worldwide desertification study.

The urgency of some global issues has caused a number of international political conventions to be convened to deal entirely with global issues. At present, more than 170 international environmental treaties exist. In a sense they represent the beginnings of global policy planning. Among the more significant are these treaties are the following:

- several agreements attempting to protect ocean species including the International Whaling Convention, the Convention on Conservation of Antarctic Marine Living Resources, and several fisheries conventions;
- the Ramsar Convention for the Conservation of Wetlands of International Importance;
- the Convention on the Conservation of Migratory Species of Wild Animals;
- the Convention on International Trade in Endangered Species of Wild Fauna and Flora;
- the United Nations Convention on the Law of the Sea (still not actually in force);
- the Montreal Protocol on Substances that Deplete the Ozone Layer.

These and similar agreements hardly add up to more than a tentative first move in the direction of truly global planning. Most of them work in the reactive or palliative mode; all lack the active boldness that might suggest global regeneration. Also lacking is a sense of broad commitment. Though the economic chasm between rich and poor countries makes this difficult, there have been some tentative efforts. Following publication of its report, *Our Common Future* (1987), the World Commission on Environment and Development (WCED) submitted to the U. N. General Assembly a proposal for a Universal Declaration and Convention on Sustainable Development, which has not been adopted. On a more fundamental level, the International Union for Conservation of Nature and Natural Resources (IUCN) published its influential *World Conservation Strategy* in 1980 and developed the basic concepts further in its *Caring for the Earth* (IUCN, UNEP, WWF, 1992). The strategy stated its purpose as helping to "advance the achievement of sustainable development through the conservation of natural systems" (IUCN, 1980, p. iv). Its three general objectives were an early avowal of the intertwined character of environment and economic development:

a. to maintain essential ecological processes and life support systems;
b. to preserve genetic diversity;
c. to ensure the sustainable utilization of species and ecosystems (ibid., p. vi).

The IUCN articulated the moral basis for its strategy with the "world ethic for sustainable living" (IUCN, UNED, WWF, 1992, p. 16) and proposed that it be developed and promulgated by coalitions of religious and environmental groups, scientists and politicians.

The IUCN's statement on the moral dimension of sustainability is an important step, especially in its recognition that our present understanding of global ecology requires a broadening of traditional ethical perspectives to include other species and indeed the whole biosphere. Nevertheless, in the hard-nosed world of international politics, moral commitment will have little effect without corresponding financial commitments. To be effective, global policymakers and planners will need the authority to manage funds. The various accords established at the United Nations Conference of Environmental Development (the Earth Summit) of 1992, though generally weak, raised the debate on most key issues to a new level; they have enormous potential power to influence the future. Though the process of negotiating international accords is slow, tedious, and imperfect in its results, it will probably remain the only avenue to global action. As Gore (1992) has pointed out, any stronger form of global governance is most unlikely.

Regional Scale

Planning at the regional scale is more highly developed, at least in some parts of the world. Its importance has been recognized by planners since Patrick Geddes (1915) first noticed that cities no longer were contained within boundaries but were tending to spread out and become regional conurbations. Geddes and those who expanded on his concepts perceived that these patterns could only be understood at the scale of regions. Growing understanding of natural processes such as the hydrologic cycle and plant and animal communities made it clear that regional order was important in nature as well.

While regional planning has become an effective process in countries such as England, Italy, and Germany, where regional levels of government exist, it has rarely succeeded in the United States. The Tennessee Valley Authority's plan in the 1930s was one major exception. During this period also, the National Resources Commission sponsored regional surveys of natural and cultural resources for the entire United States. Citizens of each region developed the information base, and the resulting surveys were published by the commission. However, the information was never used for planning purposes, and since then regional planning efforts have been scattered and sporadic. Ian McHarg has made a tireless effort to establish a new regional data-gathering program following the general principles of the National Resources Commission and applying the highly sophisticated capabilities of a computer-based Geographic Information System. So far he has had little success.

At the grass-roots level the bioregional movement has revived many of the notions of regionally focused landscape and culture first developed by Geddes and the regional planning movement in the early part of the 20th century. Since consciousness of the importance of the regional scale of thinking is growing rapidly, expressed especially in the bioregional movement, it seems likely that regional planning will again be practiced in the United States in some form. It may evolve out of the regional agencies established to deal with certain resource issues, such as water distribution, air quality, and flood control. In California the need for regional scope in efforts to improve air quality was recognized early, and the power of the regional air-quality districts has grown steadily. The fact that the Southern California Air Quality Management District is the only public agency with authority concerning land use on a regional basis may have significance for the future. As interconnections are recognized, single-purpose agencies could evolve into truly comprehensive environmental planning agencies.

The need for such planning is increasingly recognized in political circles. In 1987 the California Assembly's Office of Research recommended that a regional development and infrastructure agency be formed in each of the state's urban and urbanizing regions. The authorities of the new agencies would include air quality, transportation, water quality, water supply, housing, solid waste, and land use. They would replace all regional agencies now dealing separately with these issues, and their powers would override those of local municipal agencies. Each regional organization would be run by a governing board with a majority of members elected in the region. Other board members would include city council members and county supervisors.

The proposal was not accepted; clearly, the political obstacles were and are formidable. Very likely, however, the time for such regional agencies will arrive. They offer the only means for planning for regenerative systems in ways that can take full advantage of their integrative nature.

Subcontinental Scale

Lacking any identifiable boundaries that can be generally applied, subcontinental-scale planning is much harder to define than global or regional planning. Nevertheless, planning and policymaking at this scale has become more common and effective in recent decades. The best example is the European Community (EC), which has become a force almost as powerful in environmental matters as in economic matters. Still more common, however, are cooperative planning units determined by issues. These tend to evolve as issues evolve. An example is the International Commission for Protection of the Rhine (IRC). In the early 1960s, the river Rhine—which is flanked on both sides for hundreds of miles by industrial plants and farms, all discharging runoff and process water into the river—had reached an alarming level of pollution. Fish were dying by the thousands due to oxygen depletion and metals, toxic chemicals, and organic matter all far exceeded safe levels. In 1963 the five countries through which the river flows formed the IRC and over the next few years developed the Rhine Action Plan. The plan's goals were to reestablish the river's important species, such as salmon, to restore water quality to levels suitable for water supply, to reduce the pollutant levels in the sediments, and to protect the North Sea ecosystem. Though progress has been slow, probably due in large part to the reliance on pollution control in preference to pollution elimination, water quality in the Rhine has improved. In 1990 the water-quality goals were reevaluated by the commission and raised. Most of the existing treatment facilities were found incapable of meeting the new goals. It seems likely that a change in policy in the direction of regenerative systems will eventually prove to be the only long-term solution.

Gaia's Garden

What will a regenerative world look like? Clearly, what we have been discussing through the last nine chapters is a landscape quite different from what we are living in now. As regenerative practices and technologies come into wider use, our environment will evolve, rapidly and visibly. Over the next century the mind of nature will redesign the earth. Though it is a startling notion on first hearing, it is not unprecedented. Over the past century, the earth was redesigned in the industrial image, albeit unintentionally and with little forethought. Next time, we can do much better.

The examples described in previous chapters are pieces of the puzzle. Now the time has come to put the pieces together to envision a regenerative future. Given the difficulties and the pitfalls of prediction and the limitations of projection, metaphors are useful in thinking about the future, especially for the very large picture. Wendell Berry (1977) has pointed out that in the preindustrial period, the "governing metaphor" for the human relationship with nature was pastoral agriculture, whereas now it is the machine, symbol of mechanistic means. In the Neotechnic era the governing metaphor might well be the garden. Given the scale of thinking needed, it will necessarily be a global garden, which might be nurtured over the next century to replace the global throughput machine of the present century. Let's call it Gaia's Garden, recalling both Lovelock's concept of the earth as a single organism and the Roman Goddess of Earth whose name Lovelock borrowed.

Viewed in the large perspective, a regenerative earth will look very different from the degenerating earth of the late 20th century. The working landscape will replace much of the hardware that has dominated industrial culture; natural processes will be doing much of the work now done, unsustainably and unregeneratively, by steel, concrete, and fossil fuels. Following the 11th strategy of regenerative design, we can imagine that Gaia's garden will make those natural processes clearly visible.

Frederick Turner (1988) has suggested that the art of gardening provides the best model for the mutually energizing cognitive and emotional relationship between humans and nature that regenerative development requires:

> Any gardener will instantly recognize the state of mind I have just described. As one moves about the flower beds, weeding, propagating, pruning the apple tree, shifting the rock in the rock garden an inch or two to make room for a healthy *erica*, one becomes a subtle and powerful force of natural selection in that place, placing one's stamp on the future of the biosphere; but it feels like pottering, like a waking dream (p. 51).

Conceivably, it could be a stamp as powerful in the 21st century as that of degenerative engineering in the 20th, though Turner is careful to balance the word "powerful" with the term "subtle," which makes the stamp quite different from that of engineering practices that have dominated our relationships with land for two centuries.

Rennaissance and Baroque gardens gave eloquent expression to the ideal of human dominance within clearly defined boundaries. Leo Marx (1964) posed the powerful image of the "machine in the garden" to represent the conflict between industrial technology and the image of the countryside as perceived in American culture.

If we imagine ourselves cultivating Gaia's garden in the 21st century, then we can also imagine moving the machine out, step by step, as it is replaced by the inner processes of the landscape itself. Our ideal will be a working garden, not a pleasure garden, though we can take a great deal of pleasure in it.

Gaia's garden, like most gardens, will be green, but not a uniform green. It will be an ever varying mix of green and other colors, with each spot on earth having its own unique blend. One part will merge into another, the blending and merging occurring slowly over time; change will occur at an evolutionary pace but an evolutionary pace hastened by the human mind and hand. Green will blend into urban landscapes, with buildings and land joining together in a complex mix to replace gray conurbations. Ribbons of water will flow through, pooling into larger masses here and there, supplying and collecting, processing and knitting together large areas of the earth into complex patterns.

Boundaries will not be hard lines but gradual transitions. Distinctions between cities, agricultural areas, and natural areas will not be hard and clear as they are in the industrial world. Rather than hard edges, there will be transitions from one use and one color to another. All land will have a multiplicity of uses with subtle variations in tone.

Natural Reserves

The purest colors will be the wild reserves dotting the surface of the earth, connected by the thin green lines of ecological corridors to form an encompassing network, the areas of the garden left untended but protected. There will be no roads or other development in these areas. Every effort will be made to prevent technological influences from altering the landscape.

Wildlands have a most essential long-term role in sustaining the earth's functional integrity. They are the libraries of species, communities and ecosystems where we can continually ....renew our knowledge of how nature works without the added complications of human technology. They are the baseline ecosystems by which all human ecosystems are measured.

Ideally, a wild reserve will include at least 400 square kilometers, or roughly 160 square miles. Actual minimum size in each reserve will depend on the particular needs of the top predator species. Sullivan and Shaffer (1975) estimate the minimum size as being about 600 to 750 square kilometers. In 1990 there were 5289 protected areas in the world covering a total of 5.3 million square kilometers; thus, about 4 percent of the earth's land area was in protected status, with the average protected area covering about 1000 square kilometers, or 100,000 hectares (OECD, 1991). According to a Sierra Club survey, roughly half of that area qualified as wildlands of more than 4000 square kilometers, which the Sierra Club considers an ideal minimum size for accommodating sustainable populations of all species.

Since the total area in reserves has grown more than sevenfold since 1950 and threefold since 1970 (ibid.), we can reasonably expect it to expand further. However, given the intensifying competition with other uses, lands available for reserves are severely limited. Ultimately, as much as 10 percent of the global garden might be protected wildlands, but it is unlikely that as much as half of that will be as large as the ideal.

Biosphere Reserves

Some of these wildlands will form the central cores of biosphere reserves, which are designated by UNESCO's Man and the Biosphere program to function both as protected areas and as nuclei for innovation in regenerative management.

According to UNESCO's guidelines, a protected natural area, wild and unmanaged, is at the core of a typical biosphere reserve. Surrounding this natural core is a zone of managed landscape. The managed zone may be divided into several areas including one devoted to research, one where indigenous land-use practices are carried on, and one that is the setting for experiments in landscape rehabilitation. Local farmers and villagers continue to live and earn their livelihood within the managed zone, with advice and guidance from scientists in a local university or research institute designated as the administrative institution. Activities within the zone may include farming, grazing, hunting, fishing, recreation, handicraft production, or almost anything else that might be managed in a sustainable way. The managed zone of Monteverde Reserve in Costa Rica, for example, includes sizable dairy farms and tourist facilities. In El Triunfo Reserve in Mexico, scientists are working with farmers to terrace their sloping land to prevent erosion and to compost their cornstalks after harvesting rather than burning them. The compost promises to replace chemical fertilizers, which the small farmers can no longer afford.

Where techniques like these are successful, they soon spread among farmers in surrounding areas, and biosphere reserves become agents of change rather than isolated units. With over 300 reserves in 75 countries, this system of biosphere reserves covers a range of ecosystem types, constituting a truly global program. UNESCO hopes it will eventually include biosphere reserves in all of the world's 193 biogeographical provinces as defined by the IUCN.

If we imagine that this global network of preservation, conservation, innovation, and evolution is indeed successful, then we might expect regenerative management to spread over the landscape from its colonizing islands. If so, we will see major changes in the way the landscape functions and in the way it looks. Vast farmlands devoted to single crops will diversity to feature combinations of crops, including trees, along with animals. Spotted among the farms will be small natural enclaves—mostly streams, wetlands, steep hillsides, and other places not suitable for farming. The larger of these will be interconnected by green corridors for wildlife movement. Such corridors could multiply the habitat value of small wild patches, allowing for movement of large predators who could not live on the prey found in smaller areas. These interconnected habitats will serve important purposes, because the small percentage of the earth's surface in large reserves will be adequate to preserve only a limited number of the earth's species and communities. For a truly viable global ecosystem, the entire biosphere will have to serve as habitat, though in varied ways and to varying degrees.

Decades of degenerative management have left large areas of the earth's surface in badly degraded states. Human use has seriously degraded about 15 percent of the earth's land surface (IUCN, UNEP, WWF, 1992). The major causes are erosion and salinization brought on both by degenerative practices and by the cropping of land not suitable for agriculture in the first place. Much of this land can be restored to production by applying some of the practices described in Chapter 7. Where soils are inherently unsuitable, however, there will eventually be no choice but to cease growing crops. Given the degraded state of most such land, revitalization programs will be needed.

One marginally suitable agricultural region where crops have been grown sporadically for over a hundred years is the Great Plains of the American Midwest. Rainfall teeters on the edge of adequacy, and production is maintained only by pumping water up from underground, most notably from the immense Ogallalah aquifer. Water tables are dropping, and energy bills for pumping are rising. The days of agriculture here are limited.

Two planners have proposed returning much of this landscape to the buffalo, who once grazed it in happy union with the shortgrasses that grow naturally there. The Buffalo commons they suggest would form a broad series of grassy plains extending from northern Texas to southern Canada. The farmers who inhabit the region have not been enthusiastic about this idea; marginal though it may be, farming here is their livelihood. However, the game ranching concept, as practiced by David Hopcraft in

Kenya and described in Chapter 7, suggests it may be possible, at least to some degree, to revive the native ecosystem and harvest protein from it as well, thus providing some economic support. It is a concept that may have application in a great many of the world's landscapes that are marginal for cropping and grazing.

As single uses merge into multiple uses, boundaries between uses blur into transition zones; distinctions between what is made and managed by humans and what is natural become less clear and, in fact, unimportant. The mind of nature is an integrating, not a categorizing mind. People become physically as well as intellectually part of the landscape, and landscape becomes less a patchwork and more an ever varying continuum.

Future Cities

The keys to sustainability lie in the urban landscape. If the course of evolution moves in the regenerative way, we can expect to see cities developing in forms very different from those of the past. While the image of the compact preindustrial city, clearly defined by outer boundaries that distinguish what is urban from what is rural, is appealing, it is also a relic of the past. Cities will certainly continue to spread, though it becomes increasingly important to control where and how they spread. Regenerative cities will resemble neither neatly defined preindustrial cities nor the undifferentiated arbitrary sprawl of Paleotechnic cities. The Neotechnic city will merge into the larger pattern of the landscape as other uses do. If we can replace the concrete and hardware of industrial life-support systems with the regenerative qualities of natural processes, the merging can be a benign blending of the human and the natural.

Visions of the Neotechnic city have been developing for nearly a century. As understanding of urban ecology grew through the 20th century, most of what was learned supported the insights of Ebenezer Howard (1899), who first proposed the concept of new garden cities of limited size at the end of the 19th century. The greenbelts surrounding Howard's garden cities included most of the essential life-support functions of the urban landscape. Contrary to some later interpretations, Howard was proposing swaths of working landscape, not mere open space. His greenbelts were farms, pastures, and forests. The clustering of buildings and the arrangement of urban functions posed by Howard within working landscape would still be workable today.

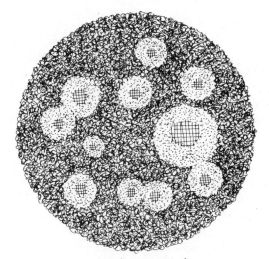

PREINDUSTRIAL

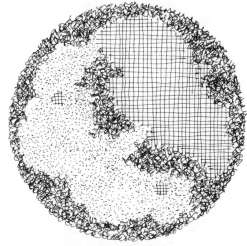

INDUSTRIAL

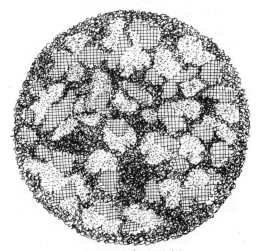

REGENERATIVE

▓▓▓ NATURAL
▒▒▒ AGRICULTURE
░░░ SETTLEMENT

EVOLUTION OF LAND USE PATTERNS

Today, however, we can no longer envision such urban units as discrete cities. Cities do not exist in such independent terms. Virtually all cities, whether we find it easy to accept or not, are dependent parts of larger urban regions, and urban regions are part of a global matrix. Thus garden cities become garden communities, and greenbelts become green networks, encompassing the communities and weaving them together. In the green networks are the processes that support life.

Michael Hough (1984) and Anne Spirn (1984) have explored the existing examples and the possibilities in considerable detail, showing that regenerative technologies have long been applied in the urban environment with dramatic success. What their many examples have suggested and what has been implied in the examples in this book is future cities in which the working landscape becomes the unifying, integrating network of urban form, rather than a decorative addition, as in the industrial city. The urban landscape will collect water when it rains and store it in ponds or tanks for future use, or allow it to infiltrate slowly into underground storage. Thus the surface will be sculpted with swales and retention ponds, some holding water through the year, some usually dry.

The working landscape will also process water, both sewage and water polluted by contact with roofs and streets, filtering it through plants in ponds and wetlands. Plants and microorganisms will assimilate nutrients and other materials, recycling them through the landscape and eliminating in many cases the need for a mechanical treatment system.

The same working landscape that filters, assimilates, and stores water and nutrients will also serve to filter, cool, and direct the flow of air. Masses of trees will be located around heavily traveled streets, industrial plants, and other sources of air pollution. They will also create microclimates within the city in all the ways described in Chapter 5.

Productivity will also be an important part of the urban landscape. Just how great the potential actually is for growing food there remains a question, but the examples of Chinese cities show that urban farms can produce a great deal of food. And certainly the biomass produced can be used in a great many ways—for composting, for energy, and for making products.

As we shift to regenerative energy sources, we can also expect to see energy-generating apparatus appearing in the urban fabric. While these will clearly not be natural forms but objects devised by humans, they can be dramatic features, as shown by the Solar Park in Case Study for Chapter 4.

In fact, making visible the ecological processes that support life will be an important part of this emerging landscape. The child who grows up in a regenerative city of the 21st century will know very well where the water she drinks comes from and where her wastes go. She will have an inner feeling for the atmospheric fluxes that make cool and warm places, and she will know how food grows and in what season. She will understand all this as part of her daily experience. She will also know that the same landscape that accomplishes all this provides a place to run, to play hide-and-seek or baseball, and to ride her bicycle to the grocery store. In the same landscape, she will see birds and squirrels and snakes, all as inhabitants of the same world she lives in.

Within this green matrix, communities will form identifiable neighborhoods. Though cities will continue to spread over the landscape, we can hope that with planning, the undifferentiated conurbation of the Paleotechnic era will give way to a pattern of discrete, identifiable, interrelated communities joined together by the working landscape. If this happens, transportation will again have a great deal to do with it. The need to use less energy will make it more desirable to walk or ride a bicycle to schools, shops, meeting places, and local services. This will pull residential, commercial and civic areas closer together. Probably, it will increase overall densities as well, although density is much less important to the consumption of resources than the pattern of land use and the design of ecologically functional urban spaces. A neighborhood of single-family homes in which walking and bicycle routes, and in some places equestrian trails, are inviting, safe, easy to use, and offer reasonably direct access to places frequently visited can be as energy-efficient as a high-density neighborhood. Cars will still be necessary for medium-distance trips, but they will assume less importance as shorter trips are commonly carried out on foot or bicycle, and most intracity trips will involve public transportation. Roads, like virtually all the elements of the landscape, will feature multiple uses as they accommodate pedestrians and bicyclists along with cars.

Within the green urban matrix, local communities will likely vary greatly in character and density. Communities in one region will be different, perhaps dramatically different, from those in other regions because the climate, landform, ecology, and culture are different. Cities everywhere, but especially American cities with their enormous ethnic and social diversity, have always featured distinct neighborhoods identified with distinct cultures. Densities will vary from highly concentrated, mid- to high-rise communities to dispersed single-family communities. Though such cities will spread over the landscape, they could be designed in the regenerative way to embrace the ecology of the landscape rather than obliterating it. Nature's processes could continue to function in concert with human culture. In such a future, the conflicts between nature and culture that characterized the Paleotechnic will no longer exist.

In regenerative cities, building will be elements of the landscape like hills or lakes or groves of trees, rather than discrete objects standing apart from the landscape. Within the green matrix they will cluster more tightly together than the buildings of industrial cities. Rather than asserting themselves and competing for attention in the manner of Paleotechnic structures, buildings will blend together more in the manner of a medieval town, forming harmonizing clusters that reflect a sense of interrelationship and community as well as a sense of rootedness in the earth. Structures within each cluster will be close enough together to avoid wasting land and to minimize circulation routes but far enough apart to allow for sunlight and air movement.

The buildings in a particular locale will have a commonality of form, reflecting the climate and landscape. Buildings in the desert will likely merge into the earth, exposing little of their skins to the desiccating sun, while buildings in the tropics will generally rise above the water-laden ground into cooling breezes.

In every climate, rooftops could be fertile and productive. Building walls could be sheathed in living green as well. In most climates, buildings will turn transparent faces southward to the sun with a variety of adjustable shading devices moving and casting shadows that vary through the seasons. The sizes of individual structures will vary from high-rise structures to single-family houses. The mass of each building will be relatively small, however, to allow for cross ventilation and natural lighting in every space.

Within each cluster, or local neighborhood, uses will be mixed. Dwellings, shops, offices, and schools will be close together, sometimes within the same structure or grouped around a plaza or courtyard. Sizes and shapes of neighborhood clusters will vary, especially since most will evolve out of cities first built during the industrial period, adapting to existing conditions. Within the clusters, outdoor spaces will be relatively small, scaled for human activity, in contrast to the larger areas of the green matrix that envelopes each cluster and knits them all together.

Nature, Garden, and City

Nature is the source and inspiration for regenerative design. This is as true of form as it is of process. The garden has long been the clearest expression of the human relationship with nature. Several times in history, forms and relationships first expressed in the garden were later translated into urban terms to become part of the basic vocabulary of urban plans. The grand *allées* of the baroque gardens of Vaux-le-Viconte and Versailles were transplanted to become the grand boulevards of Paris and other cities in various parts of the world. The pastoral greenswards of the English landscape garden became the urban parks of the 19th and 20th centuries. In similar ways, today's gardens may in some ways presage tomorrow's cities. Perhaps they provide glimpses of Gaia's Garden.

Following are a few images taken from my own garden, where I have experimented with regenerative process and form. The garden derives from the larger landscape of which it is part. The effort here is to embrace and distill ecological processes and their complexity and to give them visible expression.

The setting is at the base of the San Gabriel Mountains, a dramatically rugged range on the edge of the southern California urban area. This mountain interface zone is the setting of a dramatic and dynamic set of ecological processes at the transition between mountain and valley.

Some of the most active of these occur where water collects and moves. Under natural conditions, when water from mountain rainfall pours out of the canyons at the mountains' edge, it spreads out and flows at a slower pace over a broad depression called a wash (Figure 1), much of it percolating into underground storage along the way. Washes are important nodes for dissipating floodwaters and recharging groundwater. They are covered with rocks and dotted with plants struggling to take hold.

The analogous washes in the garden play a similar role, holding water and allowing it to percolate (Figures 2 and 3). The basic material—rock—is the same as that of the natural wash, but it is used in a

Figure 1

Figure 2

Figure 3

controlled way at a scale related to human dimensions. Thus the form of the garden wash does not mimic the natural wash, but recalls its process in human terms related to the human environment.

In the native plant forms of the foothill zone, one sees the meager but efficient water regime of a semiarid zone and an abundance of solar energy (Figure 4). They give visible expression to semidesert flows of water and energy. The leaves are small, mostly grayish green, and many of them turn their edges to meet the sun's rays, thus minimizing water loss. Most of the plants, except for the oaks, are sparse and low-growing. The plant community of the garden follows the same principles, though only a few of the plants are natives of the zone (Figure 5). The result is a complex composition of varied fine textures in shades of grayish to reddish green.

The interior environment of the small studio building that stands within the garden is also an integral part of the garden. The solarium, with south-facing glass doors, is the studio's heating system, and the plants hanging within the solarium help to clean the inside air (Figure 6). In summer the doors can be opened to allow air to flow

Figure 4

Figure 5

Figure 6

through the building. This regenerative heating and cooling system stands at the functional and aesthetic opposite end of the Neotechnic-Paleotechnic spectrum from the mechanical forced-air system.

From Garden to City

As the garden examples demonstrate, the forms that grow out of regenerative processes are dramatically different from the mechanical forms of the Paleotechnic. Figure 7 shows a typical example of the Paleotechnic way of managing urban runoff, the concrete flood-control channel. By way of contrast, Figure 8 shows an infiltration basin the city of Phoenix, designed both as a integral part of the landscape and as a clear expression of water in the landscape.

Regenerative and degenerative methods of sewage treatment provide even stronger contrasts in process and form. Figure 9 shows a conventional mechanical treatment plant, clearly an industrial form isolated from both city and nature.

The image in Figure 10 might be a garden but is not. It is actually the rock-reed filter system of the

Figure 7

Figure 8

Figure 9

Figure 10

aquatic treatment plant in Denham Springs, Louisiana. Though its location is in fact outside the town, it could easily form a very beautiful feature in the urban fabric.

Rooftops are among the most flagrantly wasted resources of cities. While they may protect those inside from the elements of nature, they also shed more water and reflect more heat than do the landscapes they replace. They are also usually barren,

lifeless places in stark contrast with the teeming, vibrant life of the landscapes they replace (Figure 11). Figure 12 shows the design for the Center for Regenerative Studies with its roof gardens that continue the basic ecological functions of the landscape. They collect water for future use, convert solar radiation to stored heat and biomass, grow food, create outdoor activity areas, and provide thermal insulation for enclosed spaces.

Figure 11

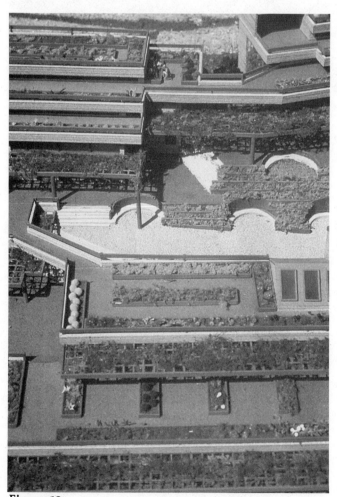

Figure 12

Grand Axis of Paris

The Tuileries Gardens in Paris and the Grand Axis that has its origin within them embody as clearly and forcefully as the garden of Vaux-le-Vicomte shown in Chapter 2 the Cartesian concept of order that ascended to intellectual dominance during the 17th century. The geometry, including the arrangement of plants, is Euclidian and absolute in its symmetry. Everything is organized around a central axis that reaches away to infinity. The scale is vast, superhuman, reflecting the vast absolute power of the Sun King whose domain this was. Human will was in control here, demonstrating how, in the new Cartesian scheme of things, humans become the masters of nature.

Landscape architect André Le Notre developed the basic forms used in the Tuileries in his earlier gardens at Vaux-le-Vicomte (see page 21) and Versailles. With the Tuileries, which Le Norte designed in the 1660s, the formal vocabulary of human intellectual dominance and control moved into the city. Soon those forms began reshaping the city. Within a few years after LeNotre laid out the gardens, he extended the axis beyond the gardens to the west. Then he planted long rows of chestnut trees to line the axis, forming a broad boulevard as an appropriate setting for the coming and going of royal chariots. A few years later the boulevard was renamed the Champs Elysées ("Elysian fields").

In 1806 Napolean began construction of the Arch of Triumph on the Grand Axis at the west end of the Champs Elysées, reflecting his own grandiose vision of empire. Over the following century, rows of commercial buildings, with fashionable shops on the ground floor, lined the boulevard on both sides and became the embodiment of the bourgeois urbanism of the 19th century.

In the mid-19th century, Baron Hausman, in his ambitious scheme to rebuild Paris, expanded the grand boulevard model of the Champs Elysées to form a grand system, superimposing the clearly articulated rational order of the formal garden on the city as a whole. The Cartesian vision of the world had become physical reality. Development of the Champs Elysées and the rest of Paris continued through the remainder of the 19th century and the first half of the 20th.

Following World War II, planners decided to extend the axis beyond the Seine with the new business center of La Defense. The name came from a monument to the 1871 defense of Paris on the site. As earlier sections of the axis had embodied the

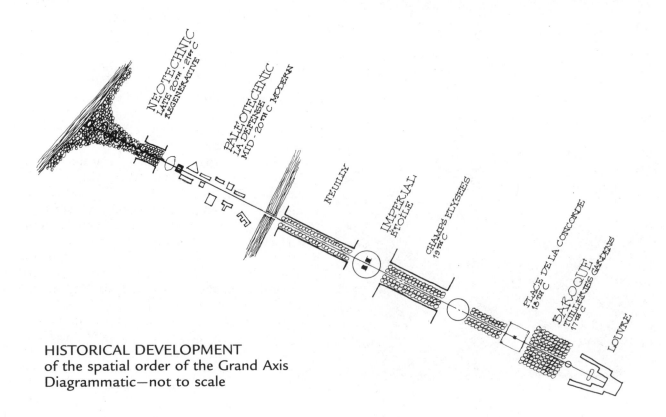

HISTORICAL DEVELOPMENT
of the spatial order of the Grand Axis
Diagrammatic—not to scale

ethos of each era, La Defense gave visible and dramatic form to the booming vision of the mid-20th century. To begin, the site was cleared and scraped bare; urban redevelopers of that period liked to start with a clean slate. Then an underground transportation system was built underneath the 1-kilometer length of the axis extension. This includes a bus station, an immense railroad station complex, several roads, and parking for 32,000 cars. On top of the transportation complex is a pedestrian mall following the axis, and along both sides of the mall are the high-rise office buildings of different international corporations, each independently representing grandeur through height or flourishes of form. There is no clearer manifestation anywhere of the urban ideal of the late Paleotechnic.

In 1991, 10 teams of planners and designers from several countries were invited to submit designs for a new extension of the Grand Axis beyond La Defense. I worked on the competition as a member of the OIKOS group, which included Italian, Austrian, and American members. What follows is the plan that I prepared for the landscape and ecological aspects of the overall scheme. It was not the scheme chosen by the jury for implementation. Nevertheless, it will serve to illustrate some of the possibilities for form and expression of regenerative processes in the urban landscape.

It is easy to imagine that the next extension of the Grand Axis might give form to the emerging new relationships between city and nature, adding a new chapter—perhaps the most important since Le Notre laid out the Tuileries—to the historical tableau of the Grand Axis. The media for the regenerative processing proposed here are two of nature's most powerful and pervasive systems, translated into human terms, clearly expressed in visual form, and integrated into the city's structure:

- the urban river
- the urban forest

The design utilizes the complex sets of interactions that characterize these two basic systems as they function in nature, adapts them to the urban environment, and augments them with the scientific and technical facility of the later 20th century. The result is a new kind of urban technology and urban structure based on natural processes.

The Urban River
The engineering of Paris' underground sewers established a model for the world in the 19th century,

and the present project offers opportunities for applying and demonstrating new biologically based processes that can play important roles in reducing pollution in rivers like the Seine. This is expressed in the plan as an urban river flowing along the axis, symbolizing the flow of the Seine through the Paris region, thus providing an aesthetic and recreational feature while also treating and purifying wastewater.

The plan proposes to establish the urban river as a natural water-processing system within the axis environment, using sewage diverted from La Defense or a nearby residential area. The system also treats the highly polluted storm-water runoff from the surrounding urban area. As described in Chapter 8, such treatment systems use the natural assimilation and filtration capabilities of vascular plants and microorganisms in various combinations. Preliminary calculations indicate that the system sketched here could treat a volume several times that produced within La Defense (which is estimated to be about 15,000 to 20,000 cubic meters per day). In addition to its functional value, this system is designed as a powerful symbol of urban regeneration and a setting for the merging of city with nature.

The sequence of flow follows nature's prevalent sequence: from source to lake to river to wetland, and then a return to the larger flow. In symbolic terms the sequence begins with the dark, still, reflective water of an urban lake immediately west of La Defense where the next section of Axis begins, forming a sacred, contemplative space with dark overtones of death and thus transition. Water moves from the lake into the winding flow of the river, suggesting the ongoing flow of life, and eventually it spreads into the teeming vitality of the primeval wetland, the regeneration of life.

Within the symbolic flow is the process of purification. After initial screening and settling to remove solid materials, the water undergoes aeration to raise the oxygen content. Accomplishing this is a waterfall: a sheet of water falling from a height of 10 meters into the lake, splashing and bubbling as it falls. At this point, quality of the water is at a level that is safe for human contact. However, if further disinfection is required, an ozonation treatment can serve the purpose.

The water rests in the lake for several days undergoing treatment by aquatic plants rooted in gravel on the lake bottom. After that, it moves into the urban river, which flows in sweeping arcs that recall the meandering course of the Seine, crossing

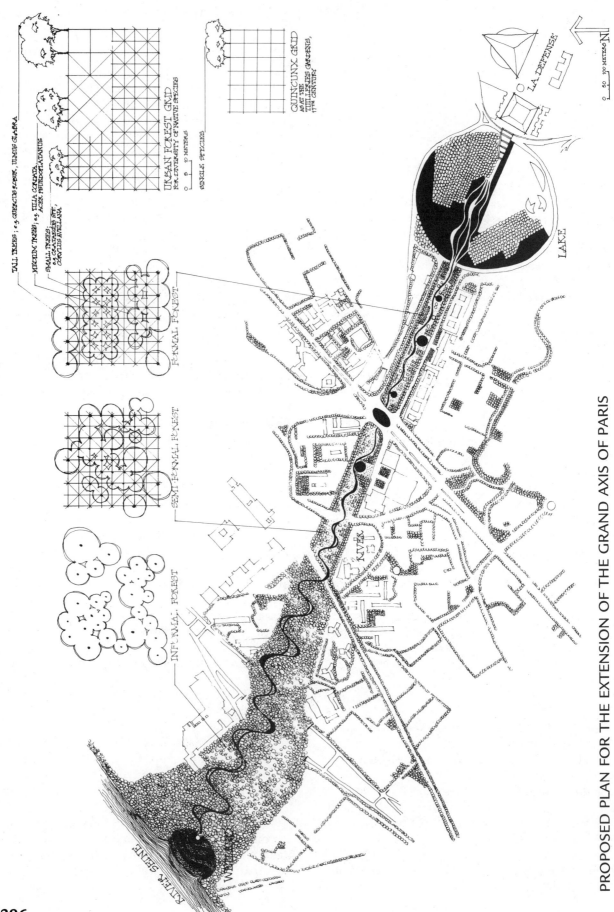

TALL TREES; e.g. QUERCUS ROBUR, ULMUS GLABRA

MEDIUM TREES; e.g. TILIA CORDATA

SMALL TREES; e.g. CRATAEGUS SP., ACER, PSEUDOPLATANUS; CORYLUS AVELLANA

URBAN FOREST GRID
FOR DIVERSITY OF NATIVE SPECIES

SINGLE SPECIES

0 5 10 METRES

QUINCUNX GRID
AS AT THE TUILLERIES GARDENS, 17TH CENTURY

FORMAL FOREST

SEMI FORMAL FOREST

INFORMAL FOREST

LA DEFENSE

N

0 50 100 METRES

LAKE

RIVER SEINE

PROPOSED PLAN FOR THE EXTENSION OF THE GRAND AXIS OF PARIS

296

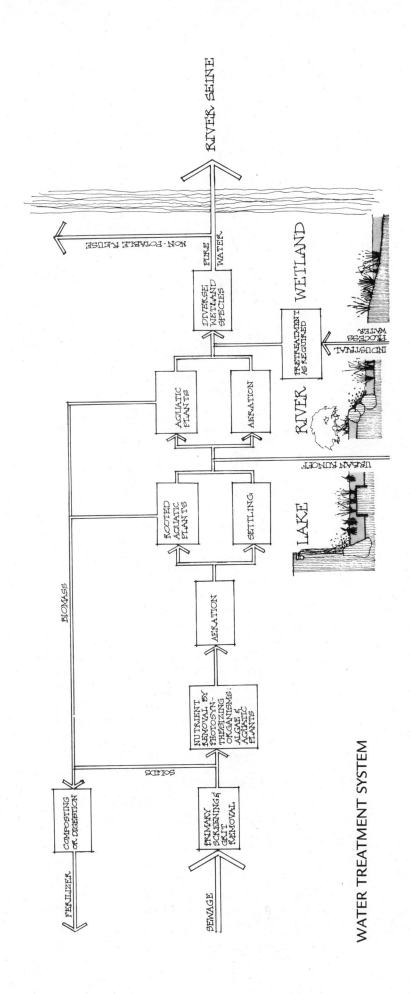

WATER TREATMENT SYSTEM

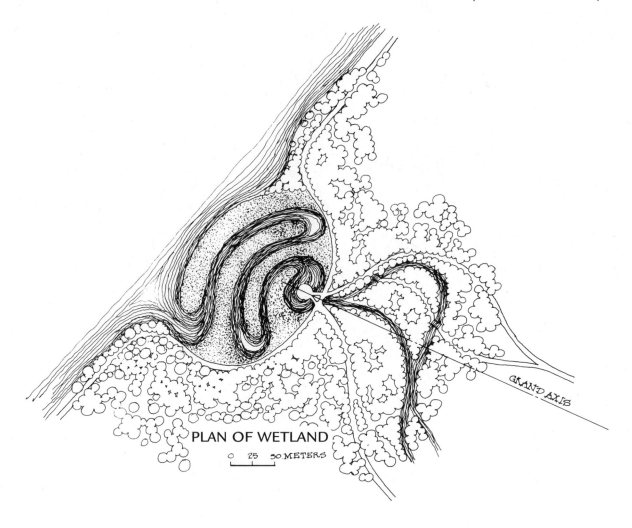

PLAN OF WETLAND

0 25 50 METERS

GRAND AXIS

and recrossing the axis. As the urban river approaches the Seine, the arcs swing wider, reflecting a return to nature's leisurely rhythms.

At intervals along its length are pools for play or for fish, and small ponds with aquatic plants for further treatment. Runoff water from the surrounding areas can be fed into these ponds with or without pretreatment. Pretreated industrial effluent can be introduced at certain points as well. Fountains, baffles, rocks, and other devices in the river create ripples and eddies for further oxidation. Fully treated effluent from other areas off the axis can join the stream along the way as this treatment approach is extended to other areas of new development in Nanterre, a suburb of Paris.

The urban river eventually flows into the river Seine through a large wetland that provides final treatment before mixing with the Seine's waters. In nature, wetlands are the complex meeting places of land and water. They are among nature's richest and most biotically productive environments, suppor-

ting large and diverse populations of birds, fish, microorganisms, and small mammals. They also are the final filters for water flowing from the land into larger bodies of water. For centuries, due to ignorance of their key ecological roles, wetlands have been filled in every part of Europe. Now, in a more ecologically enlightened time, it is an important gesture, symbolically as well as functionally, to bring biological richness into the city in the form of an urban wetland where river and city come together in mutual respect and harmony. It is especially fitting for the 21st century that the historical axis of Paris provide a symbolic home for the urban river as a primeval wellspring of life.

The Urban Forest

Trees play major roles in maintaining the quality of both air and water in all the ways described in Chapters 5 and 6, and they help to cool the city in summertime as well. To accomplish these tasks, the urban landscape must become a functioning ecosystem and not be merely a decorative feature. The plan proposes an urban forest network to encompass the axis and its environs. The community of species within the urban forest follows that of natural forests still existing around the edges of the Paris region such as the Forest of St. Germain. These natural forest communities have evolved over eons in adaptation to the conditions of this region; they are therefore well suited to growing here with a minimum of chemical inputs and other maintenance. The proposed forest community includes trees and shrubs of all sizes, thus providing a green filter at every level up to about 30 meters above the ground. At the top level are patriarchal species like oaks (*Quercus robur*) and elms (*Ulmus glabra*); in the middle are lindens (*Tilia cordata*), maples (*Acer pseudoplatanus*), and several others, and at the lower level, providing a canopy just over human height, are species such as hazelnut (*Corylus avellana*), and hawthorns (*Crataegus* spp.). Urban forests also support a diverse community of birds and small mammals, bringing wildlife back to the city. This naturally self-supporting community reduces populations of urban nuisance species such as rats and pigeons as well as many species of insects that now multiply in the absence of controlling predators.

The urban forest might eventually grow into a green network encompassing the entire urban area, perhaps eventually the entire urban region, spreading from its initial roots in the Grand Axis. In a sense it represents an expansion and restatement in contemporary ecological terms of the themes begun in the Tuilleries Garden, where the Axis originated. The trees in the Tuilleries are all one species, laid out in the simple quincux grid, an arrangement clearly expressing the simple geometry of Cartesian attitudes toward nature and form. In the plan the urban forest west of La Defense recalls the basic order of this grid, but in a much more complex form of overlaid grid modules that accommodates the diverse forest community of trees of varied types and sizes. Thus the forest merges with the geometric order of the city and gives it a new, ecological expression. The forest follows this complex grid from La Defense to its intersection with Avenue Joliot-Curies in a formal way that echoes the Tuilleries, varying its geometric order to enclose public activity spaces that are like outdoor rooms carved from the forest. As the forest spreads out from the axis to the north and south, it follows a geometric pattern along major thoroughfares such as Avenue Joliot-Curies and the esplanade to Malraux Park, recalling the grand boulevards of Paris. Where it penetrates the local neighborhoods, it departs from this geometry to adapt to local conditions and spatial forms.

Thus the urban forest also provides routes for local movement on foot and bicycle, forming a network for local nonautomobile circulation, though in many cases cars, pedestrians, and bicycles can move along the same routes.

The City in Gaia's Garden

In this example we can see some of the means by which cities can rejoin the larger landscape. The dominant features of the natural landscape—in this case the river and the forest—become also the organizing elements of urban form. The life-sustaining processes of the natural landscape—interactions among species, the ongoing renewal of flowing water, filtering and assimilation by soil plants and microbial communities—also become the life-sustaining processes of the city. Where city and nature meet, they merge gradually together.

There are few cities in the world where the relationships between city and nature have been so clearly expressed as in Paris, or where there are such grand design traditions on which to build. Nevertheless, every city in the world stands within a larger landscape that offers means for reintegration. Most of them still function on the basis of degenerative, Paleotechnic processes that increasingly demand reintegration.

CASE STUDY

The Center in the Garden

The Center for Regenerative Studies is a microcosm of Gaia's global garden, but only in the broadest sense is it a model. The community itself is not large enough to include the rich multiplicity of functions we can expect in future communities. Nevertheless, as a small community within a working landscape, it presents a limited and perhaps optimistic view of future relationships between people and nature that might take shape in the 21st century. Blending into the landscape as they do both visually and ecologically, the buildings in the model shown on pages 300 to 302 hint at the kind of forms architecture might take if, in a regenerative future, buildings become part of the earth again. Included in the model is the Center's full projected plan: dwelling and learning space for a community of 90 people. The first phase now completed, as shown on the plan on page 303, includes about 35 percent of this total, with housing for 20 students and two faculty members, lecture and seminar rooms, laboratory, and offices.

Altered conditions, along with political and financial compromises, resulted in substantial changes in the original designs as described in

Chapter 9. Arbitrarily applied building and fire regulations took a further toll. The county fire marshall, for example, required that the central pedestrian way be widened to accommodate not one but two fire engines side by side. Nevertheless, the major concepts survived. In time, most of the incompatible details can be corrected. The photographs on pages 304 and 305 show the completed first-phase buildings. In this phase the

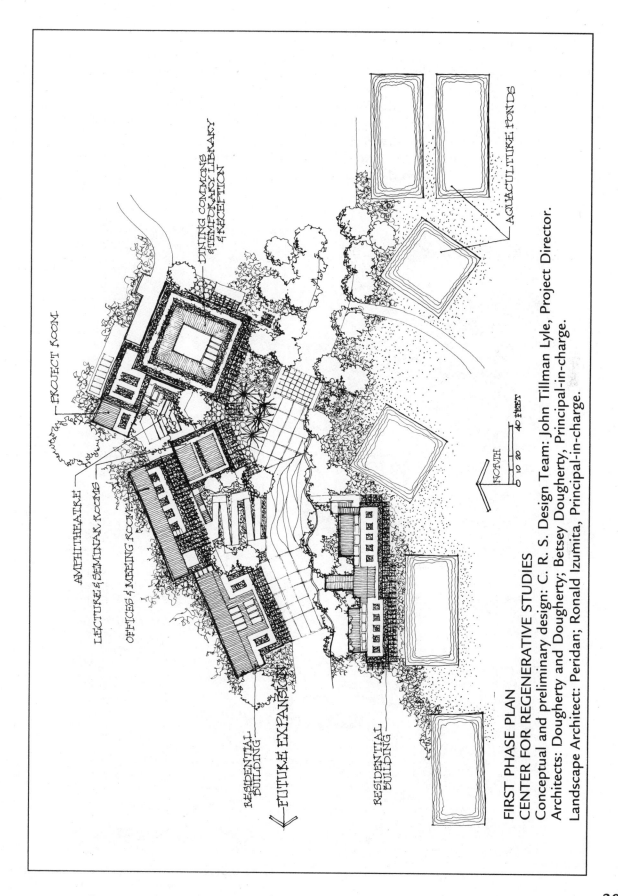

FIRST PHASE PLAN
CENTER FOR REGENERATIVE STUDIES
Conceptual and preliminary design: C. R. S. Design Team: John Tillman Lyle, Project Director.
Architects: Dougherty and Dougherty; Betsey Dougherty, Principal-in-charge.
Landscape Architect: Peridan; Ronald Izumita, Principal-in-charge.

PROJECT ROOM

AMPHITHEATRE

LECTURE & SEMINAR ROOMS

OFFICES & MEETING ROOMS

DINING COMMONS
& TEMPORARY LIBRARY
& RECEPTION

AQUACULTURE PONDS

RESIDENTIAL BUILDING

FUTURE EXPANSION

RESIDENTIAL BUILDING

NORTH

0 10 20   40 FEET

large space of the dining commons is subdivided to include offices and a project room. As the full plan is realized, these will move to their permanent locations and the dining commons will be fully operational.

Phase 1 will operate for at least two years before additional construction. The Center's faculty and designers will carefully study the operation of this initial increment will be carefully studied to provide information for design and detail of later phases.

CONSTRUCTION OF
PHASE 1 OF THE
CENTER FOR
REGENERATIVE
STUDIES NEARING
COMPLETION

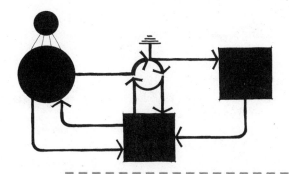

Chapter 11
Economics, Policy, and Transition

For all their promise in helping to shape a sustainable biosphere, there are two necessary conditions under which regenerative systems can fulfill that promise and become standard practice in the very practical world in which we live: They must cost no more (and preferably less) than competing technologies, and they must be supported by public policy. The subject of this final chapter is, How can we fulfill these economic and policy conditions?

Economics of Regeneration

Whenever one proposes a regenerative solution in a particular situation, the question of cost arises with astonishing immediacy. The prevailing assumption is that it must cost more. If sustainability costs no more than unsustainability, why would we still have more of the latter than the former? Though it often happens that sustainability actually costs less, simple and direct answers are elusive because of the many ways of accounting for costs. Estimating cost in this arena requires that we specify exactly what is included. If we are comparing two costs, it is important to include the same components in both. There are five ways of accounting for costs, which this section will address.

What most project sponsors mean when they ask about cost is the simplest interpretation of the term: first cost, or price including materials and labor. Given our speculative system of land development, this is the only cost that matters in most private development projects. This is because the developer usually sells the development as soon as possible, thus passing the cost of operation, maintenance, and management on to the buyer.

Buyers, along with developers who continue to operate what they develop, have reason to be concerned with costs occurring over the longer term—that is, with life-cycle costs, which include operation, maintenance, and management. The longer time frame makes life-cycle cost a more accurate measure of actual economic value. It often happens that lower first costs lead to higher costs later on. This is especially important from the resource point of view because higher costs of operation usually reflect higher consumption of materials and energy. For this reason, life-cycle cost estimating is an important conservation technique.

Private owners and developers usually have little interest in costs beyond these first two types (first costs and life-cycle costs) because the other three accounting methods include costs that, up to now, usually have been borne by the public.

The third type, which we might call total measurable cost, includes all of the actual monetary costs that can be attributed to a development practice or project regardless of who bears them. For example, a development project might increase the storm-water runoff from the site, which will place an additional burden on the city's flood-control system. Eventually, that system will have to be expanded, which represents a cost. Such costs, which are known to economists as "externalities," often add up to major economic burdens for government and thus for taxpayers. For this reason, public agencies have made some serious efforts in recent years to internalize some externalities—that is, to find ways to require both public and private developers to include such costs in their project budgets. This usually presents problems because external costs can be very difficult to measure.

Other external costs are borne by the public as a matter of government policy in the forms of subsidies, price supports, tax incentives, and others. This is especially true in the areas of agriculture, energy, and water. Whatever social benefits these subsidies may bring, they skew the cost structure and complicate comparison.

The fourth means of accounting for costs includes costs that are part of the larger economic picture, definitely part of the macro-marketplace, but nevertheless even more difficult to measure and to predict. These include such variables as numbers of jobs created by a particular technology or project, effects on income distribution, and capital concentration. These are important matters that affect the shape of society, and there are reasons to believe they can be altered by technological factors.

A fifth type of cost includes all those in the first four types and adds another kind of externality: environmental and social costs that are immeasurable or at least impossible to translate directly into monetary value, such as air or water pollution. Economists have made some efforts to quantify environmental and social costs. These have involved such techniques as surveying people to determine how much they would be willing to pay to have clean air, and measuring the cost of treatment for diseases caused by unhealthy air. The results have not been convincing. Without specific dollar costs that are explainable and convincing, it is extremely difficult to internalize such costs. Since the variables that add up to environmental quality and even those that add up to resource sustainability exist outside the marketplace, there is no reliable way to place an economic value on them. This means they are best considered as matters of public policy rather than as matters of economics.

Thus the economic implications of regenerative technologies range from relatively simple matters of comparing first costs of different types of systems to very complex matters relating to the economic structure of the society. At this point enough experience with regenerative systems exists to make some general comparisons with conventional technologies at each level. However, that experience is limited to a relatively small number of situations and thus too limited as yet for predicting anything with certainty.

First Costs

Of the five types of costs, first costs are easiest to estimate. Reasonably accurate information is available for comparing first costs of energy, water, agriculture, and waste management.

Energy

Information on the energy costs is highly developed and recent, though it is important to recognize that none of the regenerative energy technologies is yet fully operational, and that all are still in a stage of development at which improvements are frequent. In most cases this means that costs are likely to continue coming down.

As of 1990 the cost in the marketplace of energy produced by renewable means, while competitive with the cost of nuclear energy, was somewhat more than that produced by fossil fuels. For some renewable energies, such as ethanol, wind energy or solar thermal electricity, the differences between them and fossil fuels were small. For others, such as photovoltaic electricity or oil from algae, it was a matter of two or three times as much. In 1990 in California, for example, it cost utilities about $0.04 per kilowatt-hour to generate electricity in fossil-fuel-powered plants, while at that time hydropower cost about $0.03 and nuclear about $0.11. According to the Pacific Gas and Electric Company, wind-generated power then cost about $0.054 cents per kilowatt-hour. The cost of wind turbines went down by about two-thirds during the 1980s, however, and it is still declining. At this point, the cost of wind power is probably equal to that of fossil-fuel-generated power in some places.

In their newest solar thermal plants, the Luz International Corporation was generating power in 1992 for about $0.08 per kilowatt-hour. The cost of photovoltaic power was then more than three times that amount, but that will certainly come down. Photovoltaic costs dropped over 40-fold during the 1970s and another 12-fold in the 1980s.

As for petroleum substitutes, the cost of renewable fuels is again substantially higher, though not beyond the realm of practical possibility. Researchers at the Solar Energy Research Institute estimate the cost of ethanol made from agricultural waste at about $1.35 per gallon in 1991, as compared with about $0.50 for gasoline wholesale at the same time.

Water

In the area of water management, cost comparisons generally favor on-site retention, vegetative protection of watersheds, and use of reclaimed water. Shaping the landform to make swales and retention basins is far less costly than using Paleotechnic drainage systems with pipes and concrete, though the former does often require more land.

Perhaps the best cost comparison of Paleotechnic and Neotechnic water management developed so far has been made for the new town of Woodlands in southern Texas (McHarg and Sutton, 1975). The site covers 18,000 acres of flat, forested coastal plain. A conventional (Confucian-style) system would have involved underground grids of drainage tiles and storm sewer pipes as well as concrete flood-control channels. As an alternative, the planners (Wallace, McHarg, Roberts and Todd) proposed a Taoist system of human-made streams and swales. Berms and check dams were to retain the water at numerous points along its paths of flow, especially over permeable soils, to allow time for percolation into groundwater storage. This water-flow system allowed the natural vegetation to remain and established a framework for development that provided for as many units as the conventional scheme. The cost comparison showed that this Taoist system would cost less than one-quarter as much as the Confucian system. Landscape architect Ian McHarg, who was largely responsible for the plan, pointed out that "there is no better union than virtue and profit" (ibid., p. 78).

Agriculture

Another area in which first-cost comparisons are meaningful is agriculture. A number of comparisons have been made of actual costs and profit margins for regenerative and conventional farms. Among the early studies was one carried out by the Center for the Biology of Natural Systems from 1974 to 1979 (Commoner, 1990). The researchers compared productivity and profitability of 14 organic farmers and 14 conventional farms during that period. Except in their use of chemicals, the farms were very similar, growing mostly corn and soybeans. The results showed that the organic farms produced an average of 8.5 percent less than the conventional farms, but they saved almost exactly that much by not buying chemicals. Profits were essentially the same. Reports of a number of farmers who have made the change to chemical-free farming agree with this result. The Vogelsberg and Kirschenmann farms described in Chapter 7 show about the same profits as the farms of their neighbors. However, most farmers who have made the switch report going through a period of transition during which productivity declines. This period seems usually to last 2 to 5 years, after which productivity commonly levels off to a rate only marginally lower than that of conventional farms.

In the late 1980s the National Research Council (NRC, 1989) reviewed research carried out up to that time on this subject and found most of it flawed in its methodology. Then the NRC conducted a number of studies of its own. The results showed wide fluctuations from year to year and great differences among neighboring farms (as much as 50 percent) in both productivity and profitability regardless of levels of chemical use. Given these differences, the NRC researchers did not believe general conclusions were warranted (ibid.). But after studying applications of the major techniques of regenerative agriculture, they concluded that, if applied competently, all could eliminate chemical use while maintaining high levels of both productivity and profit. Crop diversification strategies especially were found effective in both decreasing input costs and increasing crop yields (ibid., p. 241).

Waste Management

Direct-cost comparisons for managing organic wastes are somewhat clearer. A study carried out for the city of Los Angeles by the 606 Studio (1988b) showed composting to be the least expensive of four means for dealing with sewage sludge.

The cost of composting is less than half that of other methods even if the value of the compost as a soil amendment is not included in the calculations.

Natural sewage treatment processes are considerably less costly than mechanical systems. In 1978 the city of Del Mar in southern California compared the cost of an aquacultural sewage treatment system using water hyacinths as an alternative to conventional secondary treatment. Cost projections showed that the total net cost of operation for aquacultural treatment, including amortization of the initial investment, would be about $244,000 as compared with $260,000 for conventional secondary treatment (Jokela and Jokela, 1978). By the sixth year of operation the comparable costs would be $284,000 and $417,000. Thus, the most significant savings would be in operational costs.

In the light of more recent experience, this analysis probably overestimated the cost of the natural treatment alternative. Most of the approximately 100 towns that had built natural treatment systems by 1990 compared the costs of alternatives before making the decision and found conventional treatment significantly more expensive. In some cases the differences have been dramatic. In Picayune, Mississippi, an aging conventional treatment system was badly damaged in a storm in 1991, and the cost of rebuilding was estimated at $11 million. The cost of replacing it with a new natural system, by comparison, was estimated at $350,000, or approximately 3 percent of the cost of the conventional system (Wolverton, 1992).

Altogether, the available information indicates that regenerative systems generally cost no more, and in some cases far less, than equivalent industrial systems that perform the same functions. This holds true even if we consider only first cost and even if we do not figure into the equation the value of resources reused or the environmental quality. When we consider that one of the basic strategies of regenerative technologies is letting nature do the work that would otherwise be done by materials that cost money, this is not so surprising. The one major exception is in providing energy, both fuel and electricity, and the reason lies in the artificially low price of fossil fuels. While all the costs figure into the price of competing technologies, fossil-fuel costs are heavily subsidized; that is, the user pays only a fraction of the actual cost. We will return to this subject shortly.

Life-Cycle Costs

In an intuitive way, life-cycle costs probably enter into most purchase decisions simply because more durable goods often have higher first costs. One means of quantifying this simple comparison is to calculate the payback period. That is, how long does it take for operational costs saved by buying the more expensive object or technology to equal the difference in first cost? The payback period for a solar water-heating system, for example, is usually 4 to 8 years. The payback period for an evaporative cooler for the kitchen in the Center for Regenerative Studies compared with a conventional air conditioner turned out to be about 2 years.

When we extend the principle to major public investments, the estimating process becomes much more complicated than simply comparing first costs, both because so many more variables are involved and because predicting the future becomes unavoidable.

One example of life-cycle budgeting on a very large scale is Gregory McPherson's economic model to measure the costs of Urban Releaf's program to plant 500,000 desert adapted trees in the city of Tucson over an 8-year period (McPherson, 1990). The cooling effects provided by each tree through shading save an average of 61 kilowatt-hours of electricity per year, which was valued at $4.39 at then-current rates. The savings per tree through evapotranspiration are considerably greater at 227 kilowatt-hours or $16.34, yielding a total saving through both effects of 288 kilowatt-hours or $20.73 per year. When compared with the cost of planting, irrigating, and maintaining the trees, this yields a benefit/cost ratio of 2.62; that is, the measurable economic benefits of planting the shade trees outweigh the costs by a ratio of 2.62 to 1. It is worth emphasizing that these calculations include only the measurable direct benefits of saving electricity. McPherson estimates that the much-harder-to-measure indirect benefits, which include water retention, reduction of atmospheric carbon dioxide, dust, and other pollutants, are probably 30 times greater than the measurable direct benefits.

Total Measurable Costs

If we expand the frame of reference one more level to include measurable externalities, or indirect costs, then the economic picture changes even further. One dramatic example involves all technologies that run on petroleum. In calculating life-cycle cost, the price of fuel is one component, though usually not a decisive one in the United States because the price of petroleum in this country is relatively low. This is at least partly due to the fact that much of its cost is paid in other ways and thus not reflected in the price. Most of these costs are paid by government and indirectly by taxpayers. Tax breaks such as the depletion allowance for petroleum and natural gas provide one example. In this way, petroleum producers are actually rewarded for hastening the depletion of a nonrenewable resource. In the case of petroleum used to power cars and trucks, much of the cost of road maintenance and that of traffic law enforcement is borne in other ways. The cost of military protection for oil fields and shipping lanes in the Middle East is paid by federal taxes. In 1990, before the outbreak of the Persian Gulf war, the Economic Strategy Institute calculated that if the costs of maintaining military forces in the Gulf and foreign aid to Middle Eastern countries were included in the price of oil, it would be about $80 per barrel, more than four times the current price (Tonelson and Hurd, 1990). Since both of these costs are attributable entirely to protecting U.S. petroleum sources, such a price would be entirely economically justified. If the price of petroleum were to go up fourfold, then most renewable sources would suddenly become cheaper in the marketplace and, assuming the principles of a free market would prevail, our entire pattern of energy use would change.

In much of the country, adjusting the price of water to include external costs would have similar effects on the pattern of water use. In the western states, where almost all agriculture is irrigated, water is supplied under federal contracts that fix its prices far below actual cost. In some cases the price is as low as $50 per acre-foot. Customers in cities pay several times that, generally $250 to $600 per acre-foot. In California, about 85 percent of all water use is for agricultural irrigation, which means that most water is paid for mostly by urban dwellers rather than by the farmers who use it. On the average, the federal government pays about 80 percent of the cost of water resource development projects in the United States (Frederick, 1991). Farmers have so far repaid only 5 percent of the costs of the hugely expensive water-diversion projects that made agriculture possible in California's Central Valley through their water purchases (Postel, 1989). Similar situations prevail in other countries with extensive irrigated agriculture. In most nonindustrial nations, farmers pay 10 to 20 percent of the cost of irrigation water (ibid.). Farmers therefore have little incentive to use less water. They cannot recover investment in water-conserving irrigation such as drip systems through money saved on water bills. Under these circumstances, overwatering makes short-term economic sense. However, where either the water or the soil contains high levels of salts, which both do in many dry regions, heavy applications of water tend to concentrate salts in the soil. Over time, heavily irrigated soils in dry regions commonly became unproductive. Throughout history, soil salinization has been a major cause of decline of civilizations founded on irrigated agriculture. What makes short-term economic sense for the farmer makes no long-term sense for society or for the farmer.

Costs and the Macro-Marketplace

While they are even harder to measure than direct externalities, the economic impacts of a project or a new technology in systemic terms can be at least equally important. Cumulatively, they can be much more important, potentially bringing major social change. The overwhelming effects that technology can have on the larger economic patterns of a society have been demonstrated with dramatic clarity by industrialization and automation over the past 200 years. Experience over the past 30 years suggests that the larger economic effects of regenerative technologies are quite different but equally significant. A number of studies have shown that regenerative technologies tend to employ more people; that is, they involve more jobs for equal amounts of capital invested than do industrial technologies serving the same functions. This is especially so in the areas of energy, agriculture, and waste management. At the same time, being generally smaller in scale, regenerative technologies require lower levels of capital investment for each enterprise.

Among major industries in the United States, those involving fossil-fuel-based energy conversion and intensive energy use show the largest amount of capital invested for each person employed. The petroleum industry invests about 10 times as much capital for each employee as those in wholesale and retail trade or textile production. For public utilities the ratio is only slightly less. For the chemical industry, the ratio is roughly four times. However, a given amount invested in solar power yields twice as many jobs as the same amount invested in conventional generating plants. The same amount invested in energy conservation yields four times as many jobs (Schachter, 1979). As it happens, the most highly capital-intensive industries are also the largest polluters. Southern California Air Quality Management District records show that the top five industrial contributors of nitrogen oxides and sulfur dioxide are oil companies. Four of the five top contributors of particulates and reactive hydrocarbons were also oil companies.

An economic analysis carried out for the Joint Economic Committee of Congress (Rodberg, 1979) showed that $115 billion invested annually in solar energy development and conservation would yield 2 million new jobs over a 10-year period. About 1.5

million of these would be in solar industries and 500,000 in conservation. However, this would bring a loss of 1 million jobs in fossil-fuel-consuming industries. If the money saved in fuel bills were invested in other areas of the economy, this would create an additional 3 million jobs. Thus, the net increase in jobs would be 4 million (ibid.).

Regenerative means of waste management show similarly larger numbers of employees than industrial alternatives. New York City's Department of Sanitation found that, while materials recycling employs about 400 to 600 people per million tons processed and composting about 225 to 325, landfilling employs about 40 to 60 and incineration about 100 to 300 (Renner, 1991). Weighed against this favorable comparison, however, is the fact that recycling will bring a loss of jobs in mining and manufacturing the products that would be made anew if they were not recycled.

For agriculture there have been few studies of employment levels related to different technologies. Perusal of the specific operations involved in regenerative farming suggests that it may require more labor, though not a great deal more. Scattered informal reports from farmers who have made the change, however, suggest the situation is probably more complex than that. Regenerative farms seem to employ more full-time help, and they particularly require more scientific and management skills. Regenerative farmers frequently express concern at the management efforts needed to operate their farms (Miller, 1992). On the other hand, the need for seasonal employees is generally considerably less. While the balance seems to tip toward a small increase in farm labor, we should not expect a reversal of the mass migration from farm to city that accompanied industrialization. More farm jobs will involve year-round employment and higher levels of thought, though not necessarily high levels of formal education.

The available studies of the subject show that, along with increasing employment, regenerative systems involve less capital investment overall and less concentration of capital. This result is partly because regenerative technologies, following the first strategy, rely more on natural processes and less on expensive hardware. More of the money spent in developing and operating them thus goes into wages and less into steel and concrete.

The dispersal of capital has much to do with scale of operation. With their built-in economies of scale, industrial operations have grown ever larger, thus requiring ever greater amounts of capital investment. Because most regenerative technologies

lack such economies of scale, they can be developed in smaller increments requiring smaller amounts of capital. Since the enactment of PURPA (the Public Utilities Regulatory Policies Act), many small companies have gone into the energy business because it is possible to operate at a small scale. Most of the new wind farms, while they add up to very large developments, are actually collections of small investments. Each wind generator is usually financed by one investor.

The implications of a shift in the pattern of capital concentration, even a minor shift, are far-reaching. It will certainly encourage small investors and entrepreneurs to involve themselves in regenerative technologies. To some degree this happened with solar technologies in the 1970s, when government support for solar energy was more nearly equal to its support for fossil fuel and nuclear energy. The results were mixed. A great many small businesses, and small divisions of big businesses, got underway. Solar technologies advanced at a rapid pace and began to make their way into the mainstream economy. However, some of the entrepreneurs proved incapable or even dishonest, and it was difficult for consumers to distinguish the competent from the incompetent in this unfamiliar territory. This situation was not unusual for a new industry and probably would have sorted itself out in a short time. But in 1980, before this could happen, government policies shifted to favor fossil fuels and nuclear energy, thus bringing on the "solar eclipse." Competing with a large, well-entrenched, and heavily subsidized conventional energy industry, the fledgling solar industry soon diminished to an insignificant level.

Reduced capital requirements for regenerative technologies will undoubtedly benefit farmers as much as small investors and entrepreneurs. The economic difficulties that have devastated farmers in recent years largely result from high levels of debt incurred to buy farm machinery, chemicals, and in some cases more land. When prices for their crops dropped during the 1980s, farmers had trouble making payments on the loans taken out for all these purposes. Untold numbers teetered on the edge of bankruptcy, and a great many fell over the edge. Access to capital accounts for most of the competitive success of the heavily capitalized agribusiness corporations. Corporate farms are not, as if often supposed, necessarily more efficient than smaller farms; they simply are better capitalized.

Increasing capital concentration and the accompanying increase in scale of organization has serious implications in other areas of technology as well.

One task force sponsored by the Rockefeller Brothers Fund (1977) took a long look at the implications of large-scale industrially based energy technologies and foresaw a number of inevitable consequences of their further development. Among these were an increasing concentration of government power to channel resources into the energy sector, to make end uses conform to the requirements of energy sources, and to override public perceptions of faults or problems with prevailing modes of energy conversion. The task force also predicted an increase in horizontally integrated corporate monopolies.

The predictions were prophetic. These ominous trends were all clearly visible in the 1980s. As they continue, change becomes more difficult. Nevertheless, regenerative technologies offer some ground for optimism. Even the relatively minor dispersion of capital they can bring would represent a counter trend and a step toward more equitable distribution of wealth in a society seriously threatened by increasing concentration of wealth and a related increase in numbers of people living in poverty. Creative energies unleashed by more equitable distribution of wealth might resound through the entire social structure. And the increase in jobs associated with regenerative technologies can potentially address the problem of hard-core structural unemployment that increasingly plagues industrialized countries. Hazel Henderson (1988) has commented that the ever increasing "productivity" brought on by industrialization and automation is really nothing more than progressive elimination of people from the work force. As discussed in Chapter 9, the reasons have much to do with the technostructure and its motivation.

Costs of Environmental Degradation and Resource Depletion

It has often been proposed that if we expand the framework for cost comparison one more time to include the whole environment, we will find ways to account for environmental degradation and resource depletion in economic terms—that is, to assign monetary values to them. Some of the most knowledgeable and articulate analysts and commentators on environmental issues have called for assigning economic value to environmental resources. Norman Myers, for example, has written that we "need to modify our traditional accounting procedures to incorporate an environmental reckoning" (1987, p. 169). Myers has assembled data to show that environmental degradation is expensive indeed. The cost of acid precipitation to the timber

industry in Germany he estimates to be about $1 billion per year and to the German economy as a whole about $2.8 billion. The total cost of pollution of all kinds to the German economy Myers calculates at around $57 billion each year (Myers, 1987).

One study carried out for the Southern California Air Quality Management District attempted to measure the costs of air pollution according to such factors as work days lost through illness due to smog and costs of hospitalization for the same reason. These costs are high indeed, far higher than the cost of reducing pollution. The researchers estimated that reduced air pollution would save $9.4 billion in health care costs alone, as compared to the $2.79 billion cost of pollution control. Because the study included only two of the nine principal air pollutants, the researchers guessed that actual savings would be much higher (Hall et al., 1989). Nevertheless, such estimates have had little impact on decisions. This is partly due to the fact that the costs are widely distributed among people whose identities are as yet unknown. A few statistically predicted cases of illness in the vaguely distant future do not seem very important in the present, which is beset with its own pressing problems. Another reason for the minimal impact of these high costs is also that such studies seem to be addressing the wrong questions in ways that are not convincing. Aside from the fact that verified means for predicting such illnesses do not exist, the economic studies miss the truly important effects, which have to do with diminished quality and quantity of life and beyond that, diminished viability of the biosphere. These are not measurable in economic terms because they exist outside the marketplace, which provides the only convincing framework for fixing costs and prices. In trying to deal with these effects, economics goes beyond its boundaries.

The academic discipline of economics provided an ideal vehicle for promoting and institutionalizing the values of the industrial era. Economic measures provided a means for quantifying success for industries and whole nations as well as for individuals. Somehow, economic measures came to represent the value system of the society. Over the past two decades, several critics have convincingly pointed out the failings of classical economic theory in dealing with larger ecological and social issues (see for example Daly, 1991; Daly and Cobb, 1989; Georgescu-Roegen, 1971; Henderson, 1988). Given the current primacy of economic thinking and the faith in its measures of efficiency, it has been hard for society's decision makers to accept the fact that economic principles are effective only within the limits of the marketplace—the realm of things regularly bought and sold. Beyond that realm, other principles apply. In the global system of ecosystem function, the flows of energy and materials include all species everywhere. Within this vast system the relatively small subsystem of economics strives to deal in quantitative terms with those segments of energy and material flows of human society that fall within the marketplace. Thus, economics is rightfully a branch of ecology and the market is one part, or subsystem, of the larger ecosystem. This relationship establishes certain modes of interaction in both system and subsystem.

According to the rules of hierarchical order, goals are established at the larger levels of a system and passed to smaller, or subsystem, levels (Feibleman, 1954). The mechanisms for achieving these goals are established at the smaller levels and passed to the larger. Thus, systems logic tells us that ecological goals should give direction to the economy, and that the economy provides one means for working toward ecological goals. However, the reverse is not true: Economic performance can be evaluated in ecological terms and not the reverse. While we can evaluate any economic operation such as a manufacturing plant or a bank in terms of its effectiveness in serving ecological purpose, we cannot measure ecological change in economic terms because economics does not incorporate a large-enough frame of reference or an adequate range of values. While some of the materials that function as parts of ecosystems are traded in the marketplace, ecosystems as functioning units are not bought and sold and cannot be measured in this way because they exist at larger, more encompassing levels of order.

The predominant position of economics in the Paleotechnic period left the industrialized world with highly developed economic institutions but without equivalent ecological institutions for serving larger purposes. Thus, human society has for some time lacked the institutional means for dealing with large systems of order that were once the province of religion. In the absence of the larger framework, economic goals tend to override ecological goals because they can by quantified in a Paleotechnic culture that greatly respects numbers and because ecological purpose is not backed by institutional authority. Moreover, economic institutions tend to defy integrative laws by trying to make ecological mechanisms serve economic purposes. The corporation, which is the quintessential organizational form of the industrial period, has only an economic purpose, not an ecological one. The profit motive, which has in some ways served capitalist

societies well in providing goods and services when and where they are needed, brings heavy exploitation when it is allowed free reign in the larger ecological realm. To control it we need a larger framework of ecological goals with solid institutional support.

Environmental organizations have played key roles in establishing such a larger framework. During the decades of the 1970s and 1980s, several of them grew to a size and level of authority that could challenge corporate power. Environmental organizations, however, can by nature be no more than special-interest groups, albeit extremely influential ones. Only government can provide the goal-setting institutional structure that is so much needed. Progress, however, has been slow. Polls consistently show overwhelming support for strong environmental policies. Nevertheless, we still have far to go in providing the kind of compelling and overriding ecological policy structure that can lead to a truly regenerative landscape at either global or national levels.

Policy for Regeneration

While policy-making efforts at the global level have begun to embrace the concept of sustainable development, environmental legislation in the United States is still generally reactive and directed at specific issues. Lacking is a policy perspective reflecting the interconnectedness of all the elements of the environment. NEPA (National Environmental Policy Act) provided a beginning in 1970 with its call for "harmony between man and the environment." Other federal legislation has included similar words, as have laws passed at other levels of government. The Subdivision Regulations of the city of Los Angeles, for example, state as their first purpose "to preserve and protect, to the maximum extent possible, the unique and valuable natural resources and amenities of the city's environment . . ." (p. 2). From NEPA to the Los Angeles Subdivision Regulations, however, the broader purpose is usually lost when it is translated into specific provisions and usually further distorted when passed on to bureaucratic regulatory processes.

The reasons for this have much to do with the magnitude and the pace of change. It has become clear that the shift from industrial to regenerative ways requires fundamental change in our ways of thinking about the world. There are many, however, who have reason not to change their ways of thinking. People and organizations, both public and private, that achieved wealth and power in the Paleotechnic era by following industrial ways are understandably reluctant to make a shift that could diminish their position even if they understand the need. As every revolutionary has learned, established interests are powerful deterrents to change. As pointed out earlier, our political system and our planning structure offer ample opportunities to deter ecological purposes.

A great many impediments to sustainability, however, result not from the pressures of established interests but simply from inertia; they are economic and legal mechanisms introduced into law or bureaucratic procedures created for some reason at one time that have simply not been removed or altered. Important among the impediments to policies supporting sustainability are degenerative subsidies, single purpose rules, and narrowly focused agencies. All of these exist due both to the entrenchment of power vested in obsolete practices and to simple inertia.

Visible and Invisible Subsidies

The illusion that the American economy is based primarily on a free market is soon dispelled by even a casual look at the complex pattern of federal subsidies that support certain industries, technologies, and practices. Most of the subsidies have developed in response to particular situations and without any basis in clearly stated policy. Critics often point out, for example, that the United States, unlike other industrial nations, has no energy policy. However, the pattern of energy subsidies suggests that there is actually a strong and effective de facto energy policy in place that promotes nuclear and fossil fuels while suppressing development of regenerative energy. This policy has been shaped not by public will but by special interests. Polls have consistently shown strong public support for renewable energy. In one 1989 nationwide poll, for example, 77 percent of Americans ranked renewables as their first or second choice for government funding. The following year the federal budget allocated $113 million for development of renewables, as compared with $718.5 million in 1980. Funding for nuclear and fossil fuels was several times that amount. Government subsidies going to hard-energy industries (mostly nuclear and fossil fuels) were estimated at $44 billion for 1984, a typical year (Flavin and Lenssen, 1990). The difference between the price of gasoline in a service station and the actual costs discussed earlier give some indication of the levels of subsidies. Federal subsidies for water use, in the form of

artificially low prices, are equally generous. If farmers paid for irrigation water at rates equalling its cost, their water bills would rise by $400 to $2000 per year per acre, which would be more than enough to pay for highly efficient irrigation systems that would reduce water use by at least 50 percent. Experience has shown that efficiency of water use rises with price. At least one authority has written that pricing structures reflecting actual cost would have greater effect than any other government policy related to water (Rogers, 1985).

Substantial subsidies for degenerative practices exist in other aspects of agriculture as well. The Federal Government leases lands for grazing at rates far less than those of comparable private lands. Federal commodity programs, which exist to stabilize farm income, also tend to discourage regenerative agricultural practices in several ways. Payments to farmers depend on base acres planted in a particular crop and average yields on those acres over the preceding 5 years. Thus, taking any of those acres out of production for crop rotation or diversification reduces the farmer's support payments. Support prices are usually set well above market levels, which also encourages farmers to apply larger amounts of fertilizers, pesticides, and irrigation water than would be justified by the market. Research shows that most farmers are strongly influenced by these subsidies in deciding what crops to plant (Miller, 1992). With over two-thirds of all agricultural land participating, the commodity support programs tend to dominate the economics of agriculture. According to the NRC (1989), they also have helped to increase land values to unjustified levels, brought about excessive capital investment in farm machinery, subsidized polluting and unsustainable cropping practices, provided funds for doubtful irrigation projects, and promoted interstate highways to the detriment of railroads.

In agriculture as in other areas, removing subsidies or shifting them in favor of sustainable practices is likely to bring a surge of invention and development of regenerative technologies. The technically inclined creative energy is available and waiting for motivation. Al Gore (1992) suggests that we further stimulate invention by improving protection provided by copyright and patent laws.

Single-Purpose Regulation

Just as most subsidies exist to serve a single purpose, determined without regard for the complexities of multiple interactions that extend the web of effect far beyond that one purpose, there are a great many rules and regulations at every level of government that originated in similar ways with similar results. Consider a few of the land development regulations in the city of Los Angeles that make it impossible to achieve the stated policy goal of preserving and protecting the "natural resources and amenities of the city's environment," especially in the sensitive foothill areas. The city's engineering standards require minimum 40-foot pavement widths for streets, which is more than double the width needed for two cars to pass and at least 15 feet more than needed for two fire engines to pass. The unnecessary paved area requires massive grading on hillside land, increases the volume of runoff water, increases ambient heat levels, and reduces vegetation cover and all the benefits that go with it. Lot-size requirements and minimum setbacks exacerbate this situation by making it extremely difficult to cluster buildings on the most suitable sites, and thus to leave undisturbed the most sensitive land and areas of wildlife habitat.

Regulations such as these are generally the most effective impediments to regenerative land development practices, greater even than conservative financing policies on the part of lending institutions. Recall the Los Angeles County requirement for two fire engines to park side by side on the small pedestrian way of the Center for Regenerative Studies. Michael Corbett, developer of Village Homes, the ecologically planned subdivision described in Chapter 5, has said that difficulties in overcoming regulations, especially minimum street widths and building setbacks, nearly forced him to abandon the project several times (Corbett, 1989). His proposals, which included narrow streets and small lots with large areas of common space and infiltration basins for runoff water, were rational improvements on prevailing practices. They were hardly radical and in no way inimical to the public interest, but they did differ from the city's engineering standards.

In most cities, zoning codes also present serious impediments to sustainable development. They commonly play a key part in the extravagant patterns of energy consumption that characterize modern cities, especially in the United States. Segregation of land uses divides daily life into tenuously related segments, making it necessary to use the automobile not only for commuting from home to work, but also for routine shopping trips and transporting children to school. Furthermore, zoning patterns rarely have any relationship with the natural character or capacities of the land.

While engineering standards and zoning codes are among the more pervasive examples, there are a great many laws and regulations at every level of government that impede regenerative practices, not by intent but as indirect results of serving other purposes. Federal laws that prohibit private ownership of wildlife populations, for example, help to protect wildlife but make game ranching extremely difficult. Since carefully planned game ranching can benefit wildlife populations by replacing extensive grazing areas devoted to exotic species, there is an obvious confusion between ends and means in the law.

We can learn important lessons from the difficulties brought on by such narrowly directed legislation and especially by the regulations written to implement it. Rapid growth in the volume of environmental legislation is all but inevitable. To be effective, each new law, rule, and standard will have to be framed within a broad context of ecological purpose rather than being directed at just one specific problem.

Single Purpose Agencies

As much as our regulatory apparatus and the layout of our cities, our governmental organization reflects the 19th-century habit of categorization and segmentation. At every level of the hierarchical structure, the responsibilities of most government agencies are narrowly defined and enclosed within boundaries that are tenaciously guarded against encroachment by neighboring agencies. While this approach to organization has important advantages in affixing responsibility and minimizing conflicts, it presents serious difficulties in dealing with systems that operationally overlap the territories of several agencies. As with other hierarchies, information flow in every direction other than from top to bottom is seriously inhibited. Planning departments, for example, are responsible for land use, but many of the factors that should determine land use, such as flood control, wildlife habitat, and public works, are in the territory of other agencies. Even within the province of a single resource, responsibilities are usually divided. For example, most cities have different departments dealing with water supply, sewage, and flood control, even though these are all integrally related in the ecological processes of water flow. In Los Angeles, even at the height of a drought period, when water imported from distant mountains is running short, it is not unusual to see storm water flowing in torrents through concrete channels to the Pacific Ocean and partially treated sewage water flow from the Hyperion treatment plant into Santa Monica Bay.

Large Scale and Long Term

Most of the subsidies and regulations that impede sustainable development, probably even many of the single-purpose agencies, are results of the common tendency within government to concentrate on the immediate and the tangible. Both the policy making and the management apparatus of government habitually focus on the short term and the small scale. The big picture is always cloudy, and the future beyond 5 years from now only a dark haze. Long-range planning is rarely carried out in practice and almost never implemented.

Numerous explanations have been offered for this. In the United States there exists a strong tradition of pragmatism that habitually dismisses abstractions and regards planning with disdain. However, both the big picture and the distant future are necessarily abstract and can be effectively engaged only through planning. Many find it difficult to exercise the imagination and conceptualization needed to deal with such abstractions. Furthermore, abstractions are easily ridiculed and dismissed because they cannot be proven to exist. The length of political terms and the local affiliations of politicians tend to limit the scope of political thinking.

Moreover, we live in a period beset by immediate problems. Government officials everywhere find themselves constantly dealing with "brushfires" that leave them no time for the larger view. Even planning departments, whose responsibilities include long-range planning, are often overwhelmed with processing requests for zoning variations and similar small, immediate problems. At the larger levels of government, agencies dealing with the longer term rarely even exist. On the private side, especially in American corporations, the tendency toward short-term thinking is even stronger.

Ornstein and Ehrlich (1989) have suggested that the roots of this dilemma go deeper, that the bias toward short-term thinking is actually built into the human brain, evolved over eons during which quick decisions dealing with immediate threats were essential to survival. Only recently have any means for influencing events long in the future become available to our species. According to these researchers the only solution is a kind of conscious evolution of the mind to incorporate long-term conceptualization.

Whatever intellectual mechanisms we may develop for addressing regeneration, it is necessarily a long-range goal that requires dealing with the future beyond 5 years from now, as far away as 50 years from now and even the indefinite unlimited future. Whether planned or not, the trajectories of resources and environment that are visible right now, including depletion of petroleum reserves, deforestation, acid precipitation, the buildup of greenhouse gases, and ozone depletion, assure us there will be major changes in the not-so-distant future. These will occur with or without planning and management, with or without any effort at human control. Virtually everyone who has seriously contemplated the resource/environment dilemma has emphasized the importance of a carefully orchestrated transition to sustainability. Without planning, the transition is likely to be painful and difficult. Though humanity will probably survive as a species, human culture may not. Even with long-range planning, there are no certainties; the situation is already serious. Optimistically, however, the transition might mark the evolution to a new post-Rennaissance cultural era with Gaia's garden as its setting.

Global and national policies of long-term regeneration can only be based on global and national commitment supported by the citizenry. The strong public support for environmental protection and long-term sustainability as reflected in a long series of surveys suggests that the federal government's reluctance to make major policy commitments in these areas does not reflect the desires of the public. When we add to the obvious benefits of conserving resources and improving environmental quality their potentials for improving social and economic conditions, it seems obvious that regenerative systems are worthy of widespread support. Increasing the number of jobs, reducing concentration of capital, and encouraging participatory decision making all promise distinct improvements in prevailing Paleotechnic conditions.

Since 1969, experience has changed our perceptions of environmental issues. The growing emphasis on sustainable development requires a proactive policy base that is conceptually a large step beyond the reactive position of NEPA. A new NEPA might reassign the primary role in environmental protection from impact analysis to ecologically based planning and design. These are the evolutionary pathfinders for both short- and long-term change.

Essential Roles of Planning and Design

In the technically oriented Paleotechnic period, engineering eclipsed planning and design in favor of singular and narrowly defined technical purposes.

Achieving sustainability will require that planning and design again become the primary vehicles for guidance into the future. This will mean reorganizing our public planning institutions to place basic emphasis on ecological order. It will require strong agencies for planning at every scale from the whole earth to local areas. In the United States it particularly will require a new structure for regional planning, probably coordinated at the state level but working within a national framework.

To function regeneratively, every project, public as well as private, will require careful and concentrated thought, far beyond the depth typical of project design in the past. Less time will be spent in gathering voluminous data for impact analyses and much more time will be spent on designing development to fit the natural context and to function ecosystematically. Requiring good regenerative design will serve the purposes of regulatory agencies far better than trying to enforce minimum standards.

In the past there has been a great reluctance on the part of private developers (and some public agencies) to spend money on planning and design. This relates to a range of factors including a pragmatic refusal to recognize their importance, the speculative nature of our development processes, and the fact that design costs often have to be paid early in the development process, before money is coming in. In development parlance, they are front-end costs. To assure good design, supervisory agencies will probably have to require that developers hire capable interdisciplinary design teams and allow them broad scope for creative and technical thinking. This may necessitate government subsidizing at least part of the cost of design, possibly in the form of incentives for resource conserving design such as those established by Ontario Hydro in Canada. It is a more effective investment than either impact analysis or enforcement of complex regulations. Furthermore, means will have to be found for relieving design and planning professionals of the liability involved in applying innovative solutions.

Removing Barriers

Key deterrents to regenerative design are the many regulations mentioned earlier that conflict with its purposes. Assuming that the political apparatus at every level can find ways to respond to the citizenry, overcome the objections of politically potent special interests with investment in environmental degeneration, and establish overriding policies of long-term regeneration, the first step will be removing the road blocks.

In 1992, as part of his economic recovery program, President Bush ordered a review of all federal regulations to seek out those that might impede economic activity and thus inhibit recovery. Though the results were not made public, the principle is an important one; government regulations tend to produce chains of unintended effects related to both ecology and economy. A similar, but more exhaustive and far-reaching effort might be directed to laws, regulations, and subsidies at every level of government to identify conflicts with long-term sustainability. Then conflicts could be resolved according to priorities reflecting common values.

Such a program would probably eliminate enough of the subsidies and regulations impeding regenerative technologies to allow most of them to compete on an equal level in the marketplace. If this were to happen, all available information on actual comparative costs suggests that regenerative technology would gradually replace industrial technology. Within a few years Gaia's garden would begin to flower.

However, the market could not provide for a total transition, at least not quickly enough. Too many decisions on these matters rest outside the marketplace. Here is where government policy again enters the picture to assure that the long-term public interest is served. Especially in cases where market forces are not adequate for the tasks of transition, subsidies and regulations could favor regenerative technologies in the same ways that they now favor industrial technologies. In addition to subsidies for regenerative technologies, there are numerous ways of forcing degenerative technologies to bear their actual costs. These include resource taxes, user fees and performance bonds to assure environmental restitution. In some areas, such as energy sources, the public interest is so overwhelmingly on the side of regenerative practices that almost any level of government intervention would be justified to assure their use. Continued burning of petroleum inevitably means faster depletion of reserves, more carbon dioxide in the upper atmosphere, more forests dying from acid precipitation, more urban smog, more international conflict, and more destruction of wildlife habitat by tanker spills, not to mention more enrichment of already wealthy foreign governments and more military spending and bloodshed to maintain access to resources. European countries have recognized this and imposed taxes that raise gasoline prices there to three to four times American levels.

Even with the best of planning, the transition period will bring disruption. Technological and social change will stimulate new enterprises but bring decline to others. Some far-sighted companies have already begun to make the transition. The Bechtel Company, which was long involved in building nuclear power plants, is now involved in dismantling them. For some companies the transition will be much more difficult, and only government programs can ease the burdens. Some companies will need help with financing technological transitions. Many will probably also need technical assistance. Programs to make these available can maximize the economic benefits of transition and turn much of the opposition into support. This applies to government agencies as well as private companies. Some agencies heavily involved in industrial technologies in the past, including the U.S. Army Corps of Engineers and the Bureau of Reclamation, have announced their intentions to change their modes of operation, shifting away from the massive engineering projects of the Paleotechnic period and toward environmentally benign projects and management. In 1987 James W. Ziglar, who was then Assistant Secretary of the Interior for Water and Science, announced that the Bureau of Reclamation was changing its primary mission as a developer of water projects in the West to that of a water resource management agency (Houston, 1970).

Among the most important problems of transition are those related to jobs. We have seen that regenerative technologies employ more people; a shift in that direction will mean higher levels of employment. However, the employment will require different skills, and much of it will be in different places. Government-sponsored retraining and relocation programs can render the changes beneficial.

Investing in Regeneration

If the deterrent subsidies and barriers can be removed and if government can provide some assistance and incentives, much of the cost of regeneration will be borne by private investment. However, there is also a great deal of work to be done on public facilities and public lands. Reversing the destructive patterns of recent centuries and reestablishing the earth's vital processes will be a very large undertaking indeed; Gaia's garden will be expensive. On the other hand, so was the global machine created by the industrial age, and so was the military machine created in the last half of the 20th century.

Economic experience since the Depression of the 1930s suggests that the American economy works best when it has a sizable sector of activity in which public funds are invested but which returns no marketable product to the economy. This provides a means for keeping money flowing without competing with private enterprise, and that money soon spreads out through the economy by means of payrolls and eventually reaches much of the population. During the Depression, various public-works programs served this function. Given the proclivities of that period, most of these involved heavy hardware—dams and highways. The unnecessary concrete channel in Pasadena's Arroyo Seco, as described on pages 162 to 166, was apparently built to create Depression-era jobs. During World War II the jobs-creation and money-distributing roles were taken over by the military and the defense industry. Throughout the Cold War these two institutions continued absorbing as much as half of the federal budget and employing up to 10 percent of the work force while producing nothing of economic value for the marketplace. However, with the dissolution of the Soviet Eastern bloc, the need for such a large military machine has dramatically diminished, with a consequent increase in unemployment.

There is no obvious reason why Gaia's garden could not replace public-works hardware projects and the military in this essential money-distributing role. Federal money could be spent on landscape rehabilitation, ecosystem renewal, and environmental management along with rebuilding cities and infrastructure in the regenerative mode. A landscape network, or green infrastructure, designed to perform ecological functions—converting energy, processing water, producing food and fiber, storing materials, providing habitat for natural communities—could replace steel and concrete over time. Infrastructure should not be all pipes and highways.

Like the military-industrial complex, such a program of regeneration could be a public-private venture employing large numbers of people on both sides. As with the military, public investment could be planned to produce no product to compete with private enterprise, though it would bring enormous public benefit. Unlike most jobs-creating programs, both civil and military, it would consume no nonrenewable resources and cause no pollution. The ratio of jobs to dollars invested would be far greater. In fact, if we invest also in work in nonindustrial countries, it might well bring full employment to most of the world through most of the next century. Al Gore (1992) has proposed a "global Marshall Plan" to "catalyze the transition to a sustainable society" (p. 301). This would involve large commitments of both financial and technological aid for third-world countries. We might see such an effort as establishing the social and economic context for Gaia's garden. The benefits could extend beyond sustainability in moving toward an ecologically integrated, socially just planet.

These few suggestions hardly begin to explore the implications of what will undoubtedly be a complex, perplexing, and challenging transition period. The important point bears a final restatement: This transition can be a new renaissance and a pathway into Gaia's global garden, or it can be a period of severe, perhaps violent, upheaval. There are many reasons to believe we have a choice, though probably not for long.

References

606 Studio. 1984. *Wind Energy Study*. Pomona. Department of Landscape Architecture. California State Polytechnic University.

606 Studio. 1986. *Design for the Etiwanda/Day Creek Area*. Pomona. Department of Landscape Architecture. California State Polytechnic University.

606 Studio. 1987. *San Jacinto Wildlife Area Development and Management Plan*. Pomona. Department of Landscape Architecture. California State Polytechnic University.

606 Studio. 1988a. *Master Plan for the Lower Arroyo Seco; for the City of Pasadena*. Pomona. Department of Landscape Architecture. California State Polytechnic University.

606 Studio. 1988b. *Regeneration of Degraded Landscapes Utilizing Composted Organic Wastes*. Pomona. California State Polytechnic University.

606 Studio. 1989. *A Management Framework for the Tijuana River Valley*. Pomona. Department of Landscape Architecture. California State Polytechnic University.

606 Studio. 1990. *Southeast Los Angeles: Urban Ecology*. Pomona. Department of Landscape Architecture. California State Polytechnic University.

Altieri, Miguel A. 1987. *Agroecology: The Scientific Basis of Alternative Agriculture*. Boulder, Colorado. Westview Press.

Altieri, Miguel, and Kat Anderson. 1986. "An Ecological Basis for the Development of Alternative Agricultural Systems for Small Farmers in the Third World." *American Journal of Alternative Agriculture*.

American Association for Vocational Instructional Materials (AAVIM). 1983. *Fundamentals of No-Till Farming*. Athens, Georgia. AAVIM.

Barney, Gerald O. (editor). 1980. *The Global 2000 Report to the President of the U.S.* New York. Pergamon Press.

Bateson, Gregory. 1979. *Mind and Nature*. New York. E. P. Dutton.

Bell, Daniel. 1973. *The Coming of the Post-Industrial Age*. New York. Basic Books.

Bernatzky, A. 1969. "The Performance and Value of Trees." *Anthos*. No. 1.

Berry, Wendell. 1977. *The Unsettling of America*. New York. Avon Books.

Boer, K. 1972. "Tree Planting Rediscovered." *Landscape Architecture*. 62(2).

Brown, Lester R. 1987. "Sustaining World Agriculture." In Linda Starke (editor) *State of the World 1987*. New York: W. W. Norton.

Brun, Magne. 1991. *Countryside in Transition: A Study of the Declining Rural Landscape*. As. Agricultural University of Norway.

Bryson, Reed. 1986. "Environmental Opportunities and Limits for Development." Leopold Centennial Lecture. June, 1986. Madison. University of Wisconsin.

Bryson, Reid A., and John E. Ross. 1972. "The Climate of the City." In Thomas R. Detweiler and Melvin G. Marens (editors). *Urbanization and Environment*. Belmont, California. Duxbury Press.

Callenbach, Ernest. 1975. *Ecotopia*. Berkeley, Banyan Tree Books.

Caudill, W., S. E. Crites, and E. G. Smith. 1951. "Some General Considerations in Natural Ventilation of Buildings." In *Research Report 22*. College Station. Texas Engineering Experiment Station.

Capra, Fritjof. 1982. *The Turning Point*. New York. Simon & Schuster.

Carson, Rachel. 1962. *The Silent Spring*. Boston. Houghton, Mifflin Company.

Clark, E. II, J. Haverkamp, and W. Chapman. 1985. *Eroding Soils: The Off-Farm Impacts*. Washington, D.C. Conservation Foundation.

Commoner, Barry. 1979. *The Politics of Energy*. New York. Alfred A. Knopf.

Commoner, Barry. 1990. *Making Peace with the Planet*. New York. Pantheon Books.

Conservation Foundation. 1984. *America's Water: Current Trends and Emerging Issues*. Washington, D.C.: Conservation Foundation.

Conservation Foundation. 1987. *State of the Environment: A View Toward the Nineties*. Washington, D.C.: Conservation Foundation.

Cook, Earl. 1971. "The Flow of Energy in an Industrial Society." In *Energy and Power*. San Francisco. W. H. Freeman.

Copeland, Claudia, and Jeffrey A. Zinn. 1986. *Agricultural Nonpoint Pollution Policy: A Federal Perspective*. Congressional Research Service Report 86-191 ENR TD 420 U.S.B. Washington, D.C. Government Printing Office.

Corbett, Michael. 1988. *A Better Place to Live*. Emmaus, Pennsylvania. Rodale Press.

Corbett, Michael. 1989. Personal communication.

Cox, George W., and Michael D. Atkins. 1979. *Agricultural Ecology*. San Francisco: W. W. Freeman.

Daly, Herman E. 1991. *Steady State Economics*. Second Edition. Washington, D.C. Island Press.

Daly, Herman E., and John B. Cobb, Jr. 1989. *For the Common Good: Redirecting the Economy toward Community, Environment, and Sustainable Future*. Boston. Beacon Press.

Day, John C., and Gerald L. Horner. 1987. *U.S. Irrigation Extent and Economic Importance*. Agriculture Information Bulletin No. 523. Washington, D.C. U.S. Department of Agriculture.

Delmendo, Medina N. 1980. "A Review of Integrated Livestock–Fowl–Fish Farming Systems." In Roger S. V. Pullin and Ziad H. Schehadeh (editors). *Integrated Agriculture-Aquaculture Farming Systems*. Manilla. International Center for Living Aquatic Resources.

Descartes, René. 1647. *Rules for the Direction of the Mind*. Translated by E. S. Haldane and G. R. T. Ross. *Encyclopaedia Britannica*. Chicago. 1971.

Dewey, John. 1916. *Democracy and Education*. New York. The Free Press.

Dover, Michael J., and Lee M. Talbot. 1989. "Feeding the Earth." *Technology Review*. February–March.

Duckworth, F., and J. Sandberg. 1954. "The Effect of Cities on Horizontal and Vertical Temperature Gradients." *Bulletin of the American Meteorological Society.*

Ebenezer, Howard. 1898. *Garden Cities of Tomorrow.* Reprinted: M. I. T. Press. Cambridge, 1965.

Evanari, Michael, and Dan Koller. 1956. "Ancient Masters of the Desert." *Scientific American* 194.

Fabos, Julius. 1985. *Land Use Planning: From Global to Local Challenge.* New York. Chapman and Hall.

Feibleman, J. K. 1954. "Theory of Integrative Levels." *British Journal of the Philosophy of Science.* 5(17).

Ferguson, Bruce. 1991. "The Failure of Detention." *Landscape Architecture.* 81(12).

Flavin, Christopher, and Nicholas Lenssen. 1990. *Beyond the Petroleum Age: Designing the Solar Economy.* Worldwatch Paper 100. Washington, D.C. Worldwatch Institute.

Frederick, Douglas D. 1991. "Water Resources: Increasing Demand and Scarce Supplies." In Frederick, Kenneth D., and Roger A. Sedjo, editors. *America's Renewable Resources: Historical Trends and Current Challenges.* Washington, D.C. Resources for the Future.

Freudenberger, Dean. 1988. "The Agricultural Agenda for the Twenty-First Century." *KIDJA, Israel Journal of Development.* 7(8).

Fukuoka, Masanobu. 1978. *The One-Straw Revolution.* Emmans, Pennsylvania: Rodale Press.

Fuller, R. Buckminster. 1981. *Critical Path.* New York. St. Martin's Press.

Galbraith, John Kenneth. 1973. *Economics and the Public Purpose.* Boston. Houghton Mifflin Company.

Geddes, Patrick. 1915. *Cities in Evolution.* New York. Harper & Row.

Georgescu-Roegen, Nicholas. 1971. *The Entropy Law and the Economic Process.* Cambridge. Harvard University Press.

Gersberg, R. M., B. V. Elkins, S. R. Lyons, and R. C. Goldman. 1985. "Role of Aquatic Plants in Wastewater Treatment by Artificial Wetlands." *Water Resources.* 20.

Geyer, John; Robert Kaufmann, David Skole, and Charles Vorosmargy. 1986. *Beyond Oil: The Threat to Food and Fuel in the Coming Decades.* Cambridge, Massachusetts. Ballinger Publishing.

Gilbert, R. G., R. C. Rice, H. Bouwer, C. P. Gerba, C. Wallis, and J. L. Melnick. "Wastewater Renovation and Reuse: Virus Removal by Soil Filtration." *Science.* 192.

Gliessman, S. R. (editor). 1990. *Agroecology: Researching the Ecological Basis for Sustainable Agriculture.* New York. Springer-Verlag.

Golueke, Clarence G. 1977. *Biological Reclamation of Solid Wastes.* Emmans, Pennsylvania: Rodale Press.

Gore, Al. 1992. *Earth in the Balance.* New York: Houghton-Mifflin.

Grinnell, Gerald E. 1988. "Fuel Ethanol: Still a Practical Option?" *National Forum.* Summer.

Grossman, Richard. 1978. "Energy and Jobs." In Stephen Lyons (editor). *Sun! A Handbook for the Solar Decade.* San Francisco. Friends of the Earth.

Hall, Jane, et al. 1989. "Economic Assessment of the Health Benefits from Improvements in Air Quality in the South Coast Air Basin." South Coast Air Quality Management District. Diamond Bar, California.

Hansen, Jame A. et al. 1988. "Global Climate Changes as Forecast by the GISS 3D Model." Journal of Geophysical Research. 17-4.

Hansen, Jame A. et al. 1988. "Global Climate Changes as Forecast by the GISS 3D Model." *Journal of Geophysical Research.* 17-4.

Hardin, Garrett. 1968. "The Tragedy of the Commons." *Science.* 167.

Henderson, Hazel. 1988. *The Politics of the Solar Age: Alternatives to Economics.* Indianapolis. Knowledge Systems.

Hill, A. C. 1971. "Vegetation: A Sink for Atmospheric Pollutants." *Journal of the American Society of Horticultural Science.* 99.

Hillman, W. S., and D. C. Culley. 1978. "The Use of Duckweed." *American Scientist.* 66.

Hopcraft, David. 1975. *Productivity Comparisons between Thompson's Gazelle and Cattle and Their Relation to the Ecosystem in Kenya.* Ph. D. Thesis. Ithaca. Cornell University.

Hopcraft, David. 1980. "Nature's Technology: The Natural Land-Use System of Wildlife Ranching." *Vital Speeches of the Day.* 46(15).

Hornick, S. B., J. J. Murray, R. L. Chaney, L. S. Sikora, J. F. Parr, W. D. Burge, G. B. Wilson, and C. F. Tester. 1979. *Use of Sewage Sludge Compost for Soil Improvement and Plant Growth.* U.S. Department of Agriculture ARM-NE-6. August.

Hough, Michael. 1984. *City Form and Natural Process.* New York: Van Nostrand Reinbold.

Hough, Michael. 1990. *Out of Place.* New Haven. Yale University Press.

Houston, Paul. 1987. "Big Dam Agency to Focus on Environment." *Los Angeles Times.* October 2.

Howard, Ebenezer. 1899. *Garden Cities of Tomorrow.* Cambridge. MIT Press.

Huat, Khoo Khay, and E. S. P. Tan. 1980. "Review of Rice-Fish Culture in Southeast Asia." In Roger S. V. Pulliam and Ziad H. Shehadeh (editors). *Integrated Agriculture-Aquaculture Farming Systems.* Manila. International Center for Living Aquatic Resources.

Hutchinson, Boyd A., Fred G. Taylor, and Robert Wendt. 1983. "Energy Conservation Mechanisms and Potentials for Landscape Design to Ameliorate Building Climates." *Landscape Journal.* 2(1).

Illich, Ivan. 1974. "Energy and Equity." In Stephen Lyons (editor). *Sun.* New York. Friends of the Earth.

International Union for the Conservation of Nature and Natural Resources (IUCN), United Nations Environmental Program (UNEP), and World Wildlife Fund (WWF). 1992. *Caring for the Earth: A Strategy for Sustainable Living.* Gland, Switzerland. IUCN, UNEP, WWF.

International Union for the Conservation of Nature and Natural Resources (IUCN), United Nations Environmental Program (UNEP), and World Wildlife Fund (WWF). 1980. *World Conservation Strategy.* IUCN, UNEP, WWF.

Jackson, Wes. 1980. *New Roots for Agriculture.* Lincoln. University of Nebraska Press.

Jackson, Wes. 1987. *Altars of Unhewn Stone. Science and the Earth.* San Francisco. North Point Press.

Jenson, K. F., and T. T. Kozlowski. 1975. "Absorption and Translocation of Sulfur Dioxide by Seedlings in Four Forest Tree Species." *Journal of Environmental Quality.* 4.

Jeavons, John. 1974. *How to Grow More Vegetables than You Ever Thought Possible on Less Land than You Can Imagine.* Palo Alto, California. Ecology Action of the Midpeninsula.

Jewel, Linda. 1980. "Alternatives for Septic Disposal on the Site." *Landscape Architecture.* November.

Johnson, James A. 1987. "Sludge Proves Effective as Fertilizer." *Biocycle.* August.

Jokela, Alice Tang, and Arthur W. Jokela. 1978. "Water Reclamation, Aquaculture, and Wetland Management." Paper delivered at Coastal Zone '78, Symposium on Technical, Environmental and Regulatory Aspects of Coastal Zone Planning and Management. San Francisco. March 14–16.

Kemp, William B. 1971. "The Flow of Energy in a Hunting Society." In *Energy and Power*. San Francisco. W. H. Freeman.

Kern, James. 1991. "Estimate of Agricultural Energy Consumption at the Institute for Regenerative Studies." Unpublished report. Pomona. California State Polytechnic University.

Kerr, Richard. 1988. "1988 Ties for Warmest Year." Science 291.

Knowles, Ralph. 1975. *Energy and Form*. Cambridge, Massachusetts. MIT Press.

Knowles, Ralph. 1992. "Solar Access." In Bob Walter, Lois Arkin, and Richard Crenshaw (editors). *Sustainable Cities: Concepts and Strategies for Eco-City Development*. Los Angeles. EHM Publishers.

Kuhn, Thomas. 1970. *The Structure of Scientific Revolutions*. Chicago. University of Chicago Press.

Legewie, H., Erika Dechert-Knarse, and Andreas Bohm. 1993. *Psychologischen Begleitforschung im Block 6*. Arbeitsgruppe Psychologische Stadtforschung. Institute f. Psychology. Tu Berlin.

Leopold, Aldo. 1949. *A Sand County Almanac*. New York. Oxford University Press.

Lovelock, James. 1988. *The Ages of Gaia: A Biography of our Living Earth*. New York. W. W. Norton and Company.

Lovins, Amory. 1977. *Soft Energy Paths: Toward a Durable Peace*. Cambridge, Massachusetts. Ballinger Publishing.

Lovins, Amory B., and L. Hunter Lovins. 1982. *Brittle Power: Energy Policy for National Security*. Andover, Massachusetts: Brick House Publishing.

Lowdermilk, W. C. 1978. *Conquest of the Land in 7,000 Years*. USDA-SCS Agricultural Information Bulletin 99. Washington, D.C. Government Printing Office.

Lowe, Marcia. 1990. *Alternatives to the Automobile: Transport for Livable Cities*. Worldwatch Paper 98. Washington, D.C. Worldwatch Institute.

Lyle, John Tillman. 1985a. "The Alternating Current of Design Process." *Landscape Journal*. 2(1).

Lyle, John Tillman. 1985b. *Design for Human Ecosystems*. New York: Van Nostrand Reinhold.

Lyle, John T. 1991. "The Utility of Semi-Formal Models in Ecological Planning." *Landscape and Urban Planning*. 21.

Lyle, John T., and Mark von Wodtke. 1974a. "An Information System for Environmental Planning." *Journal of the American Institute of Planners*. 40(6).

Lyle, John T., and Mark von Wodtke. 1974b. "Design Methods for Developing Environmentally Integrated Urban Systems." *DMG-DRS Journal: Design Research and Methods*. Berkeley, California. 8(3).

Lyle, John T. et al. 1987. *Design for the Institute for Regenerative Studies*. Pomona. California State University.

Major, Jack. 1969. "Historical Development of the Ecosystem Concept." In George M. van Dyne (editor). *The Ecosystem Concept in Natural Resource Management*. New York. Academic Press.

Marx, Leo. 1964. *The Machine in the Garden: Technology and the Pastoral Ideal in America*. New York. Oxford University Press.

May, R. H. 1973. *Stability and Complexity in Model Ecosystems*. Princeton, N.J. Princeton University Press.

May, R. H. 1975. "Stability in Ecosystems: Some Comments." In W. H. van Dobbend and R. H. Lowe-McConnell (editors). *Unifying Concepts in Ecology*. The Hague: Dr. W. Junk B. V. Publishers.

Mazria, Edward. 1979. *The Passive Solar Energy Book*. Emmans, Pennsylvania. Rodale Press.

McCormick, Kathleen. 1991. "We Don't 'Do' Wetlands." *Landscape Architecture.* 81(10).

McHarg, Ian, L., and Jonathan Sutton. 1975. "Ecological Plumbing for the Texas Coastal Plain." *Landscape Architecture.* 65(1).

McKibbon, Bill. 1989. "Reflections (The End of Nature)." *The New Yorker.* September.

McLarney, William D. 1976. "Aquaculture: Toward an Ecological Approach." In Richard Merrill (editor). *Radical Agriculture.* New York. Harper & Row.

McPherson, E. Gregory. 1990. "Economic Modeling for Large Scale Urban Tree Plantings." In *Proceedings of the ACEE 1990 Summer Study on Energy Efficiency in Buildings.* Vol. 4. Washington, D.C. American Council for an Energy Efficient Economy.

McPherson, E. Gregory, and Sharon Biedenbender. 1991. "The Cost of Shade: Cost-Effectiveness of Trees versus Bus Shelters." *Journal of Arboriculture.* 17(9).

McPherson, E. Gregory, and Paul L. Sacamano. 1992. *Energy Savings with Trees in Southern California.* Chicago. USDA Forest Service. Northeastern Forest Experiment Station.

Meier, Richard I. 1972. "Notes on the Creation of an Effiecient Megalopolis." In G. Bell and J. Tyrwhitt (editors). *Human Identity in the Urban Environment.* Harmondsworth, England. Penguin Books.

Meldan, R. 1959. "Besondere Luftechnische Aufgaben der Industrie." *Staedtebygiene.* 3(8).

Miller, Cheryl. 1992. "Which Row to Hoe? An Interim Report from the Northwest Area Foundation—May, 1992." St. Paul, Minnesota. Northwest Area Foundation.

Miller, G. Tyler. 1975. *Energy and Environment.* Belmont, California. Wadsworth Publishing.

Mollison, Bill. 1988. *Permaculture: A Designer's Manual.* Tyalgum, Australia. Tagari Publications.

Morlock, Susan. 1990. *Innovation in Subdivision Design.* MLA thesis. Pomona. California State Polytechnic University.

Mumford, Lewis. 1961. *The City in History.* New York. Harcourt, Brace and World.

Mumford, Lewis. 1966. *Technics and Human Development.* New York. Harcourt, Brace, Jovanovich.

Murphy, C. E. Jr., T. R. Sinclair, and K. R. Knoerr. 1977. "An Assessment of the Use of Forests as Sinks for the Removal of Atmospheric Sulfur Dioxide." *Journal of Environmental Quality.* 6.

Myers, Norman. 1987. "Emergent Aspects of Environment: A Creative Challenge." *The Environmentalist.* 7(3).

Myers, Norman. 1988. "Come the Day of Reckoning." *The Guardian.* February 27.

Nash, Roderick. 1989. *The Rights of Nature.* Madison. University of Wisconsin Press.

National Research Council (NRC). 1983. *Environmental Change in the West African Sahel.* Washington, D.C. National Academy Press.

National Research Council (NRC). 1989. *Alternative Aquaculture.* Washington, D.C. National Academy Press.

Needham, Joseph. 1954. *Science and Civilization in China.* Vol. IV-3, Cambridge, England. Cambridge University Press.

Nichols, Neil A. 1993. *Natural Systems Wastewater Treatment Plant at the Center for Regenerative Studies.* Pomona. California State Polytechnic University.

Nellor, Margret, et al. 1984. *Health Effects Study Final Report.* Los Angeles. County Sanitation Districts.

Novikoff, Alex B. 1945. "The Concept of Integrative Levels and Biology." *Science.* 101.

Odum, Eugene. 1971. *Foundamentals of Ecology.* Philadelphia. W. B. Saunders.

Odum, E. P. 1975. "Diversity as a Function of Energy Flow." In W. H. van Dobben and R. H. Lowe-McConnell (editors). *Unifying Concepts of Ecology.* The Hague: Dr. W. Jank B. V. Publishers.

Odum, Eugene. 1993. Personal communication.

Odum, Howard T. 1976. "Nel Energy Analysis of Alternatives for the United States." Testimony delivered before the U.S. House of Representatives Subcommittee on Energy and Power of the Committee on Interstate and Foreign Commerce, March 25 and 26.

Odum, Howard. 1988. "Self Organization, Transformity and Information." *Science.* 242.

Okigbo, Bede N. 1989. *Development of Sustainable Agricultural Production Systems in Africa.* Ibadan, Nigeria. International Institute for Tropical Agriculture.

Oldeman, L. R., V. W. P. van Engelen, and J. H. M. Pulles. 1990. "The Extent of Human-Induced Soil Degradation." Annex 5 of L. R. Oldeman, R. T. A. Hakkeling and W. G. Sombroeck (editors). *World Map of the Status of Human-Induced Soil Degradation: An Explanatory Note.* Second edition. Wageninger, the Netherlands. International Soil Reference and Information Center.

Olgyay, Victor. 1963. *Design with Climate.* Princeton, N.J. Princeton University Press.

Organization for Economic Cooperation and Development (OECD). 1991. *The State of the Environment.* Paris. OECD.

Ornstein, Robert, and Paul Ehrlich. 1989. *New World New Mind: Moving toward Conscious Evolution.* New York. Doubleday.

Orr, David. 1989. "Ecological Literacy—Education for the 21st Century." *Holistic Education Review.* Fall.

Oswald, William J., Clarence J. Golueke, and Robert W. Tryler. 1966. "Integrated Pond Systems for Subdivisions." Paper presented at the 39th Annual Conference of the Water Pollution Control Federation. Kansas City, Missouri. September 25–30.

Pearson, David. 1989. *The Natural House Book.* New York. Simon and Schuster.

Pimentel, David. 1980. "The Potential for Grass-Fed Livestock." *Science.* 207.

Pinkard, H. P. 1970. "Trees, Regulators of the Environment." *Soil Conservation.* October.

Postel, Sandra. 1989. "Water for Agriculture: Facing the Limits." Worldwatch Paper 93. Washington, D.C.: Worldwatch Institute.

Pradt, Louis A. 1971. "Some Recent Developments in Night Soil Treatment." *Water Resources.* 5.

Rajbanshi, K. G. 1980. "A Case Study on the Economics of Integrated Farming Systems: Agriculture, Aquaculture and Animal Husbandry in Nepal." In Roger S. V. Pulliam and Ziad H. Shehadeh (editors). *Integrated Agriculture-Aquaculture Farming Systems.* Manila. International Center for Living Aquatic Resources.

Rappoport, Roy K. 1971. "The Flow of Energy in an Agricultural Society." *Energy and Power.* San Francisco. W. H. Freeman.

Rees, William E. 1989. *The Ecological Meaning of Environment-Economy Integration.* Vancouver. University of British Columbia.

Regional Plan Association. 1974. *Regional Energy Consumption: Second Interim Report of a Joint Study.* New York and Washington, D.C. Published jointly by Regional Plan Association and Resources for the Future.

Riesman, David. 1964. *Abundance for What? and Other Essays.* Garden City, N.Y. Doubleday.

Renner, Michael. 1987. *Rethinking the Role of the Automobile.* Worldwatch Paper 84. Washington, D.C. Worldwatch Institute.

Renner, Michael. 1991. *Jobs in a Sustainable Economy.* Worldwatch Paper 104. Washington, D.C. Worldwatch Institute.

Robert, Karl-Henrik. 1991. "Educating a Nation." *Sun World.* 15.

Rockefeller Brothers Fund. 1977. *The Unfinished Agenda.* New York. Crowell.

Rocky Mountain Institute. 1991. *Rocky Mountain Institute Newsletter.* 7(1).

Rodberg, Leonard. 1979. *Employment Impact of the Solar Transition.* Proposed for the Joint Economic Committee, U.S. Congress. Washington, D.C. Government Printing Office.

Roderick, Kevin. 1988. "$42 Billion Needed to Avert Gridlock." *Los Angeles Times.* February 3.

Rogers, Peter P. 1985. "Fresh Water." In Repetto, Robert (editor). *The Global Possible: Resources, Development and the Century.* New Haven. Yale University Press.

Rohlich, Ted. 1992. "Waste File of Data on Pollution." *Los Angeles Times.* September 13.

Rosenfeld, Arthur H., and David Hafemeister. 1988. "Energy-Efficient Buildings." *Scientific American.* 258(4).

Runge, G. F. 1986. *The Future of the North America Granary.* Ames. Iowa State University Press.

Schachter, M. 1979. *The Job Creation Potential of Solar and Conservation: A Critical Analysis.* DOE/TEC–10250. Washington, D.C. Government Printing Office.

Schiller, John W. 1990. "The Automobile and the Atmosphere." In John L. Helm (editor). *Energy Production, Consumption, Consequences.* Washington, D.C. National Academy of Sciences.

Schneider, Stephen H. 1989. *Global Warming: Are We Entering the Greenhouse Century?* San Francisco. Sierra Club Books.

Schroeder, G. L. 1980. "Fish-Farming in Manure-Loaded Ponds." In Roger S. V. Pullin and Ziad H. Schehadeh (editors). *Integrated Agriculture-Aquaculture Farming Systems.* Manila. International Center for Living Aquatic Resources.

Schultz, Arnold. 1967. "The Ecosystem as a Conceptual Tool in the Management of Natural Resources." In S. V. Ciriacy Wantrup and James S. Parsons (editors). *Natural Resources: Quality and Quantity.* Berkeley. University of California Press.

Schumacher, E. F. 1973. *Small Is Beautiful.* New York. Harper Colphon Books.

Schweitzer, Albert. 1933. *Out of My Life and Work.* Reprint: New York. Holt, Reinhart and Winston.

Seale, Joe, and John Wolfe. 1981. "Modeling and Design of Future Bioshelters." *Journal of the New Alchemists* 7.

Sitte, Camillo. 1901. *City Planning According to Artistic Principles.* New York. Random House.

Smil, Vaclov. 1991. *General Energetics: Energy in the Biosphere and Civilization.* New York. John Wiley & Sons.

Smith, Richard A., Richard B. Alexander, and M. Gordon Wolman. 1987. "Water Quality Trends in the Nation's Rivers." *Science.* 235.

Smith, Stewart N. 1987. "Farming Near Cities in a Bimodal Agriculture." in William Lockeretz (editor). *Sustaining Agriculture Near Cities.* Ankeny, Iowa. Soil and Water Conservation Society.

Society for Range Management. 1989. *Assessment of Rangeland Conditions and Trends of the United States 1989.* Denver. Public Affairs Committee.

Soemarwoto, O. 1975. "Rural Ecology and Development in Africa." In W. H. van Dobben and R. H. Lowe-McConnell (editors). *Unifying Concepts in Ecology.* The Hague: Dr. W. Junk B. V. Publishers.

Spirn, Anne Whiston. 1984. *The Granite Garden.* New York. Basic Books.

Stammer, Larry B. 1992. "Sewage Forced Closure of 2000 Beaches in 1991." *Los Angeles Times.* July 24.

Stelfox, J. B., D. G. Sisler, and R. J. Hudson. 1984. *A Comparison of Wildlife and Cattle Ranching on the Athi Plains, Kenya.* Department of Survival Science. Edmonton. University of Alberta.

Stine, William B., and John T. Lyle. 1992. *Energy Use and Conservation Practices at the Institute for Regenerative Studies.* Research Report 92-001. Pomona. California State Polytechnic University.

Stinner, Benjamin R., and John M. Blair. 1990. "Ecological and Agronomic Characteristics of Innovative Cropping Systems." In Clive A. Edwards et al. (editors). *Sustainable Agricultural Systems.* Ankeny, Iowa. Soil and Water Conservation Society.

Stormwater Management Divison. 1984. "Maryland Standards and Specification for Stormwater Management; Infiltration Practices." Annapolis. Maryland Department of Natural Resources.

Sullivan, Arthur L., and Mark I. Shaffer. 1975. "The Biogeography of the Megazoo." *Science.* 189.

Tansley, A. G. 1935. "The Use and Abuse of Vegatational Concepts and Terms." *Ecology.* 16.

Tchobanoglous, George, Frank Maitski, Ken Thompson, and Thomas H. Chadwick. 1987. "Evolution and Performance of City of San Diego Pilot Scale Aquatic Wastewater Treatment System Using Water Hyacinths." Paper presented at the 60th Annual Conference of the Water Pollution Control Federation. Philadelphia. October 5-6.

Texas Department of Health. 1979. *Recommendations for the Construction and Operation of Hyacinth Basins for Upgrading Stabilization Pond Effluent.* Austin. Texas Department of Health.

Thayer, Robert. 1990. "Technophobia and Topophilia: The Dynamic Meanings of Technology in the Landscape." Davis, California. Center for Design Research.

Thayer, Robert. 1993. *Gray World, Green Heart.* New York. John Wiley and Sons.

Todd, Nancy Jack (editor). 1977. *The Book of the New Alchemists.* New York. E. P. Dutton.

Todd, Nancy Jack, and John Todd. 1984. *Bioshelters, Ocean Arks, City Farming: Ecology as the Basis of Design.* San Francisco. Sierra Club Books.

Toffler, Alvin. 1970. *The Third Wave.* New York. Random House.

Toffler, Alvin. 1990. *Powershift: Knowledge, Wealth and Violence at the Edge of the 21st Century.* New York. Bantam Books.

Tonelson, Alan, and Andrew K. Hurd. 1990. "The Real Cost of Mideast Oil." *New York Times.* September 4.

Townsend, A. M. 1974. "Sorption of Ozone by Nine Shade Tree Species." *Journal of the American Society of Horticultural Science.* 99.

Trank, Andrea. 1992. "Five Green Solutions." *Landscape Architecture.* 82:(1).

Turner, Frederick III. 1974. *The Portable North American Indian Reader.* New York. W. W. Norton and Company.

Turner, Frederick. 1988. "Cultivating the American Garden." *Harpers.* August.

United States Department of Energy (DOE). 1988. *Assessment of Costs and Benefits of Alternative Fuel Use in the U.S. Transportation Sector. Progress Report One: Context and Analytical Framework.* January.

United States Environmental Protection Agency (EPA). 1987. *National Water Quality Inventory, 1986 Report to Congress.* No. EPA 440/4-87-008. Washington, D.C. Government Printing Office.

United States Environmental Protection Agency (EPA). 1987. *Air Pollution Estimates: 1940 to 1986.* Washington, D.C. Government Printing Office.

United States Environmental Protection Agency (EPA). 1989. "Report to Congress on Indoor Air Quality, Vol II: Assessment and Control of Indoor Air Pollution." EPA/400/1-89/001C. Washington, D.C.

United States Environmental Protection Agency (EPA). 1990. "National Pollutant Discharge Elimination System Permit Application Regulations for Stormwater Discharges. Final Rule." *Federal Register.* 45(222).

United States Department of the Interior. n.d.a. *Public Land Statistics*. Washington, D.C. Government Printing Office.

Veblen, Thorstein. 1921. *The Engineers and the Price System*. New York. Viking Press.

von Wodtke, Mark. 1993. *Mind over Media: Creative Thinking Skills for Electronic Media*. New York. McGraw-Hill.

Wald, Matthew L. 1992. "A New Era for Windmill Power." *New York Times*. September 8.

Walter, Bob. 1992. "Gardens in the Sky." In Bob Walter, Lois Arkin, and Richard Crenshaw (editors). *Sustainable Cities: Concepts and Strategies for Eco-City Development*. Los Angeles. EHM Publishers.

Wan, David. 1990. *Biologic*. Boulder. Johnson Books.

Watson, Donald, and K. Labs. 1983. *Climatic Design*. New York: McGraw-Hill.

Weber, Max. 1927. *General Economic History*. Translated by Frank H. Knight. Glencoe, Illinois. Free Press.

Weller, Milton W. 1987. *Freshwater Marshes: Ecology and Wildlife Management*. Second edition. Minneapolis. University of Minnesota Press.

Wells, Malcolm. 1982. *Gentle Architecture*. New York. McGraw-Hill.

Wittfogel, Karl. 1956. "The Hydraulic Civilizations." In William L. Thomas, Jr. (editor). *Man's Role in Changing the Face of the Earth*. Chicago. University of Chicago Press.

Wolverton, B. C. 1979. "Engineering Design Data for Small Vascular Aquatic Plant Wastewater Treatment Systems." *Aquaculture Systems for Wastewater Treatment: Seminar Proceeding and Engineering Assessment*. Washington, D.C. U.S. Environmental Protection Agency.

Wolverton, 1992. Personal communication.

Wolverton, B. C., and John Wolverton. 1992. "Interior Plants and Their Role in Indoor Air Quality." Research report WES/100/06-92/008. Picayune, Mississippi. Wolverton Environmental Services.

Wolverton, B. C., A. Johnson, and K. Bounds. 1989. "Interior Landscape Plants for Indoor Air Pollution Abatement." Falls Church, Virginia. Plants for Clean Air Council.

Woodbridge, Sally. 1989. "Design by Community." *Landscape Architecture*. 79(8).

World Bank. 1988. *World Development Report 1988*. New York. Oxford Press.

World Commission on Environment and Development (WCED). 1987. *Our Common Future*. New York. Oxford University Press.

World Resources Institute (WRI). 1992. *World Resources: A Guide to the Global Environment 1992–93*. New York. Oxford University Press.

World Resources Institute (WRI), and the International Institute for Environment and Development (IIED). 1988. *World Resources 1988–89*. New York. Basic Books.

Index

331